"This book offers a refreshing update of Christian worldview teaching for students of Scripture. It is rigorous and deep for serious students, yet accessible for the popular reader who wants to live a muscular Christian faith in our pluralistic marketplace of world-and-life views. One of my favorite aspects of this book is its real world examples of worldview thinking and analysis from Scripture, life, entertainment, and culture—especially movies!"

Brian Godawa, author of *Hollywood Worldviews*

"It's all here: a stellar introduction to (1) the concept of worldview, (2) the contour, content, and defense of the Christian worldview, and (3) explanation and critique of alternate secular and religious worldviews. There is little new here, but new notions of basic Christian belief and practice are often misleading and sometimes profoundly false. Here the truths of Christian faith gleam with clarity and conviction. I'm impressed."

James W. Sire, author of *The Universe Next Door* and *Apologetics Beyond Reason*

"It's become fashionable in some circles to downplay the importance of worldview. *An Introduction to Christian Worldview* counters this tendency by offering a clear apologia for the value of thoughtful worldview construction and evaluation to Christian faith. Moreover, it provides a concrete comparison of a Christian worldview to alternative models found in philosophical systems and world religions. The authors make their ideas readily accessible to readers, and it is a valuable resource for all Christians who desire a deeper understanding of the conceptual foundations of our faith."

Steve Wilkens, professor of philosophy and ethics, Azusa Pacific University

T0366972

AN INTRODUCTION TO
CHRISTIAN WORLDVIEW

PURSUING GOD'S PERSPECTIVE
IN A PLURALISTIC WORLD

Tawa J. Anderson
W. Michael Clark
David K. Naugle

APOLLOS (an imprint of Inter-Varsity Press)
36 Causton Street, London SW1P 4ST, England
Email: ivp@ivpbooks.com
Website: www.ivpbooks.com

First published 2017

British Library Cataloguing-in-Publication Data
A catalogue record for this book is available from the British Library.

ISBN: 978–1–78359–597–6
eBook ISBN: 978–1–78359–598–3

Typeset in the United States of America

Inter-Varsity Press publishes Christian books that are true to the Bible and that communicate the gospel, develop discipleship and strengthen the church for its mission in the world.

IVP originated within the Inter-Varsity Fellowship, now the Universities and Colleges Christian Fellowship, a student movement connecting Christian Unions in universities and colleges throughout Great Britain, and a member movement of the International Fellowship of Evangelical Students. Website: www.uccf.org.uk. That historic association is maintained, and all senior IVP staff and committee members subscribe to the UCCF Basis of Faith.

Tawa Anderson

To Mataeo, my beloved son, God's gift — may
you always seek to know and live by God's perspective,
whatever the world throws your way

Michael Clark

To Jenny, Scout, Brooks, Tayte, and Sonora

David Naugle

To Deemie, Courtney, Mark, and Kuyper

CONTENTS

ACKNOWLEDGMENTS

Coauthoring a book is like playing in a string quartet: it's a wonderful interplay of talented artists who depend on a number of additional folks who make the whole work possible. We would like to thank some of the numerous teachers, guides, partners, friends, and encouragers who have helped bring this project to fruition.

First, we are indebted to the worldview influence of academics who have gone before us. The writings of Abraham Kuyper, Al Wolters, James Sire, Michael Goheen, and many others have transformed our thinking. The classroom impact of Ted Cabal, James Chancellor, Jim Parker, and Mark Coppenger has helped refine our study of worldview comparison and analysis.

Second, this book project began with the encouragement and prompting of the retired dean of the Hobbs College of Theology and Ministry at Oklahoma Baptist University, Dr. Mark McClellan. Mark encouraged a group of young faculty to explore writing their own material for a January term worldview course on campus. Without his leadership and prompting, the project would never have been conceived.

Third, we thank Dr. Louima Lilite, tenor extraordinaire and theological guru, for his partnership in the project. Louima has spilled blood, sweat, tears, and considerable ink to help make this book a reality.

Fourth, we thank external reviewers and commentators: Jamie Dew, James Sire, and other anonymous contributors. Our work has been strengthened by your insights and critiques.

Fifth, we thank many students and colleagues who have provided private feedback, pointing out errors, inconsistencies, and areas for improvement; of those, a special mention to James Walters, Heidi Mann,

Gunner Briscoe, Nicholas Hoffsommer, and Jonathan White for their valuable contributions.

Sixth, we thank the editorial and artistic team at IVP Academic, who have been a thorough (and professional) pleasure to work with throughout this lengthy project. To Andy Le Peau (now retired)—thank you for taking on the project and buying into the vision of what we were trying to accomplish! To Dan Reid—thank you for taking over the project midstream and shepherding us through to the finish line.

Finally, we thank our families, who have proven to be long-suffering during the many nights, days off, and vacations that have been consumed with research, writing, revising, reconceiving, rewriting, and revising again. Your love and patience (especially that of our wonderful wives, Vanessa, Jenny, and Deemie) has been a tremendous example of the patient and gracious love of God. We thank you for standing alongside us throughout.

INTRODUCTION

WORLDVIEW MATTERS

Everybody operates upon a philosophy in life, a worldview that defines for them the way the world works and how they know things and how they ought to behave. So philosophy is ultimately a practical reality for all of us. In this sense, everyone is a philosopher; some are just more aware of it than others.

BRIAN GODAWA

Christianity is a world and life view and not simply a series of unrelated doctrines. Christianity includes all of life. Every realm of knowledge, every aspect of life and every facet of the universe find their place and their answer within Christianity. It is a system of truth enveloping the entire world in its grasp.

EDWIN RIAN

Worldview is a contentious term. Some philosophers complain that it has become an abused and misused term. Others complain that worldview is regretfully neglected and overlooked in philosophical and theological conversations. Others still insist that its use is on the rise, that it has not yet hit its heyday. Still others do not even know what the concept is all about. Finally, some assert that *worldview* is simply an unhelpful term that can be dispensed with altogether without any profound loss. We are convinced that "worldview matters" matter. As the chapters that follow will make clear, we believe that thinking worldview-ishly is essential for responsible, intentional Christian discipleship.

"All truth is God's truth."[1] Arthur Holmes's ringing words exhort institutions of Christian higher education to pursue an integrated Christian worldview throughout their curricula. God is truth, and what God sees is what is true and real. As followers of God, we likewise seek acquaintance and familiarity with truth.

To that end, we pursue God's perspective on the world, for his perspective is true, reliable, and trustworthy. We desire to see things the way that God sees them—to understand ourselves, our sin, our redemption, our relationship with Christ, our relationship with fellow human beings and the rest of creation, our surroundings, and our terrestrial ball the way that God sees, understands, and knows things to be. We do not presume to have a corner on all of God's truth; we take seriously the remonstration delivered through the prophet Isaiah:

"My thoughts are not your thoughts,
   neither are your ways my ways,"
      declares the LORD. (Is 55:8)

Yet we strive and strain forward, alongside the apostle Paul (Phil 3:14), to attain a truer understanding of God, ourselves, and our world.

God's perspective on the world is, as chapter one will make clear, another way of designating God's worldview or the divine worldview. The goal of the thoughtful Christian is to pursue God's perspective—that is, to intentionally and consciously cultivate a Christian worldview. Our goal of becoming Christlike includes our goal of embracing God's perspective, seeing the world the way God sees the world. The goal is not Icarus's prideful sailing into the sun or Satan's rebellious inclination to usurp the divine throne or Adam's misguided desire to attain that which is forbidden; rather, our goal resembles a child's devoted desire to become like his heavenly Father. This book, then, is an appeal for a continued revival in Christian worldview thinking.

The book is split into three parts of approximately equal length. Part one, authored by Tawa Anderson, focuses on the theoretical side of worldview

---

[1]Arthur F. Holmes, *The Idea of a Christian College*, rev. ed. (Grand Rapids: Eerdmans, 1987), 6.

thinking. Chapter one explores the concept of worldview itself, tracing its philosophical origins and development, basic components, and universal existence. Four core worldview questions are identified as the heart of every individual and corporate worldview: (1) What is our nature? (2) What is our world? (3) What is our problem? (4) What is our end? Chapter two identifies the importance and impact of worldview on the thoughts and actions of human persons. Anderson argues that worldview exerts considerable influence through confirmation bias, experiential accommodation, the pool of live options, and life motivation. Six benefits of intentional worldview thinking are tentatively identified and explored. Chapter three outlines the process of worldview analysis, identifying three primary criteria that can help gauge the truthfulness of various worldviews and their individual components—internal, external, and existential consistency.

Part two, authored by David Naugle, expounds on the contours of a specifically Christian worldview. Chapter four outlines the narrative core of the Christian story—creation, fall, redemption, and glorification. Chapter five approaches Christian worldview through the lenses of our four core worldview questions. Chapter six applies our three criteria for worldview analysis to Christian worldview, assessing how well it stands up to rational scrutiny.

Part three, authored by Michael Clark, engages in comparative worldview analysis. Chapter seven explores three prominent Western philosophical worldview alternatives (deism, naturalism, and postmodernism), comparing them to a Christian worldview and applying the three worldview tests. Chapter eight explores two influential global religious worldview alternatives (Hinduism and Islam), comparing them to a Christian worldview and applying the worldview tests. The goal of these chapters is threefold: to better understand these significant worldviews, to subject them to intentional analysis, and to help the reader begin to gain competence at identifying worldview components and alternatives expressed by others. We then close with reflections on pursuing and living out a Christian worldview, God's perspective, in our complex pluralistic world.

Each of us writes unapologetically from within the orthodox Christian tradition. We have been transformed through our relationship with Jesus

Christ and are persuaded that Christianity is true—not just true for us but true for all people at all times in all places. We have also been greatly stretched and formed by intentional worldview thought and consideration. Our hope and prayer is that you will be challenged, convicted, exhorted, and excited by the chapters that follow.

In 2012, this project began as a way to help freshmen at Oklahoma Baptist University (OBU) pursue a biblical worldview in light of the countless worldviews that vie for their hearts. As the collaborators for the book and the reach of the book have expanded beyond the walls of OBU, our prayer remains the same: we pray that readers will be stirred to immerse themselves in God's Word and allow it to transform their hearts and minds rather than allow the world to shape them into its image.

The Christian worldview centers on Jesus of Nazareth, the God-man who was born over two thousand years ago in a humble stable in Bethlehem, lived a perfectly sinless life, was crucified on a Roman cross, and was raised from the dead in Jerusalem. We, as Christians, have embraced Jesus as Messiah and Lord. He has redeemed us, provided for us, and loved us constantly despite our flaws and failures. It is to him, and to his glory, that this book is both dedicated and devoted.

PART I

INTRODUCING WORLDVIEW

WHAT IS WORLDVIEW?

The unexamined life is not worth living.

SOCRATES

Three friends once went to a nature preserve in the African Serengeti and experienced the majestic beauty and diversity of native African wildlife—zebra, elephant, gazelle, lion, and rhinoceros. Each was awestruck by the diversity of creatures observed.

The first friend, John Luther, commented boldly: "The Lord God has definitely created an amazing array of creatures that sing his praises and declare his glory to the ends of the earth, has he not?"

The second friend, Charles Dawkins, immediately responded: "An amazing array of creatures, to be sure. But you err, my good man, in ascribing their existence to a Creator. No, these incredible animals are the result of the unguided, purposeless combination of random mutation and natural selection. We too are the product of a natural evolutionary process. Indeed, we are no different from the creatures that we see."

The third friend, Shirley Chopra, serenely replied: "I pray you both would be enlightened to the full reality disclosed by our brothers and sisters on the nature preserve. For they too bear the same spark of divinity that lies within you and me. Do you not sense them calling to you, seeking to communicate with your spirit? We are all potential gods and goddesses; we just need to awaken to our heightened state and take hold of the possibilities that lie before us."

The three friends see the same animals within the same nature preserve. Thus, they experience the same objective truth. Nevertheless, due to their vastly different perspectives, the three friends see different things. Why? Simply put, John, Charles, and Shirley are experiencing a clash of worldviews. A *worldview,* as we will define it, is *the conceptual lens through which we see, understand, and interpret the world and our place within it.* The three safari friends wear different worldview glasses; thus, although they see the same thing, they actually see the world and their place within it very differently.

In 1999, the blockbuster film *The Matrix* was released. It was followed by two sequels in 2003 and ranks as one of Hollywood's most successful trilogies. *The Matrix* (1999) envisions a hypothetical futuristic scenario where humans have made increasingly sophisticated computers, complete with artificial intelligence. Eventually, the computers develop sufficient independent intelligence to wage war against their human creators. The computers win the battle and subsequently enslave the human race. Humans, however, are generally oblivious to this reality. Why? Because they are trapped in the Matrix. The world that people experience is an illusion—the result of an intricate computer simulation. In the real world, computers breed human beings in order to hook them up to machines and suck the heat and energy out of their bodies. The real world sees human bodies grown in vast fields, hooked up to electrical inputs to harvest their resources, and also linked to visual simulators that treat them to a virtual reality. This virtual reality resembles human life on earth as we know it (in 1999, when the movie was released). The human beings attached to these machines have the vivid experience of working normal jobs, having relationships, and so forth. The virtual reality is so compelling that people do not realize they are being manipulated and deceived.

However, a group of humans who have been awakened to the true nature of reality wage a quiet rebellion against the Matrix. In the movie, the focus is on Thomas Anderson (aka Neo), a computer hacker who questions his reality but has no concept of the true world. Morpheus and Trinity, two "liberated" humans, seek to enlighten Neo. They offer him two pills: one will return him to his virtual reality life; the other will show him what is really real. Neo famously takes the red pill, which opens his eyes to the illusion, and his world is forever changed. He will never look at things the same way again. He used to have one sense of objective reality but now has a very different perspective. Neo now sees the world through a new lens, a new theoretical structure. Basically, he has a new *worldview*.

1.1 *WELTANSCHAUUNG*: THE ORIGIN OF WORLDVIEW THOUGHT

The English term *worldview* is derived from the German *Weltanschauung*, a compound word (*Welt* = world + *Anschauung* = view or outlook) first used by Immanuel Kant to describe an individual's sensory perception of the world. The term spread quickly in German idealist philosophy "to refer to an intellectual conception of the universe from the perspective of a human knower."[1] In the late eighteenth and early nineteenth centuries, German philosophers used *Weltanschauung* increasingly for the concept of answering pivotal questions regarding life, the universe, and everything. Very quickly, other German thinkers— von Ranke (history), Wagner (music), Feuerbach (theology), and von Humboldt (physics)—applied *Weltanschauung* to their own disciplines. Furthermore, *Weltanschauung* was quickly adopted in other European countries, either as a loanword or translated into the local language. The value of worldview language and thought was quickly recognized across disciplines and languages so that "since its inception in Immanuel Kant's *Critique of Judgment* in 1790, the notion of *Weltanschauung* has become one of the central intellectual conceptions in contemporary thought and culture."[2]

The roots of worldview thought are in philosophy. Nonetheless, worldview has become integral to other disciplines as well. Michael Polanyi, Thomas Kuhn, and Imre Lakatos have been instrumental in applying worldview thought to the natural sciences. Psychologists, including Freud and Jung, have utilized worldview terminology and thought. Worldview has gained importance in sociology, particularly as sociologists like Karl Mannheim and Peter Berger have raised awareness of the pretheoretical construction of individual worldviews.

Other than philosophy, the discipline that has been most influenced by worldview thought is cultural anthropology. In the mid-1900s, Robert

---

[1]David K. Naugle, *Worldview: The History of a Concept* (Grand Rapids: Eerdmans, 2002), 59.
[2]Ibid., 66.

Redfield identified culturally prevalent worldviews, arguing that worldview "is the way a people characteristically look outward upon the universe." He distinguished worldview from culture and ethos, suggesting that worldview "is an arrangement of things looked out upon, things in first instance conceived of as existing."[3] Redfield suggested common components of worldview—distinction between self and others, distinction between man and not-man, and view of birth and death. Michael Kearney, writing a generation after Redfield, continues to draw out the importance of worldview for cultural anthropologists. A cultural worldview, according to Kearney, is "a set of images and assumptions about the world" and includes components of self and other, relationship (between self and other humans and nonhumans), classification, causality, and space and time.[4]

Anthropologist Paul Hiebert defines worldview as "the fundamental cognitive, affective, and evaluative presuppositions a group of people make about the nature of things, and which they use to order their lives."[5] Hiebert sees cognitive, affective, and moral aspects to worldview and identifies six worldview functions.[6] Hiebert argues that the transformation of the nonbeliever's underlying worldview lies at the core of the missionary task.

The importance of worldview thought in other disciplines cannot obscure its centrality in philosophy. It was particularly prominent in the work of nineteenth-century German philosophers, including Johann Gottlieb Fichte, Friedrich Schelling, Georg Hegel, Wilhelm Dilthey, and Friedrich Nietzsche. Worldview thought and development continued in twentieth-century philosophy, with significant contributions from Edmund Husserl, Karl Jaspers, Martin Heidegger, Donald Davidson, and Ludwig Wittgenstein.

---

[3]Robert Redfield, *The Primitive World and Its Transformations* (Ithaca, NY: Cornell University Press, 1953), 85-87.

[4]Michael Kearney, *World View* (Novato, CA: Chandler & Sharp, 1984), 10, 68-98. See also Naugle, *Worldview*, 241-43.

[5]Paul G. Hiebert, *Transforming Worldviews: An Anthropological Understanding of How People Change* (Grand Rapids: Baker Academic, 2008), 15.

[6](1) Providing a map of reality that structures our perceptions of reality and our guide for living, (2) conveying emotional security, (3) validating deep cultural norms, (4) integrating the individual into the culture, (5) monitoring cultural change, and (6) providing psychological reassurance that the world is as we perceive it to be. Hiebert, *Transforming Worldviews*, 29-30.

Worldview has been particularly prominent in Christian philosophy since the late nineteenth century. James Orr, Abraham Kuyper, and Herman Dooyeweerd were instrumental in bringing worldview into the evangelical Christian conversation. For Orr, seeing Christianity as a worldview helps focus philosophical discussion and debate. He argues that disagreement between Christians and non-Christians is not a matter of a particular doctrine or belief but a matter of underlying worldviews. The influence of Orr and other Christian philosophers can be discerned in this text, including James Olthuis, James Sire, Ronald Nash, David Naugle, Michael Goheen, Ken Samples, Arthur Holmes, Andrew Hoffecker, Doug Groothuis, Doug Huffman, Norm Geisler, and Brian Walsh.

REFLECTION QUESTIONS

1 In the opening story, the three friends see the same animals but different realities. What are some other situations where you think people with different worldviews would interpret reality differently?

2 Why do you think worldview has had so much more prominence in philosophy than in other academic disciplines?

1.2 Christian Worldview Defined

For the purposes of this book, the concept of worldview will be approached from the perspective of Christian philosophy and education. We acknowledge the existence and value of alternative conceptions of worldview and believe that they have their rightful place within other disciplines. For example, a student preparing for foreign missions would be well advised to focus on Paul Hiebert's missiological exposition of worldview and to learn from what cultural anthropologists Michael Kearney and Robert Redfield have to say about worldview. Our primary purposes, however, are neither missiological nor anthropological. Rather, we are concerned with the holistic intellectual-spiritual formation of the Christian student—to nurture students toward loving the Lord our God with all their hearts, souls, minds, and strength. We are convinced that learning to think in terms of worldview can help students grow in their love for God. What, then, is a worldview, what does it look like, and why does it matter?

1.2.1 What is worldview? We have defined *worldview*, provisionally, as "the conceptual lens through which we see, understand, and interpret the world and our place within it." There is, however, a multitude of ways to define and explain worldview; we will survey a few of them for helpful insights.

Steven Cowan and James Spiegel define *worldview* as "a set of beliefs, values, and presuppositions concerning life's most fundamental issues."[7] They argue that the central goal of philosophy is constructing and developing a comprehensive worldview. For example, if you ask about the philosophy of René Descartes or David Hume or Socrates, what you are really asking is, what is their worldview? From this perspective, worldview is primarily an intellectual construction, a rational system of belief.

Worldview certainly has a rational component. If nothing else, worldview necessarily involves an understanding of the world that can be expressed in terms of intellectual propositions.[8] It is possible, however, to overintellectualize worldview and to think of it strictly in terms of intellectual propositions or rational systems. When this happens, worldview is equated to a formal philosophical system and becomes an abstract concept that seems applicable only to an educated elite.

More problematically, a strictly rationalistic presentation of worldview thinking misconstrues the nature of human beings by suggesting that we are primarily or exclusively thinking beings. There is no doubt that we are indeed thinking beings. Our ability to conceptualize, to theorize, to reflect, and to synthesize is an essential and nonnegotiable element of human nature. The problem arises with the implication that human beings approach the world primarily or exclusively rationally, evaluating competing truth claims and embracing those that they are convinced are the most logical and rationally compelling. It seems instead that our worldview is most commonly formed (at least initially) without

---

[7]Steven B. Cowan and James S. Spiegel, *The Love of Wisdom: A Christian Introduction to Philosophy* (Nashville: B&H Academic, 2009), 7.

[8]A proposition, simply put, is a sentence (or multiple sentences) that makes a truth claim. A proposition (e.g., Edmonton is the capital of the province of Alberta in the country known as Canada) asserts something that it claims is true of the real world. A worldview truth claim could be something like "We are all living in *the matrix*—what we think is really real, is really not real at all."

intellectual propositions or rational deliberation. A purely rationalistic picture of human beings seems to miss the prerational (or pretheoretical) and sometimes nonrational nature of worldview and worldview formation.

1.2.2 James Sire's understanding of worldview. James Sire, arguably the most influential evangelical worldview proponent over the past two generations, acknowledges that his early worldview thinking was stunted by hyperrationalism. His classic text, *The Universe Next Door: A Basic Worldview Catalog*, is currently in its fifth edition. The first three editions focused on worldview as primarily a set of basic concepts or intellectual presuppositions.[9] After rethinking his approach, Sire thoroughly revised his understanding and explanation of worldview. Sire no longer understands or explains worldview in terms of philosophical propositions alone. Instead, he provides a comprehensive and holistic definition:

> A worldview is a commitment, a fundamental orientation of the heart, that can be expressed as a story or in a set of presuppositions (assumptions which may be true, partially true or entirely false) which we hold (consciously or subconsciously, consistently or inconsistently) about the basic constitution of reality, and that provides the foundation on which we live and move and have our being.[10]

Sire's definition is helpful on several levels and deserves to be unpacked.

1.2.2.1 A matter of the heart. First, Sire notes that worldview is not simply a set of intellectual or rational ideas but rather reflects a "commitment, a fundamental orientation of the heart." The heart, on this understanding, represents the center of the human person. David Naugle notes that

> when worldview is reinterpreted in light of the doctrine of the heart, not only is its true source located, but it becomes a richer concept than its philosophical counterpart, being more than just a reference to an abstract thesis about reality, but an Hebraic expression of the existential condition of the whole person.[11]

---

[9]James W. Sire, *Naming the Elephant: Worldview as a Concept*, 2nd ed. (Downers Grove, IL: IVP Academic, 2015), 13.
[10]James W. Sire, *The Universe Next Door: A Basic Worldview Catalog*, 5th ed. (Downers Grove, IL: IVP Academic, 2009), 21.
[11]Naugle, *Worldview*, 270.

Many people are relatively unconscious of their worldview assumptions because they have developed these commitments internally and embraced them as orientations of the heart.

1.2.2.2 Propositions or narratives. Second, Sire notes that worldview can be expressed as a story or in a set of presuppositions. There has been a tendency in modern Western philosophy to reduce worldview beliefs to a propositional format, a tendency that certainly has its benefits. In reality, however, the philosophical and religious beliefs of human beings are more commonly shared and passed down through story, not through a set of philosophical propositions. We are storied creatures, responding more readily to narrative than to doctrine. From a Christian perspective, it is worth noting that the Scriptures are predominantly narrative in form. Jesus of Nazareth preferred to teach through story, utilizing the unique teaching tool of parables—brief narratives packing a powerful rhetorical punch. Thus, while Sire notes that worldview can take a narrative or a propositional format, for the vast majority of people past and present, worldview is narrative in structure.

1.2.2.3 True, false, and in between. Third, Sire observes that our worldview presumptions may be true, partially true, or entirely false. We each hold a variety of worldview beliefs, but merely holding these beliefs does not make them true. The Christian understanding that all human beings are fallen and sinful gives us reason for significant pause and epistemological humility. Knowing that we are fallen creatures and that we do not have the mind of God reminds us that we are unlikely to possess an entirely correct worldview. Worldviews will inevitably be a mixture of truth and error. This is not to say that all worldviews possess an equal proportion of truth; rather, it is to insist that no one possesses a God's-eye view of the world.

1.2.2.4 Conscious or unconscious. Fourth, Sire notes that many people maintain their worldviews consciously and explicitly while others are entirely unaware of the worldviews that they hold. Worldviews are pretheoretical in nature; they develop prior to or devoid of conscious reflection and rational deliberation. As children, our developing worldview is most strongly influenced by our parents—hence the fact that most teens inherit the worldviews of their parents. Other influences, including culture, education, media, and religion, help shape the unconscious worldview that develops. As Randy Nelson notes, "Most people take for granted the beliefs that they inherit from these sources, assuming them to be true without intentionally questioning them."[12] People are not conscious of their worldviews unless they have been challenged to think explicitly about their core beliefs and commitments. Each person presupposes a worldview, to be sure, but many people are unaware that they do and are equally unaware of what that worldview is. Along with Socrates, we hold that an unexamined life is not worth living. Accordingly, we also insist that an unexamined, unconscious worldview is not worth embracing.[13] One of the central goals in Christian philosophy is to encourage a conscious, in-depth examination of one's worldview. We are convinced that we need not remain unconscious of our worldview, unaware of what our primary heart commitments are and how they direct our lives.

1.2.2.5 Consistent or inconsistent. Fifth, Sire insists that many people hold inconsistent worldviews; their fundamental presuppositions simply do not fit together logically. Another purpose of Christian philosophy is to develop a consistent worldview by identifying and eliminating logical inconsistencies.

1.2.2.6 Ultimate reality. Sixth, Sire explains that a central component of worldview is one's perspective on "the basic constitution of reality." The core of a worldview is one's understanding of what constitutes the "really real." For a Christian, God the Father, Son, and Holy Spirit is ultimate reality. For a Muslim, Allah the Merciful and Almighty is ultimate reality. For some Buddhists, nirvana is the really real, in contrast to the desires and trials of this life, which are transitory and ultimately empty. For some Hindus, Brahman (an infinite, impersonal transcendent reality) is ultimate reality. For a materialist (atheist), the physical cosmos is the only really real. For a New Age spiritualist, the

---

[12]Randy W. Nelson, "What Is a Worldview?," in *Christian Contours: How a Biblical Worldview Shapes the Mind and Heart,* ed. Douglas S. Huffman (Grand Rapids: Kregel, 2011), 30.

[13]Sadly, I cannot take credit for this adaptation of Socratic wisdom. A similar version can be found in Norman L. Geisler and William D. Watkins, *Worlds Apart: A Handbook on World Views,* 2nd ed. (Grand Rapids: Baker Books, 1989), 9. "Socrates said, 'The unexamined life is not worth living.' And the unexamined world view is not worth living by."

divine self is ultimate reality, or at least a part of ultimate reality. One's worldview, whether in propositional or narrative form, is centered on an understood or implied foundational reality.

1.2.2.7 Life-directing. Finally, Sire notes that our worldview directs our life path by providing the foundation on which "we live and move and have our being" (Acts 17:28). Naugle points out that worldview, as a deep-seated commitment of the heart, is a motivating factor in how we live. In the first place, our cultural and contextual circumstances help shape our worldview: "Into the heart go the issues of life. . . . The life-shaping content of the heart is determined not only by nature or organic predispositions, but very much by nurture."[14] Our worldview then proceeds to shape our experience of life and our daily motivation and direction: "Out of the heart go the issues of life. Once the heart of an individual is formed by the powerful forces of both nature and nurture, it constitutes the presuppositional basis of life." The heart, the individual's worldview, is first affected by conditions and influences; in turn it influences the direction of the individual's life. Naugle identifies this interplay between one's worldview and context: "Hence the sum and substance of the heart, . . . in short, what I am calling a 'worldview,' sustains an *interactive or reciprocal* relationship with the external world."[15]

A person's worldview is developed during that person's formative years, influenced and instilled by a myriad of sociocultural forces. But worldview, once in place, becomes a fundamental heart commitment, directing one's life choices and values. Worldview beliefs, whether conscious or unconscious, serve as presuppositions on which the rest of life is based.

In summary, Sire's definition of worldview helps us grasp the strongly internal and pretheoretical nature of worldview. He points out that worldviews contain a mixture of truth and error and can be held with relative degrees of consciousness and consistency. Finally, worldview centers on a fundamental understanding of prime reality and gives direction to our life choices.

---

[14]Naugle, *Worldview*, 270-71. Naugle cites religion, culture, economic situation, friendships, marriage, family, education, work, sexual experiences, and warfare as some of the many factors that shape an individual's worldview at the heart level.

[15]Ibid. (emphasis original).

James Olthuis provides a complementary definition of worldview.

> A worldview (or vision of life) is a framework or set of fundamental beliefs through which we view the world and our calling and future in it. This vision may be so internalized that it goes largely unquestioned; it may be greatly refined through cultural-historical development; it may not be explicitly developed into a systematic conception of life; it may not be theoretically deepened into a philosophy; it may not even be codified into creedal form. Nevertheless, this vision is a channel for the ultimate beliefs which give direction and meaning to life. It is the integrative and interpretative framework by which order and disorder are judged, the standard by which reality is managed and pursued. It is the set of hinges on which all our everyday thinking and doing turns.[16]

Several pages ago, we provisionally defined worldview as the conceptual lens through which we see, understand, and interpret the world and our place within it. We will maintain that definition and use it going forward, as it concisely encapsulates the nature and scope of worldview. However, our concise definition should be understood within the enriching context provided by Sire and Olthuis.

REFLECTION QUESTIONS

1 How would you define worldview in your own words? Why provide that definition?

2 What do you think of the authors' claim that worldview is formed pretheoretically?

3 Which aspect of James Sire's expanded definition of worldview was the most helpful to you? Why?

1.3 COMPONENTS OF WORLDVIEW

Philosophers, educators, sociologists, missiologists, and anthropologists alike can agree that worldview is an important concept to understand and apply. Furthermore, scholars in each discipline agree that there is an identifiable set of common components to worldview. Scholars differ,

---

[16]James H. Olthuis, "On Worldviews," *Christian Scholar's Review* 14, no. 2 (1985): 155.

however, in regard to what those common components actually are. Their differences are sometimes related to their respective fields of study. Thus, for example, philosopher James Sire identifies classical philosophical questions as the common components of worldview.[17] Anthropologist Michael Kearney, on the other hand, highlights identification of the self and the other and sociological relationships.[18] Scholars also differ in terms of how worldview components ought to be identified. Some scholars propose categories of thought or belief as the common components to worldview. Other scholars suggest that all worldviews address a set of unavoidable common questions.

For our part, we believe that it is best to approach universal worldview components with four core questions in mind: What is our nature? What is our world? What is our problem? What is our end? On one hand, asking such questions helps to bring worldview commitments to the surface in a way that categories or classifications may not; the route of questioning embodies the still-valuable Socratic method of philosophical inquiry. On the other hand, it also seems to us that approaching worldviews via questions is more attuned to the predominantly storied or narrative structure of worldview. Thus, we believe that our worldview—conscious or not, consistent or not—answers four fundamental questions (actually, four sets of questions) about life, the universe, and everything. Each question (or set of questions) has multiple possible answers that can be given in the form of stories or propositions; together, the answers compose a comprehensive view of reality. The questions posed for and answered by every worldview have been asked by thinking persons for millennia.

A quick word of warning is in order, however. The way that we present these questions makes them seem independent of one another. In reality, this is far from the case. None of the questions exists in isolation. Like most questions and answers in philosophy and in life in general, these questions are intricately intertwined and interrelated. Answers to the first question have grave implications for the remaining questions; answers to the second question often entail necessary responses to other

---

[17]Sire, *Universe Next Door*, 22-23.
[18]Michael Kearney, *World View* (Novato, CA: Chandler & Sharp, 1984), 68-98.

questions, and so forth. Hence, one's worldview contains a holistic, wrapped-up-together set of answers to all the worldview questions.

1.3.1 What is our nature? We begin here because this is where thinking, reflective human beings begin. The question, what is our nature?, may not have logical priority, but it does have chronological and existential priority.[19] In order to ask questions about our place in the universe or the existence (or lack thereof) of a deity, one needs first to exist as a rational, reflective agent. I ask questions about my own nature and composition before asking questions about other human beings or a hypothetical deity. When I eventually ask questions about other human beings and God, I may refine or alter my understanding of who/what I am, but this does not change the fact that I ask the existential questions first. Thus, the first necessary component of worldview involves questions regarding the nature of the self, the human being.

What is our nature? Who am I? What does it mean to be human? What distinguishes me from other living creatures? Are we the product of random mutation and natural selection? Are we the handiwork of a divine Creator? Are we purely physical, material beings? Do we have an immaterial soul or spirit as well? Do we have free will, or are our actions determined by our biochemistry?

1.3.2 What is our world? When a newborn baby is unceremoniously expelled from the warm comfort of the mother's womb, I can almost hear the unexpressed words in the baby's plaintive cry: Where am I? What is the nature of this strange, cold, and bright environment? As that infant grows and is nurtured, the child gains and develops an understanding of the external world.

What is our world? What is the nature and character of the physical world? Is the physical world ordered or chaotic? Is it a closed system (deterministic) or an open system (orderable by free-willed creatures)? Is matter eternal and uncreated, divine and coeternal with deity, or temporal and created? Answering the question, what is our world?, involves an understanding of cosmology—the nature of the world. Our worldview, however, does not stop there. In answering this question, worldview proceeds to ask

---

[19]That is, this question may not be the most important question (logical priority), but it is the first one we ask (chronological/existential priority).

SCENIC VIEW

Contemporary Cultural Worldview Meditation

Star Wars and the Worldview Questions

Consider the worldview exemplified in the original Star Wars trilogy (now episodes 4-6).

What is our nature? On an individual level, Luke Skywalker's identity and nature present a pressing question throughout the trilogy: he is a Jedi prodigy, the one destined to triumph over the Sith Lord. On a global level, human beings are portrayed as merely one among a myriad of intelligent beings inhabiting a vast universe filled with sentient life.

What is our world? Again, we are part of a massive universe where science and technology reign. There are no references to spiritual beings or divine entities, only the ubiquitous midichlorians (though we don't find out that they are midichlorians until the release of episode 1), which govern the balance of the universe.

What is our problem? The Force is currently imbalanced by the domination of the emperor and his Sith partner, Darth Vader. The Empire is oppressive and suppressing, seeking to stamp out independent free-minded peoples throughout the universe, particularly through the use of their weapon of mass destruction, the Death Star.

What is our end? The purpose of humanity (actually, of sentient life) is somewhat unclear in the Star Wars films. Perhaps it is maintaining and living within the balance of the Force. Perhaps it is freedom from any autocratic government. Perhaps it is finding fulfillment in love or personal accomplishments.

questions in the realm of philosophy of religion and theology.

What is fundamental reality or ultimate reality? Is the universe all that is, all that ever was, and all that ever will be? Or is there a supernatural reality? Is this simply a physical universe, or is it a universe charged with the grandeur of God? If God exists, what is God like? Personal or impersonal? Unitary or triune? If God does not exist, what is ultimate reality?

Note the inevitable relationship between this question and the previous one. If ultimate reality is the physical universe, and there is nothing beyond it, then of necessity human beings are strictly physical creatures. If there is no spiritual or nonphysical side to the cosmos, there cannot be a spiritual or soulish side to human beings either.

1.3.3 What is our problem? The newborn infant experiences the external world as a place of discomfort. Warmth and security have been shattered by a forced move into a colder, insecure world. The child cannot help but ask, what's wrong? One constant feature of human thought and civilization has been the unshakable impression that something is amiss in the human universe.

Thus, we ask, What is our problem? What is wrong with us as human beings, and how can it be solved? What is wrong with the world, and how can it be solved? Every person and every worldview acknowledges that there is something wrong with both the world and with each person as an individual in the world. Things are not the way they ought to be. What is wrong with all human beings? Is it sinful rebellion against our Divine Maker? Is it ignorance, religious superstition, or lack of education? Is it the illusion of personal desires? Is it corrupting social, political, and economic structures? Furthermore, after identifying the problem, how can we go about fixing it?

1.3.4 What is our end? The Greek word *telos* (τέλος) carries connotations of purpose, end, goal, and destination. This final worldview question is best understood in the multifaceted light of *telos*.

What is our end? Worldview addresses our origins: What is our nature as human beings, and where did we come from? Worldview must also address our end: Where are we going? Is there any meaning and purpose in life, or are we random creatures in a purposeless, meaningless universe? Do we create our own purpose and meaning? Or do we rightly seek to fulfill some purpose for which we were created?

In addition to questions of meaning and purpose in this life, human beings also ponder their postmortem fate. What happens to us after we die? Is physical death the end of human existence? Are we absorbed into an infinite, impersonal ultimate reality? Are we judged at the throne of God Almighty for an eternity with him in heaven or an eternity without him in hell? The answers we give to these four worldview questions compose our worldview.

REFLECTION QUESTIONS

1 Why do the authors approach worldview through core questions? Do you think it's a valuable approach? Why or why not?

2 Think of a neighbor/friend who has different fundamental beliefs from yours. How do you think he or she might answer the four worldview questions?

3 Can you think of a worldview that does not acknowledge a problem with us or our world?

1.4 The Universality and Diversity of Worldview

Worldview is the conceptual lens through which we see, understand, and interpret the world and our place within it. Worldview develops in and flows through the heart, the center of the human person, and necessarily involves answers (propositional or narrative) to four sets of questions: What is our nature? What is our world? What is our problem? What is our end? Furthermore, a worldview is a person-specific matrix—a perception of reality, a filter through which everything flows as we seek to make sense of external data. The answers, conscious or unconscious, consistent or inconsistent, to the four governing questions constitute one's fundamental worldview. Each person has an answer to the four sets of questions, even if the person has never formed them into intelligible propositions or coherent narratives. Whether one looks at worldview as a set of beliefs about the structure of the world, an internal framework, or a set of glasses through which we look at reality, the bottom line is that every person possesses a worldview. We may not like it; we might deny it. We might insist that worldview is not even a rational concept. But that does not change the fact that each of us has a worldview and that one's worldview strongly affects the way that one lives.

Because everybody has a worldview, there are literally countless worldviews held by people across the globe. Each worldview is unique to its owner. No two people have precisely identical worldviews. Consider, for example, possible answers to the second worldview question, what is our world? Christians are going to answer that question with the same general answer: God's. This is my Father's world; the universe is created by and for God the Father, Son, and Holy Spirit. To this point, Christians will universally agree. But if we delve deeper, there is much more to explore.

For example, what else can we say about the God who created the universe? Some philosophers and theologians argue that we cannot say much else because God is utterly transcendent and beyond our knowledge, definition, and comprehension. Others insist that we can and should seek to understand God and that we can indeed come to know God truly (although not exhaustively). They might argue, for example, that God is omnipresent, omnipotent, omniscient, and omnibenevolent.

Imagine that we agree that God is omnipotent. Well then, what does omnipotence mean? Can God do literally anything? William of Ockham and others insist that yes, God can do literally anything. Thomas Aquinas and others insist that no, God cannot do some things. God cannot lie, because to do so would be to violate his very nature.

How about God's omnibenevolence, or all-goodness? How can we work that out? If God is all good, where does evil come from? Is evil, as Augustine argued, the absence of goodness that occurs when God's creatures fail to practice his goodness in their lives? Does evil result strictly from the sinful rebellion of man? Does God desire evil to exist in order to bring greater glory to himself through redemption? Christians have differences in these areas.

How about God's omniscience, or all-knowingness? Most Christians affirm that God knows all things, including future actions that human beings, as free-willed creatures, have not even chosen to do yet. How can this be? Augustine and Boethius argue that God exists outside of time and space, such that he experiences what is future to us as already present to himself. Thus, our future free actions are already seen by God and enable his eternally present knowledge of those events. God sees our future in the same way that we see our present. Others, including Bruce Ware, argue that God's knowledge of the future is grounded in his meticulous sovereignty, whereby he not only foreknows but foreordains what is yet to come.[20] God knows future actions because God determines what those actions shall be.

Or, consider another aspect of the second worldview question from a Christian perspective. What is the nature of reality? Christians generally agree that God has created all that is. After that, agreement can break down. Did God create the universe and everything within it a very short time ago, less than ten thousand years ago? Or did God create the universe a very long time ago, perhaps fourteen billion years ago?

---

[20]E.g., Bruce A. Ware, *God's Greater Glory: The Exalted God of Scripture* (Wheaton, IL: Crossway, 2004), 35-160.

The point here is not to engage in discussion or debate about these issues; rather, the point is simply to demonstrate that within one broad worldview perspective (that of orthodox Christian theism), there exists a wide variety of ways to work out the answers to worldview questions. The moral of the story is simply that each person possesses a worldview that is entirely unique to that person. No two Christians are going to have precisely identical worldviews. This creates somewhat of a tension within worldview thinking. On the one hand, there is such a thing as a Christian worldview—propositions, answers, or narratives that are common to all Christians at all times in all places. Baptist, Pentecostal, Catholic, and Eastern Orthodox Christians will affirm the overarching narrative of creation-fall-redemption: God created, humanity is fallen, and Jesus saves. On the other hand, Christian traditions nuance those worldview beliefs and work out other aspects of worldview differently. Examination of individual Christian believers reveals a great deal of diversity. Simply put, different Christians possess different manifestations of the Christian worldview. Despite the differences, however, there is such a thing as an overarching Christian worldview.

In some ways, this diversity in the midst of unity should not surprise us; this is just one version of the classic philosophical problem of the one and the many. For example, a typical college classroom is filled with perhaps two dozen human beings; yet each student is a different and unique example or manifestation of humanness. We all share certain essential or nonnegotiable characteristics or properties that make us uniformly human. Yet we each have other, more incidental or accidental, characteristics or properties that make us a uniquely instantiated human being. The same is true with respect to worldviews. There are certain essential characteristics to a uniformly Christian worldview, yet there are also numerous secondary characteristics that mark a uniquely fleshed-out Christian worldview.

Thus, the fact that everybody has a unique individual worldview does not prevent us from identifying a more limited number of overarching worldviews. Often these broad worldviews will be defined as philosophical systems or as religious worldviews. Some of the key worldviews prevalent in the world today include Christianity, Islam, Judaism, naturalism (atheistic modernity), existentialism, Buddhism, Hinduism, animism, New Age spirituality, and postmodernism. These overarching worldviews provide different large-picture answers to the fundamental worldview questions.

For example, a naturalistic (or atheistic) worldview claims that there is no God, the universe sprang into existence with no explanation (or else has existed eternally), life arose on primordial earth through random chemical reactions, and human life evolved through random mutation and natural selection. There is nothing particularly special about human beings compared to the rest of nature, and our primary problem is enslavement to superstitious worldviews that promote religious belief. The solution to the problem is intellectual evolution and liberation from religious oppression. After we die, we entirely cease to be, so whatever purpose we choose to pursue for our lives is the only purpose and meaning there can be.

The Christian worldview has substantially different answers. In the beginning was God the Father, Son, and Holy Spirit. All that is was created by him out of nothingness; at its creation, everything was declared good by God. Humankind was created good by God and stamped with his very image. The problems in the world are the result of humanity's rebellion and fall into sin. Instead of harmony and communion, human beings now experience broken relationships with God, self, fellow human beings, and God's creation. God provides the means for redemption through the atoning death of Jesus; broken relationships can be healed and reconciled in Christ. After death, all human beings are judged on the basis of their relationship with God in Christ; believers experience eternal life in the presence of God.

STOP & PAUSE

Biblical Worldview Insight

The eye is the lamp of the body. If your eyes are healthy, your whole body will be full of light. But if your eyes are unhealthy, your whole body will be full of darkness. If then the light within you is darkness, how great is that darkness! (Mt 6:22-23)

In the context of the Sermon on the Mount, Jesus is insisting that one must choose between the things of heaven and the things of earth—the kingdom of heaven (God) and the kingdom of earth (man). He goes on to emphasize that "no one can serve two masters" (Mt 6:24).

Given that, read Jesus' words in Matthew 6:22-23 in the context of worldview thought. If your worldview lenses are healthy, your whole body will be full of light. That is, if you are looking at the world correctly, seeing things the way that God sees them, you will live an illuminated, enlightening life. But if your worldview lenses are unhealthy, your whole body will be full of darkness. When one wears a distorted set of worldview glasses, nothing looks right, and life cannot be lived rightly.

Check your prescription! Are you wearing the right worldview? Or do you need new lenses?

The differences between the worldview matrices of naturalism and Christianity are significant and greatly affect the way that we perceive the world around us. You can, indeed, say with justification that the Christian theist and the naturalist inhabit different worlds. The conceptual lens through which the world is viewed is starkly distinct; thus, what is seen is also quite different. We consider Jesus' words in the Sermon on the Mount, understood through the filter of worldview thought, to be a fitting conclusion to this introductory chapter:

> The eye [worldview] is the lamp of the body. If your eyes are healthy, your whole body will be full of light. But if your eyes are unhealthy, your whole body will be full of darkness. If then the light within you is darkness, how great is that darkness! (Mt 6:22-23)

REFLECTION QUESTIONS

1 Do differences of opinion between Christians regarding God's omnipotence, or the way in which God created, have any importance? Why or why not?

2 What would you identify as the essential elements of an overarching Christian worldview?

3 What are the most prominent or influential worldviews in North America today? In East Asia?

4 What might be some broad differences between Baptist, Catholic, Presbyterian, and Anglican expressions of Christian worldview?

MASTERING THE MATERIAL

When you finish reading this chapter, you should be able to

✔ Provide a concise definition of worldview and explain its contours.

✔ Recount the rising importance of worldview thought, especially in Western philosophy.

✔ Identify the four core worldview questions and their subquestions.

✔ Articulate your own response to the worldview questions.

✔ Differentiate shared contours of an overarching Christian worldview and denominational/individual elements of a personal Christian worldview.

Glossary of Terms for Chapter One

cultural anthropology—A nearly independent branch of anthropology that focuses on the study of cultural variations among the human race.

inconsistent worldview—A worldview whose fundamental presuppositions do not fit together logically.

missiology—Area of practical theology that focuses on the mission, mandate, and message of the church.

narrative format—When something is told in narrative format, it takes on the framework of a story rather than a list of events.

presupposition—A belief that is assumed before any argument is made for or against it.

pretheoretical—something that arises before any theoretical considerations.

propositional format—When something is presented in propositional format, it becomes a list of main points or events rather than a narrative or story.

Weltanschauung—German word meaning "worldview" or "outlook."

worldview—the conceptual lens through which we see, understand, and interpret the world and our place within it.

Possible Term Paper Topics

✔ Trace the development of worldview thought from Kant to Kuyper.

✔ Investigate the formative/transformative power of story as it relates to worldview.

✔ Choose a prominent Christian thinker and, using that person's writings (or words), reconstruct his or her worldview at a precise level.

✔ Choose one of the core attributes of God (omnipresence, omnipotence, omnibenevolence, omniscience). Research how various theologians and philosophers have understood that attribute. Articulate and defend your own position.

Core Bibliography for Chapter One

Goheen, Michael W., and Craig G. Bartholomew. *Living at the Crossroads: An Introduction to Christian Worldview*. Grand Rapids: Baker Academic, 2008.

Naugle, David K. *Worldview: The History of a Concept*. Grand Rapids: Eerdmans, 2002.

Sire, James W. *The Universe Next Door: A Basic Worldview Catalog*. 5th ed. Downers Grove, IL: IVP Academic, 2009.

Walsh, Brian J., and J. Richard Middleton. *The Transforming Vision: Shaping a Christian Worldview*. Downers Grove, IL: IVP Academic, 1984.

THE IMPORTANCE AND
IMPACT OF WORLDVIEW

Worldview is the conceptual lens through which we see, understand, and interpret the world and our place within it. Worldview develops in and flows through the heart, the center of the human person, and necessarily involves answers (propositional or narrative) to four questions: What is our nature? What is our world? What is our problem? What is our end? Every person possesses a worldview that provides an answer or set of answers to these core worldview questions, but these individual world-views can be compiled under broad categories.

2.1 THE IMPACT OF WORLDVIEW

I greatly enjoy mysteries and detective stories, from Sherlock Holmes to Hercule Poirot, *Law & Order* to *NCIS*. When cops or crown attorneys have a working thesis concerning a particular crime, their approach to evidence is affected by how that evidence relates to their governing thesis. For example, if they suspect someone of committing a particular crime, tiny bits of evidence will strengthen their position.

One of my favorite shows was *Monk*, starring Tony Shalhoub as the obsessive-compulsive, brilliant, and dysfunctional detective Adrian Monk. In one episode, "Monk and the Astronaut," Monk investigates the murder (a staged suicide) of a former call girl who was about to publish a revealing autobiography. Monk quickly becomes convinced that the murderer is a prominent NASA astronaut and rising politician. During the investigation, Monk discovers that the woman's autobiography had included a chapter relating how, many years earlier, the suspect had been arrested and jailed for beating the now-deceased woman during their tumultuous romantic entanglement. When Monk hears this, it supports his thesis that the astronaut is "the guy." The revealing autobiography (now mysteriously erased from her computer) provides motive for the murder. The evidence is not airtight: there are no surviving manuscripts of the autobiography, no solid proof that the woman was going to "out" the suspect, no concrete evidence that the call girl was beaten by the suspect. But it doesn't take a big piece of evidence to support or maintain Monk's theory; he now has his suspect's potential motive.

I am often asked why worldview matters: What does it impact? Why bother learning about it as a concept, and one's own worldview specifically? What does it have to do with life? Throughout this chapter, I will come back to detective shows like *Monk* to help illustrate the importance of worldview awareness and thought. Simply put, worldview matters because one's worldview affects everything that one thinks and does, through *confirmation bias, experiential accommodation, the pool of live options*, and *life motivation*.

2.1.1 Worldview and confirmation bias. First, worldview affects us through a phenomenon known as confirmation bias. "Confirmation bias refers to a type of selective thinking whereby one tends to notice and to look for what confirms one's beliefs, and to ignore, not look for, or undervalue the relevance of what contradicts one's beliefs."[1] In other words, confirmation bias is the influence of worldview guiding a person to affirm what fits with his preexisting worldview. As the English philosopher Francis Bacon wrote, "It is the peculiar and perpetual error of the human understanding to be more moved and excited by affirmatives than by negatives."[2] We tend to see, dwell on, and be excited by what fits with our existing worldview beliefs. Confirmation bias is the first way in which worldview affects our approach to external data.

You can see confirmation bias at work in many different areas. For example, consider proponents of evolution. According to Darwin's original theory, the fossil record should be filled with multitudes of

---

[1]Robert Todd Carroll, "Confirmation Bias," *The Skeptic's Dictionary*, last updated June 15, 2016, accessed February 8, 2017, www.skepdic.com/confirmbias.html.
[2]Cited in ibid.

intermediate species, transitional fossils that highlight the evolutionary process from one distinct species into another. While evolutionists acknowledge that the vast fossil evidence predicted by early Darwinists is simply not there, the theory persists.[3] And every year or two, one hears the proclamation of a new fossil discovery of a possible "transitional species." There are not many intermediates, certainly not as many as predicted, but proponents trumpet each new proposed discovery as proof of evolution's truth.

Along the same lines, proponents of a worldview that claims we live in a random, purposeless universe, and that human life on earth arose strictly by chance, tend to believe that there is or ought to be life somewhere out there in the universe. If it is believed that there is life beyond the earth, then the discovery of lines that look like ancient river beds on the surface of Mars is quite exciting and serves as confirmation of that worldview. To others, it just looks like interesting lines that might indicate there used to be water on the surface of Mars—nothing earth-shattering, and certainly not proof that life could have existed on the Red Planet.

Alternatively, Christians who believe in life after death, that this physical life is only the introduction to eternity, point to studies of near-death experiences as proof that there is at least a minimal existence and consciousness after death.[4] Due to the influence of confirmation bias, it doesn't take a significant amount of corroborating evidence to reinforce the existing worldview.

Confirmation bias also affects what evidence in particular is emphasized. For example, some Westerners point to Osama bin Laden, the 9/11 attacks, ISIS, and other terrorist activities perpetrated by Muslims to conclude that Islam is a hate-filled, inherently violent religion. Others point to the Red Crescent and other Muslim charities to argue that Islam is a compassionate, inherently peaceful religion. The same evidence is seen by both parties, but each group emphasizes the data that fit with their preexisting perspective.

---

[3]See, e.g., Stephen Jay Gould, *Punctuated Equilibrium* (Cambridge, MA: Belknap Press, 2007).
[4]See, e.g., Gary Habermas and J. P. Moreland, *Beyond Death: Exploring the Evidence for Immortality* (Eugene, OR: Wipf & Stock, 2004).

Being aware of one's own (and others') worldview, then, can help identify when and where one is being affected by confirmation bias. Am I embracing these data because the data are convincing or because they fit my worldview presuppositions? Am I valuing this set of data over that set of data for objectively compelling reasons or simply because this set confirms what I already think?

2.1.2 Worldview and experiential accommodation. Second, worldview influences us by driving us to interpret new data or arguments in a manner that affirms or fits within our existing worldview. Whenever possible, we interpret new data in a worldview-affirming manner. One example is the various strata of rocks evident in the Grand Canyon. Mainstream geologists look at the data, carbon-date the rocks within the layers, and conclude quite logically that the various layers consist of sediment laid down one layer atop the other over millions of years—a conclusion that fits quite nicely within their basic belief that the earth is billions of years old and that events on earth have progressed over time through predictable and lengthy physical processes (thus answering the worldview question, what is our world?).

A minority of geologists, however, look at the same physical data and come to radically different conclusions about what these data mean. From these geologists' perspective, the layers and even the ancient appearance of the Grand Canyon are not the result of millions of years of erosion but rather represent the catastrophic effects of the global flood described in Genesis 6. The dire consequences of the flood, in their view, explain the inaccuracy of carbon-dating the rocks in those sediment strata: the flood changed the composition of the atmosphere, thereby rendering long-term past carbon-dating useless. Young-earth geologists begin with a radically different set of assumptions and thus interpret the same physical data in a radically different way.

It must be emphasized that both groups of geologists cannot possibly be right. The data of the Grand Canyon cannot mean *both* that the earth is billions of years old and the rocks are layers of sediment laid down over millions of years *and* that the earth is only thousands of years old and the evident layers are the result of a single catastrophic flood. One camp is correct in its interpretation and the other is incorrect—or, perhaps, both camps are incorrect and some other explanation is the right one. The point is that we inevitably seek to interpret new data, evidence, or arguments in a manner that fits within our existing worldview. Young-earth geologists accommodate the data to fit their prevailing worldview; old-earth geologists do the same. Most often, people will accommodate new data within their worldview rather than altering their worldview to suit new data.

In another *Monk* episode, Monk suspects a publisher of murder. However, the publisher has an alibi for the night of the murder: he was with a young woman. The woman confirms the alibi, insisting that they were together all night. Someone who believes the man was (or could be) innocent would take the alibi as conclusive proof that he could not have done it. But Monk is not convinced. Rather than allaying his suspicion, he seeks to understand how this new datum could fit within his preexisting hypothesis. He still believes the publisher to be guilty but has to explain why the woman would lie to protect him. He concludes that the man has to be paying off the young woman to provide a false alibi for him—a suspicion that is eventually proven correct. The point, again, is that we naturally seek to accommodate new data or information within our existing worldview.

Consider again the relative lack of transitional species in the fossil record. What does one do with that? It depends on the underlying worldview. The creationist simply points out that Darwin proposed a way of falsifying his theory: if the fossils were not there, his theory would be false. The fossils are not there; ergo, Darwinian evolution is false. The Darwinist is not so easily swayed. Perhaps fossils are not retained with equal frequency in various geologic ages such that most transitional fossils have simply not been preserved. Or perhaps Stephen Jay Gould was correct in proposing punctuated equilibrium as a way that Darwinian evolution could be maintained despite the absence of fossil evidence. The point is simply that the "new" evidence is dealt with differently, and the difference is determined by the underlying worldview.[5]

---

[5] I am not suggesting that the data have no impact on worldview. During the stage of worldview formation, such data can play a determinative role in answering the second worldview question (what is our world?). Indeed, there is a reciprocal relationship between the young worldview and

*Contemporary Cultural
Worldview Meditation*

Race to Witch Mountain— How About Them Aliens?

In the 2009 action flick *Race to Witch Mountain*, Las Vegas cabbie Jack Bruno (played by Dwayne Johnson) is an alien skeptic in a town of gullible people. The movie opens with Bruno driving alien-believer Dr. Alex Friedman to a UFO convention. His next fare happens to be two normal-looking teenagers, Sara and Seth—but these are no ordinary teenagers. Instead, they claim to be alien visitors returning to Earth to collect scientific data that might just save their home planet and thereby prevent the impending invasion of Earth by their people.

Bruno, however, has seen and heard it all in his cab-driving life. He is not easily persuaded that Sara and Seth are extraterrestrials. Granted, they are able to say and do some relatively odd things—make his vehicle go incredibly fast, read his mind, levitate objects in midair. But he has a lifetime of skepticism to counter these odd phenomena. He attempts to accommodate these unusual experiences within his existing worldview for as long as possible.

(continued on next page)

Being aware of one's own (and others') worldview, then, can help identify when and where one is being affected by experiential accommodation. Am I rejecting the implications of the fossil record because it conflicts with my evolutionary understanding of the world? Am I unduly emphasizing the paucity of transitional fossils solely because that supports my understanding of divine creation?

2.1.3 Worldview and the pool of live options. Third, worldview determines the pool of live options, the set of possible explanations for a given phenomenon. Worldview determines the antecedent possibility or plausibility of various explanations or theories.[6]

One might consider, for example, someone's need to explain the mysterious appearance of mail in his mailbox on a day that mail is not delivered. John returns home from attending weekly worship at his church and discovers a letter from Aunt Martha in the mailbox outside the front door of his townhouse. He is, needless to say, surprised. Mail is not normally delivered on the sabbath day. How then shall he explain this apparent mystery?

His ten-year-old son offers a potential explanation: "The postal service must

---

the data, each influencing the other. Once the worldview becomes established, however, influence flows predominantly one way—worldview directing the interpretation of data. Awareness and conscious examination of worldview can help us be more aware of this process.

[6]The phrase "antecedent possibility" refers to the possibility before consideration of data, evidence, and arguments.

have started delivering on the sabbath." His wife offers another explanation: "Yesterday's mail was probably delivered to Mr. and Mrs. Jones across the street (in 2843 Fallow Court as opposed to his 2834 Fallow Court) by mistake, and they brought it over for us today." His wide eyed seven-year-old daughter offers a third possible explanation: "Aliens stole our mail yesterday and brought it back today." His new friend Art offers a fourth explanation: "Did you not know, have you not heard, that here in the United States, mail is delivered every Saturday? It is only lazy Canadian postal workers who get the whole weekend off." (Did I forget to mention that the worship service was at a Seventh-Day Adventist Church? My apologies for the oversight.)

In the end, however, the oddities multiply, and Bruno is forced to admit what he had previously rejected out of hand: aliens exist, and they're in his cab. Bruno's experience in *Race to Witch Mountain* nicely illustrates two sides to worldview thought. (1) the impact worldview has in directing our interpretation of data and events and (2) the possibility of worldview eventually being overturned by strong enough evidence or experiences.

Each of the four explanations is, theoretically speaking, possible. None-theless, the four alternatives are not accorded the same weight of plausi-bility. Within John's own worldview, option three (aliens) will be immedi-ately discarded from the realm of possibility. His skepticism concerning the existence of extraterrestrial life forms (and his accompanying con-viction that, even if they should happen to exist, the possibility of them traveling to earth is extremely remote) rules out his daughter's suggestion. Simply put, his underlying worldview does not allow for the alien expla-nation in his pool of live options. Kelly James Clark argues, "Explanatory power is not the only factor involved in the assessment of hypotheses; hypotheses must also be judged to have some initial likelihood of being true. And judgments of initial likelihood are *conditioned by our deepest commitments*."[7] When faced with unusual phenomena or extraordinary claims, our worldview presuppositions govern their antecedent plausibility.

Imagine that Aunt Rose has been diagnosed with terminal, untreatable cancer. Her family prays for God's miraculous healing. Weeks later, the

---

[7]Kelly James Clark, "A Reformed Epistemologist's Response to Evidential Apologetics," in *Five Views on Apologetics*, ed. Steven B. Cowan, Counterpoints (Grand Rapids: Zondervan, 2000), 143 (emphasis added).

doctors find her to be entirely free from the cancer that had ravaged her body. How do you explain what happened? For the Christian theist, the answer could be quite simple. God healed Aunt Rose out of his infinite, compassionate mercy and love, in response to the humble prayers of his children. For the atheist, such an explanation is not possible. It lies outside the pool of live options. Either the initial diagnosis of cancer was mistaken, or there had been some kind of treatment that rid her body of cancer—or there is some other unknown natural explanation for her sudden healing. Whatever the case, Aunt Rose was *not* the recipient of a divine miracle. God does not exist to perform such miracles, and therefore it *cannot* be the explanation.

Consider the Christian belief in the resurrection of Jesus Christ. Worldview presuppositions determine whether the historically orthodox understanding of Jesus' resurrection is within the pool of live options. For example, prominent biblical scholar John Dominic Crossan is committed to a naturalistic worldview that denies supernatural interaction with the closed physical universe.[8] Furthermore, he insists that human life ceases absolutely and irrevocably at death. Those worldview presuppositions render the orthodox resurrection in-credible (that is, not believable). A supernatural bodily resurrection is not within the pool of live options given Crossan's worldview. Whatever explanation is given for Christian resurrection belief, Crossan's explanation (and the explanation of others holding to a naturalistic worldview) simply cannot be that Jesus was truly raised from the dead.

Crossan once engaged in a public debate with William Lane Craig regarding the resurrection of Jesus. During their dialogue, there is a fascinating and very revealing exchange. First, Craig asks Crossan, "What evidence would it take to convince you [that the resurrection really happened]? Or are your preconceived ideas about the impossibility of the miraculous and so forth so strong that, in fact, they skew your historical judgment so that such an event could never even be admitted into court?" Craig is asking Crossan what type and amount of evidence would

---

[8]See Tawa J. Anderson, "The Myth of the Metaphorical Resurrection: A Critical Analysis of John Dominic Crossan's Methodology, Presuppositions, and Conclusions" (PhD diss., Southern Baptist Theological Seminary, 2011), 80-104.

convince him that Jesus really was raised from the dead. Crossan's reply is revealing: "It's a theological presupposition of mine that God does not operate that way. . . . What would it take to prove to me what you ask? I don't know, unless God changes the universe."[9] In other words, there is no type or amount of evidence that could convince Crossan of the literal truth of the resurrection of Jesus. He has a theological presupposition that God would not do such things. It is a part of his worldview. Crossan is absolutely closed to the possibility of Jesus' bodily resurrection because it does not fit within his worldview. Worldview determines our pool of live options and thus governs the way that we interpret data that we encounter.

Another of my favorite detective shows is *Psych*, starring James Roday as Shawn Spencer, a highly observant independent investigator who pretends that his empirically driven insights are psychic visions. In one episode, "This Episode Sucks," a murder victim is found with puncture wounds on his neck and both wrists, and most of the blood drained from his body. Spencer and his "assistant" Burton Guster immediately conclude that the murder was perpetrated by a vampire; their hypothesis is just as quickly rejected by police detectives Juliet O'Hara and Carlton Lassiter. Spencer and Guster embrace a worldview wherein paranormal creatures (Bigfoot, vampires, etc.) are legitimate possibilities; for O'Hara and Lassiter, such creatures fall outside the pool of live options. There must be a different, "normal" explanation for the murder (as indeed there is in this case).

Being aware of one's own (and others') worldview, then, can help identify when and where one's pool of live options is broadened or narrowed by one's worldview. Worldview awareness also enables us to ask whether such broadening and narrowing is appropriate. Why do I reject the possibility that God healed Aunt Rose? Are there good reasons for such exclusion, or is it based merely on unexamined worldview presuppositions? Why do I reject the possibility that a vampire sucked the blood out of a victim? Do I have good reasons for disbelieving in vampires and thus concluding that vampires (as nonexisting creatures) do not commit murder, or is the exclusion based merely on unexamined worldview pre-

---

[9]Paul Copan, ed., *Will the Real Jesus Please Stand Up? A Debate Between William Lane Craig and John Dominic Crossan* (Grand Rapids: Baker Academic, 1998), 61-62.

suppositions? In other words, is there a rational justification for the contours of my pool of live options?

2.1.4 Worldview and life motivation. Fourth, worldview impacts the
way that we live. A worldview not only describes the world for us but
also directs our life in the world. It not only gives us a perspective on
how the world is (worldview's descriptive function) but also acts as a
guide for how the world ought to be and how we ought to live in the
world (worldview's normative function).

James Sire's definition of worldview emphasizes the nature of worldview
as a "fundamental orientation of the heart" and the place of worldview
in providing the foundation on which "we live and move and have our
being" (Acts 17:28).[10] The worldview that we hold is not just an intellectual, rational construct. Rather, worldview is seated deep within us; it
takes root in our hearts and then flows out of our hearts into what we
think, say, and do. As Walsh and Middleton insist,

> A world view is never merely a vision *of* life. It is always a vision for life as
> well. Indeed, a vision of life, or world view, that does not actually lead a
> person or a people in a particular way of life is no world view at all. Our
> world view determines our values. It helps us interpret the world around
> us. It sorts out what is important from what is not, what is of highest value
> from what is least. . . . A world view, then, provides a model of the world
> which guides its adherents in the world. It stipulates how the world ought
> to be, and it thus advises how its adherents ought to conduct themselves
> in the world.[11]

The Dutch theologian and educator Abraham Kuyper stressed the
nature of Christianity as a total life system. Kuyper recognized that a
Christian worldview was an all-encompassing, all-motivating system of
thought and action. He thus wrote essays working out the implications
of a Christian worldview in the areas of religion, politics, science, art, and
the future. Kuyper famously insisted that "there is not a square inch in
the whole domain of our human existence over which Christ, who is

---

[10]James W. Sire, *The Universe Next Door: A Basic Worldview Catalog*, 5th ed. (Downers Grove, IL: IVP Academic, 2009), 20.

[11]Brian J. Walsh and J. Richard Middleton, *The Transforming Vision: Shaping a Christian Worldview* (Downers Grove, IL: IVP Academic, 1984), 31-32.

Sovereign over all, does not cry, Mine!"[12] How might worldview affect life motivation? Let us briefly survey how a Christian worldview might impact three areas of life: art, science, and sex.

A Christian worldview holds that a transcendent God created the universe and everything within it out of absolute nothingness. God then created human beings in his image. As a result, Christians see human beings as inherently creative beings, granted the ability to create works of art just as God has created. Within a Christian worldview, therefore, commitment to artistic creation ought to flourish.

Christian worldview beliefs ought also to affect one's understanding and acceptance of scientific theories and hypotheses. On the one hand, a Christian worldview holds that human beings are fallen creatures. The fall affects both will and mind, meaning that (a) fallen, unredeemed human beings will tend to create scientific hypotheses (or philosophical speculations) that ignore or undermine belief in God and (b) our human knowledge, including scientific knowledge, will always be incomplete and tentative. On the other hand, a Christian worldview affirms belief in a Creator God, who brought the universe into existence *ex nihilo* (out of nothingness). There was nothing; then God created, and there was something. Holding these two beliefs, a Christian scientist will necessarily reject any scientific hypothesis that suggests that the universe is either eternal or self-created. Christians will eagerly explore the natural world to better understand God's creation, but their investigation will be guided and informed by their worldview commitments.

Similarly, a Christian worldview will hold that God created human beings to enjoy sexual intimacy within the bounds of heterosexual marriage. Sexual patience (waiting for marriage) and fidelity (being faithful to one's marriage partner) are thus highly valued as a natural outworking of the Christian view of human persons and sexuality. At the same time, the joys of faithful monogamous sexuality will be celebrated as one of God's gifts to created human beings. Sex plays an important role not only in procreation but also in relational intimacy and pleasure between self-giving spouses.

---

[12]Abraham Kuyper, "Sphere Sovereignty," cited in James D. Bratt, *Abraham Kuyper, A Centennial Reader* (Grand Rapids: Eerdmans, 1988), 488.

Other worldviews provide life motivation to their adherents as well. Skye Johnson, a missionary to the Lozi tribe along the Zambezi River in Africa, shares how the Lozi worldview affects their interpersonal relationships. Skye notes the typical Western understanding of time, possessions, and knowledge, and contrasts them with the typical Lozi worldview. For Westerners, Skye argues, time and possessions are private, while knowledge is public (shared). Thus, if you have an appointment for lunch with a friend at 12:30 p.m., it is considered disrespectful and rude to show up forty-five minutes late. It is considered stealing if you "borrow" your neighbor's vehicle on the basis that you needed transportation and they were not currently using it. On the other hand, if you know how to grow better vegetables in your garden (weeding, fertilizers, irrigation, etc.), it is appropriate and virtuous to share such knowledge with your neighbors to improve their ability to grow better produce.

The Lozi conceptions of time, possessions, and knowledge are inverted. Time and possessions are considered public (shared), while knowledge is private. Thus, it is not uncommon for Skye to arrive for a 9:00 a.m. visit with a Lozi woman only to have the woman wander in from the fields half an hour later, wash and eat breakfast, and then sit down to visit with Skye around 10:00. Their time is shared, so the Lozi have no conception of "wasting" a Western missionary's time. Similarly, when Skye and her husband have three canoes resting on the beach outside their house, neighboring Lozi feel free to "borrow" the canoes for their own use. After all, there was no way that the two Johnsons could use *three* canoes on their own anyway! Possessions are considered shared; private property is somewhat of an unknown among the Lozi.

Knowledge, on the other hand, is considered private and can be coveted quite tightly. Thus, if one of a village chieftain's multiple wives learns from a Westerner how to keep her family healthier by practicing basic hygiene, she does *not* share that knowledge with the other wives. Her special knowledge gives her power over them and enables increased access to and higher status with her husband. Accordingly, Skye argues, it is difficult to convince newly converted Lozi Christians to share their faith in Jesus with their fellow Lozi since knowledge of

Jesus' saving grace gives them a power not available to their non-Christian neighbors.[13]

There are, then, at least three ways that worldview differences are played out within the Lozi tribe. First, time-bound appointments are simply not considered; they are not a part of the cultural lexicon. Second, other people's "stuff" is free for your own use, even without seeking permission. Third, one does not share new knowledge with others; one keeps it to oneself. Worldview considerations have significant play in the day-to-day life motivation of Lozi tribespeople.

David Naugle notes that our worldview presuppositions, "though mostly hidden, and often ignored, . . . guide and direct most, if not all, of life."[14] Our worldview is, as noted in chapter one, influenced and shaped by formative sociocultural influences. Once established, however, the worldview lodging within our hearts gives shape to our values and actions. The fourth core worldview question (what is our end?) has to do with purpose, meaning, destination, and values. A person's conception of purpose and meaning in life is going to give strong direction to that person's words and deeds. If the goal of life is to accumulate personal wealth, one is likely to spend a great deal of time working and seeking to earn more money. If the goal of life is eternal life with God, money is liable to take a backseat to relationship with God. Thus, worldview affects our goals, orientations, and actions in life.

Worldview even affects the questions that we ask. For example, one of the most prominent age-old philosophical, theological, and anthropological questions is, what happens to us after we die? John Dominic Crossan answers this age-old philosophical question about mortality quite simply: "Do I personally believe in an afterlife? No, but to be honest, I do not find it a particularly important question one way or the other."[15] Crossan's disinterest in postmortem fate is determined by his worldview presumption that life absolutely ceases at death. As an analogy, consider someone who believes that God created the universe and created life on

---

[13] I am very grateful for personal conversations with Skye Johnson that informed this section.
[14] David K. Naugle, *Worldview: The History of a Concept* (Grand Rapids: Eerdmans, 2002), 272.
[15] John Dominic Crossan and Richard G. Watts, *Who Is Jesus: Answers to Your Questions About the Historical Jesus* (Louisville: Westminster John Knox, 1996), 131.

earth but nowhere else in the universe. A clear implication of this fundamental worldview is that there is no life on other planets waiting to be contacted. As a result, if this person were asked, "What do you think life on other planets would look like? Would it be carbon-based like us? Or would it be something entirely different?," the person would be entirely uninterested in the consequent discussion. Under this worldview, there *is* no life elsewhere, so speculating on the characteristics of life elsewhere would be nonsensical.

REFLECTION QUESTIONS

1 Confirmation bias can lead us to downplay evidence simply because it does not fit our worldview. But is confirmation bias necessarily a bad thing? Why or why not? If not, can you think of an example of confirmation bias generating a positive outcome?

2 Is it possible to avoid the influence of experiential accommodation? Why or why not? If so, is it wise to do so? Why or why not?

3 What factors should impact whether people ought to consider a broader pool of live options than they currently do? Why?

4 What are some other ways that a Christian worldview motivates (or ought to motivate) you to live?

5 Can you think of a TV show or movie that powerfully illustrates the impact of worldview in one or more of these ways?

2.2 WORLDVIEW CONSERVATISM AND CONVERSION

I have noted the influence that worldview exerts on us through confirmation bias, experiential accommodation, the pool of live options, and life motivation. A logical conclusion from the noted influences of worldview is simple and straightforward: *once a worldview is in place within the individual's heart, the individual tends (all other things being equal) to preserve that worldview.* That is, worldviews are inherently conservative. Individuals spend their formative years developing their worldviews through a complex interaction of sociocultural influences—for example, family, education, religion, and economic situation. A worldview may develop with some intentionality and choice, or it might arise and grow entirely unconsciously and unintentionally. Either way, once worldview is established, it is firmly entrenched and exerts tremendous influence on how a person thinks, wills, and acts.

Core worldview presuppositions tend to be stubbornly held. A small amount of contrary evidence does not convince someone to abandon one worldview and adopt a different one. In other words, worldviews are not changed unless they have to be. In the 2009 movie *Race to Witch Mountain*, Dwayne "The Rock" Johnson stars as Jack Bruno, a taxi driver who unwittingly drives two alien "teenagers" around Las Vegas. Weird things start happening right after Bruno picks them up—the teenage boy stops a pursuing car by letting it smash itself on his body—but Bruno does not immediately conclude that the teens are alien beings. After all, Bruno is convinced that aliens do not exist. Such beliefs do not change easily.

Nonetheless, worldviews (and components of worldviews) are not unalterable. If they were, then without exception individuals would adhere to their parents' religious worldviews. There are simply too many counterexamples of individuals who have moved from one worldview to another to believe that worldviews are cemented in place.[16] Worldviews change in two ways: adjustment and conversion.

2.2.1 Worldview adjustment. Given the inherent conservatism of worldview, we will always seek to accommodate new data or information within our existing worldview. Sometimes, however, this can happen only with an *adjustment* to the overarching worldview. At this point, it is helpful to distinguish between two levels of worldview beliefs.[17] At the center of one's worldview is the *worldview core*—beliefs that are so essential and nonnegotiable that to give them up entails leaving the worldview behind entirely. For example, a young Christian man who

---

[16]E.g., C. S. Lewis (from atheism to Christian theism), Antony Flew (from atheism to deism), Bart Ehrman (from Christian theism to agnosticism), and Michael Shermer (from Christian theism to robust atheism). For additional examples, see Michael R. Licona, *The Resurrection of Jesus: A New Historiographical Approach* (Downers Grove, IL: IVP Academic, 2010), 51.

[17]The following discussion is indirectly indebted to the thought of Thomas Kuhn and Imre Lakatos regarding scientific paradigms and research programs, respectively. For a summary of their thought, see A. F. Chalmers, *What Is This Thing Called Science?*, 4th ed. (Indianapolis: Hackett, 2013), 97-137.

gives up belief in the existence of a transcendent divine being ceases to hold a Christian theistic worldview; he may continue to call himself a Christian, but his worldview is not a Christian worldview. The core has been compromised, and he has moved from one overarching worldview into a different one. That new worldview may be a work in progress for a period of time, but the rejection of core worldview beliefs results in worldview conversion.

Not all beliefs, however, reside at the conceptual core of a worldview. For example, belief in an afterlife is essential to a Christian theistic worldview. When I became a Christian, my previous naturalistic worldview belief in postmortem extinction was replaced with belief in personal resurrection to eternal life. Over time, I learned that there are nuances within Christian afterlife beliefs. Some hold that immediately after one's physical death one will be raised with a new body in the presence of God, to dwell with him forever. Others hold that following one's death one will experience a period of "soul sleep"—a time of unconsciousness that will last until the second coming of Jesus inaugurates the bodily resurrection of all believers. Others hold that upon physical death one's nonmaterial soul (or spirit) experiences a period of disembodied bliss in the presence of God Almighty while awaiting the bodily resurrection that will obtain after the second coming of Christ—what N. T. Wright calls life-after-death and life-after-life-after-death.[18] Christian theists can very reasonably alter their positions on the postmortem fate of Christian believers without rejecting the core of their worldviews. That is, changing the specifics of afterlife beliefs does not result in moving from one worldview to another. Rather, it results in *worldview adjustment*.

Worldviews can be helpfully pictured as a series of concentric circles (see fig. 2.1). The central circle, the smallest one, is the worldview core, a set of nonnegotiable presuppositions, beliefs, and stories without which the worldview collapses. A naturalistic worldview might include in its core beliefs that (a) the universe is composed of only material things; (b) human beings are strictly physical creatures, composed of a material body and lacking a spiritual or soul-ish element; and (c) there is no transcendent or

---

[18]N. T. Wright, *The Resurrection of the Son of God*, Christian Origins and the Question of God 3 (Minneapolis: Fortress, 2003), 121-28.

supernatural being or god who can give direction, purpose, or meaning to life. The core beliefs of an Islamic worldview would probably focus on beliefs that (a) Allah is One, (b) Muhammad is his messenger, and (c) the Qur'an is his Word. The core beliefs of a Buddhist worldview would probably center on the Four Noble Truths and the Eightfold Noble Path.[19] The worldview core of Christian theism would focus on the narrative themes of creation, fall, and redemption.

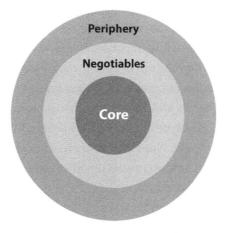

Figure 2.1. Levels of worldview beliefs

The outer two circles in our illustration represent increasingly flexible (negotiable) worldview beliefs. For a naturalistic worldview, the second tier of worldview beliefs might include things like the truthfulness of Darwinian evolution (natural selection acting on random mutation) as the explanation for the variety of life on earth. The third tier, the worldview periphery, might include beliefs like an understanding of humanity's most immediate creaturely predecessor in the evolutionary chain. The peripheral circle of worldview beliefs represents the most disposable or alterable elements of the worldview. Beliefs that fall in the outer two circles, outside the core, can be altered or replaced without affecting the overarching worldview.

---

[19]The Four Noble Truths are (1) life is suffering; (2) the source of suffering is selfish desire; (3) selfish desire can be extinguished, thereby ending suffering; and (4) the means to cessation of desire is the Eightfold Noble Path. The Eightfold Noble Path includes (1) right view, (2) right intention, (3) right speech, (4) right action, (5) right livelihood, (6) right effort, (7) right mindfulness, and (8) right concentration/meditation.

For example, the relative absence of transitional species in the fossil record has not led most evolutionary theorists to abandon their primary commitment to a purposeless, random process of evolution and common descent. Rather, the worldview periphery is slightly tweaked to explain the lack of supporting evidence. Hence, Niles Eldredge and Stephen Jay Gould proposed the idea of punctuated equilibrium, whereby new species arise very quickly with a large number of mutative changes present in them. Punctuated equilibrium is not precisely the same as classical Darwinian evolution, which requires changes to occur over long periods of time. But the fundamental worldview remains the same: the process of biological evolution occurs through random mutation and natural selection and is not governed by any type of intelligent designer.

Worldview adherents will frequently change second- and third-tier beliefs without any discernible effect on the overarching view of life, the universe, and everything. Nonetheless, sometimes changing even these peripheral beliefs will have an impact on other elements, *if* the individual thinks through the process.

For example, naturalists embrace, as a worldview core, the belief that the physical universe is all there is. As a secondary belief, they might become convinced that everything that occurs in the physical universe is the result of biochemical and physical necessity—material things responding necessarily to universal physical and chemical laws. That is, we live in a deterministic universe. They might first become convinced of this as a relatively peripheral matter, as a result of scientific inquiry and investigation. Upon philosophical reflection, however, they may acknowledge that if the physical universe is deterministic, and human beings are strictly physical creatures, then, logically, human beings are determined creatures. In other words, free will is an illusion. In reality, all our choices are the result of biochemical necessity. Such a realization would have ripple effects throughout their worldview. What begins as a peripheral adjustment, then, can filter down to other levels of the worldview.

2.2.2 Worldview conversion. Worldviews represent our understanding of the world around us. The questions involved at the core of our worldview are foundational. Such beliefs, once developed, are not easily altered. There is, however, an important distinction to be drawn.

A worldview that is held unconsciously is altered and even converted in a different fashion from one that is held consciously and intentionally.

2.2.2.1 Unconscious worldviews. Ask yourself a few questions: What are my responses to the four core worldview questions? When did I first become aware of the identity of my worldview? Why do I hold my worldview? What factors went into shaping the conceptual lens through which I see, understand, and interpret the world and my place within it? What is the justification for my worldview beliefs? Is my worldview an accurate reflection of reality? How do I know?

If you have asked those questions, and provided even tentative and partial answers to them, you have now done more worldview thinking than the vast majority of Western Christians. Unfortunately, most people do not consciously reflect on their worldview beliefs and the truth value of those beliefs. A major goal of this textbook is to stimulate conscious reflection on the reader's deep-seated worldview. For some of you, this may be the first time that you have exerted intentional effort to identify and evaluate your worldview. Many adults, even highly educated adults, have fully formed worldviews of which they are entirely unconscious. They can identify neither their fundamental worldview nor the reasons for which they hold that particular worldview.

An unconscious, unexamined worldview is more easily changed than a conscious, examined worldview. Those who have not thought through their worldview beliefs and justification will be more easily persuaded to change worldview—to undergo a paradigm shift or a complete worldview conversion. Consider Sally Smith, recently graduated from public high school. Sally has been raised within a Christian family and community and holds a broad Christian worldview. Sally, however, has never reflected on the source of her worldview or the reasons and evidence that support it. Now Sally attends a large public university where she is enrolled in freshman philosophy. Her philosophy professor rejoices in challenging and ultimately shattering the unconscious Christian worldview of incoming freshmen like Sally. He raises traditional objections to theistic belief (e.g., the problems of evil and religious pluralism) and presents philosophical defenses of naturalism (atheism) and undirected evolution. Sally's unconscious, unexamined worldview is ripe for the picking. There may have been excellent rational justifications for her theistic belief, but she had never considered them or reflected on them. Her Christian worldview may even have been an accurate representation of reality. But being confronted with an intelligent, thoughtful, articulate defender of an alternative worldview (and opponent of her own worldview) results in her rejecting Christian theism.

We believe that worldview naiveté is a significant problem in the contemporary world, particularly within the North American church.[20] The majority of young Christians are not learning to think in worldview terms, nor are they being taught why they should believe what they believe; as a consequence, they are easily swayed and can have their faith quickly deconstructed. An unconscious, unexamined worldview can be challenged and overturned. Sadly, the worldview that replaces the original one is often less coherent and less true than the original one. But it is more consciously held and thus is clung to more tightly.

2.2.2.2 Conscious worldviews. Worldviews, when consciously held, are held tenaciously. Individuals consciously holding an examined worldview will alter or convert their worldviews only in the face of what is perceived as overwhelming evidence, powerfully persuasive arguments, or existentially convincing experiences. Those who have consciously held worldviews can adjust second- and third-level beliefs—components that are not at the core of their worldviews. But the worldview core, while not absolutely immune to alteration, is certainly held very strongly.

Consider again "Monk and the Astronaut," the episode in which Monk suspects an astronaut of murdering a former call girl who was writing an autobiography revealing the astronaut's past indiscretions. Monk's primary obstacle in solving that case was the little problem of the suspect's alibi: he was in a spaceship orbiting the earth at the time of the woman's death. Alibis cannot be more airtight than that: "Not only was I out of the country; I was off the planet altogether!" How does Monk deal with that alibi? Does he say, "Oh well, the guy's got a pretty solid alibi. He must not be the guy"? No, instead Monk says, "I don't know how

---

[20]Worldview naiveté is the state of not knowing what one's worldview is and not having reflectively examined one's worldview beliefs.

he did it, but he did it. He's the guy." It takes more than an apparently airtight alibi to convince Monk to abandon his thesis. As it happens, Monk is right. The astronaut had set up the suicide scene the night before launching into space, ensuring that the woman's death would occur while he was safely beyond suspicion in the atmosphere. The point is, Monk is not dissuaded by powerful contradictory evidence.

As it is with crime, so it is with worldview. Consciously held worldviews are held tenaciously. Opposing arguments and evidence do not automatically result in worldview conversion. For example, in April 2012 I was present for a debate between Christian philosopher Gary Habermas and skeptic Michael Shermer on the question, "Is There Life After Death?"[21] Shermer began his opening statement by insisting that there is "not a shred of evidence" for life after death. Habermas then spent twenty minutes sharing evidences from near-death experiences (NDEs) and post-death apparitions (PDAs) that demonstrate the existence of personal consciousness, awareness, and intentionality during conditions of heart and brain death.

Shermer first responded to Habermas's evidence by suggesting that the NDEs Habermas cited are not of "the right type"; they show awareness of things in the patient's immediate physical proximity in cases where the patient's brain could still have been functioning and taking in information. Habermas responded by sharing a number of evidential cases where patients experienced things that occurred at a distance from their physical (and fully dead) bodies, information that was physically impossible for them to have obtained (a red tennis shoe on the hospital roof, the substance of a family's dinner table five miles away, and others). Shermer seemed to retreat to some extent, protesting that, while there might be a few such cases, there are not very many, and we should not build elaborate theories (that is, alter our core worldview understandings) on the basis of exceptions to the rule.[22] Shermer insisted that "you cannot

---

[21]The debate was the centerpiece of the Greer-Heard Point-Counterpoint Forum at New Orleans Baptist Theological Seminary April 13–14, 2012. The account that follows is derived from the audio CDs of the forum along with my personal notes and recollection of the debate. Direct quotations are transcribed from the audio.

[22]Shermer calls exceptions to the rule the "residue problem." In his view, no theory, and no worldview, will successfully account for every experience and every phenomenon.

construct a whole new worldview based on an anomaly." Habermas then noted that he could supply Shermer with dozens more such cases and asked how many of them would be sufficient to overturn Shermer's worldview presupposition that there is no life after death.

At this point, Shermer simply stated, "Well, people make stuff up all the time." In other words, he absolutely rejected the evidence that Habermas presented, presumably because the people that claim to have had and documented such NDEs are conspiring together to deceive others. The evidence presented by Habermas was not sufficient to overturn Shermer's worldview presuppositions. How much evidence would it take? I am not sure. Perhaps John Dominic Crossan's response to a different question, cited earlier, is appropriate: "What would it take to prove to me what you ask? I don't know, unless God changes the universe."[23]

Shermer holds his skeptical (naturalistic) worldview very consciously and intentionally. He has examined it over years and adheres to it very tightly. Two of his core worldview beliefs are the materiality of human beings and the cessation of conscious existence at physical death. His worldview is *not* going to be changed on the basis of a two-hour debate in which contrary arguments and evidence are presented. It is important to note that the inherent conservatism of worldview, and the stubborn clinging to a conscious, examined worldview core, does *not* imply that the fundamental worldview cannot be changed. Again, there are simply too many examples of worldview conversion for us to believe that is the case.

For example, Antony Flew was Britain's most prominent philosophical atheist in the latter half of the twentieth century. The philosophical world was shocked when, in 2004, he declared that he had rejected the core beliefs of his atheistic worldview and now embraced the existence of a deistic creator of the universe.[24] Flew's atheistic worldview had been held consciously; he had examined his worldview beliefs and in fact had written copiously on questions of divine nonexistence. Nonetheless, his worldview changed as a result of his understanding of contemporary evidence from cosmology and physics that points to the existence of an intelligent designer and creator of the universe.

---

[23]Copan, *Will the Real Jesus Please Stand Up?*, 62.
[24]Antony Flew, *There Is a God* (San Francisco: HarperOne, 2007).

Thus, we are left with three concluding thoughts. First, an unexamined and unconscious worldview is relatively easy to alter and even entirely change, even if the original worldview was accurate and largely true. Second, a consciously held, examined worldview is clung to (especially the core beliefs) very tightly and is difficult to fundamentally change. Third, though it is difficult to fundamentally change an examined, consciously held worldview, it is not impossible.

REFLECTION QUESTIONS

1 The authors argue that worldviews tend not to change. Do you think worldview conservatism is a good thing or a bad thing? Why?

2 What would you identify as the nonnegotiable elements that lie at the worldview core of Christianity?

3 Were you able to answer the questions at the start of 2.2.2.1? What does that say about your worldview and your self-awareness?

4 Do you agree with the authors' contention that worldview naiveté is a major problem in the contemporary church? Why or why not?

2.3 THE BENEFITS OF WORLDVIEW STUDY

Thus far we have surveyed the impact that worldview exerts and the possibility of worldview adjustment and conversion. One major item remains for discussion in this chapter: Why study the concept of worldview? Are worldview thought and study simply intellectually stimulating and informative? Or do they add something to our intellectual and spiritual life? Briefly and tentatively, we suggest that there are seven potential areas of benefit to understanding and studying worldview.

First, worldview study can help us live more consciously and consistently within our worldview. If we are conscious of the worldview we hold, and can identify the core beliefs within it, we can become more aware of potential or actual inconsistencies within our worldview, or between our worldview and our practice. In short, worldview study helps us to talk the talk consistently, and to walk the walk as well. Conscious reflection and logical analysis are essential elements to holding a coherent worldview and living out our worldview consistently. While some people may have no problem living inconsistently or holding an incoherent worldview, we are convinced that most people (particularly intentionally thoughtful people) desire to be consistent in their intellectual, moral, and spiritual lives.

Second, worldview study can aid us in becoming more fully self-aware. Evaluating our worldview beliefs helps to uncover what our worldview is and how it came to be what it is. Learning to think worldview-ishly helps to expose our unconscious worldview presuppositions to the light of reflective exploration and analysis. Often we will find that we were not aware of how some events or influences in our past had so strongly shaped who we are and what we believe. Examining our worldview and exposing our fundamental presuppositions to rigorous scrutiny will help us become more aware of what we believe and why we believe it. We hold this to be a self-evidently valuable goal.

Third, worldview study can strengthen our commitment to aspects of our worldview that are accurate representations of the way the world really is. When we hold our worldview unconsciously, we are liable to have that worldview challenged and overturned by a thoughtful critic. If our preexisting worldview (or at least large parts of it) was false, then of course change would be beneficial. However, if our preexisting worldview components were accurate, and are replaced by largely false beliefs and practices, then conversion is a negative outcome. For example, if our Sally Smith had engaged in worldview study and examination as part of her high school education or youth group discipleship, she could be adequately prepared for possible (and actual) objections and attacks against her faith that she encountered in college. Being aware of what she believes, how she came to believe it, and why she believes it can help her to hold more strongly to worldview beliefs that are worth holding tightly. As evangelical Christians, we are naturally convinced that the broad contours of a Christian worldview are not only meaningful and satisfactory, but also objectively true about the world. Hence, it is our desire that Christians (young and old) intentionally examine the content and reasonability of their faith—that is, that they understand their Christian worldview and be prepared to defend it.

Fourth, awareness of worldview thought can help spur the Christian to develop a more intentional and thorough Christian worldview. On the one hand, worldview thought will show us areas of life where we have failed to apply the insights of Scripture. On the other hand, worldview awareness can reduce our vulnerability to the infiltration of alien worldviews. As Michael Goheen and Craig Bartholomew note, "If we refuse to develop and indwell a Christian worldview, we will merely leave ourselves vulnerable to the influence of the worldviews present in the culture that surrounds us."[25] Worldview awareness and examination can help the disciple of Christ to live more faithfully according to a thorough Christian worldview.

Fifth, a grasp of worldview—worldview meaning, components, contours, and analysis—enables us to better understand the people around us. In my hometown of Edmonton, Alberta, Canada, there are over a million people. The Chinese community numbers over seventy thousand; there are tens of thousands of immigrants from Sudan, Ethiopia, Iran, Pakistan, India, Lebanon, and many other countries and cultures. Two blocks from my home church is 107th Avenue, known as the Avenue of the Nations for its vibrant multicultural diversity. In Edmonton we had a saying, "You don't need to go see the world; the world has come to our doorstep." Our urban centers and increasingly also our smaller towns are marked by a strong diversity, not only in ethnicity but also in worldview. Understanding that our neighbors have a worldview, and that it is quite distinct from our own, can help us a great deal in understanding the way that they think and act. We can be open-minded concerning others' beliefs and how they came to be formed, seeking to see as they see so as to know them better. So, for the purposes of loving our neighbor as ourselves, it is essential to grasp the nature and influence of worldview.

Sixth, understanding worldview and its impact can aid us in building bridges with neighbors who hold different worldviews—with those bridges ideally leading to the cross of Jesus Christ. If your neighbor comes from a Hindu or Buddhist worldview, where the goal of religious life is to escape the constant cycle of suffering, death, and rebirth

---

[25]Michael W. Goheen and Craig G. Bartholomew, *Living at the Crossroads: An Introduction to Christian Worldview* (Grand Rapids: Baker Academic, 2008), 29.

(reincarnation and samsara), sharing with them the Christian promise of eternal life may sound more like a threat than a reward. Bridges need to be built, concepts need to be understood, perhaps deconstructed, before we can effectively share the gospel.

Finally, for Christians, worldview study can help us to know and love God more truly and fully. Christians ought to desire to see the world the way that God sees the world; that is, they should want to develop a more consistently Christian worldview. Certainly we must remember that the Lord God warns us,

> My thoughts are not your thoughts,
>   neither are your ways my ways. . . .
> As the heavens are higher than the earth,
>   so are my ways higher than your ways
>   and my thoughts than your thoughts. (Is 55:8-9)

At the same time, we must remember that the Lord also entreats us,

> Come now, let us settle the matter. . . .
> Though your sins are like scarlet,
>   they shall be as white as snow;
> though they are red as crimson,
>   they shall be like wool.
> If you are willing and obedient,
>   you will eat the good things of the land. (Is 1:18-19)

So, while we will never attain to the very mind of God in all its fullness, we are nonetheless encouraged to reason with God, to develop our minds to know and understand our Lord more fully.

Indeed, developing a Christian mind and building a Christian worldview are seen as essential to our discipleship and sanctification. Jesus tells us that the greatest commandment is to "love the Lord your God with all your heart and with all your soul and with all your mind" (Mt 22:37). Sadly, the development of the Christian mind is often left behind in contemporary Christianity, to our own loss and peril.[26] Jesus' commandment is to love God with *all* our being—heart, soul,

---

[26]For a helpful discussion, see J. P. Moreland, *Love God with All Your Mind: The Role of Reason in the Life of the Soul* (Colorado Springs, CO: NavPress, 1997).

and mind. Failure to love God with our mind, to cultivate a consciously Christian worldview, is simply failing to become a mature disciple of Christ.

The apostle Paul exhorts believers to cultivate the mind of Christ: "Do not conform to the pattern of this world, but be transformed by the renewing of your mind. Then you will be able to test and approve what God's will is—his good, pleasing and perfect will" (Rom 12:2). Part of our intellectual renewal involves being conscious and wary of alternative worldviews that vie for our allegiance: "See to it that no one takes you captive through hollow and deceptive philosophy, which depends on human tradition and the basic principles of this world rather than on Christ" (Col 2:8). The Christian is to follow Paul's example: "We demolish arguments and every pretension that sets itself up against the knowledge of God, and we take captive every thought to make it obedient to Christ" (2 Cor 10:5).

Again, we must be careful to retain appropriate humility, acknowledging that we will never possess the authoritative, fully correct Christian worldview. That is to say, I will never see things exactly the way God sees things, simply because (I know this sounds shocking) I am not God. We must always be prepared to have our minds transformed by the knowledge of Christ; we must remain open to seeing the error of some of our worldview beliefs and changing our understanding accordingly. However, worldview humility and openness are not the same as worldview skepticism or tentativeness. Paul exemplifies an appropriate balance between confidence in what we are persuaded of and humility regarding what we have not yet attained:

> Not that I have already obtained all this, or have already arrived at my goal, but I press on to take hold of that for which Christ Jesus took hold of me. Brothers and sisters, I do not consider myself yet to have taken hold of it. But one thing I do: Forgetting what is behind and straining toward what is ahead, I press on toward the goal to win the prize for which God has called me heavenward in Christ Jesus.
>
> All of us, then, who are mature should take such a view of things. And if on some point you think differently, that too God will make clear to you. Only let us live up to what we have already attained. (Phil 3:12-16)

In short, we are convinced that if you (a) learn to recognize the existence and importance of worldview, (b) understand the components of your own (and others') worldview, and (c) examine your worldview for consistency and truth, you will subsequently become a more mature disciple of Jesus Christ, embracing his truth and living according to it.

REFLECTION QUESTIONS

1 The authors argue that worldview study can help one eliminate inconsistencies in one's worldview. Do you agree? Why or why not?

2 Can you identify any worldview beliefs you hold that, upon reflection, arose without your conscious intention and that you might now wish to question or reevaluate?

3 Why do the authors argue that it is important for Christians to examine their own worldviews before external critics begin to question them?

4 In what way(s) do you think worldview awareness and thought can help you become a more mature disciple of Christ?

2.4 A FEW POTENTIAL CONCERNS

In closing this section on the benefits of worldview thinking, it might be helpful to respond to a few potential concerns and criticisms regarding worldview study. While there are certainly more objections that can be (and probably have been) expressed, we will deal briefly with just three of them.

2.4.1 Worldview is irrelevant. The first potential concern suggests that worldview thought and study are irrelevant or dispensable. That is, one can jettison worldview terminology entirely and not miss out on anything. Such a concern may emerge in the following form: "I just don't see the value of talking about worldview; I don't talk about it and don't think I'm missing anything important. All the things you talk about regarding worldview—presuppositions, narratives, core beliefs, life motivation—I talk about with regard to other concepts. I don't need worldview at all."

It must first be admitted that such a statement is, in a roundabout way, absolutely correct. One can certainly derive all the benefits that we have delineated as coming from worldview thought without ever using (or referring to) the word *worldview*. One could talk about one's persona or presuppositions or driving beliefs. One could note how one has been formed by narratives that both capture one's imagination and motivate one's actions. One could insist that an understanding of how one came to embrace one's faith (or philosophy) has helped one to understand both oneself and others. One could relate how critically examining one's understanding of the world has resulted in seeing inconsistencies, and refining one's beliefs accordingly. All of this could be done without ever using the word *worldview*.

Nonetheless, while worldview may not be mentioned, worldview *thought* is certainly being employed. An analogy might help to flesh this out. Christians may talk about how thankful they are that Jesus died for their sins. They are thrilled to know that because of Jesus' crucifixion they no longer have to endure the eternal death that is the rightful consequence of sins. At the same time, Christians might object to any notion of atonement, insisting that they don't need such terminology to understand their faith. Such Christians are technically, but trivially, correct. The content and importance of atonement are already embraced in what they believe (and praise God for). Use of the specific terminology is technically unnecessary. Nonetheless, the terminology is not for that reason irrelevant or dispensable, any more so than the term *Trinity* is irrelevant or dispensable.

Similarly, Christians might classify worldview as an irrelevant or dispensable concept. If they are already thinking in worldview terms, identifying and embracing both the contours and importance of worldview without using the word, then so be it. That does not, however, mean that worldview as a concept or theme ought to be (or even can be) done away with. Rather, worldview study might help to clarify and extend Christians' understanding of what they already know.

Indeed, if this potential objection to worldview study were applied universally, one would have to conclude that specific terminology (and even entire fields of study) could be done away with. "History?

No, I have no need of that concept or that field of study. I have gotten along perfectly well talking about things that have happened in the past, what I can learn from them, and how they have shaped me without using *history* as a term or studying it as a discipline." "Music? I don't see why such a term is necessary. I enjoy listening to combinations of melody, harmony, and rhythm; I evaluate how mixtures of sounds and silence affect the human heart. But I simply don't see why you need to apply words like *music* or *musicology* to such things." The bottom line is that worldview is a legitimate, established concept, field of study, and discipline. Whether someone wants to use the term or not is irrelevant. That person is certainly already thinking worldview thoughts!

2.4.2 Worldview is overly rationalistic. James Smith, in his Cultural Liturgies trilogy, laments that worldview is often reduced to a mere intellectual enterprise. In the first installment of the trilogy, the 2009 *Desiring the Kingdom*, Smith criticizes popular worldview talk for reducing worldview to "a system of Christian beliefs, ideas, and doctrines."[27] Smith is concerned that "such construals of worldview belie an understanding of Christian faith that is dualistic and thus reductionistic: It reduces Christian faith primarily to a set of ideas, principles, claims, and propositions that are known and believed. The goal of all this is 'correct' thinking."[28] Smith proposes a philosophical anthropology that embraces the "embodied" nature of human beings. In particular, he argues that we need to understand that humans, including Christians, tend to act "not primarily on the basis of cognitive deliberation, but rather on the basis of precognitive desires."[29] In other words, Smith worries that some misrepresentations of worldview thinking depict human beings as strictly rational creatures and suggest that we need only to develop right thinking; instead, Smith argues that we are primarily "acting" and "being" creatures, shaped through our liturgies (cultural practices) rather than our minds.

---

[27]James K. A. Smith, *Desiring the Kingdom: Worship, Worldview, and Cultural Formation*, Cultural Liturgies 1 (Grand Rapids: Baker Academic, 2009), 17.
[28]Ibid., 32.
[29]James K. A. Smith, "Two Cheers for Worldview: A Response to Elmer John Thiessen," *Journal for Education and Christian Belief* 14, no. 1 (2010): 56.

In 2013, Smith published the second volume of his Cultural Liturgies project, *Imagining the Kingdom*. In *Imagining the Kingdom*, Smith argues that worldview thinkers believe that effective Christian formation and education require merely worldview training and conceptual analysis. According to Smith, such a perspective is faulty. Correct worldview thinking is not sufficient for Christian formation: our habits are shaped not by *right thinking* but by *right love* (heart orientation).[30] Worldview thinking misses the importance of worship or liturgy in determining Christian action.

Smith provides a delightful illustration to demonstrate his point. Intellectually, he embraces the thought and exhortation of Wendell Berry and Michael Pollan that Americans should eschew fast food and big-box stores in favor of local produce and small enterprise. Nonetheless, Smith finds himself reading Berry in the food court of megawarehouse Costco and pulling into the McDonald's drive-through while ruminating on Pollan's theses. Why? Smith suggests that while Berry and Pollan have captured his mind, they have not captured his practice. His cultural liturgies still follow his old habits. Right thinking is insufficient to produce right action. Right habit must also be supplied. Worldview thought, Smith charges, misses this essential component of formation.

Four things need to be said in response to Smith's critiques of worldview. First, if and when worldview is conceived as strictly rational in nature, Smith's objection needs to be taken into account. Human beings are not solely rational creatures; we are not disembodied minds. Worldview ought never to be understood just in terms of intellectual propositions that must be consciously affirmed.

However, worldview as we have presented it does not fall prey to this criticism. We have embraced Sire's definition of worldview, focusing on worldview formation within the very core of the human person, the heart. We explicitly reject any formulation or conception of worldview that presents it as solely an enterprise of the mind, as do the majority of contemporary worldview thinkers and proponents.

---

[30]James K. A. Smith, *Imagining the Kingdom: How Worship Works*, Cultural Liturgies 2 (Grand Rapids: Baker Academic, 2013), 9-10.

STOP & PAUSE

Biblical Worldview Insight

Hear, O Israel: the LORD our God, the LORD is one. Love the LORD your God with all your heart and with all your soul and with all your strength. These commandments that I give you today are to be on your hearts. Impress them on your children. Talk about them when you sit at home and when you walk along the road, when you lie down and when you get up. Tie them as symbols on your hands and bind them on your foreheads. Write them on the doorframes of your houses and on your gates. (Deut 6:4-9)

Moses emphasizes the necessity of holistic formation to the people of Israel. Israel is indeed to think rightly about the Lord. But here Moses emphasizes the way in which children are to be integrated into the community of faith. Meditate on the Lord's commandments. Teach them to your children. Talk about them, in any and every situation. Wear symbols of God's commandments. Have visual reminders of the Lord and his covenant throughout your dwelling.

Worldview is not strictly rational, and worldview formation occurs primarily at the pretheoretical level. Hence, developing thoughtful virtues is of incalculable benefit. Our lives need to be permeated with the goodness and grace of God so that our children or students simply absorb a Christian worldview.

Second, Smith is certainly correct that worldview thinking is insufficient for Christian formation and education. But I am not aware of anyone who has suggested that worldview thinking on its own is sufficient. Smith does go to some pains to emphasize that he is not denigrating or rejecting worldview thought.[31] Nonetheless, he seems to misconstrue the intent and goals of contemporary (and most historical) worldview proponents.

We agree wholeheartedly that embracing a true worldview (i.e., right thinking) is inadequate on its own to produce effective Christian practice and habit. At the same time, however, we insist that worldview thinking

---

[31]"To be very clear, this does not constitute a rejection of worldview per se. . . . However, I think there remain legitimate concerns with even the best rendition of worldview approaches insofar as these approaches tend to still conceive the task of Christian education as the dissemination of a *perspective*, a way to *see* the world." Smith, *Imagining the Kingdom*, 8.

and analysis are necessary for producing authentic followers of Jesus. In philosophical terms, worldview thought is *necessary but not sufficient* as a part of Christian education.

Third, we agree wholeheartedly that liturgy, worship, and habit are essential. At the same time, however, we insist that the cultivation and communication of virtue must be guided by deliberative reflection. Smith notes that most of our day-to-day actions are not the product of conscious thoughtfulness: we do not consider the options before us and choose the most rational one. Rather, our actions are the result of deeply ingrained practices and habits. Smith argues that his eating habits will not be changed by mere right thinking. Instead, his "environment and practices" need to be altered so that new habits replace the old ones.[32] This may be so. However, the whole process of replacing old (unhealthy) habits with new (healthy) habits is guided throughout by rational deliberation (or, for our current purposes, worldview thinking). (1) We must be convinced that the status quo is unhealthy and unacceptable. (2) We must see and acknowledge an alternative (a better way). (3) We must choose a different model. (4) Ultimately, we must seek to establish this model as a new mindless pattern. All this deliberation is required for the habit to be changed and our love to be transformed. Smith's goal is that *unhealthy mindless eating* be replaced by *healthy mindless eating*; in order for that to happen, however, *healthy mindful eating* is the necessary intermediate step. In fact, there are, arguably, two intermediate steps. First, unhealthy mindless eating must be replaced by unhealthy mindful eating. Then unhealthy mindful eating can be replaced by healthy mindful eating. Only then can Smith's goal of healthy mindless eating be achieved. We agree with the end goal of virtuous practice; we simply believe that Smith tries to take an unavailable shortcut to get there.

Fourth, finally and most fundamentally, I think Smith misconstrues the nature of the human person and the source of life motivation. The worldview model Smith criticizes elevates the mind as the source of all practice and action. Smith instead identifies habit as the source of our life practices. The model (of mysterious origin) that Smith denounces

---

[32]Ibid., 10.

emphasizes human beings as predominantly *minds* (or souls). Smith avows an alternative anthropology that emphasizes human physicality, or embodiment. Both models seem to be missing the mark. Scripture gives ample evidence of a strong reciprocal relationship between heart and mind (or soul and body). Jesus asserts that the heart is the source of the evil we say and do: "The things that come out of a person's mouth come from the heart, and these defile them. For out of the heart come evil thoughts—murder, adultery, sexual immorality, theft, false testimony, slander" (Mt 15:18-19). Furthermore, we can discern the condition of a man's heart via his actions: consider Matthew 7:15-20, culminating in Jesus' statement, "By their fruit you will recognize them." At the same time, we are exhorted to be "transformed by the renewing of your mind" (Rom 12:2). Thus, as noted in chapter one, "a worldview sustains an interactive or reciprocal relationship with the external world."[33]

Right thinking does not have the determinative power that some philosophers (notably Socrates, who argued that to know the good was to do the good) have felt it has. But rationality is not irrelevant either. If you believed, as Jains do, that all living creatures possess eternal souls, would you smack the mosquito on your arm so carelessly?[34] If you believed, as Hindus do, that the spirit of your deceased grandmother could be dwelling within that cow, would you eat it for dinner? If you believed, as many East Asians do, that deceased ancestors need earthly provisions in their afterlife and can cause you significant harm if you fail to provide it, would you go to their gravesides to give a burnt offering? If you believed, as many Christians do, that sexual intercourse with anyone other than your spouse is a sin against God, would you willfully hook up with random strangers for one-night stands?

Yes, practices shape beliefs, as Smith notes. But to at least an equal degree, beliefs drive practice. Ideas do have consequences, and what we *believe* affects what we *do*. The goal of worldview thinking is to develop a more consistent worldview and thereby to become more consistent in

---

[33]Naugle, *Worldview*, 270.
[34]Jainism is a South Asian religion similar to Hinduism; Jains do in fact hold all life sacred and seek to avoid causing harm to even the smallest living creature, including even some types of vegetables.

our practice as well. In short, worldview thinking is not the adequate, all-sufficient means to effective Christian education and formation, but it is a necessary foundation without which the edifice of a Christ-honoring life cannot be built.

2.4.3 *Worldview stunts Christian philosophy.* A third potential critique is that a focus on Christian worldview can have the unfortunate side effect of discouraging further and deeper philosophical investigation. For example, young Christians encountering worldview thought for the first time may realize that within their Christian worldview they understand human beings to be dualistic creatures (composed of body and soul) fashioned in the image of God by their divine Creator. This is all well and good, the critic might say, but will young Christians examine alternative conceptions of philosophical anthropology (or philosophy of mind)? What about physicalist (materialist, soulless) conceptions of humanity? How does a young Christian respond? Simply by saying, "Well, in *my* worldview I hold to dualism; physicalism stems from a different worldview"? If so, the critic says, the Christian has not done enough.

Again, I think the criticism is absolutely fair, if and when it accurately depicts the real situation. Ideally, however, worldview thought never leads to such a philosophically complacent (lazy?) attitude. Instead, the young Christian should actively engage with the literature promoting and defending alternative answers to the worldview question, What is our nature?, to better understand both those other positions and the reasons for which he holds his own. Perhaps his own understanding will be changed in the process. At any rate, there is no reason that worldview thought, awareness, and investigation need to thwart or discourage further philosophical investigation.

That being said, not everyone who delves into introductory worldview study and analysis will proceed into deeper analytical philosophy. Perhaps such Christians will undertake initial worldview thought but not engage with alternative philosophical anthropologies. Would it be better, from my perspective, for all students to engage in deeper philosophical study? Yes, of course. After all, I teach undergraduate philosophy because I think it's important and beneficial for all students. Not all students, however, will become academic philosophers. Would it better for those students to have studied worldview? In our opinion, yes. If worldview is as much philosophy as a student gets, it is better than none; hopefully, worldview spurs a desire to dive into the richer, deeper waters of academic philosophy as well. Thus, the potential criticism, though sometimes (perhaps) applicable, is not telling.

REFLECTION QUESTIONS

1 Are the authors correct in their argument that *history* or *music*, like *worldview*, could be eschewed as terms without losing the meaning and helpfulness of the discipline?

2 Do you have any mindless unhealthy habits that need to be transformed into mindless healthy habits? What might be the process for accomplishing that change?

3 Are there realistic dangers to worldview being presented or understood too rationalistically? Are there comparable dangers in the other direction? What balance would you like to achieve?

2.5 CONCLUSION

Worldview is the conceptual lens through which we see, understand, and interpret the world and our place within it. Worldview is not just a matter of the head (beliefs) but is "a commitment, a fundamental orientation of the heart . . . about the basic constitution of reality, . . . that provides the foundation on which we live and move and have our being."[35] A person's worldview is reinforced by confirmation bias, a tendency to see what supports existing conceptions while ignoring or downplaying evidence or arguments that question presuppositions. When confronted with new situations, data, or arguments, one tends to interpret them in a manner that fits within one's existing worldview. Worldview presuppositions determine the pool of live options. Worldview also motivates our life direction, encouraging certain actions while discouraging others. Simply put, worldview is a powerful force driving our lives in every respect.

Worldviews are inherently conservative and are especially difficult to change when they are examined and held consciously. Unfortunately, many Christians have never acknowledged their worldview, let alone

---

[35]Sire, *Universe Next Door*, 20.

examined it. Core worldview beliefs are more stubbornly held while peripheral worldview beliefs can be altered or rejected without affecting the overall structure of one's beliefs. Despite worldview conservatism, even consciously held worldviews can be changed; this tends to happen only in the face of overwhelming evidence or powerful personal experiences.

Worldview study helps one to live a more self-aware, conscious, and consistent life, which we hold to be inherently virtuous. Worldview study also aids in understanding *why* one holds a certain worldview, and helps strengthen that belief. For the Christian, worldview study furthers discipleship, helping one to develop the mind of Christ and thereby become a deeper and more consistent follower of Jesus.

Critics of worldview argue that the concept (and subject) is irrelevant and dispensable. In actuality, worldview is no more irrelevant or dispensable than atonement, history, or music. While we *may* be able to derive the benefits of worldview thought without ever using the word or studying the subject formally, our understanding will be enriched by study. Furthermore, failure to use the term or to study the subject explicitly does not entail its irrelevance.

While worldview conversation can overemphasize the rational side of things, the flip side is also true. Rejection (or downplaying) of worldview thinking can underemphasize the role of belief, doctrine, and the life of the mind. Human beings are certainly more than thinking beings, but they are not *less* than that. It is best to hold to the *whole* Christian person—to seek to love God with heart, soul, *and mind*. Beliefs matter and influence other aspects of our lives, just as our actions and practices affect our minds.

If one's philosophy stops with introductory worldview thought, then it is fair to say that one has not engaged in sufficient depth and breadth of philosophical study. It is unfair to conclude, however, that worldview thought itself stunts or discourages deeper philosophical reflection. For many students, worldview will be the gateway to further philosophy. For others, worldview will be the sum total of formal philosophy. If I may offer a terrible take on a bad cliché, "'Tis better to have worldviewed and stopped than never to have worldviewed at all." I would rather a person study worldview and not go on to further philosophical investigation than avoid studying worldview and never go on to study philosophy.

MASTERING THE MATERIAL

When you finish reading this chapter, you should be able to

✔ Identify and explain four primary ways in which worldview affects an individual.

✔ Evaluate where your worldview has imposed constraints on your understanding or interpretation of the world around you.

✔ Understand the importance of worldview consciousness and examination, especially as related to worldview conservatism and conversion.

✔ Articulate why some individuals' worldviews are more easily altered or replaced than those of others.

✔ Highlight seven benefits of worldview study and thought.

✔ Identify and respond to three common concerns about or critiques of worldview study and thought.

Glossary of Terms for Chapter Two

confirmation bias—A type of selective thinking whereby one tends to notice and to seek what confirms one's beliefs, and to ignore, not seek, or undervalue the relevance of what contradicts one's beliefs.

experiential accommodation—The drive to

interpret new data or arguments in a manner that affirms or fits within our existing worldview.

pool of live options—The set of possible explanations for a given phenomenon.

Possible Term Paper Topics

✔ Select a major historical claim that Christianity makes (e.g., Jesus' resurrection, David's kingship, the exodus from Egypt, Jesus' healing of the paralytic). Research how scholars from a range of diverse worldviews investigate that historical truth claim. Explore how the pool of live options or confirmation bias leads many skeptical scholars to downplay evidence or reject historicity. Explore how confirmation bias and life motivation work within Christian scholars, guiding them to accept evidence and historicity and apply the event to their lives.

✔ Choose a prominent historical thinker who underwent a significant worldview conversion (e.g., the apostle Paul, Augustine,

Blaise Pascal, Charles Darwin, C. S. Lewis, Antony Flew). Trace the means and method of that person's worldview conversion and assess (a) how worldview conservatism shaped the journey and (b) how consciously and tenaciously the former worldview was held.

✔ Investigate James K. A. Smith's critique of worldview as overly rationalistic. Read Smith's *Desiring the Kingdom* or *Imagining the Kingdom*, which contain his most pointed critique. Read some of the authors whom he criticizes for approaching worldview too intellectually. Arrive at a strong conclusion regarding the relationship between rationality, habit, worldview, and Christian formation.

Core Bibliography for Chapter Two

Huffman, Douglas S., ed. *Christian Contours: How a Biblical Worldview Shapes the Mind and Heart*. Grand Rapids: Kregel, 2011.

Nash, Ronald H. *Faith and Reason: Searching for a Rational Faith*. Grand Rapids: Zondervan, 1988.

Naugle, David K. *Worldview: The History of a Concept*. Grand Rapids: Eerdmans, 2002.

Smith, James K. A. *Imagining the Kingdom: How Worship Works*. Cultural Liturgies 2. Grand Rapids: Baker Academic, 2013.

WORLDVIEW ANALYSIS

A professor assigned a term paper to his students. He told the students to write on any ethical topic of their choice, requiring each student only to properly back up his or her thesis with reasons and documentation.

One student, an atheist, wrote eloquently on the topic of moral relativism. He argued, "All morals are relative; there is no absolute standard of justice or rightness; it's all a matter of opinion; you like chocolate, I like vanilla," and so on. His paper provided both his reasons and his documentation. It was the right length, on time, and stylishly presented in a handsome blue folder.

After the professor read the entire paper, he wrote on the front cover, "F—I don't like blue folders!" When the student got the paper back he was enraged. He stormed into the professor's office and protested, "F! I don't like blue folders!?!? That's not fair! That's not right! That's not just! You didn't grade the paper on its merits!"

Raising his hand to quiet the bombastic student, the professor calmly retorted, "Wait a minute. Hold on. I read a lot of papers. Let me see . . . wasn't your paper the one that said there is no such thing as fairness, rightness, and justice?"

"Yes," the student answered.

"Then what's this you say about me not being *fair, right,* and *just*?" the professor asked. "Didn't your paper argue that it's all a matter of taste? You like chocolate, I like vanilla?"

The student replied, "Yes, that's my view."

"Fine then," the professor responded. "I don't like blue. You get an F!"

Suddenly the lightbulb went on in the student's head. He realized he really *did* believe in moral absolutes. He at least believed in justice. After all, he was charging his professor with *injustice* for giving him an F simply because of the color of the folder. That simple fact defeated his entire case for relativism.[1]

The Life of Pi is an award-winning, best-selling novel by Yann Martel that was subsequently turned into an award-winning movie by the same name.[2] The novel follows the travails of young Piscine, who survives the sinking of an ocean liner and is stranded on a lifeboat with four fellow passengers — a hyena, an orangutan, a zebra, and a Bengal tiger named Richard Parker. Spoiler alert: Pi survives the shipwreck in the lifeboat for over 250 days, and by the time the story is over, the only other survivor is the tiger. At the end, authorities investigating the accident ask Pi disbelievingly how he could possibly have survived so long on the open ocean with a predatory tiger. In exasperation, Pi shares a second survival story that involves his mother and a cannibalistic ship's cook. In that story, Pi alone survives the shipwreck, and there is no tiger.

Dazed and confused, the investigators ask Pi which story is true. Pi refuses to say, instead asking the investigators, "Which story do you prefer?" In the novel, Martel expands on the thought: neither story can be confirmed; neither story can be disproved. All that's left, then, is personal preference or subjective opinion: "Which story do you prefer?" Which story is true? Doesn't matter, assuming there is such a thing as truth. What matters is what the readers prefer.

Worldview is the conceptual lens through which we see, understand, and interpret the world and our place within it. A worldview is fundamentally a pretheoretical construct resulting from cultural influences and normative nurturing. Worldview resides in and shapes the human heart, from whence it influences our thoughts, choices, and actions. Worldview can be framed as either a narrative or a set of propositions. Either way, worldview answers four fundamental questions about life, the universe, and everything: What is our nature? What is our world? What is our problem? What is our end? Like it or not, everyone has a worldview; while each person's worldview is unique, nonetheless there are a limited number of overarching worldviews, which can be categorized based on their responses to the worldview questions.

---

[1]Norman L. Geisler and Frank Turek, *I Don't Have Enough Faith to Be an Atheist* (Wheaton, IL: Crossway, 2004), 173-74.
[2]Yann Martel, *The Life of Pi* (Boston: Houghton Mifflin, 2001).

3.1 THE NEED FOR WORLDVIEW ANALYSIS

As seen in the previous chapter, worldview exerts tremendous influence over life. Hence, it is important to pursue a consistent and true worldview. As finite and error-prone creatures, we are unlikely to ever hold only true worldview beliefs with no mixture of falsity. Nonetheless, we are able to analyze worldviews—our own and those of others—to adjudicate their truthfulness and accuracy. We do not want to be as obviously self-contradictory as the moral relativist in the opening illustration.

3.1.1 What is truth? Nearly two thousand years ago, a young man was arrested on the charge of treason and sedition and brought before the governor for judgment. The governor questioned the accused, and in the written account of their encounter we overhear the following exchange:

> "What is it you have done?" [the governor asked].
>
> [The accused] said, "My kingdom is not of this world. If it were, my servants would fight to prevent my arrest by the Jewish leaders. But now my kingdom is from another place."
>
> "You are a king, then!" said [the governor].
>
> [The accused] answered, "You say that I am a king. In fact, the reason I was born and came into the world is to testify to the truth. Everyone on the side of truth listens to me."
>
> "What is truth?" retorted [the governor].

This encounter, found in John 18:35-38, ends with perhaps the most profound question Pilate could have asked at that point in time. "What is truth?" It is a question that philosophers have pondered for centuries, and in our day it has become a point of major contention. Indeed, I think it is fair to say that our postmodern society is currently embarked on a flight from truth—a running away from the notion that there is such a thing as binding truth. The flight from truth is evidenced, I believe, in the student-professor interaction in the opening illustration, as well as the ending of *The Life of Pi*. Simply put, the truth has fallen on hard times.

What exactly is this thing that we call truth? First and foremost, truth is objective and absolute. What is true is true for all people at all times in all places, whether they know it or not, believe it or not, and like it or not. For example, consider the statement "God exists." The statement is either true or false. Either God exists, or God does not exist. If God does exist, then millions of atheists are simply wrong in their metaphysical and religious beliefs. They cannot simply object, "I do not believe that God exists; therefore, God does not exist *for me*."

If, on the other hand, God does not exist, then stating that God exists is somewhat like stating that leprechauns exist—interesting but meaningless. If God does not exist, then a considerable number of people hold beliefs that are simply not true (the authors included). It is insufficient to insist that "for me, God exists; so it is true *for me* that God exists." That is akin to me insisting that it is true *for me* that leprechauns exist, or that it is true *for me* that I am the president of the United States of America. Any reasonable person would respond that my self-delusions do not result in a relativistic truth; rather, they result in me believing something that is false.

Relativism about truth simply cannot hold up under rational scrutiny. As illustrated at the opening of this chapter, relativism defeats itself. Consider the statement, there is no absolute truth. Ask the question, is that true? That is, is it true that there is no absolute truth? Or is it merely the opinion of the author? If it is the opinion of the author, why should I accept it? If it is a true statement, then the speaker has established that there is, in fact, something that is true for all people at all times in all places. The assertion that all truth is relative is itself an objective truth claim. It purports to be true and binding on all people. Hence, relativism regarding truth is self-referentially absurd. If it is true, it is false; if it is false, it is false. Either way, it is false, and not rationally compelling.

Opinion, unlike truth, is relative to the individual. "Chocolate ice cream is better than vanilla ice cream" is a statement of opinion. The sentence sounds like a truth-claiming proposition, which unfortunately confuses the issue for many hearers. It is sometimes assumed that since "chocolate ice cream is better than vanilla ice cream" and "compassion is better than murder" possess the same grammatical structure, they must also be statements of the same type. In reality, the first statement is a profession of personal opinion and preference, while the second makes an objective moral truth claim.

Note, however, that "I prefer chocolate ice cream to vanilla ice cream" is an objective truth claim and as such is either true or false (true, in this case). The sentence is expressing a personal preference (I *prefer* chocolate), but the structure of the sentence makes it a propositional truth claim rather than a statement of subjective opinion. It is either true or false that I prefer chocolate. Yes, the truth of the statement depends on the individual making the statement (and it is relative in that sense), but only because the person making the statement identifies the referent for the subject of the sentence (see table 3.1).

Table 3.1. Types of statements and truth value

Type of statement	Objectively true or false?	Relative to individual referent?	Example
Simple propositional truth claim	Yes	No	Chocolate ice cream exists.
Statement of subjective preference	No	Yes	Chocolate ice cream is better than vanilla.
Propositional statement of subjective preference	Yes	Yes	I like chocolate ice cream more than vanilla.

So, beliefs are subjective, relative to the individual, and prone to error and falsehood. Thus, the belief that God does not exist may in fact be wrong (as we believe it is). That does not make the *truth* (of God's existence) relative; rather, it makes the *belief* (about God's nonexistence) false. In the fifteenth century, when the majority of scientists believed that the sun revolved around the earth, they were objectively wrong in their beliefs. The truth is that the earth revolves around the sun; they just did not know it. The truth did not change between the fifteenth and eighteenth centuries—scientific understanding changed. Belief changes, opinion changes, and our understanding of what is true changes. What does not change, however, is truth itself. The existence of multiple perspectives and diverse beliefs should not cloud our thinking. Truth is an objective reality.

Philosophically, there are three broad conceptions of truth that bear scrutiny: correspondence, coherence, and pragmatism. Considering them will help us to grasp the fundamental nature of truth.

3.1.1.1 Truth as correspondence. The correspondence view of truth has been predominant throughout the history of philosophy. In its simplest terms, the correspondence view of truth holds that something is true if and only if it corresponds to the way things actually are in the real world. That is, truth is what is actually out there. If I say, "Canada is the northernmost country in North America," my statement is true if and only if there is a country called Canada, a continent known as North America, a direction we identify as north, and the country called Canada is in the continent of North America and truly occupies the northernmost part of said continent.

To take a different example, consider the worldview belief that there is a divine being responsible for the original creation of the universe. Under the correspondence theory of truth, that worldview belief is true only if the universe is, in fact, a created entity (i.e., it is not self-existent or self-created) and there exists a supernatural (i.e., nonmaterial) being that itself is not a part of the universe but rather created the universe.

Correspondence is a common-sense approach to the nature of truth. Indeed, it is the way we intuitively understand the concept of truth. Relativism and postmodern structuralism may have eroded acceptance of correspondence, but it is still the most valuable theory available.[3]

3.1.1.2 Truth as coherence. The coherence view of truth has increased in philosophical popularity since the late nineteenth century. According to the coherence view of truth, a belief is true if and only if it coheres with other beliefs one holds. That is, to be true something has to fit with what one already accepts as being true.

It is important to make a quick detour to explain the distinction between necessary and sufficient conditions, a distinction that we will come back to throughout the remainder of this chapter. A *necessary* condition is such that it is required in order for the outcome to be obtained. For example, one might (correctly) say that clouds are a necessary condition for snow to occur. To say that clouds are a necessary condition for snow is to say that it will never snow unless there are clouds in the sky. To use a different example, one might also say that death is a necessary condition for murder to have occurred. That is, someone cannot have been murdered if they are not in fact dead.

---

[3]Structuralism is the belief that we construct our own picture of what is true with our linguistic tools. Truth, then, has no external referent but is a structure we build ourselves. Structuralism either denies the existence of external reality or denies our ability to transcend linguistic constructs in order to know reality.

In both examples, I have identified conditions that are necessary but not sufficient. Clouds are necessary for there to be snow, and death is necessary for there to have been murder, but neither is a sufficient condition.

A *sufficient* condition is such that obtaining that condition is all that is required in order for the outcome to be obtained. For example, being enrolled and present in my epistemology class (PHIL 4653 at Oklahoma Baptist University) is a sufficient condition for being an OBU student. Taking a course this semester at OBU is sufficient to establish your identity as an OBU student.

Sometimes sufficient conditions can be established by flipping necessary conditions around. Thus, for example, I noted that death is a necessary but not sufficient condition for murder to have occurred. That is, one cannot have been murdered if one is not dead. Flip those terms around, and you can see that having been murdered is a sufficient but not necessary condition for being dead. That is, if one has been murdered, one certainly is dead.

Coherence certainly seems to be a necessary condition for truthfulness. If one holds as worldview presuppositions both (a) that the universe is composed solely of material things and (b) that human beings are dualistic compositions of material body and nonmaterial soul, then one holds fundamentally contradictory beliefs. The beliefs do not cohere together and thus cannot both be true.

Coherence is not, however, a sufficient condition for truthfulness. The primary problem with a coherence theory of truth is its inevitable relativism. One's own worldview can be examined for coherence (and hence truthfulness), but it would appear to be impossible to compare worldview beliefs for relative truth value. The Christian who believes that Jesus was raised from the dead by God the Father can hold that belief coherently within his own worldview. The Muslim who believes that Allah vindicated Jesus and rescued him from death on the cross may be able to hold that belief coherently within his own worldview. But under the coherence theory of truth on its own, one cannot judge which worldview belief (about Jesus) is true. One can only say that a set of beliefs is coherent and thus possibly true, or that it is incoherent and therefore necessarily false. Truth is necessarily coherent, but coherence does not necessarily entail truth.

3.1.1.3 Truth as pragmatism. The pragmatic view of truth holds that what works, or what is fruitful, is true. If a belief leads to further understanding or virtuous living (or whatever else is held as working or being fruitful: one of the inherent difficulties with pragmatism is delineating what conditions must be met for something to be pragmatically beneficial), then that belief is true. If a belief has no pragmatic value but rather leads to an epistemological or ethical dead end, then it is not true.

Pragmatism capitalizes on the essential insight that truth ought to have some "cash value," some identifiable benefit. The pragmatic view of truth has been particularly influential in philosophy of science where (often known as instrumentalism) it suggests that a scientific theory is more likely to be true (or approximately true) if it is fruitful for further research, predictive success, or technological improvements.

There are significant problems, however, with a strictly pragmatic view of truth. First, pragmatism holds that something is true if it works or is fruitful. But who determines or delineates what it means for a belief (or worldview) to work or to be fruitful? One person might insist that belief in God "works" because it helps that person lead a fulfilled life, with peace and joy in the midst of uncertainty and trial. Another person insists that such criteria simply demonstrate that God belief is an emotional crutch, indicating a flaw in the individual.

Second, pragmatism, like coherence, leads inevitably to a relativistic view of truth. If Christianity "works" for one person, but naturalism "works" for someone else, then both beliefs are true for the individual who holds them. Pragmatic value, then, is another necessary but not sufficient condition for truthfulness. Truth in worldview must transcend pragmatism. (For a comparison of the views of truth, see table 3.2.)

Table 3.2. Views of truth compared

View of truth	Description	Objective?	Problems
Correspondence	Truth = what matches (corresponds to) reality.	Yes	Does reality exist? What is matching/correspondence?
Coherence	Truth = what fits together.	No	Mutually exclusive but coherent views/beliefs cannot both be true.
Pragmatism	Truth = what works beneficially.	No	What counts as working? Mutually exclusive but pragmatic views/beliefs cannot both be true.

REFLECTION QUESTIONS

1 Can you think of examples in literature or cinema that, like *The Life of Pi*, downplay correspondent truth in favor of personal preference?

2 Why has the correspondence theory of truth been the most prominent throughout Western history and philosophy? Why is it increasingly questioned today?

3 Is "being an athlete" a necessary or sufficient condition for "being an NFL quarterback"?

4 Is "being born in Canada" a necessary or sufficient condition for "being a Canadian citizen"?

5 Why is coherence a necessary but not sufficient condition for truth?

6 Why is pragmatism a necessary but not sufficient condition for truth?

7 Is correspondence a necessary and sufficient condition for truth? Or is it one or the other? Or neither? Why?

3.2 CRITERIA FOR WORLDVIEW ANALYSIS

One undertakes the task of analyzing and evaluating one's worldview in order to obtain a truer understanding of reality and thereby live a more consistent life. As in other areas of life, truth in worldview is not relative to the individual but is rather an objective reality. Though the correspondence theory of truth is the superior starting point, insights can be gleaned from each of the three theories of truth.

Along with the correspondence theory of truth, we affirm that a worldview can only be true if it reflects what is actually real. Individual components of a worldview, by the same token, are true only insofar as they correspond to the objective world. Worldview beliefs are true when the answers they provide to the fundamental worldview questions reflect what is actually the case. On the other hand, if worldview beliefs are contradictory to known facts about the real world, then those beliefs are necessarily false.

Along with the coherence theory of truth, we affirm that a worldview can only be true if it is internally consistent or coherent. Individual components of a worldview, by the same token, are true only insofar as they are logically consistent with other true worldview presuppositions. On the other hand, if two beliefs within a worldview contradict one another, then at least one of those worldview components is necessarily false.

Along with the pragmatic theory of truth, we affirm that a worldview can only be true if it is livable—that is, if a person can live with integrity and purpose within that worldview. Individual components of a worldview, by the same token, are true only insofar as the individual can consistently live out those beliefs. On the other hand, if the logical implications of a worldview belief simply cannot be lived out with integrity, then that belief is necessarily false.

In order to arrive at a truer understanding of the world, one can engage in worldview analysis, evaluation, and examination. By subjecting our own worldview beliefs and those of others to various tests for truth, we can arrive at a fuller, more complete understanding of the world. If worldview is the conceptual lens through which we see, understand, and interpret the world and our place within it, then it is incumbent on us as thoughtful and intentional people to ensure that we are wearing the right lenses. Can we attain a perfectly true worldview in all its aspects? Probably not, but we can certainly evaluate the worldview we do hold and bring it into closer conformity to the truth. At any rate, our inability to attain a fully true worldview seems a poor excuse for not bothering to try. To pursue worldview truth, we suggest three worldview tests—internal consistency, external consistency, and existential consistency.

STOP & PAUSE

Biblical Worldview Insight

Those who live according to the flesh have their minds set on what the flesh desires; but those who live in accordance with the Spirit have their minds set on what the Spirit desires. The mind governed by the flesh is death, but the mind governed by the Spirit is life and peace. The mind governed by the flesh is hostile to God; it does not submit to God's law, nor can it do so. Those who are in the realm of the flesh cannot please God. (Rom 8:5-8)

Paul uses the nouns *phronousin* and *phronēma* for "minds" and "mind" in these verses. The connotation is that of having a fixed disposition, an orientation toward (in this passage) the flesh and the Spirit. If we understand worldview as a settled heart orientation that affects everything we do, then Paul here can be seen as pointing out the power of two contrary worldviews (or fixed heart orientations)—one fixated on the things of the flesh, possibly because that is all there is; the other fixated on the things of the Spirit, probably because the Spirit is seen as having unsurpassed importance and significance.

What is your mind fixed on? Does the flesh or the Spirit predominate in your mindful attention?

The three worldview tests for truth draw on insights from the correspondence, coherence, and pragmatic views of truth. Each of the worldview tests is a necessary but not sufficient condition for worldview truth. If, however, a worldview (or components of a worldview) passes all three tests with flying colors, it becomes highly probable that the worldview is an accurate, beneficial view of reality.

3.2.1 Internal consistency: logical coherence. A worldview must make sense of itself. If the tenets of a worldview fit together, that worldview (or those worldview components) is more likely to be true. If, on the other hand, two worldview beliefs are logically incoherent, those worldview components cannot possibly both be true. The worldview coherence test refers to and depends on the fundamental laws of logic—the law of noncontradiction, the law of the excluded middle, and the law of identity.

The law of noncontradiction observes that something cannot be both *A* and *non-A* at the same time and place in the same manner. For example, the red object on my office desk this morning cannot be both an apple and a non-apple.

The law of identity states with deceptive simplicity that something is what it is. According to the law of identity, then, if that red object on my desk is in fact an apple, then it must actually be an apple. It cannot be something other than what it is. If, however, it is in fact not an apple but rather a pear-apple, then it would not actually be an apple at all; rather, it would be a non-apple.[4]

---

[4] In formal terms, an apple is X, a non-apple is $\sim X$, and a pear-apple is Y. If the red object on my

The law of the excluded middle, meanwhile, is the logical observation that any proposition must be either true or false.[5] If I state, "there is a red apple on my desk right now," that statement is either true or false. It is true if, in fact, it corresponds to reality—if there really is a red apple on my desk. If there is not a red apple on my desk right now, then the propositional statement is false. What the statement cannot be is neither true nor false. If the red object on my desk is not actually an apple but rather a pear-apple, then my statement is false. Even if I am convinced that the object on my desk is an apple, when in reality it is a pear-apple, my statement is still false. If, however, I state, "I believe there is a red apple on my desk right now," then the statement would be true even if I have mistaken the pear-apple for an apple.

The laws of logic are essential for all reasoning and discourse. You cannot exchange ideas or seek to discuss intelligible matters without relying on them. Some worldview components run into immediate problems with the laws of logical thought.

For example, the anecdote opening this chapter illustrates the logical problems inherent to moral relativism. The moral relativist argues that moral standards are different for different individuals or cultures. The moral relativist goes on to insist that the difference in moral standards is not merely *descriptive* (i.e., describing the way morals are actually practiced by different people or cultures) but *prescriptive*. That is, the relativist argues that there is no overarching, objective standard of morality that delivers ethical duties and responsibilities (dos and don'ts) to individuals. Thus, if one culture practices incest while another designates it a taboo, neither culture is right in an absolute or objective sense. There is no universal standard; there are only individual or cultural standards for morality.

Relativists run into immediate problems when someone cuts them off in traffic, or fails them for a well-written philosophical position paper, or

---

desk is an apple, then it is an *X*. If it is a pear-apple, it is a *Y*, but it is also a ~*X*. We cannot say that since it is *kind of* an apple, or like an apple, that it is *both X and* ~*X*; rather, it is ~*X* because it is, in fact, *Y* instead.

[5]A proposition is a meaningful linguistic construct that makes a truth claim. That is, a proposition is a sentence, fragment, or paragraph, in verbal, written, or demonstrative form, claiming to represent reality.

punches them in the nose. Typical relativists will insist that something "wrong" has been done to them in each case.[6] To expand the problem, the relativist will also likely agree that it was wrong for the Nazis to execute millions of Jews in concentration camps, that it is wrong to cut off the left ear of every second baby girl born, and that it is wrong to own another human being as a personal slave to do with as you please. But, of course, if relativists insist that those practices are wrong, they believe that they are wrong for all people in all cultures, not just for people who hold to their personal or cultural moral viewpoint. Moral relativism, the way most individuals hold to it, is therefore incoherent; it holds two contradictory beliefs. For example:

Premise 1: Owning another human being as a piece of personal property is objectively and absolutely wrong and should not be permitted.

Premise 2: Thus (from premise 1), there is at least one moral fact that applies to all people transtemporally and transculturally.

Premise 3: There are (according to moral relativism) no absolute or objective moral standards that apply to all people transculturally and transtemporally.

Conclusion: There are no absolute moral standards, and there is at least one absolute moral standard.[7]

By the laws of logic, if your original proposition (in this case, the combination of two original worldview beliefs) generates an explicit contradiction, it necessarily entails the falsity of the original proposition (in this case, the falsity of at least one of the original worldview beliefs). Thus, moral relativists are left with a dilemma: either their worldview belief in moral relativism is false, or their worldview belief that certain actions are objectively and absolutely wrong is false. Either way, there is a contradiction within the worldview structure.

---

[6]There are, however, consistent relativists, who would emphatically deny that anything is objectively and absolutely wrong. Thus, for example, one cannot morally condemn slavery as an ethical transgression; one can only express one's own disapproval and abhorrence for such actions. Consistent moral relativists are not guilty of violating the worldview test of coherence; they may, however, be guilty of violating the third worldview test—that of existential consistency or pragmatic satisfaction.

[7]In symbolic terminology: $(\exists x)(Mx) \cdot \sim(\exists x)(Mx)$. The first half of the equation states, "There is some x such that x is an absolute, objective moral fact." The second half of the equation is the denial of the first statement: "It is false that there is some x such that x is an absolute, objective moral fact." Combining the two statements results in stating both that something is A and that something is *non-A*, an explicit violation of the law of noncontradiction.

Worldview examination can bring such internal contradictions to light and enable the individuals to discern which worldview belief lies closer to the core of their worldview, or which belief is more soundly grounded rationally, evidentially, and existentially. Worldview alteration or conversion can then follow to establish greater consistency. Unfortunately, most professing moral relativists have never examined their worldview beliefs and are entirely unaware that they are embracing an impossible contradiction.

Moral relativism is not the only worldview component to suffer from logical incoherence. Ronald Nash examines skepticism, logical positivism, determinism, physicalism, and evidentialism, exposing their violations of the law of noncontradiction. Nash's discussion of evidentialism is of particular interest. Evidentialism, as explained by W. K. Clifford, is the belief that "it is wrong always, everywhere, and for anyone, to believe anything on insufficient evidence."[8] Nash notes:

> For [Clifford], it is immoral to believe *anything* without proof. But where is the proof for his evidentialist claim? What evidence does he provide for his belief that it is immoral to believe anything in the absence of evidence? The fact is that he provides no evidence; nor could he.[9]

Evidentialism is not able to satisfy its own requirements and thus falls prey to self-refutation. As a philosophical system, it implies the truth of two contradictory propositions: (1) It is immoral to believe *any* proposition without empirical proof. (2) It is moral to believe *this* proposition, even though there is no empirical proof for it. Evidentialism, therefore, must be either revised or rejected as a component of worldview.

It is important to note that worldviews need to be altered only when there is an actual logical contradiction contained within worldview beliefs. A perceived contradiction is not the same as an actual contradiction. For example, some non-Christians insist that the Christian view of the Trinity is logically incoherent. The notion of one God existing in three persons, it is argued, makes no sense. It embraces two contradictory

[8]W. K. Clifford, "The Ethics of Belief," in *Readings in Philosophy of Religion: Ancient to Contemporary*, ed. Linda Zagzebski and Timothy D. Miller (Malden, MA: Wiley-Blackwell, 2009), 548.
[9]Ronald H. Nash, *Worldviews in Conflict: Choosing Christianity in a World of Ideas* (Grand Rapids: Zondervan, 1992), 91.

beliefs—the one-ness and three-ness of God. However, the "contra-diction" in the Trinity is only perceived, not actual. For it to be a contra-diction, the Christian belief would have to be that the Trinity is both three gods and one god, or that God is both three persons and one person. In actuality, however, the Christian belief is that the Trinity is three persons and one god. While difficult to work out conceptually, there is no actual contradiction within the belief.

If there were an actual contradiction, the logical argument would have to look something like this to demonstrate it.

Premise 1. God exists as one Being.

Premise 2. God exists as three Persons.

Premise 3. Thus, God is one divine Being who exists as three Persons.

Premise 4. Individual human persons each comprise one human being.

Premise 5. It is impossible for individual human beings to be com-posed of more than one Person.

Premise 6. Thus, it is impossible for one human being to exist as three Persons.

Conclusion 1. Thus, it is impossible for one divine Being to exist as three Persons.

Conclusion 2. Thus, if God is one divine Being, then God exists as one Person.

Conclusion 3. Thus, it is false that God is one divine Being who exists as three Persons. That is, the Christian conception of God's triunity is logically incoherent.

All six premises seem, from a Christian view, to be clearly true. What, then, might be the problem? Why doesn't the argument show that Christian trinitarianism is incoherent? The conclusion actually does not follow from the premises. In fact, nothing at all regarding divine Being and persons follows from the six premises. There needs to be an inter-mediate premise:

Premise 7. It is necessary to presume that what is true for human beings and persons also applies to divine Being and Persons.

With premise 7, you now have a connection between the six premises and the conclusions. Problem? There is no reason to accept premise 7 as true. Indeed, from a Christian perspective, there seems to be good

reason to deny the truthfulness of premise 7. Even from other super-
naturalist philosophical viewpoints, premise 7 will seem to be clearly
false. There is absolutely no reason to presume that the same conditions
and limitations that apply to human personhood and being apply in the
same way to the infinite, eternal God of the universe. C. S. Lewis provides a helpful analogy:

> You know that in space you can move in three ways—to the left or right,
> backwards or forwards, up or down. Every direction is either one of these
> three or a compromise between them. They are called the three Dimen-
> sions. Now notice this. If you are using only one dimension, you could
> draw only a straight line. If you are using two, you could draw a figure: say,
> a square. And a square is made up of four straight lines. Now a step further.
> If you have three dimensions, you can then build what we call a solid
> body: say, a cube—a thing like a dice or a lump of sugar. And a cube is
> made up of six squares. . . .
>
>   In other words, as you advance to more real and more complicated
> levels, you do not leave behind you the things you found on the simpler
> levels: you still have them, but combined in new ways—in ways you could
> not imagine if you knew only the simpler levels.
>
>   Now the Christian account of God involves just the same principle.
> The human level is a simple and rather empty level. On the human level
> one person is one being, and any two persons are two separate beings—
> just as, in two dimensions (say on a flat sheet of paper) one square is one
> figure, and any two squares are two separate figures. On the Divine level
> you still find personalities; but up there you find them combined in new
> ways which we, who do not live on that level, cannot imagine. In God's
> dimension, so to speak, you find a being who is three Persons while re-
> maining one Being, just as a cube is six squares while remaining one cube.
> Of course we cannot fully conceive a Being like that: just as, if we were so
> made that we perceived only two dimensions in space we could never
> properly imagine a cube. But we can get a sort of faint notion of it. And
> when we do, we are then, for the first time in our lives, getting some
> positive idea, however faint, of something super-personal—something
> more than a person.[10]

[10]C. S. Lewis, *Mere Christianity*, rev. ed. (New York: HarperSanFrancisco, 2001), 161-62.

The first test for worldviews, then, is the test of logical coherence or internal consistency. A worldview must make sense within itself if it is to be worth holding. We take it to be intuitively preferable to avoid holding a set of beliefs when at least one of those beliefs must necessarily be false.

3.2.2 External consistency: evidential correspondence. In addition to making sense of itself, a worldview must make sense of reality. Worldviews, as narratives or conceptual constructs, must account for what we know about the world. As James Sire notes,

> An adequate worldview . . . must be able to comprehend the data of reality
> —data of all types: that which each of us gleans through our conscious
> experience of daily life, that which are supplied by critical analysis and
> scientific investigation, that which are reported to us from the experience
> of others.[11]

Our worldview should help us make sense of the world around us rather than present cognitive or existential dissonance in the face of external reality. Thus, evidential correspondence, like logical coherence, is a necessary (but not sufficient) condition for worldview truth. External consistency is a negative truth test: absence of external consistency indicates the falsity of the worldview (or worldview components). Thus, if a worldview says that x is true of the world while we are justifiably persuaded that x is not true of the world, then the worldview is probably false in that respect. (The alternative is that our perception of the world is false in that respect; that possibility must be seriously entertained. I am assuming that the individual not only believes that x is not true of the world but has knowledge [justified true belief] that it is not true. That is, his belief is matched by reality; it is true that x is not true of the world. And he has justification [or warrant] for his belief that x is not true of the world.)

A clarification is in order. It might seem at first glance that external consistency involves testing things only in the physical world—what Nash calls the "outer world." External consistency, however, refers to all

---

[11]James W. Sire, *The Universe Next Door: A Basic Worldview Catalog*, 5th ed. (Downers Grove, IL: IVP Academic, 2009), 282.

things that are external to the worldview. The test for internal consistency sets the tenets of a worldview side by side to discern whether they are logically coherent (i.e., whether they can even possibly all be true). That test is applied only within the worldview—testing multiple beliefs within the worldview with one another to see whether they fit together. The test for external consistency sets the worldview alongside reality, and reality is outside (external to) the worldview. For example, I watch the sun rise. If my worldview declares that there are no such things as extraterrestrial bodies (stars, planets, etc.), then my undeniable observation of an extra-terrestrial body falsifies at least that aspect of my worldview. That is an external test (evidential correspondence) that relates to Nash's "outer world." If, on the other hand, my worldview declares that human beings do not need food to survive and will never experience desires for physical sustenance, then my undeniable experience of severe hunger pains after six days without food and water falsifies at least that aspect of my worldview. That is an external test for evidential correspondence that re-lates to Nash's "inner world." Both sides of reality—the outer (physical, empirical, five-senses) world and the inner (psychological, intuitive)—matter when it comes to testing a worldview for external consistency. Thus, to possess evidential correspondence, a worldview (or worldview compo-nents) must match up with the way things are in the empirically ob-servable outer world as well as the subjectively experienced inner world.[12] Failing to match up to either world reveals a lack of external consistency.

Many worldview beliefs seem to lack such evidential correspondence. For example, worldviews that deny the reality of pain and death have difficulties explaining the inner world's response to the body meeting a fast-moving bus in the outer world. The worldview does not possess factual adequacy; it does not explain the universal experience of pain and death. Consider the experience of a young boy who encountered a practitioner of Christian Science.

> Noticing that the boy seemed quite despondent, the Christian Scientist asked him, "Is everything all right, my boy?"
>
> "No, sir. I'm very sad today. My father is quite ill; my mother is worried he will die."

---

[12]Nash, *Worldviews in Conflict*, 57-62.

"Oh, no," the Christian Scientist responded. "Your father is not sick. He only *thinks* that he is sick. He must learn to counter those negative thoughts and realize that he is really healthy."

The next day the two met again on the sidewalk. The Christian Scientist asked, "How is your father doing today, my boy?"

"Today father thinks he is dead," the boy responded.[13]

Others argue that a worldview that perceives human beings as determined runs counter to the strong intuition we all have of making truly free choices. Others insist that a worldview that embraces an eternal or self-creating universe is falsified by scientific evidence demonstrating a spatiotemporal beginning to the universe at the Big Bang. Others argue that belief in a relatively young universe (less than ten thousand years) runs afoul of overwhelming scientific evidence that the universe is billions of years old. Others argue that a worldview belief that human life ends at physical death is falsified by the evidence of near-death experiences. Others insist that a worldview that denies the existence of a divine creator fails in the face of empirical evidence of transcendent design. Still others argue that a worldview that embraces the inherent goodness of all human beings is falsified by both introspection and the daily news.

Although the test of external consistency is crucial, it can be very difficult to apply. Recall that worldview is generally formed pretheoretically; that is, an individual's worldview is developed at a young age and is influenced by parents, cultural surroundings, education, and so forth. One's pretheoretical worldview affects the way that one sees the surrounding world, including what is accepted as an external fact to begin with. Thus, a naturalist with a belief that life ends at physical death will generally reject the evidential importance of near-death experiences (NDEs): the naturalist's pool of live options rejects the very possibility

---

[13]I have encountered this anecdote, which is almost certainly a fictional account, in various places and diverse forms. This version is drawn from Bill Muehlenberg, "Nothing New About 'The Secret,'" *CultureWatch*, May 23, 2007, https://billmuehlenberg.com/2007/05/23/nothing-new-about-"the-secret"/. Muehlenberg's article also printed an amusing little limerick:

There was a faith-healer from Deal,
Who said that though pain was not real,
"When I sit on a pin
And it punctures my skin,
I dislike what I fancy I feel."

that NDEs are valid. A young-earth creationist who grows up with the belief that the universe is very young sees the earth as a recent creation by God. Thus, scientific evidence pointing toward an ancient earth and universe will be either discounted (by confirmation bias) or reinterpreted (by experiential accommodation). Either way, something may seem to me an external fact requiring explanation, but to someone with a different worldview it may not be a fact requiring explanation at all, or the explanation may be very different. In this way, the pervading influence of worldview on our experience and interpretation of events and data can make it very difficult to apply the test of external consistency.

Nonetheless, all is not lost. As noted in chapter two, worldviews can be and are altered at both the peripheral and core levels. Furthermore, if someone is both conscious of his worldview and willing to engage in intentional examination of his presuppositions, then it is possible to be persuaded to accept something as an external fact that had previously been ruled out of court. Hence the importance of worldview thought and worldview study: if one is aware of one's worldview, one can engage in reflective self-examination. Why do I accept scientific evidence for the age of the universe? Why do I believe that human beings are inherently good? What are the external data that support my worldview beliefs? Do I still think that x is a fact of the external world? Or do I think there is good reason to question x? If I reject x, what impact does it have on the rest of my worldview?

In sum, it is essential to be self-reflectively aware and to expose worldview to the test of external consistency or evidential correspondence. If one's worldview does not match up with reality, one needs to adjust one's worldview beliefs accordingly.

3.2.3 Existential consistency: pragmatic satisfaction. We have seen that a worldview must make sense of itself and must make sense of the world around us. Finally, in order to be a worldview worth holding, our worldview must make sense of life. We must be able to live consistently within our worldview.

For example, consider the moral relativist depicted earlier in this chapter. Most moral relativists will insist that certain practices (slavery, torture, cold-blooded murder) are morally wrong for all people at all times, regardless of the perpetrator's own moral beliefs. However, belief in moral facts is inconsistent with the overarching embrace of moral relativism. I noted earlier that the moral relativist therefore faces a dilemma: either moral relativism is false or the relativist's moral intuitions about the objective wrongness of certain actions is mistaken. Most relativists have never examined their beliefs critically and thus have never faced this dilemma. Most relativists, when they are forced to face this dilemma, will acknowledge that moral relativism must not be absolutely true; there are, in fact, some moral standards that apply to all people in all places at all times. Other moral relativists, however, will bite the bullet and acknowledge that it is their moral intuitions that are mistaken.

Sam Harris, a contemporary atheist philosopher and author, writes of an encounter with an educated moral relativist who insisted that one cannot morally condemn even the cultural practice of plucking out the eyes of every third child at birth since there are no transcultural moral standards that are binding on everyone. Harris, himself a moral realist, is aghast that someone would continue to affirm moral relativism rather than acknowledge what ought to be rationally and existentially obvious to any educated and virtuous person—that it is wrong in all places and at all times to perpetrate such horrors on a child.[14]

How ought one respond to a moral relativist who denies the legitimacy of moral intuitions? Avicenna, a medieval philosopher, humorously noted: "Anyone who denies the law of non-contradiction should be beaten and burned until he admits that to be beaten is not the same as not to be beaten, and to be burned is not the same as not to be burned." Perhaps his advice could be adapted to apply to the moral relativist: those who deny that some things are objectively wrong should be beaten and burned for fun until they admit that it is objectively wrong to beat and burn an individual for fun. As C. S. Lewis noted two generations ago, moral relativists simply cannot live by their own precepts. Those who insist there is no transcendent right and wrong in one breath complain with their next breath that someone has treated them unfairly.

Pragmatic satisfaction, or existential consistency, is another difficult truth test for worldviews. Whereas an observer might insist that a

---

[14]Sam Harris, *The Moral Landscape: How Science Can Determine Human Values* (New York: Free Press, 2010), 43-44.

worldview is entirely unlivable, a proponent of that worldview might respond (perhaps honestly) that the worldview is quite subjectively satisfactory. Nonetheless, pragmatic *dis*-satisfaction is often a prime contributor to worldview self-examination. This was certainly the case in my own worldview journey. As a young man, I developed a strongly held naturalistic worldview. Two of the implications of my worldview, however, gave me deep existential angst—meaninglessness and postmortem extinction. The attempts by philosophers and authors like Bertrand Russell and Albert Camus to insist that an atheist could find or construct meaning and purpose in life seemed to me quite hollow, empty, and self-contradictory: if my life ceased at death, and the universe was headed for a cold death, what difference could I possibly make, and what would be the point anyway? Similarly, the reality of ceasing to exist at my physical death left me unsatisfied, with the feeling, amorphous but undeniable, that there ought to be more than this.

Similarly, some Christian theists first begin to doubt or examine their worldview because of existential inconsistency. Their worldview, unconsciously held, suggests that they ought to experience God's blessing in their life through peace, joy, health, and wealth. When suffering comes, or material security is lost, their worldview does not match up with the circumstances in their lives, and existential dissonance increases. Their worldview is not making sense of their life experience. Thus, something has to give. The belief that gives ought to be the expectation for sugar and spice and everything nice. Nowhere does God promise his children health, wealth, and a life of ease. Indeed, Jesus promises trouble and tribulation for those who sincerely follow him. See, for example, Matthew 5:10-12, Matthew 10:32-39, and 1 Peter 3:8-17.

Another aspect of existential consistency is worth mentioning, if only briefly. Philosopher Clifford Williams notes that human beings ubiquitously have numerous existential needs—he enumerates eight self-directed needs and five other-directed needs. An existentially consistent (or pragmatically satisfying) worldview will, it is argued, meet those existential needs rather than leaving them thwarted or unsatisfied. If we have unshakable yearning for a deep meaning in life, a worldview that denies the existence of meaning in life will be existentially inconsistent.

We will not be able to sustain such a worldview. It could be argued that atheistic existentialism fails the test for existential consistency since it maintains that we can (must) construct some proximate meaning/purpose for ourselves while contending that we live in a cold and absurd universe devoid of transcendent meaning.

REFLECTION QUESTIONS

1 The authors argue that it is impossible to reason without using the fundamental laws of logic. Do you agree? Why or why not?

2 Explain how moral relativism fails the worldview tests either internally or existentially.

3 Other than trinitarianism, what are some other areas of Christian worldview that might be accused of lacking logical coherence? Why?

4 In what ways might Christianity be accused of lacking evidential correspondence? How would you seek to respond to those charges?

5 In what ways might Christianity be accused of lacking pragmatic satisfaction? How would you seek to respond to those charges?

6 Which worldview test do you think is the most difficult to apply? Why?

3.3 CONCLUSION

A worldview is the conceptual lens through which we see, understand, and interpret the world and our place within it. Whether in narrative or propositional format, a worldview answers four fundamental questions about life, the universe, and everything: What is our nature? What is our world? What is our problem? What is our end? Worldview affects the way that we live, move, and have our being. Through confirmation bias, worldview determines what evidence and arguments we accept as valid and worth incorporation. Through experiential accommodation, worldview adjusts arguments and evidence to fit our preconceptions. Through the pool of live options, worldview determines what we will consider as plausible explanations for a given event or experience. And through life motivation, worldview gives direction to our thoughts, choices, and actions.

An unexamined worldview is not worth living. We all want to hold a true worldview. We may never achieve an entirely true worldview, but we dare not use that as an excuse to avoid examining our worldview. It is incumbent on thoughtful, intentional individuals to scrutinize their worldview—in its components as well as its overarching whole—to assess its truth value.

The three primary tests for worldview truth are tests of consistency: internal, external, and existential. The test for internal consistency, or logical coherence, seeks to ensure that the worldview makes sense within itself, that it is free from logical contradictions. The test for external consistency, or evidential correspondence, seeks to ensure that the worldview makes sense of the world, that it is factually adequate. The test for existential consistency, or pragmatic satisfaction, seeks to ensure that the worldview makes sense of life, that it is subjectively livable.

Thus far, our worldview thinking has been primarily theoretical and conceptual. In the rest of this book, we will move from the theoretical realm to the concrete. In part two, we will articulate and explore the contours of a Christian worldview. In part three, we will examine some major alternative worldviews. In both sections, we will be mindful that broad worldviews (or textbook worldviews) are rarely if ever fully incarnated in individuals and that one's worldview is unique to oneself. In both sections, we will apply what we have learned in this first section. We will examine broad answers to the four fundamental worldview questions: What is our nature? What is our world? What is our problem? What is our end? We will survey how the worldview affects its proponents via confirmation bias, experiential accommodation, the pool of live options, and life motivation. Finally, we will apply the worldview truth tests surveyed in this chapter to each of the worldviews we address in the rest of the book.

Part two, articulating the contours and implications of a Christian worldview, is, in our opinion, the heart of this project. While the conceptual work in parts one and three are helpful to thinkers of all stripes, part two has a specifically Christian importance. Each of the authors embraces Christian theism as the true overarching worldview, the correct conceptual lens through which we see, understand, and interpret the world and our place within it. But Christian worldview is a concept that needs to be thoroughly explored and worked out; that will be the task of the following three chapters.

MASTERING THE MATERIAL

When you finish reading this chapter, you should be able to

✔ Grasp the distinction between necessary and sufficient conditions, particularly as they apply to truth.

✔ Identify and evaluate the three main theories of truth.

✔ Understand the difference between objective and subjective statements, especially as related to truth.

✔ Articulate the nature of truth as unchanging, absolute, and objective.

✔ Explain each of the three worldview truth tests.

✔ Apply the worldview truth tests to various worldviews—your own and those of others.

Glossary of Terms for Chapter Three

descriptive—Describing the way that things actually are.

evidential correspondence—A worldview attains evidential correspondence when its premises correspond with reality.

evidentialism—The belief that nothing should be believed without sufficient evidence to support it.

existential consistency—A worldview attains existential consistency when it allows its adherents to live it out with integrity.

logical coherence—A worldview is logically coherent if all of its components fit together logically and without internal contradictions.

necessary condition—To say that A is a necessary condition for B is to say that it would be impossible for B to exist without A.

prescriptive—Established by frequent use or long-standing custom.

self-referentially absurd—statements that are false even if they are true; a self-defeating definition.

sufficient condition—To say that A is a sufficient condition for B is to say that the existence of A assures the existence of B.

Possible Term Paper Topics

✔ Research the increased skepticism regarding the correspondence theory of truth in the nineteenth, twentieth, and twenty-first centuries. Identify key thinkers who have contributed to this trend. Evaluate the merits of major veritologies

✔ Choose either moral relativism or evidentialism. After researching proponents of the position, construct a persuasive argument demonstrating its logical inconsistency.

✔ Identify one major way that the Christian worldview has been accused of failing the worldview tests of logical coherence (e.g., trinitarianism, incarnation, problem of evil), evidential correspondence (e.g., Freudian psychoanalysis and philosophy of religion, evidence of a godless random universe, Christianity's antiscientism), or pragmatic satisfaction (e.g., God as cosmic killjoy, boredom of heaven). Research how critics have argued that Christianity fails that test and how Christian philosophers and theologians have responded. Stake out your own resolution of the charge.

Core Bibliography for Chapter Three

Nash, Ronald H. *Worldviews in Conflict: Choosing Christianity in a World of Ideas*. Grand Rapids: Zondervan, 1992.

Naugle, David K. *Worldview: The History of a Concept*. Grand Rapids: Eerdmans, 2002.

Samples, Kenneth Richard. *A World of Difference: Putting Christian Truth-Claims to the Worldview Test*. Grand Rapids: Baker Books, 2007.

Sire, James W. *The Universe Next Door: A Basic Worldview Catalog*. 5th ed. Downers Grove, IL: IVP Academic, 2009.

PART II

CONTOURS OF
A CHRISTIAN
WORLDVIEW

Is there such a thing as *a* Christian worldview? Can there be just *one* Christian conceptual lens through which we must see, understand, and interpret the world and our place within it?

On the one hand, given the pretheoretical nature of an individual's worldview and the resultant diversity of worldview perspectives even among devout Christians (see section 1.4 for more), it might seem impossible to talk authoritatively about the contours of *a* or *the* Christian worldview. There is simply too much disagreement, too much diversity, to have an authoritative statement of Christian worldview.

On the other hand, call to mind the subtitle of this volume: *Pursuing God's Perspective in a Pluralistic World*. Yes, we certainly live in a pluralistic society. Christians are neighbors to Muslims, Buddhists, Hindus, Jews, agnostics, atheists, Wiccans, and many other worldviews. Within

Christendom, denominations differ on doctrines large and small. Within denominations, individual Christians disagree on major and minor points. But we are in pursuit of what is, essentially, God's worldview. A truly Christian worldview is, simply put, the way that God sees, understands, and interprets the world and our place within it. Put that way, there obviously is such a thing as *the* Christian worldview.

The only problem remains that the Christian worldview resides in (and only in) the mind of God. We do not have the mind of God. And so we stumble and bumble, as imperfect creatures, seeking after a God's-eye view of life, the universe, and everything. Yes, we are finite, fallen, and fallible (more on that in chapters four and five). Yes, we are prone to getting some things wrong—even some rather significant things. But we are also heirs of God, coheirs with Christ. We have been made alive by the Holy Spirit (if indeed we belong to Christ) and have received his gracious written Word for our instruction, edification, and (yes, we dare say it) knowledge. As we faithfully seek to use every good gift that God has given (heart, soul, mind, and strength) to pursue his perspective in a pluralistic world, we can have some tentative confidence that we will approach not only his throne of grace but also his truth about the world around us.

The faith of the saints handed down is precious. As we seek to articulate a Christian worldview, we do so in the spirit of the Apostles' Creed, C. S. Lewis's *Mere Christianity*, and John Stott's *Basic Christianity*—seeking to outline what all Christians everywhere have always believed rather than promoting our own pet doctrines and preferences.

> May these words of my mouth and this meditation of my heart
>> be pleasing in your sight,
> LORD, my Rock and my Redeemer. (Ps 19:14)

May we be found faithful in discharging our sacred task of imparting accurately the central contours of a Christian worldview.

THE NARRATIVE CONTOURS OF
A CHRISTIAN WORLDVIEW

The heavens declare the glory of God;
the skies proclaim the work of his hands.
Day after day they pour forth speech;
night after night they reveal knowledge.
They have no speech, they use no words;
no sound is heard from them.
Yet their voice goes out into all the earth,
their words to the ends of the world.

PSALM 19:1-4

I had always felt life first as a story: And if
there is a story, there is a story-teller.

G. K. CHESTERTON

In his foundational book, *The Universe Next Door*, James Sire argues that worldview can be articulated either "as a story or in a set of presuppositions."[1] In chapter five, we will examine a Christian worldview via presuppositions, or propositional claims, and see how Christianity answers our four core worldview questions: What is our nature? What is

---

[1] James W. Sire, *The Universe Next Door: A Basic Worldview Catalog*, 5th ed. (Downers Grove, IL: IVP Academic, 2009), 20.

our world? What is our problem? What is our end? Right now, however, we turn our attention to the narrative contours of a Christian worldview. As we saw in chapter one, an individual's worldview is usually formed pretheoretically, being absorbed via familial and cultural influences. Moreover, the human person is predominantly a "storied" creature; narratives and stories resonate with us more deeply than do abstract doctrinal claims.

In this chapter, then, we consider the Christian worldview by means of what God, the master narrator, has written. In other words, we will study his-story in order to seek the narrative contours of a Christian worldview. When we speak of God as the master narrator or author, when we seek his story, we are seeking to understand what God himself has revealed. The broad contours of Christian worldview, as evidenced in his story, are creation, fall, redemption, and glorification. God's revelation comes to us in two forms—natural and special revelation. Natural (or general) revelation is what God has written in the book of nature, the world around us, in penmanship legible (theoretically) to all human persons. Special revelation is what God has written in the book of Scripture, the Bible (see table 4.1).

Table 4.1. Comparing natural and special revelation

Natural revelation	Special revelation
Knowledge of God from nature	Knowledge of God from Scripture
General revelation	
Natural theology	
The book of nature	The book of Scripture
God's world / God's works	God's Word
Brings knowledge *that* God	Brings knowledge *of* God

When interpreted rightly, the two books of nature and Scripture do not disagree. There is a harmony between God's works and God's Word. In other words, there is agreement between faith and reason. We will begin, in this chapter, with a consideration of God's revelation in nature before turning to his revelation in Scripture.

4.1 NATURAL REVELATION

In natural revelation (also known as general revelation), God's reality can be discerned through observation and contemplation. The revelation of God through what he has done is sometimes called general revelation because it is for all people. It is alternatively known as natural revelation because this form of revelation comes through nature—history, the physical universe, and the conscience and consciousness of a person. More precisely, in natural revelation God makes himself known in created nature, in history, and in the human person (natural) to all (general); he is known especially through personal experience by believers, all of whom are made in God's image and likeness.

Millard Erickson defines natural revelation as "God's self-manifestation through nature, history, and the inner being of the human person. . . . It is general in two senses: its universal availability (it is accessible to all persons) and the content of the message (it is less particularized and detailed than special revelation)."[2] In light of the first sense, Erickson appropriately calls natural revelation "God's Universal Revelation."

There are many passages in Scripture that speak of a natural or general revelation. We begin in the Old Testament.

Natural revelation appears in the teaching about creation in Genesis 1–2. Like an architect who is made known in the design of a building (his or her life and heart), we would expect the sovereign Creator God to make himself known through his creation in multiple ways. We also would expect human beings, made in God's image, to be able to know such general or natural revelation.

Our knowledge is adequate to what is there. If there is a God, we can know him/it. If there are angels, we can know them. If there is a natural revelation, we can know about it. If there are atoms and molecules, we can know this too (at least theoretically). So let me repeat, our knowledge is adequate to what is there!

Upon seeing the marvels of nature and its good design, my daughter said on a recent visit to the Perot Museum of Nature and Science in

---

[2]Millard J. Erickson, *Christian Theology* (Grand Rapids: Baker Books, 1983), 1:154.

Dallas, Texas, "How could anyone not believe in God?" Only a fool, who, speaking from the heart, says there is no God (see Ps 14:1).

We have general revelation also in the next text:

> The heavens declare the glory of God;
> > the skies proclaim the work of his hands.
> Day after day they pour forth speech;
> > night after night they reveal knowledge.
> They have no speech, they use no words;
> > no sound is heard from them.
> Yet their voice goes out into all the earth,
> > their words to the ends of the world. (Ps 19:1-4)

Psalm 19 insists that God's creative activity and glory are evident to all people, not just to those who accept his Word as Scripture. In response, Christians (and other theists, like Muslims) have used natural revelation to develop powerful arguments (sometimes called theistic proofs) for the existence (and nature) of God. We will briefly outline two of them.[3]

Thomas Aquinas (1225–1274) famously articulated five ways to demonstrate the necessity for God's existence. At least two of Aquinas's arguments from natural revelation are cosmological in nature—that is, they argue from known facts regarding the physical universe (cosmos) to the existence of God. First, he notes that many things in our universe are in motion and that it is evident that nothing can be in motion unless it is set in motion by something external to itself. However, it is clear that "this cannot go on to infinity, because then there would be no first mover, and, consequently, no other mover." Therefore, "it is necessary to arrive at a first mover, put in motion by no other; and this everyone understands to be God."[4] Second, Aquinas argues nothing is the efficient (that is, actualizing) cause of itself; in other words, everything that begins to exist is brought into existence by something else. Since, once again, it is

---

[3]For treatments of these and other theistic arguments, two of the best comprehensive sources are William Lane Craig, *Reasonable Faith*, 3rd ed. (Wheaton, IL: Crossway, 2008); and Douglas Groothuis, *Christian Apologetics: A Comprehensive Case for Biblical Faith* (Downers Grove, IL: IVP Academic, 2011).

[4]Thomas Aquinas, *Summa Theologica*, II.A.2, cited in Linda Zagzebski and Timothy D. Miller, eds., *Readings in Philosophy of Religion: Ancient to Contemporary* (Malden, MA: Wiley-Blackwell, 2009), 71-72.

impossible to have an infinite series of efficient causation, there must be a first cause that itself is uncaused.[5]

Aquinas's fifth way is a teleological (or fine-tuning) argument for God's existence. Teleology, you may recall from our fourth worldview question (what is our end?), derives from the Greek τέλος (telos), which indicates purpose, function, or end. Something exhibits teleology if it appears to have been intended (made, directed) for a particular purpose (function, purpose). Teleological arguments for God's existence, then, suggest that what is known about the world around us (natural revelation) indicates purpose, design, and intentionality, which require a suprahuman (i.e., transcendent or divine) designer. Aquinas's design argument has been strengthened by philosophers and scientists like William Paley (1743–1805) and, more recently, Robin Collins.[6]

God makes his glory known through the skies, not to mention the Scriptures. Indeed, their span tells of the work of his hands, and knowledge of him is silently revealed. In wisdom, God has made all things (Ps 104:24), and all things declare his reality. No one is exempt from his self-revelation in nature.

Romans 1–2 contains another key set of verses on natural revelation. Romans 1:18-23 (perhaps the key text) reads like this:

> The wrath of God is being revealed from heaven against all the godlessness and wickedness of people, who suppress the truth by their wickedness, since what may be known about God is plain to them, because God has made it plain to them. For since the creation of the world God's invisible qualities—his eternal power and divine nature—have been clearly seen, being understood from what has been made, so that people are without excuse.
>
> For although they knew God, they neither glorified him as God nor gave thanks to him, but their thinking became futile and their foolish hearts were darkened. Although they claimed to be wise, they became fools and exchanged the glory of the immortal God for images made to look like a mortal human being and birds and animals and reptiles.

---

[5]Ibid., 72. The argument from causation has a long history in Jewish, Christian, and Muslim natural theology and most recently has been developed with intricate and exhaustive (and exhausting) detail by William Lane Craig in *The Kalam Cosmological Argument* (Eugene, OR: Wipf & Stock, 2000).

[6]See, e.g., William Paley, *Natural Theology*, Oxford World's Classics, ed. Matthew D. Eddy and David Knight (New York: Oxford University Press, 2008), chaps. 1–3; and Robin Collins, "The Teleological Argument," in Zagzebski and Miller, *Readings in Philosophy of Religion*, 39-50.

In Romans 1, Paul highlights many implications of God's natural revelation. First, God is stirred to anger by all of humankind's ungodliness and unrighteousness. Our sin, Christian and non-Christian alike, makes God very angry, and he lets us know that he is angry (Rom 1 and elsewhere). I would be too, if people rejected me and my creation. God created a beautiful and good world and gave us all we need to enjoy it and him forever. Instead, humanity wandered off from him and all things that he designed. Just as Adam and Eve wandered away from God in the garden (Gen 3), we also wander off by our daily sinning. God knows our sinfulness and lets us know that he knows and isn't pleased.

Second, Paul accuses sinful humanity not just of rebelling against God in unrighteousness and ungodliness but of actually suppressing the truth that is known. The Greek word for "suppress" is *katechō*, which comes from *kata* and *echō,* meaning "to hold back, restrain and hinder." Humankind, then, is guilty of holding back God's self-revealed truth in our unrighteousness (the biblical story explains why, as we will see shortly). The truth has been revealed through creation, and by other means, but we do not want it. So we suppress this truth in wickedness—sometimes consciously, sometimes unconsciously, but always with sinful blameworthiness. But God's revelation is like a coil spring on a car, in that it keeps on thrusting its way into consciousness. In other words, God continues to reveal himself through natural revelation, even if it is rejected.

Third, natural revelation makes known God's eternal power and divine nature. God's power or omnipotence (after all, God is the Cause and Designer of all things) and some of his attributes (his divine nature) are known to all through the creation. Paul insists that what has been made clearly displays God's power. As Aquinas's Five Ways argue, there is no way to account for motion, causation, and teleology without a prime mover, an uncaused first cause, and a transcendent intentional designer.

A fourth implication of natural revelation, Paul says, is that since God has made himself so clearly known through creation (natural revelation), people have no excuse in this matter of God's judgment. When I drive down the highway, I am responsible for knowing the speed limit, as there is ample signage giving me knowledge of the law. If I profess ignorance, the law will hold me to be culpably ignorant: I have no excuse for my failure to know the speed limit. Similarly, Paul argues that humans are without excuse when it comes to the knowledge of God's existence, eternal power, and divine nature. We might claim to have insufficient evidence for God's existence, as British philosopher Bertrand Russell famously proclaimed, and we may even honestly think that to be the case. But God insists that the speed limit signs are posted for all to see, and our failure to heed the signs points not to his nonexistence or failure to self-reveal but to our inexcusable suppression of the truth.

Fifth, Paul suggests that natural revelation results in a knowledge of God, even when the person suppresses or denies such knowledge. This is an important point since many thinkers (Christian and non-Christian alike) insist that the created order does not provide enough for people to come to belief in God. According to Karl Barth, for example, God is too vast and humanity too small for natural revelation to result in any actual knowledge of God's existence and nature. Thus, we might ask, in what sense do we *know* God through general and natural revelation? After all, Paul elsewhere insists that before becoming Christians we "did not know God," but now we have come to know God (Gal 4:8-9). Perhaps it is best to understand that Paul is distinguishing a generic knowledge from a salvific knowledge of God. While natural revelation provides a general knowledge of the existence and nature of God, special revelation is necessary to establish a personal, relational, and redemptive knowledge of God. That is, natural revelation provides enough to *know about God*, while the ultimate goal is to *know God*. Such a distinction helps explain Paul's emphasis in Romans 1—that God's self-revelation in nature provides knowledge of him, such that we are without excuse—in light of texts suggesting that the non-Christian does not know God. Joe Rigney puts it well:

> Of course, because of human sin, our ability to interpret creation has been marred and corrupted. Our eyesight is poor, our minds are distorted, and our hearts are depraved. We can't see the light of the glory of Christ in the gospel, let alone in the natural world [or creation]. Only through the restoration accomplished by the new birth are we able to rightly interpret the Scriptures and thus rightly interpret the world. Unless we are born again,

we cannot see the kingdom. . . . But having been born again, and having immersed ourselves in Scripture and thus learned the basics of God's language, we are then free to seek to faithfully discern God's meaning everywhere else.[7]

Sixth, God gives people up to themselves, meaning their sin, especially in the sexual realm (see Rom 1:24-27). One of the worst things a parent, in our case, God the Trinity, can do is leave children to themselves. Ask those who have been abandoned in one way or another. Furthermore, if we do not worship the triune God, then false worship and commensurate ways of life are sure to follow, including gross sexual immorality!

Seventh, as the passage continues in Romans 1:28-32, God gives us over to a depraved mind to do those things that we acknowledge as wrong according to the moral law written on our hearts—an implication that becomes clearer in our next text.

> Indeed, when Gentiles, who do not have the law, do by nature things required by the law, they are a law for themselves, even though they do not have the law. They show that the requirements of the law are written on their hearts, their consciences also bearing witness, and their thoughts sometimes accusing them and at other times even defending them. (Rom 2:14-15)

This general revelation text is pregnant with meaning. Those who do not know God (the Gentiles) instinctively perform according to the law and act as a law to themselves. The moral law of God is written on everyone's heart, and our conscience either accuses or defends. Regardless, this natural revelation of morality makes public morality in general possible. For example, morality is possible in legal matters in which right and wrong is debated. It also means that a public morality is possible throughout all cultures. Do not steal or kill. Do not even spit on the sidewalk. This is all very practical. We all know about sin, even if it goes by another name.

It is in currently in vogue to question the existence of universal or objective morality. It is fashionable to suggest that moral standards are

---

[7]Joe Rigney, *The Things of Earth: Treasuring God by Enjoying His Gifts* (Wheaton, IL: Crossway, 2015), 63-64.

determined by personal preference or cultural consensus and to insist that there is no natural moral law written on the hearts of all people. A Christian worldview will respond quite emphatically that God declares (in Rom 2:14-15 and elsewhere, like Jer 31:31-34) that he *has* stamped his moral code on us. But we can do more. C. S. Lewis has much to say about God's natural moral revelation in his classic works *Mere Christianity* and *The Abolition of Man*. Lewis first notes that the fashionable denial of objective morality is really only skin deep; that is, even the professing moral relativist does not truly reject the existence of a universal moral code.

> Whenever you find a man who says he does not believe in a real Right and Wrong, you will find the same man going back on this a moment later. He may break his promise to you, but if you try breaking one to him he will be complaining "It's not fair!" before you can say Jack Robinson.[8]

Indeed, Lewis notes that his former atheistic worldview was founded, to a large extent, on perceived unfairness and injustice in the world. That is, Lewis noted grievous injustice in the world and supposed that if God were all good and all powerful, he would not permit such injustice to occur. Lewis continues:

> My argument against God was that the universe seemed so cruel and unjust. But how had I got this idea of *just* and *unjust*? A man does not call a line crooked unless he has some idea of a straight line. What was I comparing this universe with when I called it unjust? If the whole show was bad and senseless from A to Z so to speak, why did I, who was supposed to be part of the show, find myself in such violent reaction against it? . . . Of course, I could have given up my idea of justice by saying it was nothing but a private idea of my own. But if I did that, then my argument against God collapsed too—for the argument depended on saying that the world was really unjust, not simply that it did not happen to please my fancies. Thus in the very act of trying to prove that God did not exist— in other words, that the whole of reality was senseless—I found I was forced to assume that one part of reality—namely my idea of justice—was full of sense.[9]

---

[8]C. S. Lewis, *Mere Christianity*, rev. ed. (New York: HarperSanFrancisco, 2001), 6.
[9]Ibid., 38-39.

Lewis argues (quite rightly) that our profound intuitions of justice and injustice are ingrained, innate, and reflective of God's natural moral law. We simply cannot escape our knowledge that, as Paul insists in Romans 2, there is a moral code by which we are bound. Lewis concludes:

> If no set of moral ideas were truer or better than any other, there would be no sense in preferring civilised morality to savage morality, or Christian morality to Nazi morality. In fact, of course, we all do believe that some moralities are better than others. We do believe that some of the people who tried to change the moral ideas of their own age were what we would call Reformers or Pioneers—people who understood morality better than their neighbours did. Very well then. The moment you say that one set of moral ideas can be better than another, you are, in fact, measuring them both by a standard, saying that one of them conforms to that standard more nearly than the other. But the standard that measures two things is something different from either. You are, in fact, comparing them both with some Real Morality, admitting that there is such a thing as a real Right, independent of what people think, and that some people's ideas get nearer to that real Right than others. . . . If your moral ideas can be truer, and those of the Nazis less true, there must be something—some Real Morality—for them to be true about.[10]

That "Real Morality" is the natural law—the moral code that God has revealed in his natural revelation, available to (indeed imprinted within) all people. In *The Abolition of Man*, Lewis writes: "It is the doctrine of objective value, the belief that certain attitudes are really true, and others really false, to the kind of thing the universe is, and the kind of things we are."[11] In natural revelation, then, God has disclosed not only his eternal power and divine nature but also his holiness, his moral reality.

Acts 14:15-17 is another important text on natural revelation.

> Friends, why are you doing this? We too are only human, like you. We are bringing you good news, telling you to turn from these worthless things to the living God, who made the heavens and the earth and the sea and everything in them. In the past, he let all nations go their own way. Yet he

---

[10]Ibid., 13.

[11]C. S. Lewis, *The Abolition of Man or Reflections on Education with Special Reference to the Teaching of English in the Upper Forms of Schools* (1944; repr., New York: Simon & Schuster, 1996), 31.

has not left himself without testimony: He has shown kindness by giving you rain from heaven and crops in their seasons; he provides you with plenty of food and fills your hearts with joy.

Paul and Barnabas have been preaching the risen Jesus in Lystra. The men to whom they were speaking called Barnabas Zeus, and they called Paul Hermes since he was the main speaker. Furthermore, the men of Lystra wanted to offer sacrifices to Paul and Barnabas (note that people are indeed religious in general!), but the missionaries, with great difficulty, restrained them from doing so. Instead, Paul and Barnabas insisted that they were the same kind of human beings as the people to whom they were speaking. Paul and Barnabas were just preachers of the gospel as they encouraged people in Lystra to turn from vanity to the living God who created all things.

Paul then articulates elements of natural revelation to the men of Lystra. First, although God allowed the nations their freedom to make even bad choices (as outlined in Rom 1:18-32 earlier), he did not leave himself without a witness (here "without witness" in the Greek is *amartyron*, and this word is related to the English word *martyr*—a reminder that you might become a martyr if you witness!). Second, God's residual witness, evident to all men, consists of rain, fruit, food, and gladness. God demonstrates his love for humanity even in the mundane realities of natural revelation. We normally do not think of these things—rain, fruit, food, and gladness—as expressions of God's love and gifts, but they are! So says James 1:17: "Every good and perfect gift is from above, coming down from the Father of the heavenly lights, who does not change like shifting shadows."

Acts 17:22-29, part of Paul's Mars Hill address delivered to the leading philosophers (Areopagus) of Athens, also speaks of natural revelation:

Paul then stood up in the meeting of the Areopagus and said: "People of Athens! I see that in every way you are very religious. For as I walked around and looked carefully at your objects of worship, I even found an altar with this inscription: TO AN UNKNOWN GOD. So you are ignorant of the very thing you worship—and this is what I am going to proclaim to you.

"The God who made the world and everything in it is the Lord of heaven and earth and does not live in temples built by human hands. And he is not served by human hands, as if he needed anything. Rather, he himself gives everyone life and breath and everything else. From one man he made all the nations, that they should inhabit the whole earth; and he marked out their appointed times in history and the boundaries of their lands. God did this so that they would seek him and perhaps reach out for him and find him, though he is not far from any one of us. 'For in him we live and move and have our being.' As some of your own poets have said, 'We are his offspring.'

"Therefore since we are God's offspring, we should not think that the divine being is like gold or silver or stone—an image made by human design and skill."

Several points are relevant in Paul's appeal. First, Paul recognizes the religiosity, or faith, of the men of Athens, including some of the Stoic and Epicurean philosophers. As already noted, people are inherently religious—an empirical reality evident to all of us. Faith can be placed in reason, science, math, and philosophy, and even in the worship of an unknown god or an idol, as in Athens. Second, however, Paul argues that the men of Athens were worshiping in ignorance (they were not unintelligent, just ignorant). Thus, Paul redirects their attention to the lordship of the Creator God who neither dwells in temples nor is served in any way by human hands as if he were needy.

Third, Paul notes that this self-revealing God has not left himself without witness; he makes his existence clear in that he gives "life and breath and everything else" (Acts 17:25) to humanity. As Creator, this God has made all nations from one, having determined "their appointed times in history and the boundaries of their lands" (Acts 17:26). Fourth, Paul argues that God established the nations in order that people would look for him, investigate him, and perhaps discover him. Indeed, Paul declares that God is close by, citing the ancient philosopher Epimenides: "For in him we live and move and have our being" (Acts 17:28).[12]

Fifth, Paul notes than even the Athenian poet Aratus acknowledges this natural revelation, declaring: "We are his offspring" (Acts 17:28).[13]

---

[12]Epimenides was a philosopher who lived (we think) around 600 BC. The quotation is from his poem *Minos and Rhadamanthus*.

[13]Paul is citing Aratus, a Greek poet ca. 315-245 BC, from the opening invocation of his poem *Phaenomena*.

Indeed, we are, at least by creation. All people are God's children in the sense that he created us. However, only the redeemed are actually children of God as we are adopted into his family. Sixth and finally, the Athenians should note that God is not made of precious metals like gold or silver, nor is he lifeless like a stone, nor is he an image crafted by the art and thought of humanity. In Acts 17:30-31, Paul says that God over-looked the times of ignorance and calls all to repent since he will justly judge, having provided proof for all people by Jesus, whom he raised from the dead (an item of special revelation).

Concerning natural revelation, John Calvin (1509–1564) argued that "God has given us an objective, valid rational revelation of himself in nature, history, and human personality."[14] Calvin also urged that in order to avoid instability and vacillation, "we ought to seek our conviction [that the Bible is God's Word and thus that Christianity is true] in a higher place than human reasons, judgments, or conjectures [but] in the secret testimony of the Holy Spirit."[15] Calvin believed that the Holy Spirit would give us the assurance we need.

We have seen that a great deal can be gleaned about God from natural revelation, the works of God that are evident to all human beings. We have surveyed numerous biblical passages discussing the reality and insights of natural revelation. But as we conclude this discussion of natural revelation, it is important to emphasize, as Calvin did, that while we can *know that God is* via natural revelation, we can *know God* (as redeemer) only through special revelation. That is, by his grace God makes himself known to us in a personal, intimate, saving manner. We can know that God is by means of general revelation and natural theology, but we can know who God is (or know God) only via special revelation. Through general revelation and natural theology, all people know of God's power, his goodness, and his righteous judgment of our sin, but it is only through special revelation that we come to know God personally and know the forgiveness offered through Jesus Christ.

---

[14] John Calvin, quoted in Erickson, *Christian Theology*, 1:170.

[15] John Calvin, *Institutes of the Christian Religion*, Library of Christian Classics 20, ed. John T. McNeill, trans. and indexed Ford Lewis Battles (Philadelphia: Westminster Press, 1960), 78.

REFLECTION QUESTIONS

1 What is natural revelation? Why do we call it natural revelation?

2 How helpful are Aquinas's five ways in convincing skeptics of God's existence?

3 Why does Paul argue (in Rom 1:20) that humanity is "without excuse" for their disbelief and idolatry? Do you agree? Why or why not?

4 How does humanity's belief in an objective morality provide evidence for God's existence?

5 How does Paul's Areopagus address in Acts 17 utilize natural revelation to build bridges to the gospel?

6 What are the contributions and limits of natural revelation? That is, what can we discern about God from natural revelation, and what are we unable to discern about God from natural revelation?

4.2 SPECIAL REVELATION

If we are to know God, if we are to gain the contours of a truly Christian worldview, we need more than natural revelation; we require something in addition to God's evident works in nature. We need special revelation, God's spoken and written Word to humanity. The core source of a Christian worldview, then, is the Bible—God's *inspired* and *authoritative* Word delivered to the church. The Bible is the perfect record of God's self-revelation to mankind. Because of his deep and abiding love for his creation, God has chosen to reveal himself—his being, character, will, and purposes—to us, the crown of his creation. God desires for us to come to know him through his self-revelation.

Biblical revelation presupposes the existence of God and implies that we humans are finite and fallible creatures who cannot figure life out on our own, despite God's clear self-revelation in nature. We pant, we are tired, we need help. Biblical revelation supplies this help. It teaches, much to our chagrin, that the Judeo-Christian God is the sovereign Creator God. We do not want anyone, even (or especially) God the sovereign Creator, to hamper our lifestyle. Biblical revelation also implies that there is one way—its way. We may not always like the message of special revelation, but it is what it is! All of God's revelation begins with him. He takes the initiative.

4.2.1 The inspiration of Scripture. We begin with a definition. Special revelation is the very breath and Word of God. As 2 Timothy 3:16-17 declares, "All Scripture is God-breathed and is useful for teaching, re-buking, correcting and to niving for righteousness, so that the servant of God may be thoroughly equipped for every good work." "God-breathed" is from the Greek θεοπνευστος (*theopneustos*), which is sometimes translated "inspired" and means literally that Scripture is God's very breath. Hence the Bible is the inspired Word of God. As such, it is not merely a human document, written by holy and faithful God-worshipers. Rather, as they were spurred on by the inspiration of the Holy Spirit, people wrote the principles, phrases, and words that God desired to communicate through them. The apostle Peter declares, "Above all, you must understand that no prophecy of Scripture came about by the prophet's own interpretation of things. For prophecy never had its origin in the human will, but prophets, though human, spoke from God as they were carried along by the Holy Spirit" (2 Pet 1:20-21).

Nonetheless, God's breath in Scripture is not conveyed mechanically. Instead, God's inspired Word displays the authors' full humanity while God superintends the authors. God speaks to the authors of Scripture, and he speaks to us through the voices of those human authors. Thus Peter can write of Paul's letters:

> Bear in mind that our Lord's patience means salvation, just as our dear brother Paul also wrote you with the wisdom that God gave him. He writes the same way in all his letters, speaking in them of these matters. His letters contain some things that are hard to understand, which ignorant and unstable people distort, as they do the other Scriptures, to their own destruction. (2 Pet 3:15-16)

The human authors were not mechanical robots, writing down God's precise dictation.[16] To say that God's Word is reflective of the personality

---

[16]It must be noted that on occasion they actually were recording directly words from God—such as when Moses wrote down the law (Ex 21:1; 31:18) and when the prophets spoke and wrote the words of God (e.g., Jer 31:15; 51:1; Ezek 31:1; Hos 4:1). Elsewhere we see the ubiquitous introductory

of the human author is not, however, to downplay the significance or divinity of the Bible. Rather, it is to express that there are two authors behind each book of the Bible: the human author who wrote the words down, and the Holy Spirit who inspired and guided the human author to write God's Words. Each word in the Bible is there because God desires it to be there—there is nothing written that God did not desire to be a part of his revelation, and there is nothing left out that God desired to reveal to us.

4.2.2 The truthfulness of Scripture. As the inspired Word of God, the Bible is a complete source of truth. In all that it intends to impart to the reader, it conveys the truth, the whole truth, and nothing but the truth. As such, Scripture is entirely without error. That does not mean, however, that every word in the Bible must by necessity be accurate in a precise scientific sense. In the parable of the mustard seed, Jesus states, "The kingdom of heaven is like a mustard seed, which a man took and planted in his field. Though it is the smallest of all seeds, yet when it grows, it is the largest of garden plants and becomes a tree, so that the birds come and perch in its branches" (Mt 13:31-32). The mustard seed is not technically the smallest of all seeds that can be planted, nor does it grow to literally be the largest of all garden plants. The parable of the mustard seed, however, is not intending to convey agricultural truth regarding seed and trees. Rather, it conveys principles concerning the kingdom of God, and so the truth contained within the parable is inescapably true—a large (the largest) plant can grow from a small (the smallest) seed; the kingdom of God spreads from just one person (Jesus Christ) into the billions of believers throughout history. One ought not to apply God's Word to academic disciplines that it was never intended to address.

In affirming the complete truthfulness of the Word of God, we also affirm its historical accuracy—what the Bible records as history is truthful in its entirety. There are places at which the historical account in the Bible is evidently incomplete, such as the account of creation given in Genesis 1–2. However, we should not interpret incompleteness as

---

formulae in the prophets, along the lines of "The word of the Lord that came to . . ." (see, e.g., Is 8:1; Jer 1:4; 13:1; Ezek 6:1; Hos 3:1; Joel 1:1; Amos 1:13; 2:1; Jon 1:1; Mic 1:1; 6:1; Hab 1:1; Zeph 1:1; Zech 1:1; 8:1; Mal 1:1).

untruthfulness. Rather, in such cases we understand that the Word of God does not give us the full account. For example, when God declares that he created living creatures "according to their kinds" (Gen 1:24-25), I do not take that to mean that God created all animals at exactly the same moment in time and placed them all on the earth simultaneously; but I do take that to be a statement that God designed and superintended each species of animal especially and uniquely.

4.2.3 *The authority of Scripture.* Special revelation in Scripture, which is to God's people in the church, or his family as a whole (their love letter), has many specific advantages. It is especially clear and exact. It also tells us about Jesus as God incarnate (see Jn 1:14), who brings us salvation. Indeed, Jesus is the central message and focus of all of Scripture. Paul says about his preaching of Jesus in 1 Corinthians 2:2, "For I resolved to know nothing while I was with you except Jesus Christ and him crucified."

God's Word is our authority for both faith and practice. Our understanding of God must be rooted in Scripture, the source of God's self-revelation to us. We cannot base our understanding of God's nature, character, will, and purpose on our own human experience or the writings of other men and women (even good and admirable ones such as Corrie ten Boom or Martin Luther). Rather, our knowledge of God must be founded on the Word of God.

The authority of God's Word requires that it is paramount over and above human traditions. Hence we find Jesus at once affirming the authority and permanence of God's Word and rejecting the way that God's Word had been interpreted and added on to by the tradition of the Jewish leaders.[17] Jesus recognized that the eternal, perfect Word of God had been altered by the accumulations of centuries of human tradition and interpretation. In Matthew 15 Jesus is accosted by the Pharisees and teachers of the law: "Why do your disciples break the tradition of the elders? They don't wash their hands before they eat!" (Mt 15:2). He lashes back:

---

[17]"Do not think that I have come to abolish the Law or the Prophets; I have not come to abolish them but to fulfill them" (Mt 5:17); and "You have heard that it was said, 'Love your neighbor and hate your enemy.' But I tell you, love your enemies and pray for those who persecute you" (Mt 5:43-44).

*Contemporary Cultural
Worldview Meditation*

Abortion and Alberta Politics

When I (Tawa) first became a Christian as a seventeen-year-old high school senior, there were many things in my life that did not line up with God's Word. There were many areas where I needed to change. Many of those changes took place very gradually. Not long after I became a Christian, there was a provincial election in Alberta, and I got involved volunteering for the Liberal candidate in Sherwood Park. During the campaign, abortion became an issue. Liberal leader Laurence Decore was asked his thoughts on abortion, and he answered honestly that he felt abortion was abhorrent, it involved killing unborn babies, and he was personally very opposed to abortion. Conservative Premier Ralph Klein was asked his thoughts on abortion, and he answered that it was a matter between "a woman, her doctor, and God"—basically, that it was a matter of personal choice. (The irony was that, historically, Liberals are generally much more pro-choice than their pro-life Conservative counterparts.) As a new Christian, I was appalled at Mr. Decore's comments, and I could not believe that he was

(continued on next page)

You nullify the word of God for the sake of your tradition. You hypocrites! Isaiah was right when he prophesied about you:

"These people honor me with
    their lips,
  but their hearts are far from me.
They worship me in vain;
  their teachings are merely
    human rules." (Mt 15:6-9)[18]

As Christ-followers seeking God's perspective in a pluralistic world, we must constantly be on our guard against allowing our human traditions to overrule the Word of God, as the Pharisees did with regard to the tradition of hand washing.

4.2.4 The books of Scripture. The inspired, truthful, authoritative Word of God is composed of sixty-six books—thirty-nine in the Old Testament (the Hebrew Scriptures) and twenty-seven in the New Testament (the Greek Scriptures).[19] The canon

---

[18]Jewish ceremonial hand washing before meals did not originate, as many people think, in the Mosaic (Old Testament) law; rather, it began during the Babylonian Exile. Living as strangers in a strange land, a land of pagan idol worshipers, the Jewish religious leaders began the practice of ceremonially washing their hands at the end of the work day to cleanse away the pagan filth and pollution that they had come into contact with during the day. After the ceremonial hand washing, they were once again "pure." Gradually the ceremonial hand washing became established tradition, expected of all faithful Jews, to the point here in the gospels where the divine Son of God is accosted for his failure to make his disciples ceremonially wash their hands before eating. Tradition became expected behavior.

[19]It should be noted that there are some slight differences between the traditional Protestant understanding of the biblical canon outlined above and the canons embraced by the Roman Catholic and Eastern Orthodox traditions. In short, Catholic churches often accept some intertestamental books (written between the Old and New Testament time periods) as

(authoritative list of biblical books) is closed, in that there is no possibility of new books being added to the Bible and no option of deleting "undesirable" books (Martin Luther famously wanted to do away with the book of James which he termed the "epistle of straw"). The canon was collected by faithful followers of God, guided by the Holy Spirit to incorporate those books that God had inspired as a part of his revelation to humankind. The criteria considered for incorporation into the New Testament were apostolicity (written by or closely associated with apostles), universality (accepted by all the churches throughout the Roman Empire), and orthodoxy (teaching in accordance with the rule of faith handed down through church leaders). Just as God guided the process of the human authors recording his Word, so too God guided the process of humans collecting his Word together and canonizing it. These sixty-six canonical books, from Genesis to Revelation, compose the inspired, truthful, authoritative Word of God, the sole foundation of faith, the only guide to life.

going to lose the election because of his condemnation of abortion. I also remember my mother coming to me in the midst of that election campaign and asking me about Mr. Decore's comments. I tried my best to explain them away, arguing that this issue was not really going to be very important anyway and that our Liberal candidate certainly did not share Mr. Decore's opposition to abortion (which was true—he was pro-choice). At that point in my life, in my new Christian walk, I never stopped to consider what God's perspective on abortion was—whether God had anything to say about whether abortion was right, wrong, or indifferent. I just figured, well, maybe it would not be right for me, but if someone else wants to get an abortion, okay.

In the succeeding years, I began to learn more about God's Word and began to understand more of God's nature and character. I learned of God's heart for the poor, the underprivileged, and the defenseless. I came to understand God's love for each human life, no matter how old or young, rich or poor. I also began to understand the science of conception and pregnancy, and I came to believe that a fetus was, in fact, a fully human being, viable in every way—simply an unborn baby. Gradually I concluded that abortion was wrong in the eyes of God because it was taking the life of an innocent, helpless baby. It was easy to recognize that abortion was wrong "to me," that I would never want my girlfriend or wife to get an abortion, no matter what the circumstances were. Eventually, however, I came to hold that not only is abortion wrong for me, but abortion is just wrong, period. If it was wrong in the eyes of God for me to get an abortion, it was also wrong in the

(continued on next page)

"deuterocanonical"—helpful for the faith of believers but not to be treated on the same level as the rest of Scripture.

eyes of God for someone else to do so. Honestly, I struggled intensely coming to that conclusion because I did not want to have to get there. I knew that most of my peers and family members felt strongly that abortion was a matter of personal choice and that no one should force their pro-life views down the throats of others. But as my own character and worldview was gradually being shaped by God's Word, I had no choice. If, as I believed, God's Word was authoritative, then I had to accept the conclusions that I saw the Bible was driving me to, including unpopular conclusions that I would have preferred to avoid at that time. That is the power of the authority of Scripture—the Word of God is the source for our faith and practice. As God's Word made it clear to me that abortion was wrong, my life and my beliefs needed to reflect that. I could not pretend that something was morally permissible once I came to see that the Bible said it was wrong in the eyes of God.

4.3 THE TRIUNE GOD: THE CENTER OF A CHRISTIAN WORLDVIEW

A Christian worldview begins (and ends) with God (the alpha and omega, the beginning and the end). God exists. He is that than which nothing greater can be conceived, as Anselm says in his *Proslogion*.[20] God, that is, possesses every positive attribute in the maximal possible degree. Strength (or power) is a positive attribute, and God possesses maximal power; he is omnipotent. Similarly, God possesses all and only knowledge; he is omniscient. God is filled with maximal love; he is omnibenevolent. Existence is a positive attribute, so God is both present everywhere and at all times (omnipresent) *and* his existence is not dependent on anything outside of himself; he is a necessary self-existent being. He cannot not be, and his existence is not dependent on any other beings or states of affairs. Goodness or holiness is a positive attribute, and God is morally perfect—without fault, without flaw, without sin.

The self-revealing God of Scripture is also personal, relational, and triune. He is personal in community as Trinity—Father, Son, and Holy Spirit. In other words, he is one God in three divine Persons. He is holy and unsurpassable in both his being and his morality. The divine attribute of absolute perfection means that God lacks nothing. He is worthy of our worship; God possesses worth-ship.

The God at the center of a Christian worldview is both immanent and transcendent. He is our Father, desiring to be in intimate relationship

---

[20]Anselm, *Basic Writings*, trans. S. N. Dean (La Salle, IL: Open Court, 1962), 7.

and communion with his created children (immanent). But he is also utterly other, wholly outside of our ability to fully comprehend (transcendent). Finally, God is utterly free, bound only by his own perfect nature and character. His creation of the universe and his relationship with humanity do not stem from any inherent need on his part (as if he could gain anything from our service and worship).

God is a self-revealing God—revealing himself in both his works (natural revelation) and his Words (special revelation).

> He who forms the mountains,
>> who creates the wind,
>> and who reveals his thoughts to mankind, . . .
>> the LORD God Almighty is his name. (Amos 4:13)

Indeed, God speaks in a powerful way as strong as creation!

The narrative that God reveals in his Word, the Bible, is the grand story of creation, fall, redemption, and glorification. The Christian worldview narrative can be symbolized by a check mark. We started at creation, we had a great fall, and then we are propelled upward to redemption and glorification, all through Jesus.

REFLECTION QUESTIONS

1 Why is the Bible such an important source of knowledge for a Christian worldview?

2 What does it mean to say that the Bible is "God-breathed"?

3 Why is God the first consideration in a Christian worldview?

4 What are some of God's attributes that we can discern from the Bible?

4.4 THE NARRATIVE OF A CHRISTIAN WORLDVIEW

4.4.1 Creation. Has the world lost its true story? Indeed, it has. I am out to recover it—creation, the fall, redemption, and finally glorification. A Christian worldview begins at the beginning—with our creation. We must make the wonderful rediscovery of the world as God's creation, loving both the Creator and his creation well. This is a key to real, lasting happiness. As I once wrote, "This grand union of God, ourselves, and the whole cosmos in a sacred synthesis of rightly ordered love constitutes the deep meaning of happiness."[21]

The creation narrative, as the first installment of the world's true story, is found in Genesis 1–2. Here we learn many things about the world in which we live. It is a creation, nothing more, nothing less: "In the beginning God *created* the heavens and the earth" (Gen 1:1). If it is a creation, then through cause and effect, science, which is based on cause and effect, tells us that there must be a Creator. The Scriptures tell us this as well, cosmologically. As Hebrews 3:4 says, "For every house is built by someone, but God is the builder of everything."

In the beginning, the earth, to which the writer of Genesis 1 directs our attention, is both formless and void. The remainder of Genesis 1 relates how God brings first form and then content (fullness) to what was previously without form and content. The six days of God's creative activity, then, can be seen as two parallel sets of three days. During the first three days God establishes form, or structure; on the second three days God provides content, or fullness.

In the first three days of creation, God forms the formless world in creating light and darkness (day number one), the sky and seas (day number two), and land and plants (day number three). And God declares that it is all good.[22] Then on the second three days, God fills the formed but still empty or void world. Some commentators say God put rulers in the realms he formed.

On day one, God creates light and darkness, the structure or form of the expanse (the heavens). On day four, God puts lights in the expanse, including the sun, the moon, and the stars, providing fullness to the form of the expanse. On day two, God creates the sky and the seas, the structure or form of the upper and lower (nonterrestrial) expanses. On day five, God puts fish and sea monsters in the waters, and birds in the sky, creating the content to fill the structure. On day three, God creates

---

[21]David K. Naugle, *Reordered Love, Reordered Lives: Learning the Deep Meaning of Happiness* (Grand Rapids: Eerdmans, 2008), 23.

[22]For day 1, see Genesis 1:3-5. For day 2, see Genesis 1:6-8. For day 3, see Genesis 1:9-13. God affirms the goodness of all he has made in Genesis 1:4, 10, and 12.

the land and vegetation. On day six he creates animals and humankind, corresponding to the land and plants he created. Again, God declared that his creation is all good.[23]

Figure 4.1. The six days of God's creation in Genesis 1-2

After the six days of active creation, Genesis recounts that God rested on the seventh day, not because he was tired but because he was finished. This seventh day (Gen 2:1-3) became the basis of the sabbath law in Exodus 20.

When God created humanity in his own image, he gave them an original commission, often referred to as the "cultural mandate," in Genesis 1:26-28.

> Then God said, "Let us make mankind in our image, in our likeness, so that they may rule over the fish of the sea and the birds in the sky, over the livestock and all the wild animals, and over all the creatures that move along the ground."

---

[23]For day 4, see Genesis 1:14-19. For day 5, see Genesis 1:20-23. For day 6, see Genesis 1:24-31. God affirms the goodness of all he has made in Genesis 1:18, 21, and 25.

> So God created mankind in his own image,
>   in the image of God he created them;
>   male and female he created them.

> God blessed them and said to them, "Be fruitful and increase in number; fill the earth and subdue it. Rule over the fish in the sea and the birds in the sky and over every living creature that moves on the ground."

Could it be that the Great Commission, with which we are so familiar, is a republication of this original commission?

> Then Jesus came to them and said, "All authority in heaven and on earth has been given to me. Therefore go and make disciples of all nations, baptizing them in the name of the Father and of the Son and of the Holy Spirit, and teaching them to obey everything I have commanded you. And surely I am with you always, to the very end of the age." (Mt 28:18-20)

What does it mean to "make disciples of all nations"? Does disciple making not involve bringing the blessings of God to bear among the peoples and cultures of the world? Might it be appropriate to see the process of making disciples to be the role of filling the earth, subduing the earth, and ruling over the earth as God's image bearers and vice regents? This is what it means to make disciples of all the nations. We are called to be cultural creatures in this original commission in Genesis 1 and in the Great Commission in Matthew 28. We are undoubtedly culture makers and culture formers.

Then God gave the initial pair of human beings something to eat, in the form of green plants. It seems that the original humans were vegans or, at least, vegetarians! After the creation of human beings, Genesis 1:31 declares: "God saw all that he had made, and it was very good." This is the clarion call, the declaration that resides at the center of a Christian worldview understanding of what God has made. Creation is good; God doesn't make junk. The whole creation was and still is truly great, or as Albert Wolters writes, "Creation before and apart from sin is wholly and unambiguously *good*."[24] To embrace a fully Christian worldview, we must make the wonderful rediscovery of this world as God's very good creation and esteem both the Creator and creation appropriately.

---

[24]Albert M. Wolters, *Creation Regained: Biblical Basics for a Reformational Worldview*, 2nd ed. (Grand Rapids: Eerdmans, 2005), 48.

King David added a poetic commentary to the creation decree in Psalm 8:

LORD, our Lord,
  how majestic is your name in all the earth!

You have set your glory
  in the heavens.
Through the praise of children and infants
  you have established a stronghold against your enemies,
  to silence the foe and the avenger.
When I consider your heavens,
  the work of your fingers,
the moon and the stars,
  which you have set in place,
what is mankind that you are mindful of them,
  human beings that you care for them?

You have made them a little lower than the angels
  and crowned them with glory and honor.
You made them rulers over the works of your hands;
  you put everything under their feet:
all flocks and herds,
  and the animals of the wild,
the birds in the sky,
  and the fish in the sea,
  all that swim the paths of the seas.

LORD, our Lord,
  how majestic is your name in all the earth!

God wanted humanity, who bears his image and likeness, to do as he had done—that is, to form the earth culturally by having dominion over it, and to fill it with more and more images and likenesses of God by being fruitful and multiplying. Brian Walsh and Richard Middleton see our creation in God's image as related to our rule over the earth (among other things).[25] Indeed, in Genesis 2:15, God takes the man and places

---

[25]Brian J. Walsh and J. Richard Middleton, *The Transforming Vision: Shaping a Christian World View* (Downers Grove, IL: IVP Academic, 1984), 53-54.

him in God's garden to cultivate and to keep the garden. God gives humanity cultural and environmental responsibilities. The narrative continues in Genesis 2 and says that the man was to eat from the trees of the garden, minus one, lest he eat from that particular tree and die.

According to Genesis 2, it was not good for the male to be alone, the only thing in creation that was not good. So God made a woman from the side of the man, and the man poetically proclaimed:

> This is now bone of my bones
> and flesh of my flesh;
> she shall be called "woman,"
> for she was taken out of man. (Gen 2:23)

God is a relational God, who enjoys intimate communion within the triune Godhead; human beings, created in his image, are created also to enjoy intimate communion—not only with the Lord God but also with one another. The marriage relationship is intended to be the most intimate of all human relationships. Marriage was the purpose of the creation of the female. Hence, God says in Genesis 2:24-25,

> That is why [in marriage] a man leaves his father and mother and is united to his wife, and they become one flesh.
> Adam and his wife were both naked, and they felt no shame.

The man leaves his parents and cleaves to his wife. And there is nakedness yet without any embarrassment or shame. The phrase "one flesh" indicates a total life union; the man and woman become a united whole, no longer separable into discrete lives. "One flesh" includes a sexual relationship but points to a much deeper intimacy. There was ideal communication between the man and the woman in their marriage. They were naked but unashamed.

Creation is the first component in the larger biblical story; it includes a setting (the creation itself), characters (Adam and Eve) as actors, and a purpose (to be culture makers). Who knows how much knowledge is conveyed about the divine design for human life in these first two chapters in the Bible? Our treatment here just scratches the surface.[26] In

---

[26]There is much more elsewhere, for example, Psalm 104:24, Proverbs 8:22-31, and Colossians 1:16.

any case, humanity (Adam and Eve, the first human couple) had a personal relationship with God in the garden. But the fall in Genesis 3 disrupted this relationship.

4.4.2 Fall. The second component of a Christian worldview narrative, after God's creation, is the fall of humanity—the major conflict that explains why we and the world are in such a mess, both physically and spiritually. Genesis 3 brings us to act two (creation is act one)—the fall of humanity and creation into sin.

Genesis 3 begins with a temptation after it notes the craftiness of the serpent (the embodiment of Satan). The temptation comes in the form of Satan questioning God's self-revelation: "Did God really say, 'You must not eat from any tree in the garden'?" (Gen 3:1). Satan has been questioning God's word ever since. The woman answers in Genesis 3:2-3, with only partial accuracy: "The woman said to the serpent, 'We may eat fruit from the trees in the garden, but God did say, "You must not eat fruit from the tree that is in the middle of the garden, and you must not touch it, or you will die."'" Was the woman the first legalist by adding that they were not even to touch the forbidden tree and its fruit? (God's command in Genesis 2:17 was simply "you must not eat from the tree of the knowledge of good and evil.") Perhaps she was! How else did the woman answer incorrectly? She erred by claiming that God had forbidden them to eat the fruit "from the tree that is in the middle of the garden," whereas God had only forbidden eating from *one* of the two trees in the middle of the garden (the tree of the knowledge of good and evil). Adam and Eve were invited to eat the fruit from the *other* tree in the middle of the garden, the tree of life (see Gen 2:9).

The trees were pleasing to the sight, which is the aesthetic component, as well as good for food, which is the nutritional component. Both components are in Genesis 2:9. Adam and Eve were at liberty to eat freely from them all, except one (Gen 2:16-17). God was not (and is not) a scrooge. He invited Adam and Eve to eat freely from the permitted trees of the garden; he just wanted them to remain on his side of a huge battle, rather than seeking a self-endangering autonomy or independence. As a loving heavenly Father, God had Adam and Eve's best interests at heart: he knew what was best for them in a way that they could not. God granted the human couple liberty within boundaries established by love—much in the same way that human parents grant (or should grant) their children growing liberty within firm boundaries put in place for the children's protection, growth, and flourishing. God warned Adam and Eve what would happen if they ate from the forbidden tree and its fruit: "you will certainly die" (Gen 2:17).

The devil was ready with a response. He assured Eve, "You will not certainly die. . . . For God knows that when you eat from it your eyes will be opened, and you will be like God, knowing good and evil" (Gen 3:4-5).

The funny thing (perhaps it is not so funny) is that the woman was already like God, bearing his very image and likeness. But she did not know good and evil on her own, autonomously or independently. She was not a law unto herself. In fact, she was under God: she was submissive to, under the authority of, the Lord God. She and her husband were subject to God's law. However, Satan is a liar and the father of all lies (see Jn 8:44). Satan depicts God as stingy or withholding something from her: God wants to keep her eyes closed, but (Satan promises) if she will disobey God's command and take control of her own life, her eyes will be opened and she will become more than, better than, what God has allowed her to be. Such is always the deceptive implication and promise of Satan's temptation. God is keeping something good from us; if we will rebel against God, we will experience the really good stuff. Satan assures Eve that she will not surely die (Gen 3:4), just as the devil assures us today that there will not really be any negative consequences for disregarding our heavenly Father's path. But the devil lied and contradicted God's word. Eve would, indeed, die! So too, the path that Satan would pull us down today looks good, but leads to death: "Enter through the narrow gate. For wide is the gate and broad is the road that leads to destruction, and many enter through it" (Mt 7:13).

But Eve's flesh got the better of her. She saw that the tree was good for food (lust of the flesh), that it delighted her eyes (lust of the eyes), and that it was desirable to make one allegedly wise (boastful pride of life). This triumvirate of temptations—the lust of the flesh, the lust of the eyes, and the boastful pride of life—are likewise highlighted in 1 John 2:16 and are the focus of the Gospel accounts of Jesus' temptation in Matthew 4.[27] Eve succumbed to the tempter. She took and ate the forbidden fruit and gave some also to her husband with her, and he ate too. Indeed, their eyes were opened, they knew they were naked, and they tried to cover up their shame and sin with fig leaves.

Adam and Eve had to choose between submitting to God's word and heeding the devil's claim. They chose the words of Satan over the Word of God. There were several consequences for their actions.

First, there is a separation from God—the *theological* or *spiritual* consequence of humanity's sinful rebellion:

> Then the man and his wife heard the sound of the Lord God as he was walking in the garden in the cool of the day, and they hid from the Lord God among the trees of the garden. But the Lord God called to the man, "Where are you?"
>
> He answered, "I heard you in the garden, and I was afraid because I was naked; so I hid." (Gen 3:8-10)

The man and his wife hid themselves from the presence of God among the trees of the garden when God took a long walk in the cool of the day. They fled from him (Gen 3:8), but God knew exactly where they were (Gen 3:9). The fall of man from his original created state breaks the intimate communion he previously had with God; we are now separated from God, alienated from our Creator and Father.

Second, the fall results in separation from the self—the *psychological* or *mental* consequence of humanity's sinful rebellion. The man heard the sound of God in the garden. And he was afraid (fear) because he knew himself to be naked (shame), and thus he hid himself (guilt) (Gen 3:10). All these destructive emotions of fear, shame, and guilt replaced the shalom or soundness, wholeness, and well-being for which God had created man.

Third, the fall results in a separation between man and woman— the *social* or *relational* consequence of humanity's sinful rebellion. If

---

[27]"For everything in the world—the lust of the flesh, the lust of the eyes, and the pride of life— comes not from the Father but from the world" (1 Jn 2:16). The three temptations of Jesus in the desert appeal to (1) the lust of the flesh: "tell these stones to become bread," in order to satisfy Jesus' intense physical hunger; (2) the lust of the eyes: "throw yourself down," in order that the people might see Jesus' miraculous survival and adore him; and (3) the pride of life: "all this I will give you, . . . if you will bow down and worship me" (Mt 4:3, 6, 9).

parenting, or teaching undergraduates, divulges any clue, this is a big area. After asking the man how he knew he was naked, and if he had eaten the forbidden fruit from the forbidden tree (though God already knew he had), the man blames God first, then the woman, for his own sin. The woman, in turn, blames the serpent. We read in Genesis 3:12-13,

> The man said, "The woman you [thus it's your fault, God] put here with me—she gave me some fruit from the tree [thus it's her fault, not mine], and I ate it."
> Then the LORD God said to the woman, "What is this you have done?"
> The woman said, "The serpent deceived me [thus it's his fault, not mine], and I ate."

She blames the serpent. In other words, the devil made her do it! The social/relational consequences of Adam and Eve's sinful rebellion results in a threefold curse.

The serpent takes it on the chin. He bit the dust, literally. He was cursed supremely more than any beast of the field. He went to his belly from an upright position, and now he eats dust all his life.

> The LORD God said to the serpent, "Because you have done this,
> "Cursed are you above all livestock,
>   and all wild animals!
> You will crawl on your belly
>   and you will eat dust
>   all the days of your life." (Gen 3:14)

In the middle of the cursing of the serpent, there is also a promise from God, contained in Genesis 3:15, which theologians and scholars of the Old Testament call the first preaching of the gospel itself—the *protevangelium*. There is conflict or enmity between the two offspring, and in this conflict, the offspring of the woman will defeat the serpent/Satan with a fatal wound to his head. In the process the offspring of the woman will be bruised significantly on the heel. In Genesis 3:15 we read,

> And I will put enmity
>   between you and the woman,
>   and between your offspring and hers;
> he will crush your head,
>   and you will strike his heel.

Along with the cursing of the serpent, there are curses on the woman and Adam. Both curses involve a role and a relationship: the woman in her role as a mother and in her relationship with her husband, and the man in his role as culture maker and in his relationship to the earth. The woman's curse is found in Genesis 3:16 and comes in the form of increased pain in the childbearing process.

To the woman he said,

"I will make your pains in childbearing very severe;
    with painful labor you will give birth to children.
Your desire will be for your husband,
    and he will rule over you." (Gen 3:16)

The man mistakenly heeded the voice of his wife and ate from the forbidden tree and its fruit. The first man failed in his role as spiritual leader; he meekly stood by as Eve was tempted to not trust God's word. As a result, the ground was cursed and Genesis 3:18 says essentially it will now resist his attempts at making culture.

To Adam [God] said, "Because you listened to your wife and ate fruit from the tree about which I commanded you, 'You must not eat from it,'

"Cursed is the ground because of you;
    through painful toil you will eat food from it
    all the days of your life.
It will produce thorns and thistles for you,
    and you will eat the plants of the field.
By the sweat of your brow
    you will eat your food
until you return to the ground,
    since from it you were taken;
for dust you are
    and to dust you will return." (Gen 3:17-19)

His role as culture maker has changed significantly. Only by the sweat of his face will he eat bread. He is reminded that he is but dust. Death awaits him. Adam's relationship to the earth has changed significantly.

Now ironically, Adam calls his wife's name "Eve," which means "life" or "living." He believed in God's promise that from a woman's offspring would come one who would bring life and life abundantly (Jn 10:10). God responded to Adam's faith by sacrificing animals to clothe their nakedness with garments of skin from the innocent lives of animals: "The LORD God made garments of skin for Adam and his wife and clothed them" (Gen 3:21).

Thus far we have seen three catastrophic consequences of Adam and Eve's fall (alienation from God, self, and fellow human beings), plus three curses. Finally, the fall results in a separation between humankind and Eden/paradise—the *creational* consequence of humanity's sinful rebellion. (For the fourfold consequences of sin, see fig. 4.2.) It is important to remember that we came from (and were created for) a paradise. Before the fall, Adam and Eve dwelt in a perfect, blissful garden with God. Adam and Eve's disobedience affected not only themselves; they subjected all of creation to the curse of the fall. Consider Paul's words in Romans 8:18-23, as he speaks of the catastrophic consequences of sin on creation, along with the glorious hope for redemption that creation shares with humanity:

> I consider that our present sufferings are not worth comparing with the glory that will be revealed in us. For the creation waits in eager expectation for the children of God to be revealed. For the creation was subjected to frustration, not by its own choice, but by the will of the one who subjected it, in hope that the creation itself will be liberated from its bondage to decay and brought into the freedom and glory of the children of God.
>
> We know that the whole creation has been groaning in the pains of childbirth right up to the present time. Not only so, but we ourselves, who have the firstfruits of the Spirit, groan inwardly as we wait eagerly for our adoption to sonship, the redemption of our bodies.

As believers, we are headed to a glorious paradise in the new heavens and the new earth, a restored and remade creation (see Rev 21–22). We are not designed to be or remain in a fallen world, but we are glad that Jesus has conquered: "Take heart! I have overcome the world" (Jn 16:33).

As a result of the fall, human beings became independent of God in knowing good and evil. We began making up the rules of life autonomously, as a law to ourselves. While in the Garden of Eden, we could live

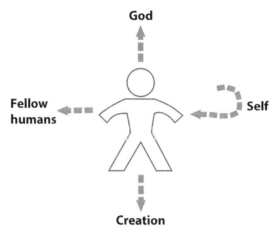

Figure 4.2. The fourfold consequences of the fall

forever by eating from the tree of life. To allow us to survive without the tree of life, God sent a merciful judgment in driving us out of the Garden of Eden where we would work the ground from which we were taken. To make sure we did not return to the paradise of Eden, and eat from its tree of life and live forever, God placed an angel and a flaming sword to stand guard to keep humanity from eating from it.

> And the LORD God said, "The man has now become like one of us, knowing good and evil. He must not be allowed to reach out his hand and take also from the tree of life and eat, and live forever." So the LORD God banished him from the Garden of Eden to work the ground from which he had been taken. After he drove the man out, he placed on the east side of the Garden of Eden cherubim and a flaming sword flashing back and forth to guard the way to the tree of life. (Gen 3:22-24)

After the fall of Adam and Eve, things in creation go from bad to worse. First, Cain commits the brother-on-brother murder of Abel, a fratricide (Gen 4); then God brings a worldwide flood because evil has become rampant (Gen 6–9). Next, the building of the tower of Babel prompts God to descend and scatter the people (Gen 11).

We have seen the fourfold consequences of the fall: the sinful rebellion of Adam and Eve results in alienation of man from God, alienation of human from self, alienation between a human and fellow humans, and alienation of humanity from creation. In closing, we must emphasize that the consequences of the fall are both ubiquitous and universal; that is, sin affects everything and everyone. There is neither person nor place in all of creation that remains unstained by the presence and power of sin. As Paul reminds us:

> "There is no one righteous, not even one;
>   there is no one who understands;
>   there is no one who seeks God.
> All have turned away,
>   they have together become worthless;
>   there is no one who does good,
>   not even one."
> "Their throats are open graves;
>   their tongues practice deceit."
> "The poison of vipers is on their lips."
>   "Their mouths are full of cursing and bitterness."
> "Their feet are swift to shed blood;
>   ruin and misery mark their ways,
>   and the way of peace they do not know."
>   "There is no fear of God before their eyes." (Rom 3:10-18)

As a result, "There is no difference between Jew and Gentile, for all have sinned and fall short of the glory of God" (Rom 3:22-23). All human beings are born into sin as a result of the fall of Adam and Eve: "Sin entered the world through one man, and death through sin, and in this way death came to all people, because all sinned" (Rom 5:12). Our sinful rebellion has grave consequences: "The wages of sin is death" (Rom 6:23). In our misery, we cry out with Paul: "What a wretched man I am! Who will rescue me from this body that is subject to death?" (Rom 7:24). Thanks be to God, there is a divine response to the fall—God's glorious redemption, by grace, through faith in Jesus Christ.

4.4.3 Redemption. Creation and fall mark the first two acts of the Christian worldview narrative. With redemption, we come to the good news, the third act in Christian worldview, displayed in three stages or scenes. The first scene is the history of the nation of Israel, the nation God chose for a special revelatory relationship. The second and third scenes focus on the person and work of Jesus Christ: redemption already (realized eschatology) and glorification not yet (future eschatology). While Genesis 1–3 relates the first two acts (creation and fall), the bulk of the Bible (Gen 4–Rev 20) covers redemption. The Bible is, for the most part, holy history, or his-story, of redemption and glorification with a three-chapter introduction: two chapters on creation (Gen 1–2), and one on the fall (Gen 3)

4.4.3.1 Redemption and the nation of Israel. Israel's history is up and down—mostly down. There are lots of twists and turns, positives and negatives, and starts and stops.

Paul says that being Jewish has certain advantages: "What advantage, then, is there in being a Jew, or what value is there in circumcision? Much in every way! First of all, the Jews have been entrusted with the very words of God" (Rom 3:1-2). Paul does not continue with a second of all. Had he, he might have been specific in listing the overall redemptive-historical narrative of the nation of Israel—the calling out of the nation of Israel through the patriarchs Abraham, Isaac, and Jacob (see Gen 12–50), the law given through Moses (see Ex 19–24), the sacrificial system to enable relationship with God (see Leviticus), the tabernacle and temple and their services (see Ex 25–30, 35–40 on the tabernacle and 1 Kings 8–9 on the temple), and God's dwelling with Israel in the tabernacle and temple (Ex 40; 1 Kings 8–9). God called the prophets—Samuel, Elijah, Elisha, Isaiah, Jeremiah, Ezekiel, Daniel, and others—and inspired them to speak on his behalf to his people, alternately delivering words of warning, rebuke, correction, comfort, and promise. He inspired the poetical wisdom books of Job, Psalms, Proverbs, Ecclesiastes, and Song of Songs. Though his chosen nation Israel continually strays and sins, God remains faithful to his covenants with them and pursues them in a redemptive-historical relationship. But Paul is utterly realistic in charging not just Gentiles but also Jews with sin (see Rom 3:9-20).

The Old Testament is equally realistic about the sinful rebellion of Israel. Judges 21:25 is an Old Testament example of moral deterioration: "In those days Israel had no king; everyone did as they saw fit." Amid the depressing rebellions, King David is a bright spot (1–2 Sam; 1 Kings 1–2). David defeated the enemy warrior Goliath (1 Sam 17). He was the sweet

SCENIC VIEW

*Contemporary Cultural
Worldview Meditation*

Rex Murphy vs. Justin Trudeau on Religious Beliefs in Politics

In 2014, Justin Trudeau, leader of the Liberal Party of Canada, required that all Liberal Party members vote pro-choice in Parliament or be removed from the party caucus. Trudeau insists that a woman's right to control her own body is a nonnegotiable element of the party platform.

Rex Murphy, a distinguished political commentator (or a grumpy old curmudgeon, depending on who you ask), suggests that this is an unwise and untenable requirement (*National Post*, June 21, 2014). Murphy notes, in ways that resonate with the imperatives of this textbook, that "if a Christian is a politician, then his public conduct, his thinking and voting on matters of public concern will naturally, inescapably, seek the polar star and guidance of his religious understanding. Religion is not an accessory to one's occupation and career. It has a core relationship to all of life." Murphy acknowledges that worldview commitments permeate all of life, including political perspectives.

Murphy then asks, "What kind of politics are they which require an MP to renounce his deepest moral commitments; indeed, to go beyond renunciation and declare himself positively in favour of ideas and actions that his faith condemns, his Church forbids, and his conscience cannot abide?"

Trudeau expects his Liberal Party members to "leave their faith at the door." For Christians, this is simply not an option. Our Christian faith is to permeate every aspect of our lives, even our political views.

psalmist of Israel (2 Sam 23:1) and wrote many of the comforting biblical psalms (e.g., Ps 23). The destiny of the human race depended on him (2 Sam 7:19). The messianic promise was given to David and fulfilled in Jesus: the promised Messiah will sit on the throne of David his father (or ancestor) forever and ever (see Lk 1:31-33). The New Testament considers David to be significant; indeed, he is mentioned fifty-eight times in the New Testament.

While God works particularly with and through his chosen nation of Israel in the Old Testament, there is always the promise of a future in which God's covenant will extend to all people, not just Israel. Even in the calling of Abraham, God promises that "all peoples on earth will be blessed through you" (Gen 12:3). God's scope is always global, his grace desiring the redemption of all people in all nations.

4.4.3.2 Redemption and realized eschatology (already). The second scene in redemption has to do with Jesus, who was born a Jew from Israel. As he taught, "salvation is from the Jews" (Jn 4:22). Jesus' central message, especially in the Synoptic Gospels of

Matthew, Mark, and Luke, was about the kingdom of God. Mark 1:14-15 is a good example: "After John was put in prison, Jesus went into Galilee, proclaiming the good news of God. 'The time has come,' he said. 'The kingdom of God has come near. Repent and believe the good news!'"

We believers are pretty good at proclaiming the gospel from the epistles, but not so good at this task when it comes to the Gospels themselves. So we must ask several questions.

First of all, was the kingdom of God in the Old Testament? Yes, the kingdom of God was in the Old Testament (see Ps 145:11-13). God shows himself sovereign over all things in creation, including Israel, over whom he reigns as king. God has always been King, but he became King in a real and tangible way in Jesus' ministry.

Second, what is the kingdom of God? The kingdom of God is the royal rule and kingship of God in dynamic action against all evil in the world. New Testament scholar C. H. Dodd (1884–1973) says the kingdom denotes that God reigns as king. The kingdom is God's sovereign power. Dodd writes the following words, explaining,

> But there can be no doubt that the expression before us [the kingdom of God] represents an Aramaic phrase well-established in Jewish usage, "The *malkuth* [kingdom] of Heaven." *Malkuth* . . . is properly an abstract noun, meaning "kingship," "kingly rule," "reign," or "sovereignty." The expression "the *malkuth* of God" connotes the fact that God reigns as King.[28]

The kingdom of God is his power, his mighty acts, and his dominion. God's empire strikes back against sin, Satan, and death. We frequently mistake the notion of the kingdom of God for a realm or land, but its active and dynamic meaning is the most important. The parallelism in Psalm 145:11-13 helps define the word *kingdom*. Note the italicized words.

> They tell of the glory of your *kingdom*
>   And speak of your *might*,
> so that all people may know of your *mighty acts*
>   and the glorious splendor of your *kingdom*.
> Your kingdom is an everlasting *kingdom*,
>   and your *dominion* endures through all generations.

---

[28]C. H. Dodd, *The Parables of the Kingdom* (London: Nisbet, 1935), 21.

Can there be any doubt about what the Jews, including Jesus, believed about the kingdom of God? I like what George E. Ladd says about the kingdom: "The 'kingdom' that Jesus appointed for his disciples is [God's] 'royal rule.'"[29]

In his gospel, Matthew frequently designates the kingdom of God as "the kingdom of heaven(s)," a phrase that Ladd points out is used thirty-two times in Matthew. Because Matthew was probably written for a primarily Jewish audience, "the kingdom of heaven" (*ouranos*—in Mt 4:17) was a substitute for "the kingdom of God." Matthew is showing deferential courtesy to Jews, who would not speak or write the name of God (the name of God is written YHWH, or יהוה in Hebrew, the tetragrammaton). So, in other words, the kingdom of heaven and kingdom of God are synonymous expressions.

Third, what is the nature of the kingdom of God? Essentially, it is a revealed mystery. Jesus himself spoke of the mysteries of the kingdom of God or heaven in the context of kingdom parables.[30] Paul also spoke of this mystery: "God has chosen to make known among the Gentiles the glorious riches of this mystery, which is Christ in you, the hope of glory" (Col 1:27). Christ himself is the kingdom, and the kingdom is a revealed mystery that has been hidden for long ages past but is now made known to all the nations, leading to the obedience of faith. The mystery has now been uncovered:

> Now to him who is able to establish you in accordance with my gospel, the message I proclaim about Jesus Christ, in keeping with the revelation of the mystery hidden for long ages past, but now revealed and made known through the prophetic writings by the command of the eternal God, so that all the Gentiles might come to the obedience that comes from faith— to the only wise God be the glory forever through Jesus Christ! Amen. (Rom 16:25-27)

Fourth, why did the kingdom of God come? The kingdom of God came because people and all creation were in a tight spot under sin,

---

[29]George Eldon Ladd, *A Theology of the New Testament*, rev. ed. (Grand Rapids: Eerdmans, 1993), 61.
[30]See, e.g., Luke 8:10: "He said, 'The knowledge of the secrets of the kingdom of God has been given to you.'" See also Matthew 13:11: "[Jesus] replied, 'Because the knowledge of the secrets of the kingdom of heaven has been given to you, but not to them.'"

Satan, and death. As seen in the previous section, the entire human race and the whole of creation are afflicted. As non-Christians, we have burdens that are hard to bear (Lk 11:46), and as sinners our lives are filled with cursing and bitterness (Rom 3:14). We sigh and we cry out because of our bondage and slavery (Heb 2:15). We stand guilty before a holy God (Jas 2:10). We are helpless, and hopeless, and we see no way out of our desperate situation (Eph 2:12). Creation itself groans (Rom 8:22).

Paul affirms that, though we were formerly far off, in Christ we have been brought near through his blood: "But now in Christ Jesus you who once were far away have been brought near [to God] by the blood of Christ" (Eph 2:13).

Indeed, the whole world and the entire human race are in bondage and slavery. The whole creation and the entire human race are under futility and desire freedom (Rom 8:18-25). The good news of the gospel is that all will be liberated, at last! Whatever happens to believers happens to the creation. When we are enslaved, so is creation (Rom 8:18-25). When we are set free, so is creation. After all, we came from the earth, and the first couple brought it down (see Gen 1–3). In grace and mercy, Jesus redeemed all things. So, as created, fallen, and yet redeemed people, we live in a created, fallen, and yet redeemed world.

How did this unfortunate spiritual situation come about? Because of the fall of humanity and creation into sin in Genesis 3. We had a great fall. We have to understand the whole story of the cosmos—the narrative of a Christian worldview—and interpret our lives and our many confusions in light of the larger story. It is the world's true narrative: creation, fall, redemption, and glorification.

We have surveyed the nature of and the need for the kingdom of God. A fifth and final question concerning redemption and God's kingdom is this: how did the kingdom come? The means of the coming of the kingdom is a part of the mystery revealed. It came in a relatively simple way: through the person and work of Jesus of Nazareth. Here are, in brief, six aspects of the kingdom's coming in Jesus Christ.

First, the kingdom arrived in Jesus' birth and incarnation. The divine Word became human, or flesh, and dwelt among us (Jn 1:1-14; Lk 2). The kingdom entered the human stage in the least of all kingly acts: Jesus' humble birth in a stable. Second, Jesus lived a perfectly righteous life and taught well (1 Pet 2:22). Third, he died on a Roman cross as an atoning sacrifice for sin (Rom 5:8). The kingdom conquered sin and death through another lowly, kingly act—agonizing death by crucifixion. Fourth, Jesus was buried in a borrowed tomb (Lk 23:50-56). Fifth, he was raised from the dead in a glorious bodily resurrection (this is the gospel; see 1 Cor 15:3-5). Sixth, he ascended to the right hand of God's throne (Acts 1:9-10). The Age to Come had come, and we have henceforth been transferred to God's kingdom (Col 1:12). The Christ event *in its entirety* constituted the first coming of the kingship of God. The empire of God struck back against sin, Satan, and death; and it will come again in glory!

In light of the fact that the kingdom of God came in such a humble manner, it is no wonder Jews ask for a sign and Greeks seek wisdom, but with no results. To the Jews Jesus is a stumbling block, and to Greeks Jesus is foolishness, but to believers Jesus Christ is the power of God and wisdom of God.

> Jews demand signs and Greeks look for wisdom, but we preach Christ crucified: a stumbling block to Jews and foolishness to Gentiles, but to those whom God has called, both Jews and Greeks, Christ the power of God and the wisdom of God. For the foolishness of God is wiser than human wisdom, and the weakness of God is stronger than human strength. (1 Cor 1:22-25)

Indeed, the kingdom came as a mystery but is now revealed in Jesus.

4.4.4 Glorification (future eschatology). When considering the kingdom of God, we have looked at the nature of the kingdom, the need for the kingdom, and the means by which the kingdom came. We come now to the third scene of redemption (itself the third act of the great Christian worldview narrative) and consider a final kingdom question: when does the kingdom come? The nature and timing of the kingdom of God are both present and future: realized eschatology and future eschatology. New Testament theologians say the kingdom is already in terms of redemption but not yet in terms of glorification.

New Testament scholar Oscar Cullmann likes to compare it to D-day and V-E Day in World War II. On D-day (June 6, 1944) the Allied Forces landed at Normandy, ensuring Adolf Hitler's defeat, but that final defeat did not come until about a year later on V-E Day (May 8, 1945). Cullmann writes: "The hope of the final victory is so much more vivid because of the unshakably firm conviction that the battle that decides the victory has already taken place."[31] Similarly, Jesus' victory came at his first coming when he defeated sin, Satan, and death.

> In him you were also circumcised with a circumcision not performed by human hands. Your whole self ruled by the flesh was put off when you were circumcised by Christ, having been buried with him in baptism, in which you were also raised with him through your faith in the working of God, who raised him from the dead.
>
> When you were dead in your sins and in the uncircumcision of your flesh, God made you alive with Christ. He forgave us all our sins, having canceled the charge of our legal indebtedness, which stood against us and condemned us; he has taken it away, nailing it to the cross. And having disarmed the powers and authorities, he made a public spectacle of them, triumphing over them by the cross. (Col 2:11-15)

But, however you work out the details eschatologically (which is important), the final defeat, when all sin and its consequences will be conquered, will not occur until Christ returns a second time. This second coming of Jesus we call, in a Christian worldview narrative, glorification.

The parable of the weeds (Mt 13:24-30) and Jesus' subsequent interpretation of the parable (Mt 13:36-43) show how the kingdom is both already and not yet. In Matthew 13:30, Jesus says: "Let both [wheat and weeds] grow together until the harvest. At that time I will tell the harvesters: First collect the weeds and tie them in bundles to be burned; then gather the wheat and bring it into my barn.'" The wheat (believers redeemed by God's grace through faith in Christ) is already present but is not yet bundled purely together. Instead, the weeds grow together with the wheat until the harvest—as believers will mix and interact with nonbelievers until the second coming of Christ.

---

[31]Oscar Cullmann, *Christ and Time: The Primitive Christian Conception of Time and History*, trans. Floyd V. Filson, rev. ed. (Philadelphia: Westminster, 1964), 87.

The already-but-not-yet tension is the theological structure of the entire New Testament (see "is coming" and "now . . . have come" in 1 Jn 2:18; cf. Jn 4:23):

> Dear children, this is the last hour; and as you have heard that the antichrist is coming, even now many antichrists have come. This is how we know it is the last hour. (1 Jn 2:18)

> Yet a time is coming and has now come when the true worshipers will worship the Father in the Spirit and in truth, for they are the kind of worshipers the Father seeks. (Jn 4:23)

Jesus has already completed his work of redemption and will return again to wrap things up (see 1 Cor 15:25-26; Rev 21–22), but this glorification has not yet been fully realized.

So we have been redeemed. The creation has been redeemed. This is realized eschatology. The future is present now, and we live at the hyphen in the already-not yet. There is also hope, as a certainty, for the future in glorification. We believers are already redeemed but not yet made perfect; we are already forgiven but not yet sinless. Our future, including the world's future, is captured nicely in a portion of the Lord's Prayer in Matthew 6:10:

> your kingdom come,
> your will be done,
>   on earth as it is in heaven.

REFLECTION QUESTIONS

1 What does the parallelism of days 1-3 and days 4-6 of creation in Genesis 1 suggest about both the nature of God's creative activity and the text of Genesis 1?

2 What does God's declaration of creation's goodness mean for us today? How, if at all, is creation's goodness affected by the fall?

3 What aspects of human life are affected by Adam and Eve's fall? How are those effects felt today?

4 What is the nature of the kingdom of God? How is Jesus connected to the kingdom?

4.5 SUMMARY

The hymn writer David Clowney, at the tender age of sixteen, I am told, got the biblical narrative just right when he composed the hymn "God, All Nature Sings Thy Glory," sung to the chorus of the last movement of Beethoven's Ninth Symphony. The overarching biblical narrative is found in the following lyrics.

[Creation:]

God, all nature sings thy glory, and all thy works proclaim thy might;
ordered vastness in the heavens, ordered course of day and night;
beauty in the changing seasons, beauty in the storming sea;
all the changing moods of nature praise the changeless Trinity.

Clearer still we see thy hand in man whom thou hast made for thee;
ruler of creation's glory, image of thy majesty.
Music, art, the fruitful garden, all the labor of his days,
are the calling of his Maker to the harvest feast of praise.

[Fall:]

But our sins have spoiled thine image; nature, conscience only serve
as unceasing, grim reminders of the wrath which we deserve.

[Redemption:]

Yet thy grace and saving mercy in thy Word of truth revealed
claim the praise of all who know thee, in the blood of Jesus sealed.

[Summary:]

God of glory, power, mercy, all creation praises thee;
we, thy creatures, would adore thee now and through eternity.
Saved to magnify thy goodness, grant us strength to do thy will;
with our acts as with our voices, thy commandments to fulfill.[32]

"This is my story, this is my song," wrote a blind Fanny J. Crosby (1820–1915) in another hymn, "Blessed Assurance." Before we do anything, we must ask, what is my story? The story of the Christian worldview, as

---

[32]Lyrics by David Clowney, 1960. Performance available on Eric Graef, *Preach to Yourself*, digital album (Downers Grove, IL: InterVarsity Press, 2012), accessed February 9, 2017, https://ericgraef.bandcamp.com/track/god-all-nature-sings-thy-glory.

revealed by God in Scripture, is the fourfold narrative of creation, fall, redemption, and glorification. This is the world's true story. And do not forget the check mark as an emblem of the biblical narrative.

MASTERING THE MATERIAL

When you finish reading this chapter, you should be able to

✔ Explain general revelation and special revelation.

✔ Tell the biblical story, especially how creation, fall, redemption, and glorification affect all things.

✔ Outline the kingdom of God (what? why? how? when?).

✔ Explain the already-but-not-yet structure of the kingdom of God.

✔ Articulate what is the gospel or the good news.

✔ Explain how Jesus' life, death, burial, and resurrection relate to the kingdom of God.

Glossary of Terms for Chapter Four

cosmological arguments—Arguments for God's existence based on the existence or origins of the universe.

creation—What God has made. Refers to the world not being random or unintended but rather the intentionally designed creative act of God.

eschatology—Having to do with the end of time, or after physical death. Within a Christian worldview, this includes both redemption (already—realized eschatology) and glorification (not yet—future eschatology).

fall—Man's rebellion against God, through disobedience to his revealed will.

Five Ways—Thomas Aquinas's five arguments for the existence of God based on natural revelation.

kingdom of God—God's rule/reign on earth, both now and in the age to come.

natural revelation—God's world: what God has revealed about himself through what he has made; knowledge that God exists (and

some about his nature) that can be ascertained by all people through an investigation of the natural world.

objective morality—Moral values and duties that are binding on all people in all places at all times, whether or not people acknowledge or obey those moral values and duties.

special revelation—God's Word: what God has revealed about himself through what he has said; knowledge about God and his purposes that can be ascertained only by submissively reading his spoken and written Word (the Bible).

teleological (fine-tuning) arguments—Arguments for God's existence based on the apparent purposiveness or intricate design of the universe or its component parts.

triunity—Refers to God's trinitarian nature: three persons, one God. Three unique persons (Father, Son, and Holy Spirit) compose one divine Godhead or Being—not three gods, not one person.

Possible Term Paper Topics from Chapter Four

✔ Lay out the logical steps of either a cosmological or teleological argument for God's existence from natural revelation. Defend the truthfulness of the premises and the significance of the conclusion.

✔ Discuss the nature and contours of natural revelation. What is natural revelation? What can it tell us? What are the limits and boundaries of the knowledge available through natural revelation? How helpful could natural revelation be in bringing non-Christians to a knowledge of God?

✔ Discuss the nature and contours of special revelation? What is special revelation? What does it tell us? Why does God supplement natural revelation with special revelation? How helpful is special revelation in bringing non-Christians to a knowledge of God?

✔ Research Christian views on the interpretation of the days of Genesis 1. Defend a particular approach to the timing and extent of God's creative activity.

✔ Blaise Pascal argued that only the Christian doctrines of creation and fall could make sense of human self-understanding and experience—our simultaneous feeling of nobility and depravity. Is Pascal right? How do other worldviews explain human self-understanding?

✔ Examine the already-but-not-yet structure of the kingdom of God. How is the kingdom already come? How is the kingdom yet to come? How does the balance or tension inherent in the already-but-not-yet nature of God's kingdom affect the daily life of the Christian?

Core Bibliography for Chapter Four

Demarest, Bruce A. *General Revelation: Historical Views and Contemporary Issues*. Grand Rapids: Zondervan, 1982.

Erickson, Millard J. *Christian Theology*. 1st ed. 3 vols. Grand Rapids: Baker Books, 1983.

Jenson, Robert W. "How the World Lost Its Story." *First Things*. October 1993. www.firstthings .com/article/1993/10/002-how-the-world -lost-its-story.

Wolters, Albert M. *Creation Regained: Biblical Basics for a Reformational Worldview*. Postscript coauthored by Michael W. Goheen. 2nd ed. Grand Rapids: Eerdmans, 2005.

THE PROPOSITIONAL CONTOURS
OF A CHRISTIAN WORLDVIEW

The Christian story provides us with a set of lenses,
not something to look at but to look through.

Lesslie Newbigin

Worldview is the conceptual lens through which we see, understand, and interpret the world and our place within it. We have seen, in the first part of this book, the importance and benefit of worldview study and the impact that worldview exerts on us. In chapter four, we surveyed the contours of a Christian worldview from a narrative perspective, examining the grand story of creation, fall, redemption, and glorification revealed in God's Word. We now move on to see how a Christian worldview answers our four core worldview questions: What is our nature? What is our world? What is our problem? What is our end?

As emphasized in the last chapter, the contours of a Christian worldview are delineated by God's special revelation—his revealed Word in the Bible. Hence, a Christian worldview is necessarily a biblically faithful worldview, the contours of which are determined by the clear teachings of Scripture—in short, a biblical worldview. Hence, while many Christian college students have heard of a Christian worldview, or they have heard of the elements that make up a Christian worldview story from special revelation, we still have to ask, "Is your 'Christian' worldview that biblical?"[1] Insofar as your worldview does *not* line up

---

[1]Brian J. Walsh and J. Richard Middleton, *The Transforming Vision: Shaping a Christian World View* (Downers Grove, IL: IVP Academic, 1984), 93-95.

with Scripture, it is *not* a Christian worldview. Critical self-examination is crucial if we desire (as we ought) to pursue God's perspective in a pluralistic world.

So, in this chapter we will cover the propositional contours of a Christian worldview, beginning with a view of our nature (theological or philosophical anthropology), which necessarily includes a discussion of the Christian God. A Christian worldview begins with God the Trinity and ourselves.

5.1 What Is Our Nature?

The first of our worldview questions concerns our nature as human beings. What am I? What does it mean to be human? What distinguishes me from other living creatures? We begin here in our articulation of Christian worldview simply because, as self-reflective creatures, this is where we naturally begin. We find ourselves asking questions, and we each take note of the reality that *I* am asking questions. So worldview examination begins with the chronologically prior question, what is our nature?

Within a Christian worldview, however, a discussion of our human nature necessarily begins with a discussion of the nature of the triune God of the Bible. Given that human beings are created in the image of God (more on that presently), in order to understand our nature we must first understand his nature. God is the ultimate reality within Christian worldview—the foundation on which all else is built and according to which all else is understood. So I consider him first, and then on to our nature.

5.1.1 Doctrine of God. God has revealed himself to be triune. He is eternally existent as Father, Son, and Holy Spirit—not three gods but One God; not a monad but a divine Trinity. The three persons of the Trinity are distinct but not separate; they are of the same substance and nature and yet are not commingled.

God the Trinity—the Father, the Son, and the Holy Spirit—is all-determinative. He can be diagrammed as illustrated in figure 5.1. This illustration of God's triunity is common and important to understand. There are four central truths to articulate regarding the Trinity:

- The Father, the Son, and the Holy Spirit are all God; that is, there is one divine substance. This is monotheism (one God).

- *God the Father* is not God the Son or God the Holy Spirit (*the Father* is a Person or consubstantial Person or hypostasis: one of three).
- *God the Son* is not God the Father or God the Holy Spirit (*the Son* is a Person or consubstantial Person or hypostasis: one of three).
- *God the Holy Spirit* is not God the Father or God the Son (*the Holy Spirit* is a Person or consubstantial Person or hypostasis: one of three).

We have one What (or Substance, the first truth) subsisting in three Who's (or Persons or consubstantial Persons—all three in italics above). Similarly, the first point in this list is different from the following three.

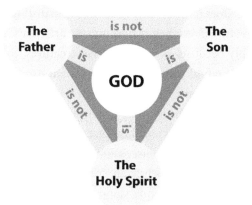

Figure 5.1. The Trinity

The Fourth Lateran Council, called the greatest of the medieval councils by Pope Innocent III, was convened on April 19, 1213, and dealt in large measure with the nature of God. The council declared of the monotheistic substance of the Trinity that "there is only one true God." Later, the council described the place and function of the three persons in the Trinity: "the Father begetting, the Son being begotten, and the Holy Spirit proceeding."[2]

The Athanasian Creed (from the fourth century) nicely sums up my expression of trinitarian belief:

[2]John Leith, ed., *Creeds of the Churches: A Reader in Christian Doctrine from the Bible to the Present*, 3rd ed. (Atlanta: John Knox, 1982), 56-57.

We worship one God in Trinity, and Trinity in Unity; neither confounding the persons nor dividing the substance. For there is one person of the Father, another of the Son, and another of the Holy Spirit. But the Godhead of the Father, of the Son, and of the Holy Spirit is all one, the glory equal, the majesty coeternal. Such as the Father is, such is the Son, and such is the Holy Spirit. The Father uncreated, the Son uncreated, and the Holy Spirit uncreated. The Father incomprehensible, the Son incomprehensible, and the Holy Spirit incomprehensible. The Father eternal, the Son eternal, and the Holy Spirit eternal. And yet they are not three eternals but one eternal. As also there are not three uncreated nor three incomprehensible, but one uncreated and one incomprehensible. So likewise the Father is almighty, the Son almighty, and the Holy Spirit almighty. And yet they are not three almighties, but one almighty.

So the Father is God, the Son is God, and the Holy Spirit is God; and yet they are not three Gods, but one God. So likewise the Father is Lord, the Son Lord, and the Holy Spirit Lord; and yet they are not three Lords but one Lord. For like as we are compelled by the Christian verity to acknowledge every Person by himself to be God and Lord; so are we forbidden by the catholic religion to say; There are three Gods or three Lords. The Father is made of none, neither created nor begotten. The Son is of the Father alone; not made nor created, but begotten. The Holy Spirit is of the Father and of the Son; neither made, nor created, nor begotten, but proceeding.

So there is one Father, not three Fathers; one Son, not three Sons; one Holy Spirit, not three Holy Spirits. And in this Trinity none is afore or after another; none is greater or less than another. But the whole three persons are coeternal, and coequal. So that in all things, as aforesaid, the Unity in Trinity and the Trinity in Unity is to be worshipped.[3]

God reveals himself in his Word to be a triune God. He is revealed to humanity as eternally existent as Father, Son, and Holy Spirit. All three are God, members of the divine Godhead; and yet it is not three gods that we worship, but one. Although the theological term *Trinity* does not occur in the Scriptures of the Old or New Testaments, the Bible is exceedingly clear about the true triune nature of the triune God.

---

[3]Athanasian Creed, points 3-27, from the bishop Athanasius, a defender of orthodox Christianity against the heresies of Arianism. For full text online, see, e.g., www.ccel.org/creeds/athanasian .creed.html, accessed February 10, 2017.

Popularly speaking, God the Father is the Person to whom people usually refer when they talk about God generically. The Father is eternally preexistent and is usually understood to be the creative agent of the Trinity. The love of God is expressed to his people in terms of fatherhood, whereby God the Father possesses the fullness of true fatherly love for all his sons and daughters. The Father reigns in complete sovereignty over all of creation and governs all of human history.

> In the beginning was the Word, and the Word was with God, and the Word was God. He was with God in the beginning. Through him all things were made; without him nothing was made that has been made. In him was life, and that life was the light of all mankind. The light shines in the darkness, and the darkness has not overcome it. . . .
>
> He was in the world, and though the world was made through him, the world did not recognize him. He came to that which was his own, but his own did not receive him. Yet to all who did receive him, to those who believed in his name, he gave the right to become children of God. . . .
>
> The Word became flesh and made his dwelling among us. We have seen his glory, the glory of the one and only Son, who came from the Father, full of grace and truth. (Jn 1:1-5, 10-12, 14)

The Bible affirms unhesitatingly the divinity of Jesus Christ, the Son of God. Despite the rash of heresies throughout Christianity denying the divinity of Jesus Christ, orthodox Christianity has, since the life, death, and resurrection of Christ, affirmed that Jesus Christ is God, come to earth in the flesh in order to redeem humankind.

Jesus Christ himself confirms, on numerous occasions, his divine nature.

> Jesus replied, "If I glorify myself, my glory means nothing. My Father, whom you claim as your God, is the one who glorifies me. Though you do not know him, I know him. If I said I did not, I would be a liar like you, but I do know him and obey his word. Your father Abraham rejoiced at the thought of seeing my day; he saw it and was glad."
>
> "You are not yet fifty years old," [the Jews] said to him, "and you have seen Abraham!"
>
> "Very truly I tell you," Jesus answered, "before Abraham was born, I am!" At this, they picked up stones to stone him, but Jesus hid himself, slipping away from the temple grounds. (Jn 8:54-59)

Jesus claims to have been around before Abraham was born, even though Abraham lived and died more than four thousand years earlier. How could this be, unless Jesus is the eternal God of the universe? Jesus finishes his claim by invoking God's self-designation from the Old Testament—"I AM" (Ex 3:14). "Before Abraham was born, I am!" Jesus claims to be God, come to earth in human form.

> At that time Jesus said, "I praise you, Father, Lord of heaven and earth, because you have hidden these things from the wise and learned, and revealed them to little children. Yes, Father, for this is what you were pleased to do.
>
> "All things have been committed to me by my Father. No one knows the Son except the Father, and no one knows the Father except the Son and those to whom the Son chooses to reveal him." (Mt 11:25-27)

Jesus is the Son, the only one who fully knows God the Father, and the mediator of knowledge of God to all humankind.

> The high priest said to him, "I charge you under oath by the living God: Tell us if you are the Messiah, the Son of God."
>
> "You have said so," Jesus replied. "But I say to all of you: From now on you will see the Son of Man sitting at the right hand of the Mighty One and coming on the clouds of heaven."
>
> Then the high priest tore his clothes and said, "He has spoken blasphemy!" (Mt 26:63-65)

Jesus openly claims to be God in the flesh. He goes on to claim for himself the divine right to forgive the sins of all men and women (e.g., Mt 9:2-6; Lk 7:36-50; Jn 8:1-11) and the right to judge the souls of all humankind (Mt 25:31-46). He professes to be the source of eternal life (Jn 3:16; 10:24-28; 11:25). I appreciate Lewis's summary of the nature of Christ.

> I am trying here to prevent anyone saying the really foolish thing that people often say about Him: "I'm ready to accept Jesus as a great moral teacher, but I don't accept His claim to be God." That is the one thing we must not say. A man who was merely a man and said the sort of things Jesus said would not be a great moral teacher. He would either be a lunatic —on a level with the man who says he is a poached egg—or else he would be the Devil of Hell. You must make your choice. Either this man

was, and is, the Son of God: or else a madman or something worse. You can shut Him up for a fool, you can spit at Him and kill Him as a demon; or you can fall at His feet and call Him Lord and God. But let us not come with any patronizing nonsense about His being a great human teacher. He has not left that open to us. He did not intend to.[4]

Jesus was truly divine. But he was also truly human. His conception was miraculous: he was not conceived of the sexual union between a man and a woman; rather, he was planted in the womb of the virgin Mary by the power of the Holy Spirit. However, his birth was entirely natural and normal; he proceeded through Mary's birth canal and into the world. Jesus possessed a fully human body and went through the normal stages of human development. The hymn to Christ contained in Philippians 2:6-11 beautifully sums up the sacrifice that it was for the divine, glorious, eternal Son of God to descend to earth and take on human form:

Who, being in very nature God,
    did not consider equality with God something to be used to his own
        advantage;
rather, he made himself nothing
    by taking the very nature of a servant,
    being made in human likeness. (Phil 2:6-7)

As John 1:14 reminds us, "the Word became flesh and made his dwelling among us." Christ, God the Son, came down from heaven to earth for our sake. In the fullness of his humanity, he experienced all the emotions and needs that we face—hunger (Mt 4:2), thirst (Jn 19:28), pain and suffering (Mt 26:36-46; Jn 18–19), tiredness (Mt 8:23-25), grief (Jn 11:35), anger (Mt 21:12-14; 23:1-39), compassion (Mt 9:36), and love (Mk 10:21). However, Christ experienced them in their true fullness, in the full humanity that God intended for all human beings to experience these emotions. Christ also experienced his full humanity without sinning. Although he experienced the same temptations that we face (Mt 4:1-11; 16:21-23; 26:36-46), he lived a perfectly sinless life, never departing from the express will of his Father in heaven. Thus, as Hebrews 4:14-16 encourages us,

---

[4]C. S. Lewis, *Mere Christianity*, rev. ed. (New York: HarperSanFrancisco, 2001), 52.

Since we have a great high priest who has ascended into heaven, Jesus the Son of God, let us hold firmly to the faith we profess. For we do not have a high priest who is unable to empathize with our weaknesses, but we have one who has been tempted in every way, just as we are—yet he did not sin. Let us then approach God's throne of grace with confidence, so that we may receive mercy and find grace to help us in our time of need.

Because of his divine nature, his full humanity, and his perfectly sinless life of obedience, Jesus Christ was able to die as a substitutionary sacrifice in our place. Through his death on the cross he atoned for the sins of all creation. As the Nicene Creed states,

> For our sake he was crucified under Pontius Pilate;
> he suffered death and was buried.
> On the third day he rose again
> in accordance with the Scriptures;
> he ascended into heaven
> and is seated at the right hand of the Father.
> He will come again in glory to judge the living and the dead,
> and his kingdom will have no end.

Through his atoning death, creation is reconciled to God.

While Jesus was both divine and human, he was also clearly a separate person (though of the same substance) from God the Father. Jesus prays to the Father (Mt 11:25-26), differentiates his role from the Father's (Mt 11:27), and insists that God the Father possesses knowledge inaccessible to God the Son in his humanity (Mt 24:36). Thus, the Father and the Son are not merely different modes or expressions of the same divine Person; rather, they are unique divine Persons within the one triune Godhead.

The Holy Spirit proceeds from the Father and the Son and is the Spirit of God. The inspiration of God's Word was given through the Holy Spirit—even when the human authors were unaware of the giver of the inspiration. The Holy Spirit was also the instrument of God's communication with the Old Testament prophets and kings:[5]

---

[5]Consistently in the Old Testament we are met with the words, "and the Spirit of God came upon" a prophet. See, e.g., Numbers 24:2-3: "When Balaam looked out and saw Israel encamped tribe by tribe, the Spirit of God came on him and he spoke his message"; 2 Chronicles 20:14: "Then the Spirit of the LORD came on Jahaziel son of Zechariah."

But as for me, I am filled with power,
with the Spirit of the LORD,
and with justice and might,
to declare to Jacob his transgression,
to Israel his sin." (Mic 3:8)

The Holy Spirit is not just some kind of impersonal force that God uses to work within his creation—like a wind, or thunder, or lightning, or Star Wars. Rather, the Holy Spirit is personal; in fact, the Spirit is the third person of the Trinity—God working within the hearts and lives of his people. Isaiah 63:10-14 describes God's relationship with his people Israel through his Holy Spirit in exceedingly personal terms:

Yet [Israel] rebelled
and grieved his Holy Spirit.
So he turned and became their enemy
and he himself fought against them.
Then his people recalled the days of old,
the days of Moses and his people—
where is he who brought them through the sea,
with the shepherd of his flock?
Where is he who set
his Holy Spirit among them,
who sent his glorious arm of power
to be at Moses' right hand,
who divided the waters before them,
to gain for himself everlasting renown,
who led them through the depths?
Like a horse in open country,
they did not stumble;
like cattle that go down to the plain,
they were given rest by the Spirit of the LORD.

The Holy Spirit speaks directly to Christians:

While Peter was still thinking about the vision, the Spirit said to him, "Simon, three men are looking for you. So get up and go downstairs. Do not hesitate to go with them, for I have sent them." (Acts 10:19-20)

Similarly, the Holy Spirit speaks in Acts 13:2:

> While they were worshiping the Lord and fasting, the Holy Spirit said, "Set apart for me Barnabas and Saul for the work to which I have called them."

The Holy Spirit also guides and directs God's people—sometimes even preventing them from going a certain direction:

> Paul and his companions traveled throughout the region of Phrygia and Galatia, having been kept by the Holy Spirit from preaching the word in the province of Asia. When they came to the border of Mysia, they tried to enter Bithynia, but the Spirit of Jesus would not allow them to. (Acts 16:6-7)

The Holy Spirit is given as our counselor, our guide, our illuminating light, our seal of salvation, and our constant divine presence.

> And I will ask the Father, and he will give you another advocate to help you and be with you forever—the Spirit of truth. The world cannot accept him, because it neither sees him nor knows him. But you know him, for he lives with you and will be in you. I will not leave you as orphans; I will come to you. . . . But the Advocate, the Holy Spirit, whom the Father will send in my name, will teach you all things and will remind you of everything I have said to you. (Jn 14:16-18, 26)

The Holy Spirit interacts with us in an intensely personal and intimate manner. God desires to speak with us, to instruct us, and to guide us, and he does this through the Holy Spirit, who dwells within the heart of all who accept salvation by the grace of God through faith in Jesus Christ.

On the very first page in his famous book *Knowledge of the Holy*, A. W. Tozer (1897–1963), a pastor, author, editor, and mentor, says this about God and ourselves:

> What comes into our minds when we think about God is the most important thing about us.
>
> The history of mankind will probably show that no people has ever risen above its religion, and man's spiritual history will positively demonstrate that no religion has ever been greater than its idea of God. Worship is pure or base as the worshiper entertains high or low thoughts of God.
>
> For this reason the greatest question before the Church is always God Himself, and the most portentous fact about any man is not what he at a given time may say or do, but what in his deep heart conceives God to be like.[6]

---

[6]A. W. Tozer, *Knowledge of the Holy* (1961; repr., New York: HarperOne, 2009), 1.

As Tozer continues with this stream of thought, he covers the following attributes of God (which he simply defines as "something true about God"): incomprehensibility, triunity, self-existence, self-sufficiency, eternality, infinitude, immutability, omniscience, wisdom, omnipotence, transcendence, omnipresence, faithfulness, goodness, justice, mercy, grace, love, holiness, and sovereignty. Tozer ends with an urgent exhortation: "acquaint yourself with God." There is more to know about God than we can ever hope to fully comprehend, but we have the privilege of pursuing a personal and intimate knowledge of him.

In his classic work *Knowing God*, J. I. Packer expounds numerous characteristics of God. Packer covers these attributes of God (among other things): God as the Only True God, God Incarnate (in Jesus), God Unchanging (God's immutability), the majesty and wisdom of God, the truth and grace of God, God's goodness and severity, God's jealousy, God as judge, God's wrath, God's gospel, and, finally, God's adequacy.[7]

Finally, a standard (and widely used) philosophy of religion textbook includes the following qualities of God: (1) perfect and worthy of worship; (2) necessary and self-existent; (3) personal and free Creator; (4) all-knowing, all-powerful, and perfectly good; and (5) eternality—timeless or everlasting.[8]

God is omnipotent or all-powerful, insofar as his own nature allows. For instance, he can't cease to be and he cannot sin, since his nature is necessary (he cannot not be) and perfectly good morally (he is perfect). He is omniscient, knowing all things in one timeless act of knowing, and he never knows anything false. He is also omnibenevolent or all good, or he is simply kind, just, merciful, and loving. We can add God's omnipresence to this list of divine attributes; God is everywhere present in his fullness. He is also with us, a God close by, what theologians call his immanence. He is also above and beyond us, a God far off, or what theologians call God's transcendence. By the way, people today are looking for something above and beyond them. People are looking for transcendence (not just immanence)! If you don't believe me, just go to

[7]J. I. Packer, *Knowing God,* 20th anniv. ed. (Downers Grove, IL: InterVarsity Press, 1993).
[8]Michael Peterson et al., *Reason and Religious Belief: An Introduction to Philosophy of Religion*, 5th ed. (New York: Oxford University Press, 2013), 135-56.

a football game featuring your favorite team (mine is the Dallas Cowboys) or a rock concert featuring your favorite band (mine are U2 and Switchfoot). He can also be very kind, but he is also severe (as Rom 9–11 makes plain; see especially Rom 11:22). Regardless, as Anselm (1033–1109), the archbishop of Canterbury, said of the greatness of the triune God in his *Proslogion*, "He is that than which nothing greater can be conceived."[9]

Obviously, the Christian theistic God, the Trinity, is our ultimate reality, and ultimate reality is the touchstone of any worldview. In a Christian worldview, God affects everything, including our understanding of human nature.

5.1.2 Doctrine of humanity. "Humankind's greatness and wretchedness are so evident that true religion must necessarily teach us that there is in humankind some great principle of greatness and some great principle of wretchedness."[10]

The Christian doctrine of humanity begins necessarily with God the Father, Son, and Holy Spirit. After creating the heavens and the earth, and filling the waters, the skies, and the land with all manner of living creatures, God creates human beings in his own image (the *imago Dei*).

> Then God said, "Let us make mankind in our image, in our likeness, so that they may rule over the fish in the sea and the birds in the sky, over the livestock and all the wild animals, and over all the creatures that move along the ground."
>
> So God created mankind in his own image,
>   in the image of God he created them;
>   male and female he created them. (Gen 1:26-27)

A Christian worldview answers the question, what is our nature?, with an initial emphatic declaration that human beings are created in the image of God. There are numerous logical implications of the *imago Dei*. First, since God is the greatest Good, the truest True, and the purest Beautiful, human beings bear inherent dignity, value, and worth. God possesses ultimate value; as his image-bearers, we possess derivative, but

---

[9]Anselm, *Basic Writings*, trans. S. N. Dean (La Salle, IL: Open Court, 1962), 7.
[10]Blaise Pascal, *Pensées*, trans. A. J. Krailsheimer (London: Penguin, 1995), *pensée* 149, p. 46.

real and high, value. The Christian worldview thus grounds the modern notion of innate human dignity and universal human rights.

Second, since God is a noncorporeal (spiritual, not physical) Being, humanity is a unique union of physical body (created from the dust) and nonphysical soul (God-breathed). That is, there is more to the human person than a physical body. A Christian worldview thus has a fundamentally different conception of our nature than a naturalistic or atheistic worldview, in which the human person is a strictly material (physical) creature. The biblical picture of the human person is dualistic insofar as humans are composed of body and soul (traditionally called "body-soul dualism").[11] But the human person is also unitary, in that we are not fully human (complete) unless we are both body and soul—that is, the Gnostic/Platonic/Cartesian picture of the human person as essentially an immaterial soul that happens (unfortunately) to be planted in a material body is not biblical (it is antibiblical, in fact).[12] In short, the biblical picture of human composition (what are we made of?) is holistic dualism. We are an essential unity of a physical body (which God created good) and an immaterial soul.[13]

---

[11]For some of the major biblical texts indicating or supporting body-soul dualism, see Genesis 2:7; 1 Samuel 28:1-20; Job 19:25-27; Isaiah 14:9-11; 26:19; Jeremiah 31:31-33; Ezekiel 37:1-14; Daniel 12:2-3; Matthew 5:29-30; 10:28; 17:1-13; 22:23-33; 27:50; Luke 16:19-31; 23:42-43; 24:37-39; John 5:28-29; Acts 2:25-31; 23:5-8; Romans 8:10-11, 18-25; 1 Corinthians 7:34; 15:12-58; 2 Corinthians 4:7-18; 5:1-10; 12:2-4; 1 Thessalonians 4:13-18; 5:23; Hebrews 12:22-24; 1 Peter 1:9; 3:18-20.

[12]The Gnostics were an ancient (first century BC to third century AD) philosophical-religious group known for their radical body-soul dualism. Some schools of Gnosticism adopted a semi-Christian stance in the early years of the church, holding Jesus to be a divine imparter of knowledge who only put on human flesh like a coat. Gnosticism held that one is saved, and liberated to live eternally in the spiritual realm, via the acquisition of esoteric knowledge (the Greek gnōsis means "knowledge").

Plato was an ancient Greek philosopher (ca. 428–348 BC) known for his radical body-soul dualism. He understood the human soul to be eternal, and to have lived previously in a realm of "forms" along with other abstract perfections. The soul is currently trapped in a degraded physical body; the goal of life is to be liberated from physical embodiment through contemplation and to be reunited with the realm of the forms.

René Descartes was an early modern French philosopher (1596–1650) best known for his cogito, ergo sum (I think, therefore I am) argument for the existence of an independent and nonphysical self. Descartes's Christian faith emphasized God as creator and humanity as created in the image of God; but he also tended to denigrate humanity's physicality and embodiment.

[13]Note that the Christian doctrine of eternal life involves a resurrection body—the physical nature of human beings persists past our physical death. For more on holistic dualism, including biblical, scientific, and existential arguments, see John W. Cooper, *Body, Soul, and Life Everlasting: Biblical Anthropology and the Monism-Dualism Debate* (Grand Rapids: Eerdmans, 2000).

Third, if human beings are created in God's image, then it stands to reason that we share in many of God's attributes. James Sire notes several ways in which human beings are like God:

> Like God, we have *personality, self-transcendence, intelligence* (the capacity for reason and knowledge), *morality* (the capacity for recognizing and understanding good and evil), *gregariousness* or social capacity (our char-acteristic and fundamental desire and need for human companionship—community—especially represented by the "male and female" aspect) and *creativity* (the ability to imagine new things or to endow old things with new significance).[14]

Walsh and Middleton argue that God's image has both a "wide" and a "narrow" sense. The wide sense means something structural or static (like reason); the narrow sense has to do with a relational or dynamic approach (like measuring up to match God's image). They note that "the Scriptures are themselves the primary source of understanding of what it means to be in God's image." They believe that bearing God's image and likeness is closely tied to "our dominion over the earth, and the religious choice of serving God or idols."[15] In other words, their definition is linked to Genesis 1–2 and Genesis 3—that is, to culture and cult. Being made in God's image and likeness is directly tied to what we worship, and what we worship is connected to what we make of the world. We worship either God or idols.

The Christian conception of humanity as bearing the image of God does not mean that we are God or are just like God. Many of God's attributes—omnipotence, omniscience, omnibenevolence, omnipresence, for example—are *incommunicable*; that is, they are not able to be shared by anyone or anything other than God. Humanity, then, shares only in God's *communicable* attributes—those divine characteristics that are capable of being borne by his image-bearers.

Another crucial communicable attribute of God is love, or desire. Basically, we want and desire things. We are, indeed, created in the image and likeness of a God who wants and desires things, especially that we

---

[14]James W. Sire, *The Universe Next Door: A Basic Worldview Catalog*, 5th ed. (Downers Grove, IL: IVP Academic, 2009), 32, 34-35.
[15]Walsh and Middleton, *Transforming Vision,* 53.

love him supremely and that we love others as ourselves. So said Augustine (354–430), C. S. Lewis (1898–1963), and, most importantly, the Scriptures (see 1 Jn 4:7-12). A contemporary poet, David Hopes (b. 1950), speaks of our many wants and desires:

> we are of one ambition and one lineage:
> *Want.* Want not in proportion to any need,
> *want* unreasonable and overflowing,
> our days and nights overshadowed with *desire.*[16]

Calvin College philosopher James K. A. Smith says we have habits that are very powerful, and that we are what we love.[17] Unfortunately, most of our desires are disordered because we are sinful in nature and in practice. Sin is part of us. Of the many Scriptures that teach that we desire things in a disordered way, three will have to do.

We have worldly desires: "But the worries of this life, the deceitfulness of wealth and the *desires* for other things come in and choke the word, making it unfruitful" (Mk 4:19).

Some desire same-sex relations: "In the same way the men also abandoned natural relations with women and were inflamed with lust for [i.e., *desired*] one another. Men committed shameful acts with other men, and received in themselves the due penalty for their error" (Rom 1:27).

All our choices as non-Christians are made in the desires of the flesh (flesh is not physical but ethical): "So I say, walk by the Spirit, and you will not gratify the *desires* of the flesh" (Gal 5:16).

Our desires, then, are misplaced because of the pervasive influence of sin. However, our desires do not have to be completely negative. *We can take delight in God with positive results in terms of desire*: "Take delight in the LORD; / and he will give you the *desires* of your heart" (Ps 37:4).

Why are so many passages about desire negative in their teaching? The answer, I think, is the culture surrounding us and the culture's celebrities. We know about these celebrities, even if we haven't seen them in person

---

[16]David Brendon Hopes, "The Invalid of Park Street," in *Upholding Mystery: An Anthology of Contemporary Christian Poetry*, ed. David Impastato (New York: Oxford University Press, 1997), 205-6 (emphasis added).

[17]James K. A. Smith, *You Are What You Love: The Spiritual Power of Habit* (Grand Rapids: Brazos Press, 2016).

or been to one of their concerts! I have conducted research regarding our knowledge of popular culture, and the research has shown we all know the prominent celebrities (at the very least we watch *Entertainment Tonight*). For example, we know about Lady Gaga (b. 1986) though we probably have never been to one of her concerts (or if you have, you may have left early). Regardless, we are held captive by our culture, especially of the popular kind. And popular culture includes radio, TV, music, films, sex, fashion, the mall, and on and on the list could go. It's in the air we breathe. Popular culture trains our desires well.

In short, as 1 John 2:16 says, we succumb to "the lust of the flesh [or *sensualism*—sex, food, and fashion], the lust of the eyes [or *materialism*—money, wealth, and possessions], and the pride of life [or *egotism*—pride, accomplishments, and bragging]." These are not from God the Father but are from the fallen world and its culture. However, in addition to possessing wrong desires, believers are also redeemed. Believers are new creations in Christ. As 2 Corinthians 5:17 says, "Therefore, if anyone is in Christ, the new creation has come: The old has gone, the new is here!"

James Smith is known for saying "we are not just brains on a stick." As divine image-bearing lovers, we are ensouled bodies—not disembodied souls.[18] We are not just Auguste Rodin's statue *The Thinker*, though we are certainly not less. We are, indeed, lovers with hearts and minds! We need emotion and sympathy, not just explanation; we operate based on desires, not just syllogisms. Yet, there is no anti-intellectualism here. After all, we are to love God intellectually with all of our minds (see Mt 22:37). Still, above all, we want and desire things even if those wants and desires are disordered in sin.

Smith summarizes a critical component of his understanding of human nature:

> We have now articulated an alternative to the person-as-thinker and the person-as-believer in the person-as-lover model. We have highlighted four key elements of this model: Human persons are intentional creatures whose fundamental way of "intending" the world is love or desire. This

---

[18]James K. A. Smith, *Desiring the Kingdom: Worship, Worldview, and Cultural Formation*, Cultural Liturgies 1 (Grand Rapids: Baker Academic, 2009), 76.

love or desire—which is unconscious or noncognitive—is always a vision of the good life, some particular articulation of the kingdom. What primes us to be so oriented—and act accordingly—is a set of habits or dispositions that are formed in us through affective, bodily means, especially bodily practices, routines or rituals that grab hold of our hearts through our imagination, which is closely linked to our bodily senses.[19]

According to Smith, the body is significant epistemically (I once went to a U2 concert where I *felt* the music in my body as well as heard it with my ears; perhaps you have had the same experience at different concerts), a thought echoed by Pope John Paul II (1920–2005) in his "theology of the body."[20] Furthermore, Smith also says the shopping mall is particularly influential in cultural formation. Don't forget, we want things! What better place is there than a mall to buy the things we want?

Indeed, Smith's model represents something of a paradigm shift, especially in regard to higher education, when considering human identity. In fact, a central claim of Smith's *Desiring the Kingdom* "is that liturgies [which are any kind of worship]—whether 'sacred' or 'secular'—shape and constitute our identities by forming our most fundamental desires and our most basic attunement to the world. In short, liturgies make us certain kinds of people, and what defines us is what we *love*."[21] Traditions of various kinds have formed our liturgies. It behooves us to reflect on the liturgies that mark our lives, the habits that prompt them, and to ask whether they demonstrate a love and desire for God and his kingdom, or for the kingdom of this world.

We are created in the image and likeness of God who is love (1 Jn 4:8, 16). By divine design, then, we are lovers.

> *What* do you love [your objects]? *How* do you love the things that you love [your methods]? What do you *expect* to receive from the things you love [your expectations]? There aren't too many questions more important than these. Why? Because as we love in our hearts, so are we. We reap

---

[19]Ibid., 62-63.

[20]John Paul II, *The Theology of the Body: Human Love in the Divine Plan* (Boston: Pauline Books & Media, 1997); see also the websites for Theology of the Body Institute, http://tobinstitute.org/, and Theology of the Body Evangelization Team, http://tobet.org/, both accessed February 10, 2017.

[21]Smith, *Desiring the Kingdom*, 25.

what we love. Indeed, wherever we go and whatever we do, it is our loves that move us and take us there.[22]

Paul, Augustine, and C. S. Lewis all believed in the order of the loves (the *ordo amoris*). For example, Paul believed that what and how we loved controlled us:

> And this is my prayer: that your love may abound more and more in knowledge and depth of insight, so that you may be able to discern what is best and may be pure and blameless for the day of Christ, filled with the fruit of righteousness that comes through Jesus Christ—to the glory and praise of God. (Phil 1:9-11)

C. S. Lewis, though separated by many centuries, read the same book. Lewis once said this about people, whom he valued greatly:

> There are no *ordinary* people. You have never talked to a mere mortal. Nations, cultures, arts, civilization—these are mortal, and their life is to ours as is the life of a gnat. But it is immortals whom we joke with, work with, marry, snub, and exploit—immortal horrors or everlasting splendours. . . . Next to the Blessed Sacrament itself, your neighbour is the holiest object presented to your senses.[23]

In other words, *all* lives matter (whatever their color or ethnicity); Christian kindness to all is proper. We are all precious in his sight.

New Testament thought builds on the Old and sees humanity united and one in Christ, and that is a creation-restored reality. Sin broke humanity apart into fragments, but in Christ our unity and oneness can be restored: "For we were all baptized by one Spirit so as to form one body—whether Jews or Gentiles, slave or free—and we were all given the one Spirit to drink" (1 Cor 12:13).

What is our nature? Human beings are created in the image of God, endowed with dignity, value, and worth—composed of a good physical body and an immaterial soul. We possess personality, agency, intelligence, and creativity, and we are driven by loves and desires.

---

[22]David K. Naugle, *Reordered Love, Reordered Lives: Learning the Deep Meaning of Happiness* (Grand Rapids: Eerdmans, 2008), xi. See also Augustine, *Confessions*, trans. F. J. Sheed, 2nd ed. (Indianapolis: Hackett, 2006), 294-95, §13.9.

[23]C. S. Lewis, *The Weight of Glory and Other Addresses*, rev. ed., Collected Letters of C. S. Lewis (New York: HarperCollins, 2001), 46.

REFLECTION QUESTIONS

1 Why do the authors begin their discussion of Christian worldview with "what is our nature?"

2 Why is an understanding of the nature of God essential to understanding the nature of human persons?

3 What would you identify as some essential characteristics of God that are a necessary part of a faithful Christian worldview?

4 Blaise Pascal believes that the Christian doctrines of creation and fall are clearly evident in human nature and experience. Why? Do you agree? Why or why not?

5.2 What Is Our World?

Our world is created, fallen, and redeemed, and one day it will be glorified. What we want is the world's true story. God exists. As the eternally existing God, he has made known by revelation (the Bible) that he is the Maker of heaven and earth (Gen 1–2). In other words, the world is his creation and not just nature, as a naturalistic worldview would hold. We live in an enchanted universe—a universe charged with the grandeur of God. If creation were nature alone, then all would be random—time, energy, matter, and chance. As it is, there is nothing purposeless or meaningless or truly random (though it might appear random to us) in creation. All is intended by the God who creates and presides over his creation. It is evident, then, that the Christian and the naturalist (atheist) live in fundamentally different world(view)s!

The first fact about our world is that it is created. At the same time, the world is also deeply fallen. People are angry, and so is God (see Rom 1:18). After all, we wandered off from him and sought self-rule (autonomy) instead of submitting to his loving lordship. However, Jesus Christ has redeemed both believers and the world as a new creation. As Jonathan R. Wilson says,

> In the coming together of God's work of creation and redemption in life, our vision is directed forward to the new creation. Thus, creation and redemption may be known by faith to be one in their "end" [in the sense

of fulfillment] in the new creation. . . . We may say simply that God works creation and redemption for this: the new creation.[24]

In different words, we can say, salvation in Christ is holistic in scope (see Rom 8:20-21). There is a oneness in Scripture. For example, here's a short story. A friend of mine and I were driving down the highway not long ago and came upon a church advertising itself as Full Gospel. Of course, we both knew what was meant, but my friend said, half-jokingly, "Well, who would want a half-gospel church!" I answered, "Apparently, lots of Christian people do! They go all out for a two-chapter gospel in the fall and redemption, instead of a four-chapter gospel of creation, fall, redemption, and glorification! The two-chapter gospel of fall and redemption only—that's a half gospel." Returning to the church sign, I laughed and said, "I guess that's why they say Full Gospel."

Our world is a dual world: natural and supernatural. We certainly do not want to ascribe negativity to the natural world as God's creation (see Gen 1:31; he creates it "good"!). Obviously, there is the natural, physical world—stars, sun, moon, earth, trees, oceans, plants, and animals. The natural world operates according to physical (natural) laws that God ordained and instituted, and thereby reflect God's glory (Ps 19:1). Humanity was made as God's image to rule over it.

> Then God said, "Let us make mankind in our image, in our likeness, so that they may rule over the fish in the sea and the birds in the sky, over the livestock and all the wild animals, and over all the creatures that move along the ground."
>
> So God created mankind in his own image,
>   in the image of God he created them;
>   male and female he created them.
>
> God blessed them and said to them, "Be fruitful and increase in number; fill the earth and subdue it. Rule over the fish in the sea and the birds in the sky and over every living creature that moves on the ground." (Gen 1:26-28)
>   The LORD God took the man and put him in the Garden of Eden to work it and take care of it. (Gen 2:15)

---

[24]Jonathan R. Wilson, *God's Good World: Reclaiming the Doctrine of Creation* (Grand Rapids: Baker Academic, 2013), 53.

The physical world, then, is created by God, declared good, and entrusted to humanity's stewardship.

Along with the natural, physical world, there is also a supernatural or spiritual world. This world above, then, must also be taken into consideration when developing a biblical/Christian worldview. The question is how these two worlds—the physical, natural world God made and the supernatural world of God—relate to each other? A number of things can be said about this relationship. The first has been said already, in that the original creation is fulfilled in Christ. Creation has its final end or *telos* (fulfillment) in him who brings a new creation (see also Gal 6:15).

STOP & PAUSE

Biblical Worldview Insight

And Elisha prayed, "Open his eyes, LORD, so that he may see." Then the LORD opened the servant's eyes, and he looked and saw the hills full of horses and chariots of fire all around Elisha. (2 Kings 6:17)

The King of Aram has sought to capture Elisha, and Elisha's servant is frightened by the assembled army of horses and chariots outside of Elisha's city. But Elisha sees what his servant cannot—that the armies of the Lord are protecting Elisha from potential harm. Sometimes what we see is dependent on what we are willing to see.

Sight is used with exquisite irony in 2 Kings 6. After God opens the eyes of Elisha's servant, he responds to Elisha's further prayer by striking the Aramean army with communal blindness and handing them over to the king of Israel.

Allow God to guide your sight! Are you willing to see his world?

Second, the eternal, spiritual world of God shines through this physical world, like architects do in their buildings. I call this arrangement a "sacramental perspective" (see Is 6:3). All things are holy (see Col 1:16-20). You best take off your shoes. Third, we get to know God, "treasuring God"—as Joe Rigney and John Piper say[25]—through his creation. No one has spoken about this sacramental arrangement better than Alexander Schmemann in *For the Life of the World*:

---

[25]Joe Rigney, *The Things of Earth: Treasuring God by Enjoying His Gifts*, foreword by John Piper (Wheaton, IL: Crossway, 2015).

All that exists is God's gift to man, and it all exists to make God known to man, to make man's life communion with God. It is divine love made food, made life for man. God *blesses* everything He creates, and, in biblical language, this means that He makes all creation the sign and means of His presence and wisdom, love and revelation: "O taste and see that the Lord is good."

"*Homo sapiens*" "*homo faber*" . . . yes, but, first of all, "*homo adorans*." The first, the basic definition of man is that he is *the priest*. He stands in the center of the world and unifies it in his act of blessing God, of both receiving the world from God and offering it to God—and by filling the world with this eucharist, he transforms life, the one that he receives from the world, into life in God, into communion with Him. The world was created as the "matter," the material of one all-embracing eucharist, and man was created as the priest of this cosmic sacrament.[26]

Fourth, in this world, God has become man. Planet Earth, our created home, is the visited planet. "Do you mean to tell me," said the little angel, "that [God] stooped so low as to become one of those creeping, crawling creatures of that floating ball?"[27] Theologically speaking, God the Son becoming man, without the diminishment of either the divine or human, is called the incarnation (see Jn 1:14). Christ has deep meaning, as a former pope once declared: "In Christ and through Christ man has acquired full awareness of his dignity, of the heights to which he is raised, of the surpassing worth of his own humanity, and of the meaning of his existence."[28] The dignity of human persons arising out of the mystery of the incarnate Christ is the cornerstone of the Christian humanistic worldview, the implications of which embrace the totality of life.

Fifth and finally, our world possesses a balance of immanence and transcendence. God is preeminent and utterly transcendent (above and beyond the physical universe). Yet he does invade this world from above.

---

[26]Alexander Schmemann, *For the Life of the World: Sacraments and Orthodoxy*, rev. ed. (Crestwood, NY: St. Vladimir's Seminary Press, 1973), 14, 15. *Homo sapiens* means "wise man," and *homo faber* means "man the maker," while *homo adorans* means "man the worshiper."

[27]J. B. Phillips, "The Angel's Point of View (or 'The Visited Planet')," *Grace and Truth*, March 25, 2014, https://graceandtruth.me/2014/03/25/the-angels-point-of-view-or-the-visited-planet/.

[28]John Paul II, *The Redeemer of Man: Redemptor Hominis*, encyclical letter (Boston: Pauline Books & Media, 1979), 20-21. For a discussion of the pope's vision of Christian humanism, see Andrew N. Woznicki, *The Dignity of Man as a Person: Essays on the Christian Humanism of His Holiness John Paul II* (San Francisco: Society of Christ Publications, 1987).

The incarnation is just one example. All miracles, like crossing a dry Red Sea, healing the sick, and the resurrection of Jesus, are examples of the transcendent God making himself immanent in our physical reality. If you believe in God as Creator, then miracles are not only possible but to be expected! As many would say, we live in an open universe, not a closed universe. A closed universe would be one wherein everything that occurs is the result of a physical cause: there is nothing outside of the physical box of cause-and-effect in a closed universe to bring about effects in the physical world. In an open universe, the physical box is open to the involvement of causal agents that exist outside (transcendent to) that box. In other words, an open universe holds that God, who created the physical universe, can and will act within the physical universe, while a closed universe holds such divine intervention/action to be impossible. In short, our world is God's world—created, sustained, and directed by God the Father, Son, and Holy Spirit.

REFLECTION QUESTIONS

1 Why does the author say that there is nothing random in our world?

2 What are the two natures, or two sides, to reality embraced by a Christian worldview?

5.3 WHAT IS OUR PROBLEM?

> Is it not . . . clear as day that man's condition is dual? The point is that if man had never been corrupted, he would, in his innocence, confidently enjoy both truth and felicity, and, if man had never been anything but corrupt, he would have no idea either of truth or bliss. But unhappy as we are (and we should be less so if there were no element of greatness in our condition) we have an idea of happiness but we cannot attain it. We perceive an image of the truth and possess nothing but falsehood, being equally incapable of absolute ignorance and certain knowledge; so obvious is it that we once enjoyed a degree of perfection from which we have unhappily fallen.[29]

---

[29]Pascal, *Pensées*, pensée 131, 35.

In brief, the problem according to a Christian worldview is sin, which results in life in a fallen world. Adam and Eve rebelled against God in Genesis 3. What are the consequences of their capitulation to the temptations of the devil?

First, there is a spiritual or theological result: we humans are separated from God in our sin. The text in Genesis 3:8 says that we hid ourselves from God among the trees of the garden. In sin, we separate ourselves from our Maker. The second result is that human beings are separated from themselves, psychologically. The text in Genesis 3:10 says that the man was afraid (fear) because he was naked (shame), so he hid himself (guilt). Fear, shame, and guilt replaced peace with God and all things in creation (in Hebrew, *shalom*). As a result, we are psychologically broken. Third, the man blamed the woman, and this is the origin of our marital and relational problems. In Genesis 3:12, the man first blamed God and then his wife, and finally he admitted his own sin: "The woman you put here with me—she gave me some fruit from the tree, and I ate it." The fourth and final consequence of sin is that we are separated from the paradise of the garden. Genesis 3:22-24 declares that man would no longer be permitted to reside in Eden and eat from the tree of life.

Not only are the consequences of human sin and rebellion catastrophic; the consequences are also universal. We live in a fallen world, amid fallen people. "There is no difference between Jew and Gentile, for all have sinned and fall short of the glory of God" (Rom 3:22-23). Furthermore, we are utterly unable to rectify our fallen nature on our own accord. We need God's redemptive intervention: "For it is by grace you have been saved, through faith—and this is not from yourselves, it is the gift of God—not by works, so that no one can boast" (Eph 2:8-9).

Like the first human beings, however, we have been trying to cover our own sin with inadequate fig leaves, trying to make it into God's heaven on our own steam. But this leaves us despondent. We have failed miserably at trying to overcome our own sin (which is autonomy or lawlessness; see 1 Jn 3:4), and we have failed in multiple ways. We imagine God asking, "Is your sin covered? Why should I let you into my heaven?"

Human beings have traditionally pursued three paths in their efforts to save themselves. First and most prominently, we have tried to save ourselves through our good works. We desire our sins to be covered and to get into God's heaven. For example, I went to a funeral once where the minister valorized the deceased person because he delivered Meals on Wheels. Delivering meals to shut-ins is a good endeavor, but it will not cover your sin. Good works alone do not count. So strike one.

Second, we hope to cover our sins and go to heaven when we die by being a good, moral person. At least I am not as bad as the other person. However, Jesus told a parable to people "who were confident of their own righteousness and looked down on everyone else" (Lk 18:9). The moral of the parable is that he who thinks he is righteous is farthest from redemption, while he who acknowledges his own sinfulness is redeemable (Lk 18:14). It is good to be morally good, but this will not cover your sin or get you into heaven. Thus, being a good, moral person doesn't count. So strike two.

Third, we hope to cover our sins and go to heaven when we die by going to church, at least twice a year. "At least I go to church on Christmas and Easter!" But there are a lot of CEOs—Christmas and Easter only Christians—out there. Again, going to church is a good thing, but it won't cover your sin or get you into heaven. So strike three. You're out, literally! You cannot get yourself there, but Jesus can.

I am exhibit A. I grew up in church, but I didn't know who Jesus was. I knew he played an important role, but if he were to have asked me, "Who do *you* say that I am?," I wouldn't have had a clue (see Mt 16:13-20). That is, until I watched a Billy Graham Crusade on TV at my mother's encouragement, and Billy Graham (b. 1918) told me about Jesus. Graham said Jesus lived, died on a cross, and rose from the dead to cover our sins so that we could go to heaven when we die (see 1 Cor 15:3-4). Theologians emphasize that Jesus' death was an atoning sacrifice and a propitiation. *Atonement* carries the connotations of righting (making reparation for) a wrong, while *propitiation* means turning away wrath. In both senses, Jesus did for us what we could not do—paid the price for our sin ("the wages of sin is death," Rom 6:23) and turned away the righteous wrath of God expressed against sin (Rom 1:18).

Like John Wesley, when I heard these words, I felt my heart strangely warmed. I believed in Jesus, and I asked him to be my Savior and Lord.

He has been ever since, thanks be to God, and he can be yours too, when you believe! I embarked on a lifelong journey of discipleship and spiritual growth. With a new mindset and a new set of loves, I was developing a new worldview.

> Amazing grace! How sweet the sound
> That saved a wretch like me!
> I once was lost, but now I'm found;
> Was blind, but now I see.
>
> . . .
>
> My chains are gone
> I've been set free
> My God, my Savior has ransomed me.[30]

As we consider the worldview question (what is our problem?), we are inescapably drawn to a discussion of ethics and morality. Asking what is wrong with the world (what is our problem?) requires that there be such a thing as right and wrong. Identification of rightness and wrongness involves ethical adjudication and moral determination.

C. S. Lewis used a fleet of ships to illustrate different aspects or branches of ethics. Each individual boat must know how to keep shipshape. That is the realm of personal ethics. Boats also need to keep from bumping into each other. That is the realm of social or political ethics. Finally, the entire fleet needs to know where it is heading. That is, ethically speaking, the greatest or highest good (or *summum bonum* in Latin). As Lewis says, we do not want to aim for New York but wind up in Calcutta.[31]

Worldview shapes our view of ethics, like it does everything else. For example, the existence of God (or lack thereof) affects morality. If there is a God, ethics are given foundation and shape. His will, Word, and character are the final source in determining that which is good. If there is not a God, morality is still affected. We human beings (individually or

---

[30]Chris Tomlin, "Amazing Grace (My Chains Are Gone)," incorporating the words of "Amazing Grace," by John Newton, *See the Morning*, Sparrow/sixsteps, 2006.
[31]Lewis, *Mere Christianity*, 69-75.

corporately) would then be on our own to make up the rules of the game of life. In other words, God's existence or the lack thereof is ethically determinative.

Within a Christian worldview, God the Father, Son, and Holy Spirit serves as our touchstone proposition, our ultimate reality. Thus, if there are red lights (stop that) and green lights (go for it) that govern the moral traffic of human affairs, such signals must be put in place by God. Two questions follow: Is everyone aware of these red and green lights? And, where do the red and green lights originate—God's Word or God's essence?

A Christian worldview holds that we are all aware of the red and green lights in the universe. It seems that all humans recognize that there is something terribly wrong with each one of us. As C. S. Lewis notes in *Mere Christianity*, we know that there is a moral law, and we know that we constantly break it (sin). The moral law noted by Lewis governs the realm of ethics, and Lewis even saw morality as a clue to the meaning of the universe. The belief that there is an inborn sense of morality is called natural law. We have a built-in or natural sense (it comes as standard equipment with the car, or it's the default mode on the digital device) of right and wrong: "They [Gentiles] show that the requirements of the law are written on their hearts, their consciences also bearing witness, and their thoughts sometimes accusing them and at other times even defending them" (Rom 2:15).

Where then does the moral law originate—God's Word (will) or God's essence? I say that it's both his Word and his essence. Is something right or wrong because it conforms to God's essence, or did God simply say what is right and wrong, without anyone telling him what to say or do? As Norman Geisler opined once (I don't think this was Geisler's opinion), God could have just as easily decreed hatred and cruelty as ethical norms instead of love and justice. Is something righteous and just because God willed it (called voluntarism because the ethical word springs from him voluntarily), or does God will something because it is right (called essentialism because it aligns with God's essence)? Could it be both his will and essence? I have suggested this!

Is there a way of combining these two schools of thought? For example, surely the divine commandments prohibiting adultery and fornication do not apply to God himself. Hence, these commandments must stem from God's will alone. At the same time, they are a reflection of his righteous character, and also come from God's understanding of human nature. Perhaps other divine laws of prohibition, permission, and obligation show forth both God's will and holiness in a synchronous way. The Scriptures, then, suggest that the divine realities of who God is and what he has chosen as the basis for the ethics revealed in Scripture and in nature (Deut 32:3-4; Rom. 9:11). Regardless, God whispers his divine will naturally to us in our consciences, and Scripture clarifies what he expects of his people in the more clear and precise commandments of the Bible.[32]

Since the moral requirements that come from God's word and essence in special revelation were covered in chapter four, only one verse will be given here: "Be perfect, therefore, as your heavenly Father is perfect" (Mt 5:48).

However, perfection comes later. Remember, neither we nor the world has been glorified . . . yet. Remember that redemption comes in two stages: the already (realized eschatology) and the not yet (future eschatology). In the meantime, we continue to battle our fallen condition and the sinful nature within us. As Paul declares:

> The acts of the flesh are obvious: sexual immorality, impurity and debauchery; idolatry and witchcraft; hatred, discord, jealousy, fits of rage, selfish ambition, dissensions, factions and envy; drunkenness, orgies, and the like. I warn you, as I did before, that those who live like this will not inherit the kingdom of God. (Gal 5:19-21)

Similarly, Augustine's magisterial *The City of God* emphasizes the ubiquity of our struggle against ongoing sin:

> Carking anxieties, agitations of mind, disappointments, fears, frenzied joys, quarrels, disputes, wars, treacheries, hatreds, enmities, deceits, flattery, fraud, theft, rapine, perfidy, ambition, envy, murder, parricide, cruelty, savagery, villainy, lust, promiscuity, indecency, unchastity, fornication, adultery, incest, unnatural vice in men and women (disgusting acts too filthy to be named), sacrilege, collusion, false witness, unjust

---

[32]David K. Naugle, *Philosophy: A Student's Guide*, Reclaiming the Christian Intellectual Tradition (Wheaton, IL: Crossway, 2012), 77.

SCENIC VIEW

*Contemporary Cultural
Worldview Meditation*

"Ka-Ching!" and *The Big Short*— The Love of Money

Pop star Shania Twain's 2002 hit single "Ka-Ching!" takes a playfully critical look at consumerism and greed in North America. Twain sings:

> We live in a greedy little world,
> That teaches every little boy and girl
> To earn as much as they can possibly,
> Then turn around and
> Spend it foolishly
> We've created us a credit card mess
> We spend the money that we don't possess
> Our religion is to go and blow it all
> So it's shoppin' every Sunday at the mall
> All we ever want is more
> A lot more than we had before
> So take me to the nearest store.[a]

The lyrics, music video, and genre are full of self-deprecating irony, as Twain performs draped in expensive clothing and jewelry, criticizing the very motivations that fuel her own stardom. The love of money is indeed a powerful idol!

The 2015 Adam McKay film *The Big Short* highlights the same idolatrous desire. The movie stars Christian Bale, Steve Carrell, Ryan Gosling, and Brad Pitt as "four denizens in the world of high finance [who] predict the credit and housing bubble collapse of the mid-2000s, and decide to take on the big banks for their greed and lack of foresight."[b]

(continued on next page)

judgment, violence, robbery, and all other such evils which do not immediately come to mind, although they never cease to beset this life of man—*all these evils belong to man in his wickedness, and they all spring from that root of error and perverted affection which every son of Adam brings with him at his birth.*[33]

We do live in a messy, fallen world and desire all sorts of things other than he whom we were created to desire. Kyle Idleman, launching from John's threefold division of worldly desires ("the lust of the flesh, the lust of the eyes, and the pride of life"; 1 Jn 2:16), identifies three main centers of idolatrous desire in contemporary life: pleasure (food, sex, entertainment), power (success, money, achievement), and love (romance, family, self).[34] Certainly one of the many things we want in our messiness is money and lots of it, something sternly rebuked by Paul: "The love of money is a root of all kinds of evil" (1 Tim 6:10).

So we have sinned and wandered off from God. Genesis 3

---

[33] Augustine, *Concerning the City of God Against the Pagans*, trans. Henry Bettenson (New York: Penguin, 1984), 1065, §22.22 (emphasis added).
[34] Kyle Idleman, *Gods at War: Defeating the Idols That Battle for Your Heart* (Grand Rapids: Zondervan, 2013).

and Romans 1 tell the sad story well. We live in a fallen, messy world. These are our problems. Sin and its effects ravage individuals, societies, and all of creation. "What a wretched man I am! Who will rescue me from this body that is subject to death? Thanks be to God, who delivers me through Jesus Christ our Lord!" (Rom 7:24-25).

REFLECTION QUESTIONS

1 What is the origin of sin and evil in the world according to a Christian worldview?

2 Outline the fourfold consequences of sin and the fall.

3 What do you think are some prominent contemporary examples of fallen pursuit of wrong desires?

Andrew Trotter, Christian film critic and head of the Consortium of Christian Study Centers, writes of *The Big Short*:

> The unrelenting greed that the bankers of Wall Street played in this scandalous blot on American business history comes in for some much-needed direct approbation, and any Christian should be glad of that. If nothing else, it is a wonderful study in idol-making (from a number of different perspectives) and explores the sins of both materialism and acquisitiveness at deep levels."[c]

Jesus warns us, "No one can serve two masters. . . . You cannot serve both God and money" (Mt 6:24). Has our Christian worldview been compromised by an undue attachment to the riches of this world rather than to our eternal riches in Christ? Examine your priorities and your gods!

---

[a]Shania Twain, "Ka-Ching!," *Up!*, Mercury Nashville, 2002.
[b]*The Big Short*, directed by Adam McKay (Plan B Entertainment and Regency Enterprises, 2015). IMDb, www.imdb.com/title/tt1596363.
[c]Andrew Trotter, "The Big Short," *Consortium of Christian Study Centers* (blog), December 29, 2015, https://studycentersonline.org/blog-2/.

5.4 WHAT IS OUR END?

When we consider the final worldview question, we need to remember that "our end" is intended in two ways: our ongoing purpose of life and our final destination (what happens after we die).

The Westminster Shorter Catechism (1646–1647) holds the answer to the first question. The catechism first asks, "What is the chief end of man [or we might say, humanity]?" It answers that humanity's chief end "is to glorify God, and to enjoy him forever." This is our purpose, ongoing throughout life and beyond. Within a Christian worldview, the chief end of man is a nonnegotiable!

For the most part, the catechism is correct, but it needs expansion. Our chief end is to glorify and honor God in all we do. The church is a called people, called by God to bring him glory and honor (see, e.g., 1 Cor 1:2). This calling is comprehensive or holistic and includes work, play, family life, and free time. You name it, and we are called to glorify and to honor him in it (see Col 3:17). Two examples will suffice. You are called in all your work: "Work at it with all your heart, as working for the Lord, not for human masters" (Col 3:23). You are called in family life: if you are a son or daughter, then honor your parents, or if you are a father, don't provoke your children to anger (Eph 6:1-4). This is our purpose in life, bringing glory and honor to God in all things.

The meaning of life is found in another familiar quote that includes almost the entire Christian story. Augustine's spiritual autobiography, *Confessions*, begins with one of the best-known lines in Christian literature: "For Thou hast made us for Thyself [creation] and our hearts are restless [fall] til they rest in Thee [redemption]."[35] It turns out, when you add God, revelation, and glorification to this quotation, you have not only the complete Christian worldview story but also the meaning of life . . . in God. We rest in him.

God is the meaning of life, but not all people know God, belong to God, or find meaning in God. Despite frequently being used as synonyms, *purpose* and *meaning* are not the same. Purpose and meaning are as different as the material is from the spiritual. You can have a purpose in life (even the wicked and non-Christians do: see Prov 16:4) without having the meaning of life in salvation in God. Again, the meaning of life is found in God the Trinity, through Jesus Christ in the power of the Holy Spirit. In other words, the gospel of Christ is the meaning of life. Believe in Christ, and you will have meaning and you can develop a new worldview: saved and with meaning!

What is our end, our *telos*, in terms of meaning and purpose? For a Christian worldview, our end is the glory of God, serving him and enjoying him forever. What about our *telos* in terms of final destination? What happens when we die? Where are we going?

---

[35] Augustine, *Confessions*, trans. F. J. Sheed, 2nd ed. (Indianapolis: Hackett, 2006), 3, §1.

The Apostles' Creed indicates our future too. It closes, some people seem to assume, as follows (pay close attention): "I believe in the Holy Spirit; the holy catholic Church, the communion of saints; *the eternality of the soul*, and life everlasting. Amen."

But wait! That's not in the Bible, the line in italics! Rather, that's Platonistic otherworldliness, an unconscious embrace and exaltation of Plato's forms in the otherworldly heavenlies (put on your thinking caps here). The implication (explicit in Plato) is that all things "below," in our created, physical world are merely poor, corrupt images of the real thing(s) (Plato's forms). So if there is life after death, it must be (and we should want it to be) a disembodied eternal soul-life in the realm of the forms. At least this is what Plato said. The moral of this story is do not follow Plato on this point.

The Apostles' Creed really concludes like this: "I believe in . . . the communion of saints; the forgiveness of sins; *the resurrection of the body*; and the life everlasting. Amen." The resurrection of the body is the biblical depiction of our after-death destination. What happens when we die? We are resurrected—some to eternal life with God, some to eternal damnation apart from God (see, e.g., Mt 25:46).

It has always been popular to question the existence of hell, where the resurrected bodies and spirits of unredeemed sinners experience torment and anguish in their eternal separation from God. Never has disbelief in hell been more popular than in contemporary Western society; such disbelief has even permeated many branches of the Christian church, such that followers of Christ shy away from talking about the reality of hell, instead desiring to talk about the niceness of heaven. While an appeal to salvation should always be based on the love of God and the promise of eternal life in his presence in heaven, we need to have a balanced, biblical presentation of eternity. Difficult though it may be, such a balanced presentation of the eternal destination of human beings includes a forceful discussion regarding the fact that there is a real place called hell, where the souls of the damned will forever experience torment, punishment, and separation from all the goodness of God.[36]

---

[36]For some biblical passages about the reality and nature of hell, see Matthew 5:29-30; 13:40-42, 47-50; 18:8-9; 25:31-46; Luke 16:19-26; 2 Thessalonians 1:6-9; Jude 6-7, 13; Revelation 14:9-11; 20:7-15.

While unredeemed humans will experience eternal separation from God in hell, those who are found in Christ will be resurrected to eternal life in a renewed heavens and earth. Contrary to Platonic otherworldliness, Christianity valorizes or values the physical or material world. Indeed, a Christian worldview values the physical more highly than does any other major world religion. When God creates, he repeatedly declares of his physical creation, "it is good" (Gen 1:10, 12, 18, 25, 31). God's redemption of the world through Christ is not merely a spiritual (or soul-oriented) salvation. All of physical creation eagerly anticipates redemption and glorification (Rom 8:19-21). Our own redemption is a redemption of the *whole* person (body and soul); our glorification likewise will involve not just a redeemed soul but a resurrected body. New Testament scholar N. T. Wright helpfully calls our resurrection body "transphysical," indicating both its continuity with our created earthly body (physical) and its discontinuity with our predeath bodily experience (trans).[37]

In Philippians 3, Paul says that we wait for Jesus from heaven, where lies our true citizenship (so much for nationalism), and that one day we will have a new, resurrected body like Christ's (called "glorification" in this book). Note how this passage combines the spiritual and the physical worlds:

> But our citizenship is in heaven. And we eagerly await a Savior from there, the Lord Jesus Christ, who, by the power that enables him to bring everything under his control, will transform our lowly bodies so that they will be like his glorious body. (Phil 3:20-21)

Furthermore, 1 Corinthians talks extensively about the nature of the believer's resurrection body, based on Christ's own resurrection.

> But Christ has indeed been raised from the dead, the firstfruits of those who have fallen asleep. For since death came through a man, the resurrection of the dead comes also through a man. For as in Adam all die, so in Christ all will be made alive. . . .
>
> So will it be with the resurrection of the dead. The body that is sown is perishable, it is raised imperishable; it is sown in dishonor, it is raised

---

[37]N. T. Wright, *The Resurrection of the Son of God*, Christian Origins and the Question of God (Minneapolis: Fortress, 2003), 3:711.

in glory; it is sown in weakness, it is raised in power; it is sown a natural body, it is raised a spiritual body. . . .

Listen, I tell you a mystery: We will not all sleep, but we will all be changed—in a flash, in the twinkling of an eye, at the last trumpet. For the trumpet will sound, the dead will be raised imperishable, and we will be changed. For the perishable must clothe itself with the imperishable, and the mortal with immortality. (1 Cor 15:20-22, 42-44, 51-53)

Concerning Paul's discussion of the resurrection in 1 Corinthians, N. T. Wright says:

This is the point above all where Paul is trying to teach the Corinthians to think eschatologically, within the Jewish categories of "apocalyptic"—not of an "immanent expectation" of the end the world, but of the way in which the future has already burst into the present, so that the present time is characterized by a mixture of fulfillment and expectation, of "now" and "not yet," pointing towards a future in which what happened at the first Easter will be implemented fully and the true God will be all in all.[38]

There is a future in which the whole world, including ourselves, will be renewed and glorified (see Rev 21–22). We are calling that future day "glorification." It is not that God will make *new things*; rather, it is that God will make *all things new*. This reminds me of a saying that is worth repeating: "God does not make junk and He does not junk what he has made."[39]

But, if I understand him correctly, Plato might think that God does make junk! After all, God created physical matter, and to Plato physical stuff is junk. A lot of contemporary Christianity is just "Platonism for the 'people,'" as Friedrich Nietzsche once wrote in the preface to *Beyond Good and Evil* (1886).[40]

Some hymns are just "Platonism for the 'people,'" too. Hear these partial lyrics to "I'll Fly Away," and tell me if the song is biblical or Platonic in content (you have to admit, the tune is rather catchy):

---

[38]Ibid., 333.
[39]Albert M. Wolters, *Creation Regained: Biblical Basics for a Reformational Worldview*, 2nd ed. (Grand Rapids: Eerdmans, 2005), 57.
[40]Friedrich Nietzsche, *Beyond Good and Evil: Prelude to a Philosophy of the Future*, trans. Helen Zimmern (1907; repr., New York: Tribeca, 2010), 2.

When the shadows of this life have gone,
I'll fly away;
Like a bird from prison bars has flown,
I'll fly away (I'll fly away).

Chorus

I'll fly away, O Glory
I'll fly away (in the morning);
When I die, hallelujah, by and by,
I'll fly away (I'll fly away).[41]

Which hymn is more faithful to a Christian worldview—"I'll Fly Away"
or "This Is My Father's World"?

This is my Father's world,
and to my listening ears
all nature sings, and round me rings
the music of the spheres.
This is my Father's world:
I rest me in the thought
of rocks and trees, of skies and seas;
his hand the wonders wrought.[42]

The bottom line is this: we must pay more attention to the lyrics of
hymns and songs we sing in church! Some hymns and songs just may be
reading the Bible through Platonic lenses, and end up dead wrong theologically. The composers may be Platonists without realizing it. We must
listen and sing very carefully, else we succumb to the same fate as the
composers of the hymns and songs we sing. Self-examination is crucial!

So our choices are a Platonic otherworldliness or a down-to-earth
Christian worldview that embraces the goodness of physical creation.
Which choice shall be for you? Personally, I hope you enjoy God and his
creation forever, and bring glory to him forever, in a resurrected body
forever, in the new heavens and earth, forever and ever! Amen!

When we survey our meaning and purpose within a Christian worldview,
as well as our ultimate destination (eschatology), we cannot help but also

---

[41]Albert E. Brumley, "I'll Fly Away," *Wonderful Message*, Hartford Music, 1932.
[42]Maltbie Davenport Babcock, "This Is My Father's World" (original poem), *Thoughts for Every-Day Living*, 1901.

speak of history. We begin by noting that God himself in his attributes is the standard of history, for history is his-story, especially his story of creation, fall, redemption, and glorification. In other words and in short, history is theistic in nature. It is not cyclical as the Hindus would have us believe (see chapter eight). As a Christian, one sees history on a line (or linear) in perspective, leading to glorification or a final fulfillment in Christ.

Within history, we all have been endowed with a measure of historical power, or the power to shape history. Some have more historical power than others. Some shape their families, their workplace, and their communities; others, like the president of the United States, shape the whole world. The president has been endowed with loads of historical power.

People have the ability to shape history to some extent. Redemptive history, however, is within the purview of God alone. Redemptive history, or the story of God's redemptive work among humanity, starts with Adam's faith in the promise of the woman's offspring (Gen 3:15), continues through Noah (Gen 6–9) and Abraham and Israel in the Old Testament (Gen 12–50 and elsewhere), and culminates in Jesus and his church in the New Testament. Believers are part of this salvation history as seen in the book of Acts. James Sire says of history:

> In short, the most important aspect of the theistic concept of history is that history has meaning because God—the Logos, meaning itself—is behind all events, "sustaining all things by his powerful word" (Heb. 1:3) but also "in all things . . . [working] for the good of those who love him, who have been called according to his purpose" (Rom. 8:28). Behind the apparent chaos of events stands the loving God sufficient for all.[43]

REFLECTION QUESTIONS

1 What does the Westminster Catechism say about the "chief end" of man? Do you agree? Why or why not? How would you articulate our end within a Christian worldview?

2 What does a Christian worldview hold with regard to what happens to human beings after physical death?

---

[43]Sire, *Universe Next Door*, 43-44.

3 How does a Christian view of time and history differ from a Hindu view of time and history? Why does it matter?

5.5 Summary: The Motivation of a Christian Worldview

One's worldview does not merely provide a conceptual understanding of life, the universe, and everything. A worldview also supplies an individual's priorities and informs his commitments and actions. In short, as argued in chapter two, worldview determines our life motivation. Within a Christian worldview, believers are motivated by their calling in Christ. In Ephesians 4:1 Paul writes, "As a prisoner for the Lord, then, I urge you to live a life worthy of the calling you have received."

Believers are also motivated by their walk in the Holy Spirit, as Paul writes in Galatians 5:16-17. "So I say, walk by the Spirit, and you will not gratify the desires of the flesh. For the flesh desires what is contrary to the Spirit, and the Spirit what is contrary to the flesh. They are in conflict with each other, so that you are not to do whatever you want." There is a war inside, but we will win it because of a strong calling and the indwelling of the Holy Spirit; if we possess and live a Christian worldview, these are our strongest motivators.

STOP & PAUSE

Biblical Worldview Insight

Galatians 5:16-26 is a well-known passage that contrasts the "desires of the flesh" with the "fruit of the Spirit":

So I say, walk by the Spirit, and you will not gratify the desires of the flesh. For the flesh desires what is contrary to the Spirit, and the Spirit what is contrary to the flesh. They are in conflict with each other, so that you are not to do whatever you want. But if you are led by the Spirit, you are not under the law.

The acts of the flesh are obvious: sexual immorality, impurity and debauchery; idolatry and witchcraft; hatred, discord, jealousy, fits of rage, selfish ambition, dissensions, factions and envy; drunkenness, orgies, and the like. I warn you, as I did before, that those who live like this will not inherit the kingdom of God.

But the fruit of the Spirit is love, joy, peace, forbearance, kindness, goodness, faithfulness, gentleness and self-control. Against such things there is no law. Those who belong to Christ Jesus have crucified the flesh with its passions and desires. (Gal 5:16-24)

In Galatians 5:25, Paul concludes: "Since we live by the Spirit, let us keep in step with the Spirit." Paul is encouraging the Galatian Christians to have their lives oriented toward God, not the world. Our lives are to be motivated by obedience to God and his Word rather than being marked by rebellion and disobedience.

In this chapter, we have outlined a Christian worldview in propositional form. What is our nature? We are created in the image of God; as his image-bearers, we are a holistic union of body and soul, possessing personality, creativity, and agency. We are driven by desires and loves. What is our world? This is our Father's world, created by him with intricate beauty; the universe reflects and manifests his glory and awesomeness. What is our problem? Sin and its ravaging effects. What is our end? Our purpose is to glorify God and enjoy him forever.

MASTERING THE MATERIAL

When you finish reading this chapter, you should be able to

✔ Explain why ultimate reality is the leading proposition of any worldview.

✔ Articulate what it means to be created in God's image.

✔ Explain what worldliness is from a Christian/biblical vantage point.

✔ Articulate how a Christian worldview answers the four core worldview questions.

✔ Explain a biblical view of ethics and history.

✔ Understand how a Christian worldview motivates one's life and actions.

Glossary of Terms for Chapter Five

communicable and incommunicable attributes—Attributes (or characteristics) of God that *can* (communicable) or *cannot* (incommunicable) be shared by other persons/things in his creation. Rationality is a communicable attribute; omnipotence is an incommunicable attribute.

dualism (body-soul dualism)—The Christian worldview perspective that the human person is a union of a physical body and a nonphysical soul.

ethics—Branch of investigation and learning that focuses on moral principles, values, and duties.

immanence and transcendence—God is close (immanent) to his creation, in intimate relationship with his creatures; God is also above and beyond his creation, superior (transcendent) to it and utterly other than what he has made.

omnibenevolence—All-goodness; God possesses all and only love for all he has made.

omnipotence—All-powerful; God's ability to do all things, or all things that are logically possible.

omnipresence—All-present; God is fully and equally present in all places (and times) at once.

omniscience—All-knowing; God knows all and only truths; God knows all things that are true, and all of his beliefs are true beliefs.

triunity—Refers to God's trinitarian nature: three persons, one God. Three unique persons (Father, Son, and Holy Spirit) compose one divine Godhead or Being. Not three gods; not one person.

Possible Term Paper Topics

✔ What are some ways that the doctrine of the Trinity has been misunderstood in the past? Research past heresies like Arianism, docetism, partialism, and Sabellianism. How can one describe or explain God's triunity without being guilty of either logical incoherence or doctrinal error?

✔ Investigate philosophical and theological attempts to articulate what aspects of human nature are involved in the *imago Dei* (image of God). What characteristics or essences are included in or referred to by the image of God? What would you identify as non-negotiable elements of the image of God in humans?

✔ Compare ancient Platonism, Gnosticism, and Christian theism with regard to the goodness of the created world. Why does a Christian worldview hold that the world is good? Is the world's goodness conditional or unconditional, total or partial?

✔ How do other prominent or influential worldviews today address the problem of humankind? What solutions do they offer? Consider researching Hinduism, Buddhism, naturalism, deism, postmodernism, and Islam.

✔ One of the effects of the fall is alienation of man from man. Evaluate the impact of man's fallenness in a specific cultural area or social institution (e.g., music, marriage, economics, politics).

Core Bibliography for Chapter Five

Augustine. *Confessions*. Translated by Henry Chadwick. Oxford World Classics. New York: Oxford University Press, 2008.

Lewis, C. S. *Mere Christianity*. Rev. ed. New York: HarperSanFrancisco, 2001.

Packer, J. I. *Knowing God*. 20th anniv. ed. Downers Grove, IL: InterVarsity Press, 1993.

Smith, James K. A. *You Are What You Love: The Spiritual Power of Habit*. Grand Rapids: Brazos Press, 2016.

TESTING A CHRISTIAN WORLDVIEW

Only let us hold true to what we have attained.

Philippians 3:16, ESV

In the past two chapters, we have surveyed the narrative and propositional contours of a Christian worldview. We saw that Christianity begins and ends with belief in the triune God—Father, Son, and Holy Spirit—who reveals himself in both his works (natural revelation) and his Word (special revelation). The biblical narrative covers the grand story of creation, fall, redemption, and glorification. In chapter five we surveyed how the Christian worldview answers the four core worldview questions. However, both the narrative and propositional contours of a Christian worldview have come under considerable questioning and doubt from those both inside and outside the church. It is incumbent on us, therefore, to call to mind the tools for worldview analysis (covered in chapter three) and apply their critical lenses to the Christian worldview we have outlined over the last two chapters.

The worldview analysis tools outlined in chapter three are truth tests—means of testing the consistency of a worldview. The test for internal consistency checks the logical coherence of worldview components. The test for external consistency examines the evidential correspondence of the worldview to known facts about the world. The test for existential consistency evaluates the pragmatic satisfaction (livability) of the worldview. Together, the three truth tests help illuminate the ability and adequacy of a worldview in accounting for itself, the world, and human experience.

Our worldview tests for truth are not the only possible tools for worldview analysis. Whatever worldview truth tests are adopted, however, there are some general considerations to note prior to applying them. James Sire, after articulating analytical tools, advocates an attitude of humility (which, he says, is not skepticism). Why humility? Because of human finitude. Sire says, "whatever our humanity turns out to be, [it] will keep us from total accuracy in the way we grasp and express our worldview and from completeness or exhaustiveness."[1] Worldviews are works in progress. Worldviews, like science, are human and thus fallible. We must be humble about them. God's Word is infallible, but we are not. Thus we examine our Christian worldview not merely in order to establish the truthfulness of its primary contours; we examine our individual Christian worldview in order to identify inconsistencies that have crept in. Where we find inconsistencies, we can make corrections. After all, we desire not to cling stubbornly to our preexisting perspective but to pursue God's perspective on the world. That pursuit requires an openness to change, a willingness to critically examine our existing, pretheoretical worldview (using tools for worldview analysis), and a desire to change where change is needed. The goal is to obtain God's truth—to possess, so far as we are humanly capable, a God's-eye view of life, the universe, and everything. Without humility, without a willingness to acknowledge our fallibility and finitude, we will never adopt the change that is needed.

As we pursue worldview analysis, we must be cognizant of a natural problematic tendency. We cannot help but analyze a worldview (any worldview, including our own) from within our own worldview. Our natural tendency (call to mind section 2.1 "The Impact of Worldview," especially 2.1.1 "Worldview and confirmation bias" and 2.1.2 "Worldview and experiential accommodation") is to minimize or ignore potential problems in our worldview while highlighting or exaggerating potential inconsistencies in other worldviews. It's no wonder, then, that our own worldview tends to come out of this judgment smelling like a rose while all other worldviews stink.

---

[1] James W. Sire, *The Universe Next Door: A Basic Worldview Catalog*, 5th ed. (Downers Grove, IL: IVP Academic, 2009), 281.

An illustration from C. S. Lewis may be helpful. As he says in his short but meaningful article "Meditation in a Toolshed," it is one thing to stand and look *at* a beam of bright sunlight that breaks into the darkness in a toolshed from a crack in the door. It is another thing entirely to stand *in* the beam of light and see other things by it. As Lewis puts it, "Looking along the beam, and looking at the beam are very different experiences."[2]

In the toolshed you can never judge one worldview except from the vantage point of another. You can never know darkness (their worldview) except from the vantage point of the light (your worldview) or about the light (your worldview) except from the vantage point of the darkness (their worldview). Inevitably, we evaluate all things from the perspective of our vantage point, in particular *race* (whatever the color or ethnicity), *gender* (male or female), and *class* (lower, middle, or upper and variations thereof). Or as Lewis points out, "you can step outside one experience only by stepping inside another."[3] What we know as true about reality is always from the inside of one experience or another. So there is no view from nowhere. All conversation, all analysis, is worldview dependent. Worldview matters, even in testing worldview for truth!

Lewis then adds this sobering point to his examination: "Therefore, if all inside experiences [which is all there is] are misleading, we are always misled."[4] With Martin Heidegger (1889–1976), we might say that we all have "the forestructure of understanding." Heidegger argues that we are all interpretative beings, and interpretation is always an attempt to understand structurally "something as something."[5] That is, understanding is always by means of what he calls a "fore-having," a "fore-sight," and a "fore-conception." Heidegger insists: "Interpretation is never a presuppositionless grasping of something previously given."[6] We all have our presuppositions, traditions, and prejudices. In other words, we all have a worldview!

---

[2]C. S. Lewis, "Meditation in a Toolshed," in *God in the Dock: Essays on Theology and Ethics*, ed. Walter Hooper (Grand Rapids: Eerdmans, 1970), 212.

[3]Lewis, "Meditation," 215.

[4]Ibid.

[5]Martin Heidegger, *Being and Time*, trans. Joan Stambaugh (Albany: State University of New York Press, 2010), 144.

[6]Ibid., 145-46.

Given that each of us has a worldview and cannot help but operate according to that worldview, is it therefore impossible to fairly evaluate worldviews for truth? If that were the case, it would be a hopeless situation indeed; there would be no purpose in public dialogue, critical examination, or even education. Fortunately, by being self-aware and open (teachable, humble), we are able to mitigate our prejudices. As Heidegger says, "What is decisive is not to get out of the circle, but to get in it in the right way."[7] But how? Glad you asked!

First, we must be aware and mindful or recognize that the circle (the tendency to evaluate worldviews from within our own worldview) does, indeed, exist. We can (and must) come to the process of testing for truth in the right way, with awareness and mindfulness. Do not let the culture around you have an excessive influence on you, especially culture of the popular kind, in order to prevent being held captive to the culture without realizing it.

Second, we must come to the circle by realizing that nothing is stronger than God's Word. God's powerful Word helps us come to the circle with awareness. For example, I once heard a short story about a town skeptic and the parishioners of a local church, who wondered how he would get along with their new pastor. After the pastor completed his very first sermon, he stood at the back door, met, and greeted the people. The skeptic approached him. As he listened to the objections of the skeptic, the new pastor repeatedly told the young skeptic, "Young man, it is appointed to man once to die and then comes the judgment (Hebrews 9:27). What will you do on the day of judgment?" That's all the new pastor said. That afternoon, all the young skeptic could think about was Hebrews 9:27, and the new pastor's follow-up question. The skeptic was converted to Jesus that very day.

Third, finally and fortunately, we do have evidence that demands a verdict, as Josh McDowell would say.[8] That is, the Christian worldview is supported by an impressive array of internal, external, and existential consistency. A fair examination of Christianity will vindicate its truthfulness.

---

[7]Ibid., 148.

[8]Josh McDowell, *Evidence That Demands a Verdict: Historical Evidences for the Christian Faith*, rev. ed., 2 vols. (Nashville: Thomas Nelson, 1992, 1999).

Though we will never have a God's-eye point of view, we can still argue for our point of view, even though we do argue in a not-so-vicious circle.

Now, at last, let's go on to apply the three worldview truth tests to the Christian worldview. Our three tests, again, are related to the consistency of worldview internally, externally, and existentially. The three worldview truth tests are based on the three theories of truth (discussed in chapter three)—coherence, correspondence, and pragmatic. Along with Socrates, we hold that an unexamined worldview is not worth holding. Let us examine our Christian worldview critically, to ascertain as best we can whether it makes sense within itself (internal consistency), makes sense in the world as we know it (external consistency), and makes sense of human life as it is lived out (existential consistency).

6.1 INTERNAL CONSISTENCY (LOGICAL COHERENCE)

Along with the coherence theory of truth, we affirm that a worldview can only be true if it is internally consistent or coherent. Individual components of a worldview, by the same token, are true only insofar as they are logically consistent with other true worldview presuppositions. On the other hand, if two beliefs within a worldview contradict one another, then at least one of those worldview components is necessarily false. Does a Christian/biblical worldview possess internal consistency and logical coherence? Is it rationally consistent?

William James (1842–1910), a proponent of philosophical pragmatism, speaks about religious choices. He notes the passionate nature of human beings, analyzes claims of scientific all-sufficiency, and notes that there will always be insufficient evidence for religion to be rationally compelling. Thus, he writes:

> If religion be true and the evidence for it be still insufficient, I do not wish, by putting your [scientific and or skeptical] extinguisher upon my nature ... to forfeit my sole chance in life of getting upon the winning side—that chance depending, of course, on my willingness to run the risk of acting as if my passional need of taking the world religiously might be prophetic and right.[9]

---

[9]William James, "The Will to Believe," in *Philosophy of Religion: An Anthology*, ed. Louis P. Pojman (Belmont, CA: Wadsworth, 1987), 433.

James seems to be suggesting that there is more to religious decision making than logical analysis. He is almost certainly correct. But still, logic matters. While there is more than logical coherence to worldview truth, there certainly cannot be less than logical coherence if a worldview is to be even possibly true. Again, the test for internal consistency is a negative truth test: where a worldview fails the test for internal consistency, the worldview is necessarily mistaken in some fashion; passing the test for internal consistency only establishes that the worldview is more likely to be true. As Keith Yandell writes, "If a conceptual system contains as an essential element a (one or more membered) set of propositions which is logically inconsistent, it is false."[10]

It is incumbent on us, then, to subject our Christian worldview to logical analysis, to test its contours for internal consistency. While we cannot cover every proposed logical inconsistency in this brief section, we will examine three of the most common objections: the incompatibility of God's existence with evil in the world, the logical impossibility of the incarnation, and the irrationality of faith (or the incompatibility of faith and reason).[11]

6.1.1 The problem of evil. Evil and suffering have long been cited as powerful reasons to question the existence (or at least goodness) of God: volcanic eruptions destroying villages and killing villagers, tsunamis wiping out entire islands, the Crusades, the Holocaust, mass murderers, child rapists. From ancient to contemporary times, the world has been replete with violence, strife, death, and suffering. In short, everybody hurts, sometimes as a result of their own sin, sometimes as a result of the sins of others, sometimes as a result of living in a fallen world. And to many (Christian and non-Christian alike), the existence, extent, and experience of evil and suffering demonstrate that the Christian God cannot be.

Comedian George Carlin says this about God and evil:

When it comes to believing in God, I really tried. I really, really tried. I tried to believe that there is a God, who created each of us in His own

---

[10]Quoted in Sire, *Universe Next Door*, 281.
[11]Another proposed internal inconsistency (possibly the most frequently cited logical objection to Christianity) is the triune nature of the Christian God. For a discussion of that objection, see section 3.2.1.

image and likeness, loves us very much, and keeps a close eye on things. I really tried to believe that, but I gotta tell you, the longer you live, the more you look around, the more you realize . . . something is wrong here. War, disease, death, destruction, hunger, filth, poverty, torture, crime, corruption, and the Ice Capades. Something is definitely wrong. This is not good work. If this is the best God can do, I am not impressed. Results like these do not belong on the résumé of a Supreme Being. This is the kind of [stuff] you'd expect from an office temp with a bad attitude.[12]

To put it another way, why does God (if God exists) allow bad things to happen to good people? If God is all-powerful, all-knowing, and all-loving, why is there such deep and senseless evil and suffering on earth? David Hume, the eighteenth-century atheist philosopher, stated the problem of evil when he revived Epicurus's ancient complaint and inquired: "Is [God] willing to prevent evil, but not able? Then He is impotent. Is He able, but not willing? Then He is malevolent. Is He both able and willing? Whence then is evil? Is He neither able nor willing? Then why call Him God?"[13] According to Hume, and to many skeptics since, an all-powerful and loving God would not permit the existence of the evil that we perceive and experience. The argument is basically thus: "If the Christian God exists, then evil would not be. Evil is; therefore God is not." In logical format, the argument looks something like this:

- If God exists, then evil does not exist.
- Evil exists (i.e., it is false that evil does not exist).
- Therefore, God does not exist.

The second premise seems clearly true (unless one adopts a worldview that perceives physical appearances and personal experiences as fundamentally illusions—Christian Science and some forms of Hinduism, perhaps). The first premise, however, needs to be expanded, as it is not immediately apparent that God's existence disallows the existence of any and all evil. Perhaps J. L. Mackie's version would work:

---

[12]George Carlin, cited in James S. Spiegel, *The Making of an Atheist: How Immorality Leads to Unbelief* (Chicago: Moody, 2010), 62.

[13]David Hume, *Dialogues Concerning Natural Religion*, ed. Martin Bell (London: Penguin, 1991), 108-9.

1. If God exists, he is omnipotent (possesses all power), omniscient (has all knowledge), and omnibenevolent (is completely good/loving).

2. An omnipotent being has the ability to prevent evil.

3. An omniscient being has the knowledge of how to prevent evil.

4. An omnibenevolent being has the desire to prevent evil.

5. Therefore, if God exists, there is no evil.

6. There is evil.

7. Therefore, God does not exist.[14]

Epicurus, Hume, and Mackie believed that the logical problem of evil demonstrates that the existence of evil disproves the existence of the Christian God. But does their argument do so? Is Christian belief in God and evil logically incoherent? Must we give up either belief in God or acknowledgment that there is evil in the world? In a word, no.

Christians will generally affirm that God has a prima facie desire to prevent evil—that is, a desire to prevent evil, all other things being equal. But why should we assume that all other things are equal, or that there is nothing else worth considering? As the prophet Isaiah reminds us, God's ways are not our ways; neither are God's thoughts our thoughts (Is 55:8). Perhaps it would be better to affirm in Mackie's point four that an omnibenevolent being has the prima facie desire to prevent evil. Might there be something that overrides this prima facie desire to prevent evil? Certainly. Here are two suggestions.

First, perhaps God is accomplishing some greater good through evils that he permits to occur. Thus, Cowan and Spiegel argue, "God allows evil in order to *bring about some greater good*—a good which could not be brought about unless evil existed as its precondition."[15] Some good outcomes, perhaps, can be achieved only by permitting a degree of evil to occur.

---

[14]This formulation of the logical problem of evil is found in Steven B. Cowan and James S. Spiegel, *The Love of Wisdom: A Christian Introduction to Philosophy* (Nashville: B&H Academic, 2009), 295-96. The argument is articulated in J. L. Mackie's famous article, "Evil and Omnipotence," *Mind* 64, no. 254 (1955): 200-212. A much more developed articulation and defense is found in Nick Trakakis, "Evidential Problem of Evil," *The Internet Encyclopedia of Philosophy*, accessed February 10, 2017, www.iep.utm.edu/evil-evi/.

[15]Cowan and Spiegel, *Love of Wisdom*, 297.

We can find support for that line of thinking in common human experience. For example, parents take their infant to the doctor to receive shots. The infant indubitably experiences shots as an evil, something the child would rather not encounter. Without a doubt, the shots hurt the young child. Why, then, do parents subject their children to such evil? Because the shots are achieving a greater good, inoculation against deadly diseases, that could not be attained without the apparent evil of the shots. The evil is achieving something better. What Christians believe occurred on Good Friday, similarly, is an appalling evil (the unjust conviction, torture, and execution of Jesus of Nazareth) that God permitted and utilized to accomplish an infinitely greater good (the atonement of sin, the redemption of human beings). Thus, the Christian can argue in place of Mackie's point four that an omnibenevolent being "has a morally sufficient reason to permit evil, and thus an *ultima facie* desire not to prevent evil (i.e., a desire that overrides his *prima facie* desire to prevent it)."[16] If it is the case that an all-loving God has sufficient reason to permit evil, then there is no logical contradiction between the existence of God and the presence of evil in God's creation. This response to the logical problem of evil is known as the greater-good defense.

There is a second path Christians can take to respond to the logical problem of evil, a path known as the free-will defense. Perhaps the greater good that justifies God's permitting evil is the creation of significantly free creatures. Alvin Plantinga thus argues that "a world containing creatures who are significantly free (and freely perform more good than evil actions) is more valuable, all else being equal, than a world containing no free creatures at all."[17]

But, the skeptic might argue, why didn't God create free creatures who always (or at least more frequently than they do) choose to do good? It seems that it is at least logically possible for God to have created such creatures. Nonetheless, Plantinga points out, even an omnipotent God cannot create just any logically possible world. After all, God could not create a world in which God does not exist because God is, by traditional definition, a necessarily existing being. Either he exists in all possible

16Ibid., 298.
17Alvin C. Plantinga, *God, Freedom, and Evil* (Grand Rapids: Eerdmans, 1977), 30.

worlds, or he does not exist at all. Thus, although it is logically conceivable for God to create a world in which he does not exist, such a world is not actualizable; that is, God cannot bring it into existence. God cannot create a world in which he does not exist. An omnipotent (all-powerful) God still has logical limits or boundaries to his power: he cannot bat (baseball) more than 1.000; he cannot have a save percentage (hockey) above 1.000; nor can he create a world in which he does not exist.

It seems likely that even an omnipotent God could not have created a world in which significantly free creatures always chose to do good. Why not? Because in such a scenario, those creatures would seem to be not significantly free after all. If people never had the ability to do evil, then they would not possess robust freedom (what philosophers call libertarian freedom, also known as the power of contrary choice or the ability to have done other than what they actually did do). Thus, the Christian argues that the skeptic's second premise (an omnipotent being has the ability to prevent evil) also needs to be refined: an omnipotent being possesses all power, but it is not logically possible to create a world with free-willed creatures who will always freely choose good. That is, God cannot create a world with moral good but without moral evil.[18]

Both of these Christian responses to the logical problem of evil—the greater-good defense and the free-will defense—successfully show that there is no logical contradiction between the existence of God and the existence of evil. God and evil can both exist without incoherence.

The skeptic may not be finished questioning the Christian worldview, however. Perhaps the *logical* presentation of the problem of evil fails, but there might be opportunity for an *evidential* version of the problem of evil. For example, atheist philosopher William Rowe acknowledges that the existence of God is compatible with the existence of evil. For Rowe, it seems that the type and amount of evil that we experience in the world make God's existence highly improbable. Rowe and others believe that God's existence is inconsistent with gratuitous evil—evil that does not serve some greater good. Rowe grants the cogency of the greater-good defense but argues that it is still likely that God does not exist. Thus:

---

[18]See ibid., 30-45.

(a) If God exists, there would be no pointless evil.

(b) There is pointless evil (i.e., it is false that there is no pointless evil).

(c) Therefore, God does not exist.[19]

Rowe and others acknowledge that shots and even Christ's crucifixion can theoretically be evils that are used to accomplish some greater good that otherwise would be unattainable. Rowe believes, however, that there are numerous examples of evil in the world that are not accomplishing any greater good. Such evil is known as gratuitous. It is evil that does not make a point, does not serve a greater purpose, and does not accomplish some greater good. Gratuitous evil, Rowe argues, is logically incompatible with the existence of God. One of the two must go.

Rowe is confident that there are gratuitous evils in the world. To support his contention, he invokes what we might call a "noseeum" inference.[20] In short, a noseeum inference states:

- I cannot see an X.

- Therefore, there probably is no X.

With regard to the problem of evil, Rowe argues that there are countless occurrences of evil wherein we cannot discern any greater good that is being accomplished: that is, from our perspective, the evil is gratuitous. Given that we cannot see a greater good, employing the noseeum inference permits the conclusion that there probably is no greater good; and, given the earlier argument (a-c above), God (probably) does not exist. Is Rowe's argument more successful than the Hume/ Mackie version? No.

The success of a noseeum inference requires that it be reasonable to presume that we would be able to see X if X were to actually exist. If I open my refrigerator and look for a gallon of milk (X) but am unable to see one (noseeum), then I can reasonably conclude that there is no gallon

---

[19]See William L. Rowe, "The Problem of Evil and Some Varieties of Atheism," *American Philosophical Quarterly* 16 (1979): 335-38.

[20]This might sound so trite that you suspect it is not a real thing, an intellectually responsible invocation. You would be mistaken! Noseeum inferences are widely utilized and accepted, and the principle is strenuously defended across the worldview spectrum. See, e.g., Trent Dougherty, "Skeptical Theism," first published January 25, 2014, *The Stanford Encyclopedia of Philosophy* (Stanford, CA: Metaphysics Research Lab, Center for the Study of Language and Information, 2016), http://plato.stanford.edu/entries/skeptical-theism/.

of milk in my fridge. If, on the other hand, I open my refrigerator and look for a dust mite (X) but am unable to see one (noseeum), then it would not be reasonable to conclude that there is no dust mite in my fridge. Common sense dictates that a gallon of milk should be easy to spot in a fridge, while a dust mite would be impossible to spot (at least with the naked eye) even if there were thousands of them present.

The relevant question is this: Which is God's potential purpose (greater good) in evil more like—the gallon of milk or the dust mite? Is it reasonable to expect that human beings would grasp the reason that God has for allowing each and every occasion of evil in the world, if God indeed has such reason? After all, God is transcendent, omniscient, and omnipresent, while we are earthbound, limited in knowledge, time, and space. God does not see as we see, and we do not see all that he sees. Should we presume that we, as finite and selfish creatures, can understand the full range of thought of the infinite eternal Creator? Is it not more reasonable to expect that God might often have purposes that far exceed our ability to discern and comprehend?

Go back to the example of parents inoculating infants against diseases through the perceived evil of shots. Can infants understand why their supposedly loving parents allow them to suffer so? Absolutely not! The infant has insufficient intellectual capacity and an undeveloped base of experience on which to draw. In reference to God, we stand in much the same relationship. We have insufficient knowledge and experience to understand God's intentions and dealings when he permits particular instances of evil and suffering. Thus, perhaps it is quite appropriate to conclude that even when we cannot see what God is accomplishing through a particular evil, God is nonetheless accomplishing something, and the evil is not truly gratuitous. Therefore, within a Christian worldview we can reasonably question premise b; perhaps, after all, there is no pointless evil. At the very least, it seems we cannot be certain that God does not have a purpose for permitting the evils we experience.

Might we go even farther? William Rowe suggests that God and pointless evil are logically incompatible. Let us agree with him, just for the sake of argument; that is, let us grant the truth of premise a, that "if God exists, there would be no pointless evil." Given theistic arguments, however, I have great confidence in the existence of God. My knowledge of God's existence is based on the general and special revelation discussed in chapter four, as well as my own experiential awareness of God's reality and presence in my life. Thus, I believe that (b') God exists.

I certainly have more confidence in the truthfulness of b' than of Rowe's b. If, however, it is true that God exists, then given premise a, a different conclusion follows:

(a) If God exists, there would be no pointless evil.
(b') God exists.
(c') Therefore, there is no pointless evil.

In other words, if I am confident in the existence of God, I can accept Rowe's claim that God and pointless evil cannot coexist and yet reject his conclusion. Instead, I will be led to believe that there is no pointless evil, and in cases where I cannot see the greater good that God is accomplishing through an apparently pointless evil, there nonetheless is a greater good. Once again, we see that there is no logical contradiction between the existence of God and the existence of evil. We may not know all that we wish to know, but nonetheless we can be confident that God has a purpose in the world's evils.

STOP & PAUSE

Biblical Worldview Insight

I pray that the eyes of your heart may be enlightened in order that you may know the hope to which he has called you, the riches of his glorious inheritance in his holy people, and his incomparably great power for us who believe. (Eph 1:18-19)

Paul indicates that grasping the glory of the gospel of Jesus Christ requires an enlightenment of the "eyes of your heart." Whereas once our hearts perceived the world through the stone-cold eyes of rebellion, the Holy Spirit can awaken our spirit to see the illumination of a world bathed in God's redemptive activity. Without that Spirit-enabled heart orientation, Christ-honoring living will be impossible.

Has your worldview, your heart orientation, been revived by the divine Holy Spirit? Has God opened the eyes of your heart?

There are other helpful considerations when examining the logical coherence of the Christian worldview in light of the problem of evil. First, a crucial part of a Christian worldview story is sin and life in a fallen world. Second, evil can be used as an argument for God's existence, for you can't say something is truly evil (say, the Holocaust or 9/11) unless an absolute standard of goodness exists, namely God. Third, God has done something about evil in the incarnation, life, death, resurrection, and ascension of Jesus (and this gospel is not to be overlooked). Fourth, no one response is satisfying in defending the just ways of God to humanity. Fifth, there is the justice response (in the new heavens and the new earth, all will be made right; see Rev 21–22). I employ all these arguments. In any case, we must work out a response, and in the final analysis, Jesus Christ will be at the heart of our answer.

6.1.2 The incarnation: the dual human-divine nature of Jesus. Jesus Christ will lie at the heart of our response to the problem of evil, partly because Jesus lies at the heart of everything within a Christian worldview! Indeed, the person of Jesus Christ poses another significant logical challenge to Christianity's internal consistency. Orthodox Christianity emphasizes the dual nature of Jesus as both fully divine and fully human. Many (again, both Christian and non-Christian) suggest (or fear) that the dual nature of Jesus is rationally inconsistent.

However, this question was settled long ago! The Chalcedonian Creed of 451 (following the Council of Chalcedon) articulated the hypostatic union of Jesus Christ. The pertinent part of the creed reads as follows:

> We, then, following the holy Fathers, all with one consent, teach men to confess one and the same Son, our Lord Jesus Christ, the same perfect in Godhead and also perfect in manhood; truly God and truly man, of a reasonable soul and body; consubstantial with us according to the manhood; in all things like unto us, without sin; begotten before all ages of the Father according to the Godhead.

The creed continues to explain,

> one and the same Christ, Son, Lord, Only-begotten, to be acknowledged in two natures, inconfusedly, unchangeably, indivisibly, inseparably; the distinction of natures being by no means taken away by the union, but rather

the property of each nature being preserved, and concurring in one Person and one Subsistence, not parted or divided into two persons, but one and the same Son, and only begotten, God the Word, the Lord Jesus Christ.

The Chalcedonian Creed was a high watermark in the intellectual life of the earlier Christian world. The framers of the creed knew the logical objections to Christ's dual nature; after all, the council was called in part to respond to heresies (theological errors) like Apollinarianism (which states that Jesus had no human rational mind but instead had only a divine mind), Nestorianism (which states that there were two separate persons in Jesus, one human and one divine), and Eutychianism (which states that at times the human nature of Christ was overcome by the divine, or that Christ had a human nature but one unlike the rest of humanity). The Christ-oriented heresies arose because of the difficulties early Christians had in understanding how Jesus could be both truly God and truly man, fully divine and fully human. It seemed most reasonable to presume that one—either the divine or the human—had to be dismissed or diminished in order to avoid logical contradiction. In response, the Chalcedonian Creed articulated the orthodox position that Jesus was one complete person and two absolute natures, both human and divine. Therefore, Jesus had a human rational mind. He was only one person, yet of two complete natures.

A key logical distinction can help us see how Christ's incarnation avoids being guilty of internal inconsistency. You and I are both (I trust) fully human.[21] Jesus was also fully human. You and I are also both (I am confident) not divine—in that we have a different nature from that of Jesus. Furthermore, you and I are both (again, I am confident) merely human; that is, *human* exhausts our essence, our nature. Here, Jesus is unique: he is the only human who was not merely human. Instead, he was fully human but also fully divine, in a way that we can neither experience nor fully grasp. In a similar fashion, a Swiss Army knife is fully a

---

[21]This is, in some ways, debatable. Some might suggest that Adam and Eve were the only two "fully human" persons. As sons and daughters of Adam and Eve, post-fall we inherit their sinful nature, which makes us not more than but rather less than what they were. In other words, perhaps we are all (post-Eden) less than fully human. We will set that debate aside and assume for the sake of argument that you and I are both fully human.

pocketknife, but it is not merely a pocketknife; it is also a bottle opener, a screwdriver, and a variety of other things. The incarnation of Jesus, like the trinitarian nature of God (see discussion in section 3.2.1 Internal consistency: logical coherence), may be difficult to work out conceptually, but it is not logically incoherent.

6.1.3 Faith and reason: is Christianity irrational? Critics will definitely say that a Christian worldview is, if not silly and superstitious, at least contradictory or out of sync rationally. They may be partially right. We would agree, for we formulators of a Christian worldview are prone to mistakes theologically and biblically, and in life (literally, missed-takes).

Tertullian (ca. 145–220) reportedly said in *De carne Christi* (known to modern readers as *On the Flesh of Christ*)[22] that he believed in Christ because it was "absurd." "Absurd" is a legitimate translation of the Latin word *ineptum*, from which we English speakers get *inept*. Peter Holmes translates the relevant passage as follows: "The Son of God was crucified; I am not ashamed because men must needs be ashamed of it. And the Son of God died; it is by all means to be believed because it is absurd [*ineptum*]. And he was buried, and rose again; the fact is certain because it is impossible."[23]

Is Tertullian disregarding reason in favor of faith? Tertullian is known as a fideist (i.e., "religious belief systems are not subject to rational evaluation")[24] and famously asked, "What has Athens [Greek philosophy] to do with Jerusalem [Christian church]?"[25] Is Tertullian espousing faith alone? Is that what he was saying when he allegedly said, "I believe because it is absurd"? For him, does a Christian or a biblical worldview hang together rationally? Is the Christian faith logically or rationally consistent for him?

How did "it is by all means to be believed because it is absurd" become "*I believe* because it is absurd"? I really don't know. But I do know this,

---

[22]Tertullian, *On the Flesh of Christ*, in *Latin Christianity: Its Founder, Tertullian. Three Parts: I. Apologetic; II. Anti-Marcion; III. Ethical*, ed. A. Cleveland Cox, vol. 3 of *Ante-Nicene Fathers*, ed. Alexander Roberts and James Donaldson (Peabody, MA: Hendrickson, 1994), 3:521-43, chap. 5.
[23]Tertullian, *On the Flesh of Christ*, trans. Peter Holmes, in *Ante-Nicene Fathers*, 3:525, chap. 5.
[24]Michael Peterson et al., *Reason and Religious Belief: An Introduction to the Philosophy of Religion*, 5th ed. (New York: Oxford University Press, 2013), 65.
[25]Ibid., 60.

earlier in chapter five of the same *On the Flesh of Christ*, Tertullian writes: "But, after all, you will not be 'wise' unless you become a 'fool' to the world by believing 'the foolish things of God.'"[26] Tertullian's reference is obviously to 1 Corinthians 1:25, "For the foolishness of God is wiser than human wisdom, and the weakness of God is stronger than human strength."

Tertullian was not rejecting reason per se. He believed in the logical or rational consistency of a biblical belief system, worldview, or faith. Tertullian "was not an exponent of bare faith alone. His own writing is evidence to the contrary."[27] He used reason time and time again to debunk many heresies and alternative philosophies. If he believed in Christ because it was absurd, foolish, inept, or incongruous, it was simply because such belief, though contrary to the wisdom of the world, embraced the wisdom of God with whom all things are possible. Even though it is impossible for human beings, it is possible with God (see Mk 10:27). We need his grace.

We also need to defend the Christian faith, an endeavor known as apologetics and founded on the biblical apologetic mandate in 1 Peter 3:15: "Always be prepared to give an answer to everyone who asks you to give the reason for the hope that you have." However, we can see that apologetics is not the only reason for the study of philosophy. The study of philosophy also aids the development of a conscious, consistent, coherent, and comprehensive Christian worldview. Perhaps this is philosophy's primary purpose. Another way to put this is that the study of philosophy is number two, and theology, in general, is number one. Theology is the queen of the sciences.

Referencing Clement of Alexandria (ca. 150–215), who saw philosophy in a positive, even redemptive, light, Christian philosopher Nicholas Wolterstorff writes: "It is then the calling of Christian intellectuals to go beyond apologetics and incorporate the truth proclaimed by Christ into a larger picture—a more comprehensive philosophy, if you will."[28] That is, into a

---

[26]Tertullian, "Chapter 5. Christ Truly Lived and Died in Human Flesh," *On the Flesh of Christ*, rev. and ed. Kevin Knight for New Advent, from *Anti-Nicene Fathers*, vol. 3, trans. Peter Holmes, accessed February 10, 2017, www.newadvent.org/fathers/0315.htm.

[27]Nicholas Wolterstorff, "Tertullian's Enduring Question" (paper presented at Lilly Fellows Program in Humanities and the Arts Eighth Annual National Conference, University of Notre Dame, October 1998), 7, www.lillyfellows.org/media/1406/nicholas-wolterstorff-1998.pdf.

[28]Ibid., 8.

worldview! Philosophy can crown worldview. Of my own calling, I have
frequently said that my calling from God is to develop a biblical worldview,
from all the sources—globally, biblically, and otherwise. I am Clementine.

Philosophy (logic especially) helps worldview thinkers to be logically
and rationally consistent with their own principles. It also helps believers
to live in accordance with their worldview (see Eph 4:1). A Christian
must also walk the walk. Philosophy should help us to attain a walk
worthy of the calling with which we have been called.

A Christian worldview must make sense of itself; it must be internally
consistent, or logically coherent. We have seen that two of the traditional
accusations of logical incoherence (the problem of evil and the incarnation of Jesus) do not uncover actual incoherence. Some contours of a
Christian worldview may be difficult to work out conceptually, but they
are not illogical or irrational. Our faith is indeed a reasonable faith.

REFLECTION QUESTIONS

1 Sketch out the logical problem of evil, premises through conclusion.

2 How does the distinction between prima facie and ultima facie
play into the author's response to the problem of evil?

3 Do you think there are any gratuitous evils in the world? What
sorts of life events might qualify as gratuitous evils?

4 How does the distinction between fully human and merely human
help resolve the apparent inconsistency of Christ's incarnation and
dual nature?

5 Can you think of any other areas where a Christian worldview
might be accused of internal inconsistency?

6.2 EXTERNAL CONSISTENCY (EVIDENTIAL CORRESPONDENCE)

A worldview must make sense internally; in addition, it must make sense
of the world. Along with the correspondence theory of truth, we affirm
that a worldview can only be true if it reflects what is actually real. Individual components of a worldview, by the same token, are true only

insofar as they correspond to the objective world. Worldview beliefs are true when the answers they provide to the fundamental worldview questions reflect what is actually the case. On the other hand, if worldview beliefs contradict known facts about the real world, then those beliefs are necessarily false.

A true worldview covers all the facts. Does a Christian or a biblical worldview do this? When it comes to this second worldview truth test, Walsh and Middleton ask: "As a vision of life, does it elucidate all of life? Can it open up all of life to those who adhere to it? Is it truly a *world* view? Or does it tend to open up only some aspects of life, ignoring others? Does it over emphasize or idolize one thing at the expense of another?"[29]

James Sire argues that

> A second test of an adequate worldview is that it must be able to comprehend the data of reality—data of all types: that which each of us gleans through our conscious experience of daily life, that which are supplied by critical analysis and scientific investigation, that which are reported to us from the experience of others. All these data must, of course, be carefully evaluated on the lowest level first (is it veridical? is it illusory?). But if the data stand the test, we must be able to incorporate them into our worldview.[30]

Here are Sire's examples. "If a ghost [or demon, angel, god(s), goddess(es), or God] refuses to disappear under investigation, our worldview must provide a place for it. If a man is resurrected from the dead, our system must explain why that could happen."[31] Worldviews must account for what we find to be true about our world.

As Ronald Nash notes, what we know to be true about the world by experience includes the "outer world" and the "inner world." Nash writes: "Just as a [worldview] must pass the test of reason, it must also satisfy the test of experience. . . . World-views should throw light on our experiences of the world. They should explain our experiences easily and naturally."[32]

---

[29]Brian J. Walsh and J. Richard Middleton, *The Transforming Vision: Shaping a Christian World View* (Downers Grove, IL: IVP Academic, 1984), 37.

[30]Sire, *Universe Next Door*, 282.

[31]Ibid.

[32]Ronald H. Nash, *Faith and Reason: Searching for a Rational Faith* (Grand Rapids: Zondervan, 1988), 55.

Nash suggests that our typical test for human experience is empirical in nature. Empirical tests have to do with sensed experiences—what can be known via the five senses: sight, hearing, smell, touch, and taste. But Nash argues that the test for external consistency must go beyond these empirical tests, which he calls tests of the "outer world." A worldview must also be consistent with what we know to be true about the "inner world"—"what we know about ourselves."[33] If we know things about human nature (e.g., that we have thoughts, feelings, desires, and needs) from introspection, then a worldview must successfully account for those realities.

While there is much that can and should be said when it comes to testing the Christian worldview for external consistency, we will limit our attention to three specific areas. First, we will respond to the accusation from scientific naturalism that Christianity does not account for what is known about the physical universe. Second, we will evaluate the external evidence for the existence of miracles and the historicity of Jesus' resurrection. Third, we will consider evidence from the "inner world" of religious desire and experience.

6.2.1 Christianity and scientific naturalism. Naturalism is a worldview that insists that the physical world is all that exists (see section 7.4 Naturalism). Scientism insists that the scientific method is the only means to gaining (reliable) knowledge (see the conclusion). The combination of the naturalistic worldview with scientism results in a widespread contemporary perspective known as scientific naturalism, in which science is the authoritative discipline that helps us to understand the physical reality around us and to see that physical reality is the only reality.

Scientific naturalism seems to be the predominant, almost default, worldview in much of secular higher education. It is broadly assumed that science gives us truth and that science shows that reality is exhausted by physical reality. Given that, scientific naturalism charges a Christian worldview with external inconsistency: our perspective does not correspond to the evidence. Christianity claims that God created the

---

[33]Ibid., 56.

universe; science demonstrates that the universe is neither designed nor created. Christianity claims that humanity is a special creation by God, created in his image; science demonstrates that humans have descended from a common ancient ancestor via an unbroken chain of unintended, purposeless, naturalistic evolution. Christianity claims that Jesus healed the blind, the lame, the leper, and even the dead; science demonstrates that the only way to heal people is through medical science and technological advances. Christianity claims that homosexual activity is unnatural, contrary to God's created design, and sinful; science demonstrates that homosexuality is the natural result of genetic tendencies and dispositions. Christianity claimed that the sun revolves around a flat earth; science demonstrates that a spherical earth revolves around the sun. Christianity claims that Jesus was raised from the dead; science demonstrates that dead men stay dead. On these and many other counts, it is argued, Christianity fails the test of external consistency while science provides the necessary corrective.[34]

Science is a tremendous gift from God to his people. We have the privilege and ability to investigate the world God has made (his natural revelation), to learn truths about the created order and the natural laws that govern it, and to know God better through that scientific knowledge. But, science is not the same as scientism. We must acknowledge that science does not (indeed, cannot) explain everything. In other words, science is not an omnicompetent epistemology, or way of knowing. Science is a relative good, but not the absolute good: the triune God alone is the

---

[34]For the record, the proper response to these objections runs as follows (understanding that there is a lot more that needs to be said): Science does not demonstrate that the universe is undesigned and uncreated; if anything, it shows the opposite. Science does not (at least not conclusively) demonstrate that humans have evolved from a common ancestor; and even if it did, it would be impossible for science to demonstrate that such descent was undirected, unintended, and purely random—such claims are philosophical/theological arguments that are immune to empirical proof or disproof. Science does not demonstrate the impossibility of miraculous healings; again, if anything, empirical observation demonstrates the opposite. Science does not demonstrate the genetic predetermination of homosexuality. Christianity does not teach (and never has taught) that the earth is flat; the medieval Christian belief that the sun revolves around the earth was driven by Aristotelian science, not theological concerns. Christianity does not dispute that dead men generally stay dead; but science is incapable of demonstrating that all people stay dead at all times in all places.

absolute good. Science has its limits as a way of knowing. Something more is needed.

In a classic debate on the existence of God between Christian philosopher William Lane Craig and atheistic philosopher Peter Atkins, Atkins famously claimed that "science is omnipotent" and asked Craig whether he denied the ability of science to "account for everything."[35] Craig emphatically asserted that there are "a good number of things that cannot be scientifically proven, but that we're all rational to accept." He proceeds to list five.

> Logic and mathematical truths cannot be proven by science. Science presupposes logic and math, so that to try to prove them by science would be arguing in a circle.
>
> Metaphysical truths, like *there are other minds other than my own* or that *the external world is real* or that *the past was not created five minutes ago with an appearance of age* are rational beliefs that cannot be scientifically proven.
>
> Ethical beliefs about statements of value are not accessible by the scientific method....
>
> Aesthetic judgments . . . cannot be accessed by the scientific method because the beautiful, like the good, cannot be scientifically proven.
>
> And finally, most remarkably, would be science itself. Science cannot be justified by the scientific method. Science is permeated with unprovable assumptions.[36]

The final point deserves some elaboration. Science, as we have said, is not an omnicompetent (omnipotent, in Atkins's words) discipline. Specifically, science cannot justify science. Philosophers of science have long noted that science is riven with philosophical presuppositions—assumptions, philosophical in nature, that must be made in order to successfully do science at all! For example, Cowan and Spiegel note five necessary presuppositions of the scientific enterprise: (1) the laws of thought (logic),

---

[35]William Lane Craig vs. Peter Atkins, "What Is the Evidence for/against the Existence of God?" Carter Presidential Center, Atlanta, GA, April 1998 (emphasis original). The exchange, along with the transcribed comments that follow, occurs around the 1:10:00 mark of the debate, during the "Craig Rebuttal" section. See transcription of the debate at www.reasonablefaith.org/debate -transcript-what-is-the-evidence-for-against-the-existence-of-god#section_4, accessed February 13, 2017.
[36]Ibid.

(2) the general reliability of sensory perception, (3) the law of causality (things do not happen without a cause), (4) the uniformity of nature (the regularity of natural operations), and (5) the existence and importance of ethical values.[37] In other words, science can operate only on external philosophical presuppositions, which themselves cannot be established or supported by the scientific method. It is literally impossible for science to be an omnicompetent discipline. Scientism as a perspective, then, is self-refuting.

It is helpful to note, however, that the philosophical presuppositions necessary for the operation of science are amply supported by a Christian worldview. The Christian doctrine of creation by a good God supports the law of causality, the general reliability of sensory perception, and the uniformity of nature. The Christian understanding of God's nature, likewise, undergirds the laws of logic and the existence of values. Other worldviews, like naturalism, can certainly utilize these presuppositions but cannot establish their reasonability. In a significant way, then, the modern scientific enterprise is dependent on the truth of a Christian worldview. That might help explain why modern science is borne out of a deeply Christian European worldview and not a Chinese Buddhist worldview or an Arabic Muslim worldview (let alone a tribal animistic worldview).

Furthermore, we must remember that science is a human endeavor and institution, and like all human endeavors and institutions it is subject to error, the fluctuations of history, psychological pressure from others, and even contemporary fads (what's in style and what isn't). Indeed, some scientific discoveries, such as the chemical structure of benzene, have even come in dreams.[38]

According to Thomas Kuhn (1922–1996), a Massachusetts Institute of Technology philosopher and historian of science, all scientific discoveries come in history (what else is there?) and are deeply influenced by their historical context.[39] Science inevitably works within a paradigm,

---

[37]Steven B. Cowan and James S. Spiegel, *Loving Wisdom: A Christian Introduction to Philosophy* (Nashville: B&H Academic, 2009), 105-6.

[38]Doug Stewart (The Doc), "7 Great Examples of Scientific Discoveries Made in Dreams," *Famous Scientists: The Art of Genius* (blog), accessed February 13, 2017, www.famousscientists.org/7 -great-examples-of-scientific-discoveries-made-in-dreams/.

[39]Thomas S. Kuhn, *The Structure of Scientific Revolutions*, 2nd ed., International Encyclopedia of Unified Science 2, no. 2 (Chicago: University of Chicago Press, 1970).

an operative framework that dictates presuppositions, models, and methods. Indeed, Kuhn's paradigms have been equated by some observers with the traditional understanding of worldview. What Kuhn is arguing, then, is that science is necessarily directed by worldview. Along the same lines, Michael Polanyi (1891–1976), taking a cue from Augustine, said that all science is governed by presuppositions and the tacit dimension.[40] All knowledge, including scientific knowledge, is therefore personal knowledge. This is why medical doctors *practice* medicine (i.e., take a long, good look and make an educated and experienced guess). A recent study says most Americans will be misdiagnosed at least once in their lives.[41] Putting it differently, we get the "scientific facts" wrong. Science, so long as it is practiced by finite, fallible, and fallen human beings, can never be an error-free, omnipotent discipline.

Finally, it is important to note that contemporary scientific discoveries do far more to support than to question the truth of the Christian worldview. Here are just three brief examples. First, the discovery of red shift and cosmic background radiation confirms the Big Bang theory of the universe's origin—namely, that the space-time universe began to exist a finite period of time ago. This discovery implies the necessity of an external agent causing the universe to come into being.[42]

Second, modern physics has identified a number of physical constants that govern things like the rate of the universe's expansion, the force of gravity, the attraction of atoms to one another, and the strength of

---

[40]Michael Polanyi, *Personal Knowledge: Towards a Post-Critical Philosophy*, corrected ed. (Chicago: University of Chicago Press, 1962), 266-67. This book is based on Polanyi's Gifford Lectures, delivered at the University of Aberdeen in 1951-1952. See also Polanyi, *The Tacit Dimension* (Garden City, NY: Doubleday, 1966).

[41]Lena H. Sun, "Most Americans Will Get a Wrong or Late Diagnosis at Least Once in Their Lives," *Washington Post*, September 22, 2015, www.washingtonpost.com/news/to-your-health /wp/2015/09/22/most-americans-who-go-to-the-doctor-will-get-a-wrong-or-late-diagnosis-at -least-once-in-their-lives-study-says/?utm_term=.9fbc4d5fce7c.

[42]See, e.g., William Lane Craig, *Reasonable Faith*, 3rd ed. (Wheaton, IL: Crossway, 2008), 100-105; John D. Barrow and Frank J. Tipler, *The Anthropic Cosmological Principle* (Oxford: Clarendon, 1986), 368-69; John Jefferson Davis, *The Frontiers of Science and Faith: Examining Questions from the Big Bang to the End of the Universe* (Downers Grove, IL: InterVarsity Press, 2002), 27-28; Stephen Hawking, *A Brief History of Time: From the Big Bang to Black Holes* (New York: Bantam, 1988), 50; Paul Davies, *Cosmic Jackpot: Why Our Universe Is Just Right for Life* (Boston: Houghton Mifflin, 2007), 24; and Hugh Ross, *The Creator and the Cosmos: How the Greatest Scientific Discoveries of the Century Reveal God*, 3rd ed. (Colorado Springs, CO: NavPress, 2001), 50-53.

electromagnetism. All these constants must be set in an extremely narrow band within a very large range of possibilities in order for life to exist anywhere in the universe (let alone on earth). The possibility of these constants being what they are by random chance (without an intelligent designer) is so infinitesimally small as to be rationally laughable— pointing to the reasonability of belief in a transcendent divine designer.[43]

Third, the advance of modern genetics has uncovered the digital language of DNA—a language far more complex (and impactful) than human languages and computer coding. The intricacy of genetic language renders it virtually impossible that DNA is the result of unguided naturalistic processes—pointing again to an intelligent transcendent designer of the biological world.[44]

Thus, in the end, the enterprise of modern science does not undermine the truthfulness of Christianity. Science does not show that the Christian worldview lacks external consistency. Rather, the evidence supports Christianity!

6.2.2 The outer world: the evidence for miracles and Jesus' resurrection. The dead are raised. Food is multiplied. Lepers are cleansed. The sick are healed. The sea is calmed. An axe head floats. The waters are parted. The sun stands still. The Bible is replete with miracle claims. At the heart of a Christian worldview lies belief in miracles, including the central miracle of Easter Sunday—the bodily resurrection of Jesus of Nazareth. The question is, are miracle claims rationally and evidentially defensible? Critics of Christianity launch a twofold accusation. First, miracles do not happen, or, more strongly, miracles are impossible. They not only do not happen; they cannot happen. Second, the resurrection of Jesus Christ is an article of faith that is not supported by the external evidence. The accusation was eloquently set forth by New Testament scholar Rudolf Bultmann (1884–1976): "It is impossible to use electric

---

[43]See, e.g., Patrick Glynn, *God—The Evidence: The Reconciliation of Faith and Reason in a Postsecular World* (Roseville, CA: Prima, 1999), 22-23; Davies, *Cosmic Jackpot*, 54; Hawking, *Brief History of Time*, 123; Hugh Ross, "Why I Believe in the Miracle of Divine Creation," in *Why I Am a Christian: Leading Thinkers Explain Why They Believe*, ed. Norman L. Geisler and Paul K. Hoffman, rev. ed. (Grand Rapids: Baker Books, 2006) 148-51; and Ross, *Creator and the Cosmos*, 43-46.

[44]See, e.g., Francis S. Collins, *The Language of God: A Scientist Presents Evidence for Belief* (New York: Free Press, 2006), 109-42.

light and the wireless and to avail ourselves of modern medical and sur-
gical discoveries, and at the same time to believe in the New Testament
world of spirits and miracles."[45]

6.2.2.1 The reasonability of belief in miracles. The classical articulation
of the philosophical argument against miracles comes from the skeptical
Scotsman David Hume (1711–1776). In his essay "Of Miracles," Hume
makes two primary claims. First, he argues that miracles are impossible
by the very nature of the case. Second, he argues that, even if miracles
were philosophically (logically) possible, yet there has never been (and
could never be) sufficient external evidence to justify believing a miracle
has actually occurred. Hume's critique is theoretically directed toward
miracles in general, but he provides indications throughout that Jesus'
resurrection lies in the crosshairs of his philosophical argument.

Before assessing whether the evidence supports belief in miracles, we
must define miracles. What is it that Hume is saying can or cannot occur?
Hume defines a miracle as "a violation of the laws of nature." He proceeds
to argue that, "as a firm and unalterable experience has established these
laws, the proof against a miracle, from the very nature of the fact, is as
entire as any argument from experience can possibly be imagined."[46]
Hume insists that "it is no miracle that a man, seemingly in good health,
should die on a sudden"; however, "it is a miracle, that a dead man should
come to life; *because that has never been observed in any age or country*."[47]
Hume has, essentially, defined miracles out of existence, deciding the
matter a priori. (1) The laws of nature are established by universal observation and experience and cannot be violated. (2) If miracles occur, they
are violations of the laws of nature. (3) Therefore, miracles do not occur.
Hume's initial statement of the argument against miracles is in fact a
linguistic sleight of hand.

---

[45]Rudolf Bultmann, "New Testament and Mythology: The Mythological Element in the Message
of the New Testament and the Problem of Its Re-interpretation," in *Kerygma and Myth: A Theological Debate*, ed. Hans Werner Bartsch (New York: Harper & Row, 1961), 5.

[46]David Hume, "Of Miracles," in *An Enquiry Concerning Human Understanding* (Chicago: Paquin,
1963), 126.

[47]Ibid., 126-27 (emphasis added). Note how Hume immediately predetermines the discussion
concerning Christ's resurrection—a man rising from the dead *would* be a miracle because such
has *never* been observed, including, of course, by the purported eyewitnesses to Jesus' resurrection in the New Testament.

> When anyone tells me, that he saw a dead man restored to life, I immedi-
> ately consider with myself, whether it be more probable, that this person
> should either deceive or be deceived, or that the fact, which he relates,
> should really have happened. I weigh the one miracle against the other . . .
> and always reject the greater miracle.[48]

Hume's argument against the possibility of miracles is built on his
definition of a miracle as "a violation of the laws of nature." Hume
insists that those laws of nature are inviolable—thereby rendering
miracles impossible. But Hume's definition is not only prejudicial (deciding the case before considering any evidence, an unusual procedure
for an empiricist like Hume); it is also widely rejected in favor of more
nuanced definitions. Even the sympathetic Antony Flew, a supporter
of Hume's general position, insists that miracles should be defined
with more nuance: according to Flew, a miracle "must involve an overriding of a law of nature, a doing of what is known to be naturally
impossible by a Power which is, by this very overriding, shown to be
supernatural."[49] Flew's definition leaves open the possibility of miraculous events, even though Flew himself believes none have ever actually occurred. If one uses the more neutral definition, then the actual
possibility of miracles becomes tied to the existence of a divine being
(Flew's "supernatural Power").

Thus, one ought to rightly reject Hume's definition of miracles (as a
"violation of the [inviolable] laws of nature") in favor of Flew's more open
definition of miracles involving "an overriding of a law of nature, a doing
of what is known to be naturally impossible." At that point, we can
evaluate the actual evidence and ask whether there is sufficient reason to
believe that a miracle has ever occurred. Within a Christian worldview,
we could immediately leap to special revelation and insist that the Bible

---

[48]Ibid., 128. The unstated conclusion drawn by Hume is that it is more likely that the disciples'
testimony concerning Jesus' resurrection from the dead is false.

[49]Antony Flew, "Neo-Humean Arguments About the Miraculous," in *In Defense of Miracles: A
Comprehensive Case for God's Action in History*, ed. R. Douglas Geivett and Gary R. Habermas
(Downers Grove, IL: IVP Academic, 1997), 46. My own considerably longer definition of miracles follows: "A miracle is a purposeful event, which appears to supersede (or transcend, or
suspend, or interrupt, or contravene) the normal working of nature, which event is impossible
under any natural (i.e., material/physical/naturalistic) explanation, which event can therefore
only be understood as the action (directly or indirectly) of a supernatural (i.e., divine) agent."

is filled with accounts of miracles that occurred in history. However, someone who does not share our Christian worldview will dispute the trustworthiness of the biblical miracles. Hence, it is more helpful if we are able to provide reasons and evidence from outside of Scripture that point to the actuality of miracles.

Hume, for one, thinks that such an endeavor will fail. He develops four arguments against the reliability of historical miracle claims. First, miracles have never historically been attested by a "sufficient number of men" whose "good-sense, education, . . . learning, . . . undoubted integrity, . . . credit and reputation" place them above doubt.[50] Second, Hume notes the natural human credulity toward miracle claims.[51] Third, Hume asserts that "it forms a strong presumption against all supernatural and miraculous relations, that they are observed chiefly to abound among ignorant and barbarous nations."[52] Finally, Hume suggests, without supporting argumentation, that the various miracle claims of different religions cancel one another out.

Hume seems to be arguing that testimony may in theory be capable of establishing a historical miracle, but in actuality no such miracles have been sufficiently attested. It is instructive to note that Hume gives no indication of having carefully examined and weighed any, let alone all, historical miracle claims to have come to such a comprehensive conclusion against their veracity. More compelling, however, is that later in his article Hume reverts to simply defining miracles out of existence.

Hume considers the raft of miracles attested to at the tomb of François de Pâris in the Saint-Médard neighborhood of Paris. Hume acknowledges that "the curing of the sick, giving hearing to the deaf, and sight to the blind" were claimed; moreover, "many of the miracles were immediately proved upon the spot, before judges of unquestioned integrity, attested by witnesses of credit and distinction, in a learned age, and on the most eminent theatre that is now in the world." In other words, Hume's four criteria for reliable miracle attestation were all met in the case of the

---

[50]Hume, "Of Miracles," 128.

[51]Ibid., 129-31. It is interesting to note that this credulity does not seem to be operative in our contemporary society. Rather, there seems to be an underlying *in*credulity toward miracle claims.

[52]Ibid., 131-34.

Abbé Paris. Nonetheless, Hume refuses to accept the miracle claims as factual, claiming instead that they are impossible by definition.

> And what have we to oppose to such a cloud of witnesses, but the absolute impossibility or miraculous nature of the events, which they relate? And this surely, in the eyes of all reasonable people, will alone be regarded as a sufficient refutation.[53]

In other words, miracles may be theoretically possible, but there can never be a sufficient body of evidence to prove one historically. Notice that this makes Hume's entire argument viciously circular. (1) Miracles do not happen because, if they did, they would be violations of the laws of nature. (2) The laws of nature cannot be violated. (3) We know that nature's laws cannot be violated because they have never been observed to have been violated. (4) Any time it seems as if the laws of nature have been violated, somebody (the person testifying to the miracle's occurrence) is either deceived or deceiving. (5) We know that the miracle claim must be intentionally deceptive or the result of someone having been deceived, because miracles do not happen. (6) We know that miracles do not happen, because if they did happen, they would be violations of the laws of nature . . . and we are right back where we started.

Throughout, Hume's implicit target has been the death and resurrection of Jesus. At the conclusion of his essay, Hume focuses on his target more directly by drawing a contemporary analogy.

> But suppose, that all the historians who treat of England, should agree, that, on the first of January 1600, Queen Elizabeth died; that both before and after her death she was seen by her physicians and the whole court . . . and that, after being interred a month, she again appeared, resumed the throne, and governed England for three years: I must confess that I should be surprised at the concurrence of so many odd circumstances, but should not have the least inclination to believe so miraculous an event. I should not doubt of her pretended death, and of those other public circumstances that followed it: I should only assert it to have been pretended, and that it neither was, nor possibly could be real. You would in vain object to me the difficulty, and almost impossibility of deceiving the world in an affair of

---

[53]Ibid., 138.

such consequence. . . . All this might astonish me; but I would still reply, that the knavery and folly of men are such common phenomena, that I should rather believe the most extraordinary events to arise from their concurrence, than admit of so signal a violation of the laws of nature.[54]

Hume explicitly affirms that resurrection from the dead is absolutely impossible. Miracles fall outside the pool of live options of Hume's worldview. There is absolutely no set of evidence, public or private, that could convince Hume of the veracity of a resurrection—of Queen Elizabeth in AD 1600 or of Jesus Christ in AD 30.

What if, however, we approach the question of miracles with a more open mind? Would we ever be able to say that there is sufficient evidence to establish the reality of miracles? Those were the questions that prompted New Testament scholar Craig Keener to launch an investigation into contemporary miracle claims around the world. Keener's meticulous and sober research leads him to some startling conclusions that conclusively falsify Hume's antimiracle position.

Whereas Hume argues that "a firm and unalterable experience has established [natural] laws" as being inviolable, Keener establishes that "there is no such uniform experience against miracles."[55] Instead, Keener notes that in the United States, 34 percent of the population (50 percent of evangelical Christians) claim to have either witnessed or personally experienced a divine miraculous healing. Globally, "hundreds of millions of persons alive today claim that they have *witnessed* or *experienced* miraculous healings. One might disagree with all of these claims, but one cannot simply arbitrarily exclude all the claimants from the modern world."[56] Hume suggests that since no one today observes miracles, we should assume that past miracle claims are fabricated: "It is strange, a judicious reader is apt to say, upon the perusal of these wonderful historians, that such prodigious events never happen in our days. But it is nothing strange, I hope, that men should lie in all ages."[57] Keener's

---

[54]Ibid., 142.
[55]Craig S. Keener, *Miracles: The Credibility of the New Testament Account* (Grand Rapids: Baker Academic, 2011), 1:156.
[56]Ibid., 1:204-5. For Keener's calculations, arriving at a conservative estimate of at least 200,000,000 miracle claims, see ibid., 205-38.
[57]Hume, "Of Miracles," 133-34.

research demonstrates that miracle claims are not restricted to ancient cultures and ignorant peoples; indeed, miracle claims are abundant, even ubiquitous, in human experience.

Keener proceeds to recount what he considers to be some of the best-evidenced miracle claims from around the world, including curing blindness, seeing the lame walk, and raising the dead.[58] Geographically, Keener recounts miracles that have occurred in Asia (Philippines, India, Sri Lanka, Nepal, Indonesia, South Korea, China), Africa (Nigeria, Mozambique, Congo), Latin America (Cuba, Ecuador, Chile), and the West (United States, Canada, England, Germany).[59] In numerous cases, Keener is able to access and evaluate medical documentation confirming a miraculous healing.[60]

Keener articulates two primary theses in his magisterial work. His primary thesis is that, contra Hume, "eyewitnesses do offer miracle claims," and do so in massive numbers. His secondary thesis is that "supernatural explanations, while not suitable in every case, should be welcome on the scholarly table along with other explanations often discussed."[61] In summarizing his findings, Keener argues that "there is some sufficiently strong evidence today to meet an open-minded non-supernaturalist's bar of proof, if never that of a closed-minded antisupernaturalist."[62] In other words, the external evidence demonstrates that miracles can and do happen and that only the most closed-minded individual, who absolutely refuses to follow the evidence where it leads (at least if the evidence leads to the existence of miracles), will insist that miracles do not happen. And, if miracles happen around the world today, then it is quite reasonable to accept that the miracle accounts in the Old and New Testaments could be true accounts.

6.2.2.2 The reasonability of belief in Jesus' resurrection. Given the actuality of miracles in the world today, and the reasonability of believing in biblical miracles, what can we say about the central miracle claim of Scripture—the resurrection of Jesus Christ? In addition to the general

[58]Keener, *Miracles*, 1:511-79.
[59]Ibid., 1:264-506.
[60]See ibid., 2:712-27.
[61]Ibid., 1:1.
[62]Ibid., 2:607.

argument in favor of miracles, we can now go further: we can show that our belief in the bodily resurrection of Jesus corresponds with the external (historical) evidence. The argument is best set forth by N. T. Wright, Michael Licona, William Lane Craig, and Gary Habermas.[63] Using accepted principles of historical inquiry, we are able to distill six essential historical facts (data points) that are best explained by the bodily resurrection of Jesus. The six historical facts are agreed on by the vast majority of scholars, including the vast majority of non-Christian, skeptical scholars. We are not cherry-picking!

1. Jesus was crucified, died, and was buried.

2. On the third day after his crucifixion, Jesus' tomb was found empty by some of his female disciples, including Mary Magdalene.

3. After Jesus' death, many of his disciples claimed to have seen Jesus, risen from the dead. These appearances are physical in nature and occur in individual, small-group, and large-group contexts.

4. Jesus' half brother James, who was skeptical of Jesus' nature and mission prior to his death, converts on the basis of a resurrection appearance and emerges as a key leader in the early church.

5. Saul (Paul) of Tarsus, a vehement opponent and persecutor of the early church, converts and becomes a follower of Jesus on the basis of a resurrection appearance and emerges as a key leader in the early church.

6. The disciples are radically transformed by their professed resurrection appearances, from fearfully hiding to becoming bold, open proclaimers of the risen Jesus. The transformed disciples preach the gospel in Jerusalem, the very city where Jesus had been crucified and buried, soon after his death.

Historians must identify plausible explanations that adequately account for all six facts. While skeptics have sought to suggest alternatives—swoon

---

[63]See N. T. Wright, *The Resurrection of the Son of God*, Christian Origins and the Question of God 3 (Minneapolis: Fortress, 2003); Michael R. Licona, *The Resurrection of Jesus: A New Historiographical Account* (Downers Grove, IL: IVP Academic, 2010); William Lane Craig, *The Son Rises: The Historical Evidence for the Resurrection of Jesus* (Eugene, OR: Wipf & Stock, 1981); and Gary R. Habermas, *The Risen Jesus and Future Hope* (Lanham, MD: Rowman & Littlefield, 2003).

theories, disciples' deception, hallucination, and others—none of the offered hypotheses account for the data with explanatory scope and power.[64] In the end, the historical evidence confirms the external consistency of the crucial Christian miracle claim, the resurrection of Jesus Christ. Not only is it reasonable to believe in miracles in general, but belief in *the* miracle is strongly evidenced and eminently reasonable. In short, the Christian worldview's embrace of the miracle of Jesus' resurrection demonstrates not external inconsistency (lack of evidential correspondence) but precisely the opposite.

6.2.3 *The inner world: the evidence of religious desire and experience.* We have looked at two outer-world aspects of the evidential correspondence of the Christian worldview—(1) faith and science and (2) miracles. Let us turn our attention to an aspect of the inner world and see whether Christianity corresponds to what we know about human nature and experience. Again, there is much to be said, but we will focus on the unquenchably religious spirit of human beings—human religious desire and experience of the divine.

As John Calvin says, we have a *sensus divinitatis*—the sense or awareness of divinity—and the *semen religionis*—the seed of religion.[65] The *sensus divinitatis* and the *semen religionis* give rise to the multiplicity of religions and mythologies in the world. On this issue C. S. Lewis and Alvin Plantinga have a great deal to contribute.

The search for experience of the divine, or religious joy, was the "central story" of Lewis's life. He wrote about it often, for example, in his autobiography *Surprised by Joy*.[66] For Lewis, this spiritual experience, even apart from its fulfillment, was sweeter than the actual fulfillment of any human desire. In another place Lewis wrote: "This poverty [is] better than all other wealth."[67] Moreover, Lewis argued that the desire to experience God (or the transcendent, the divine) was a natural human

---

[64]See Licona's *The Resurrection of Jesus* for a particularly in-depth analysis of alternative hypotheses for the historical facts.

[65]John Calvin, *Institutes of the Christian Religion*, ed. John T. McNeill, trans. Ford Lewis Battles, Library of Christian Classics 20 (Philadelphia: Westminster, 1960), 43, 47, 1.3.1 and 1.4.1.

[66]C. S. Lewis, *Surprised by Joy: The Shape of My Early Life* (New York: Harvest, 1955), 17.

[67]C. S. Lewis, *The Pilgrim's Regress: An Allegorical Apology for Christianity, Reason, and Romanticism* (1958; repr., Grand Rapids: Eerdmans, 1977), 7; and see through 10.

desire—something not taught but innate. Given that the desire is natural, it would then seem to have a source of potential satisfaction. After all, all our other natural desires (for food, water, sex, community, etc.) can be satisfied by something that exists in reality. Yet we can find nothing in this physical world to satisfy our religious desires. Hence, Lewis claims: "If I find in myself a desire which no experience in this world can satisfy, the most probable explanation is that I was made for another world."[68] That is, the world of God is behind the physical, natural world. We were made for both worlds. We do not want to forsake God's creation or the natural world for the world above. We want to care for both rightly in a reordered manner at the very same time. But as Lewis insinuates, and Augustine famously proclaims, we are made for God, and our hearts will be restless until they find rest in him.

Alvin Plantinga (b. 1932) has erected an entire system of knowledge and apologetics on the *sensus divinitatis*, arguing that we can believe in God even without arguments.[69] Why try to argue for what people already believe in? Instead, our Christian worldview can be embraced as properly basic—a foundation on which everything else is based rather than something that we argue to. Along the same lines, a number of philosophers have spoken of religious experience as a kind of empirical evidence for God—among them, Teresa of Ávila (1515–1582), William James (1842–1910), and William P. Alston (1921–2009).

Some thinkers, according to Bernard Ramm, have specifically developed apologetic systems for Christianity on the basis of "subjective immediacy," or an empirically adequate notion.[70] According to Ramm, thinkers who have developed such apologetic systems on the basis of the "Christian experience of grace" (Ramm's words) include Blaise Pascal (1623–1662), Søren Kierkegaard (1813–1855), and Emil Brunner (1889–1966). Christian experience of God and his grace constitutes the chief experience.

---

[68]C. S. Lewis, *Mere Christianity*, rev. ed. (New York: HarperSanFrancisco, 2001), 136-37.
[69]See, e.g., Alvin Plantinga, "Reason and Belief in God," in *Faith and Rationality: Reason and Belief in God*, ed. Alvin Plantinga and Nicholas Wolterstorff (Notre Dame, IN: University of Notre Dame Press, 1983), 16-93.
[70]Bernard Ramm, *Varieties of Christian Apologetics: An Introduction to the Christian Philosophy of Religion*, Twin Brooks (Grand Rapids: Baker Books, 1974).

Do Martin Luther's *feelings* at conversion qualify as an empirical experience or as evidence of external consistency and evidential correspondence? After all, upon being born again, Luther said: "And straight way I *felt* as if I were born anew." In other words, the empirical experience becomes an empirically adequate test of faith and of a Christian worldview.

We have surveyed the external consistency of a Christian worldview in three areas—science, miracles, and faith—and have found that it passes the worldview truth test with flying colors.

REFLECTION QUESTIONS

1 What is Ronald Nash's distinction between the inner world and outer world when considering external consistency?

2 List at least five philosophical presuppositions that are necessary in order to do modern science. Why are they necessary for science? And why is science unable to ground them?

3 Why is Hume's argument against miracles guilty of circular reasoning?

4 Are you persuaded by Calvin's argument that all humans possess an internal sense of the divine (*sensus divinitatis*)? Why or why not?

6.3 EXISTENTIAL CONSISTENCY (PRAGMATIC SATISFACTION)

Along with the pragmatic theory of truth, we affirm that a worldview can only be true if it is livable—that is, if a person can live with integrity and purpose within that worldview. Individual components of a worldview, by the same token, are true only insofar as the individual can consistently live those beliefs out. On the other hand, if the logical implications of a worldview belief simply cannot be lived out with integrity, then that belief is necessarily false.

Does any worldview have *existential power*, including biblical Christianity? Is a given worldview "subjectively satisfactory"? Sire illustrates "subjective satisfaction," as he calls it, by saying, "it must meet our sense of personal need as a bowl of hot oatmeal breaks the fast of a long night's sleep."[71] Thus, we might ask, is a Christian/biblical worldview existentially consistent and livable? Does a Christian/biblical worldview possess existential consistency or pragmatic satisfaction?

Not if those who say Christianity is a crutch are right. But here I will make one observation and ask one question. My observation is this: we all depend on something! My question is this: what do you depend on? Do you depend on drugs, porn, possessions, your dog, boyfriend, girlfriend, or anything else under the sun? What do you depend on? A man with a broken leg depends on a crutch to help him get where he needs to go; if he depended on a pocketknife for the same purpose, he would be sorely disappointed. For a human being with a broken soul, what is better to rely on to get us where we need to go (for healing)? A risen Savior or an idolatrous substitute?

A Christian worldview is not existentially consistent if the hypocrites are right! If hypocrisy ruled in a Christian worldview, then it wouldn't be a solid worldview. But as regards hypocrisy, I just want to say, join the club. Our lives are often inconsistent, and our beliefs and principles certainly are. Since worldviews are human constructs, they, like science, are likely to err. Worldviews and life, as everyone recognizes, are works in progress.

Here's another story. Paul Simon of Simon and Garfunkel fame (a 1970s music duo) was having a conversation once upon a time with noted Christian leader John Stott (1921–2011). Simon was complaining to Stott vociferously about hypocrisy in the church. Stott let him go on for quite a while and then said quietly, "Let's now talk about Jesus of Nazareth." He "committed no sin, and no deceit was found in his mouth" (1 Pet 2:22). In other words, Jesus and a Christian worldview are not the source of the hypocrisy; instead, we and our inconsistency are! Our lives and our principles are radically out of sync with each other.

Walsh and Middleton ask about this worldview test of existential consistency and pragmatic satisfaction, does any worldview open up life? (Deut 30:15-20). They add: "Does this [world]view bring life or death[,] blessing or curse?"[72] To be sure, a Christian/biblical worldview does

[71]Sire, *Universe Next Door*, 283.
[72]Walsh and Middleton, *Transforming Vision*, 38.

bring life and blessing. Walsh and Middleton give examples from unlikely sources about gratitude from the Japanese and about land from the
Dene (North American Native Americans). They conclude we can learn
much from other worldviews. From them, we can learn practical life
lessons—namely, about gratitude and land. Common grace strikes again!

We can say for sure that a Christian worldview is certainly challenging.
We have to do many things that are contrary to our fallen, though re-
deemed, nature. *Challenging* is the operative word, especially ethically.
Obeying the Ten Commandments and the ethical teachings of Jesus the
Messiah and the apostle Paul are challenging. Here are some ethical ex-
amples from the Old Testament, from Jesus, and from Paul:

First, see this example from the Old Testament, and part of the Ten
Commandments:

> Honor your father and your mother, so that you may live long in the land
> the LORD your God is giving you.
>
>   You shall not murder.
>
>   You shall not commit adultery.
>
>   You shall not steal.
>
>   You shall not give false witness against your neighbor.
>
>   You shall not covet your neighbor's house. You shall not covet your
> neighbor's wife, or his male or female servant, his ox or donkey, or any-
> thing that belongs to your neighbor. (Ex 20:12-17)

Next are several examples from Jesus himself in his Sermon on the
Mount. (Please read the whole sermon!)

> But I tell you that anyone who is angry with a brother or sister will be
> subject to judgment. Again, anyone who says to a brother or sister, "Raca,"
> is answerable to the court. And anyone who says, "You fool!" will be in
> danger of the fire of hell. (Mt 5:22)
>
>   But I tell you, love your enemies and pray for those who persecute you,
> that you may be children of your Father in heaven. He causes his sun to
> rise on the evil and the good, and sends rain on the righteous and the
> unrighteous. If you love those who love you, what reward will you get?
> Are not even the tax collectors doing that? And if you greet only your own
> people, what are you doing more than others? Do not even pagans do
> that? (Mt 5:44-47)

Be careful not to practice your righteousness in front of others to be seen by them. If you do, you will have no reward from your Father in heaven. (Mt 6:1)

Do not judge, or you too will be judged. For in the same way you judge others, you will be judged, and with the measure you use, it will be measured to you. (Mt 7:1-2)

So in everything, do to others what you would have them do to you, for this sums up the Law and the Prophets. (Mt 7:12)

By their fruit you will recognize them. Do people pick grapes from thornbushes, or figs from thistles? Likewise, every good tree bears good fruit, but a bad tree bears bad fruit. A good tree cannot bear bad fruit, and a bad tree cannot bear good fruit. Every tree that does not bear good fruit is cut down and thrown into the fire. Thus, by their fruit you will recognize them. (Mt 7:16-20)

Therefore everyone who hears these words of mine and puts them into practice is like a wise man who built his house on the rock. The rain came down, the streams rose, and the winds blew and beat against that house; yet it did not fall, because it had its foundation on the rock. But everyone who hears these words of mine and does not put them into practice is like a foolish man who built his house on sand. The rain came down, the streams rose, and the winds blew and beat against that house, and it fell with a great crash. (Mt 7:24-27)

Now we have ethics from Paul, first from Romans, and then 1 Corinthians (you see, a Christian worldview is challenging, but existentially consistent):

Love must be sincere. Hate what is evil; cling to what is good. Be devoted to one another in love. Honor one another above yourselves. Never be lacking in zeal, but keep your spiritual fervor, serving the Lord. Be joyful in hope, patient in affliction, faithful in prayer. Share with the Lord's people who are in need. Practice hospitality. (Rom 12:9-13)

Or do you not know that wrongdoers will not inherit the kingdom of God? Do not be deceived: Neither the sexually immoral nor idolaters nor adulterers nor men who have sex with men nor thieves nor the greedy nor drunkards nor slanderers nor swindlers will inherit the kingdom of God. And that is what some of you were. But you were washed, you were sanctified, you were justified in the name of the Lord Jesus Christ and by the Spirit of our God. (1 Cor 6:9-11)

> Love is patient, love is kind. It does not envy, it does not boast, it is not proud. It does not dishonor others, it is not self-seeking, it is not easily angered, it keeps no record of wrongs. Love does not delight in evil but rejoices with the truth. It always protects, always trusts, always hopes, always perseveres. (1 Cor 13:4-7)

Substitute your name for the word *love* in this last ethical text from Paul in 1 Corinthians 13 for added meaning and challenge.

We will crash and burn if we add the ethics of the apostles Peter, James, and John to this list. Perhaps read the New Testament before you make a commitment to Christ; look before you leap and see how challenging the gospel can be. It is livable. Thank God, literally, for the Holy Spirit who gives us power to live out a biblical worldview.

6.4 Summary

The burden of this chapter has been to subject the Christian worldview to the critical scrutiny of the three worldview tests for truth. We assessed the logical coherence of Christianity in light of the problem of evil and the incarnation of Jesus and found that it possesses internal consistency. We examined the evidential correspondence of the Christian worldview in relation to scientism, miracles, and religious desire and found that it possesses external consistency. Finally, we considered the pragmatic satisfaction of the Christian worldview in relation to dependence, hypocrisy, and ethical demands and found that it possesses existential consistency. We have barely scratched the surface when it comes to worldview analysis, but at least in our introductory inspection, Christianity looks like a worldview worth holding. It is now time to turn our attention to some alternative worldviews, to seek an understanding of those perspectives and subject them to the three tests for truth.

MASTERING THE MATERIAL

When you finish reading this chapter, you should be able to

- ✔ Discern the tests of any worldview, especially a Christian worldview.
- ✔ Explain why we test and critique all things within our own worldview.

✔ Explore the *sensus divinitatis* and the *semen religionis* in Calvin's *Institutes* as evidence of empirical adequacy and evidential correspondence.

✔ Outline a historical argument supporting the resurrection of Jesus Christ.

✔ Expound on Christian responses to the logical and evidential problem(s) of evil.

✔ Give details on the ethical challenge of a Christian worldview.

Glossary of Terms for Chapter Six

evidential problem of evil—The skeptic's argument that the presence of gratuitous evil in the world serves to disprove (or render less likely) God's existence.

gratuitous evil—Evil or suffering that serves no greater purpose, evil that has no redemptive impact.

incarnation—The birth of God the Son on earth in the person of Jesus of Nazareth.

logical problem of evil—The atheist's argument that the existence of God is incompatible with the existence of any amount/type of evil in the world.

miracle—An event that involves an overriding of a law of nature, a doing of what is known to be naturally impossible.

noseeum inference—An informal logical argument that if you cannot see something, *x*, that you have good reason to think you should be able to see, then it is likely that *x* does not exist.

scientism—A perspective insisting that the scientific method is the only means to reliable knowledge, or that science is capable of gaining all truths about the world.

sensus divinitatis—An innate sense or awareness of the existence of a divine being. John Calvin argues that all human beings possess a *sensus divinitatis*.

Possible Term Paper Topics

✔ Read J. L. Mackie's article "Evil and Omnipotence," *Mind* 64, no. 254 (1955): 200-212, and Alvin Plantinga's response in *God, Freedom, and Evil* (Grand Rapids: Eerdmans, 1977). How else can a Christian respond to the logical problem of evil?

✔ This chapter contains a brief synopsis of scientific discoveries and evidence that support the truth of the Christian worldview (Big Bang cosmology, cosmic constants and fine-tuning, DNA fine-tuning). Research some additional areas where science supports Christian belief and present a strong thesis for the truthfulness of Christian worldview.

✔ Survey Craig Keener's *Miracles: The Credibility of the New Testament Accounts*. Assess the strength of the belief that miracles can and do happen today. What impact does your conclusion have on the historicity of Jesus' bodily resurrection?

✔ The chapter argues that historical evidence supports the Christian belief that Jesus was raised from the dead. Research some alternative hypotheses (e.g., Michael Licona, *The Resurrection of Jesus*) that attempt to account for the data. Assess where they fail to sufficiently deal with the historical facts.

Core Bibliography for Chapter Six

Geisler, Norman L. *Christian Apologetics*. Grand Rapids: Baker Books, 1976.

Keener, Craig. *Miracles: The Credibility of the New Testament Accounts*. Grand Rapids: Baker Academic, 2011.

Kuhn, Thomas S. *The Structure of Scientific Revolutions*. 2nd ed. International Encyclopedia of Unified Science 2, no. 2. Chicago: University of Chicago Press, 1970.

Licona, Michael R. *The Resurrection of Jesus: A New Historiographical Approach*. Downers Grove, IL: IVP Academic, 2010.

Plantinga, Alvin. *The Nature of Necessity*. Oxford: Clarendon Press, 1974.

Polanyi, Michael. *Personal Knowledge: Towards a Post-Critical Philosophy*. Corrected ed. Chicago: University of Chicago Press, 1962.

Ramm, Bernard. *Varieties of Christian Apologetics: An Introduction to the Christian Philosophy of Religion*. Grand Rapids: Baker Books, 1974.

PART III

ANALYZING WORLDVIEWS

WESTERN PHILOSOPHICAL ALTERNATIVES

DEISM, NATURALISM,
AND POSTMODERNISM

In the first two parts of this book, we examined the concept of worldview and the contours of a Christian worldview. Now we turn our attention to focus specifically on alternative worldviews. Our purpose is twofold: (1) to understand the worldviews that our friends and neighbors profess and embrace and (2) to subject those worldviews to intentional analysis, scrutinizing them through the filter of our three criteria for worldview evaluation.

Three significant Western philosophical alternatives to Christian worldview include deism, naturalism, and postmodernism. Even though deism as a movement died out two or three centuries ago, a large percentage of the 91 percent of Americans that affirm belief in God or "a universal spirit"[1] could probably be classified as deists. Generally, deism affirms the existence of a creator god, but he (or it) is not involved in the world. He (or it) created the world with physical laws and has let it run on its own. Traditionally, deists have held that people can discover what they need to know about god and morality through reason alone; there is no need for supernatural revelation nor the miraculous.

Though most Americans affirm belief in God or a universal spirit, many affirm a naturalistic worldview that rejects the idea that God exists.

---

[1]Forum on Religion & Public Life, *"Nones" on the Rise: One-in-Five Have No Religious Affiliation*, Pew Research Center, October 9, 2012, 48, www.pewforum.org/files/2012/10/NonesOnTheRise -full.pdf.

Almost 15 percent of the world's population is nonreligious, meaning they are either agnostic or atheistic.[2] In the United States alone, research done by the Pew Research Center in 2012 shows that 6 percent of the population describe themselves as atheist or agnostic.[3] Naturalism provides the worldview for many atheists and agnostics because it asserts that all that exists is material "stuff"; there are no spiritual or supernatural entities. Therefore, God does not exist. As we will see, many have used Charles Darwin's theory of evolution to explain the world, thereby removing the need for the creator god of the deists.

This chapter will apply the four worldview questions to deism and naturalism: What is our nature? What is our world? What is our problem? What is our end? Then the issue of life motivation within deism and naturalism will be discussed. In other words, what is the guiding principle or aim that drives the everyday lives of adherents of deism and naturalism?

Next, this chapter will address postmodernism. Postmodernism is not technically a worldview but rather is an influential approach to knowledge and language, which ultimately leads to skepticism and relativism. Though postmodern thought is most commonly found in colleges and universities, its influence extends far beyond campus life and into American culture.

Because postmodernism is not a comprehensive worldview—it actually eschews worldviews—it does not address the four worldview questions, nor does it provide a guiding principle or aim in life. Because postmodernism is silent on these matters, it would be unreasonable to try to answer worldview questions from the postmodern perspective. Therefore, instead of answering the four worldview questions and discussing life motivation for postmodernism, a general overview of postmodern thought will be included. Finally, after describing deism, naturalism, and postmodernism, each will be analyzed for (1) internal consistency and logical coherence, (2) external consistency and evidential correspondence, and (3) existential consistency and pragmatic satisfaction. These three methods of analysis can be used to test any kind

---

[2]Patrick Johnstone, *The Future of the Global Church: History, Trends, and Possibilities* (Colorado Springs, CO: Biblica, 2011), 65.
[3]Forum on Religion & Public Life, *"Nones" on the Rise*, 9.

of truth claim. They are not limited to analyzing worldviews. Therefore, even though postmodernism is not a fully developed worldview, it is appropriate to apply these tests to postmodern thought.

7.1 Deism

Deism was largely a seventeenth- and eighteenth-century phenomenon, though many today could accurately be called deists. In *The Oxford Companion to Philosophy*, J. C. A. Gaskin defines deism as "belief in a god established by reason and evidence (notably by the design argument) without acceptance of the special information supposedly revealed in, for example, the Bible or Koran."[4] In *The Cambridge Dictionary of Philosophy*, William J. Wainwright provides a more concise definition by stating that deism is the belief that "true religion is natural religion."[5] In other words, true religion is found not in any kind of special revelation from a deity but rather in creation itself. God has not communicated to humanity except through nature. God has not only been silent, but he is not even involved in his creation. Anthony Thiselton argues that deism "denotes a rationalist concept of God as the source of Creation who remains above and beyond it, but is not immanent within it."[6] In other words, God is an absentee God. He created the world as a clockmaker creates a clock; he created it and now lets it run on its own.

Many trace the origin of deism to the Englishman Herbert of Cherbury (1583–1648). Lord Herbert argued that all religions shared five common principles. These five principles later became known as the five articles of deism: (1) God exists; (2) as Supreme Being, God is worthy of worship; (3) piety and virtue characterize religion; (4) repentance expiates sin; and (5) justice demands reward or punishment in postmortal existence.[7] Other prominent English deists include John Toland (1670–1722), Anthony Collins (1676–1729), Matthew Tindal (1657–1733), and Thomas

---

[4]J. C. A. Gaskin, "Deism," in *The Oxford Companion to Philosophy*, ed. Ted Honderich (New York: Oxford University Press, 1995), 182.

[5]William J. Wainwright, "Deism," in *The Cambridge Dictionary of Philosophy*, ed. Robert Audi, 2nd ed. (New York: Cambridge University Press, 1999), 216.

[6]Anthony C. Thiselton, *A Concise Encyclopedia of the Philosophy of Religion* (Grand Rapids: Baker Academic, 2002), 61.

[7]Ibid.

Chubb (1679–1747). Though influenced by the Christian worldview, these writers rejected belief in the supernatural and any uniqueness of Christianity among the other religions of the world. They argued that Christianity was essentially a moral religion that could be discovered through reason alone. For example, in *Christianity Not Mysterious*, John Toland argued that Jesus was simply a preacher of a simple and moral religion, and that any mysteries in the Gospels came from "the intrusion of pagan ideas and priestcraft."[8] Similarly, Matthew Tindal wrote in *Christianity as Old as Creation* that Christianity was an eternal natural religion based on reason and morality, and not on revelation.[9] Tindal's work, which rejected the fall, original guilt, and the need for atonement, became "the Bible of Deism."[10]

Deism also took root in continental Europe and the United States. Voltaire (1694–1778) and Hermann Samuel Reimarus (1694–1768) were prominent deists in Europe. Voltaire, an influential figure of the French Enlightenment, believed in the existence of God because of the design in the universe but rejected the idea of innate moral laws, insisting, however, that God gave us the ability to identify natural moral laws. Reimarus was part of the German Enlightenment; he rejected the idea of a purely mechanistic world but also rejected supernatural divine revelation and miracles. He argued that miracles were unworthy of God because God carries out his purposes through a "rationally intelligible system."[11]

In the United States, some of the prominent deists include Thomas Paine (1737–1809) and Elihu Palmer (1764–1806). Thomas Paine argued for a First Cause based on the laws of mechanics requiring an origin of motion but was a harsh critic of the Bible. Of the Bible he wrote, "It is incumbent on every man who reverences the character of the Creator, and who wishes to lessen the catalogue of artificial miseries, and remove the cause that has sown persecutions thick among mankind, to expel all ideas of revealed religion, as a dangerous heresy and as an impious

---

[8]Colin Brown, *From the Ancient World to the Age of Enlightenment*, vol. 1 of *Christianity and Western Thought: A History of Philosophers, Ideas and Movements* (Downers Grove, IL: IVP Academic, 1990), 205.
[9]Thiselton, *Concise Encyclopedia of the Philosophy of Religion*, 62.
[10]Brown, *From the Ancient World to the Age of Enlightenment*, 207.
[11]Ibid., 124.

fraud."[12] Elihu Palmer was a former Baptist preacher who ended up rejecting the deity of Christ and wrote *Principles of Nature* (ca. 1801), which became "the Bible of American Deism."[13] Although deism began in England, it eventually became far more popular in the United States. For instance, Thomas Jefferson and many other framers of the Constitution were deistic. Jefferson wrote, but never published, what has become known as *The Jefferson Bible*, in which he presented Jesus as simply a teacher of morality by cutting and pasting the Gospels together, removing references to miracles, the Holy Spirit, and the resurrection. These examples might suggest that every deist was hostile to Christianity, but this was not exactly the case.

In *The Universe Next Door*, James Sire rightly classifies some deists as "cold deists" and others as "warm deists."[14] Cold deists were hostile to Christianity, while warm deists were not. Warm deists, or Christian deists, kept more elements of the Christian worldview. For example, they retained belief in divine revelation but argued that it could be learned through natural religion. In contrast, cold deists rejected organized religion, arguing that religion finds its origin in "credulity, political tyranny, and priestcraft," which corrupts reason and pulls people away from true religion.[15]

Although not many would claim to be deists today, there are many who would rightly be called by such name. Sire identifies three forms of modern deism: (1) sophisticated philosophical deists, (2) sophisticated scientific deists, and (3) popular deists.[16] He argues that cold deism still exists among many scientists and philosophers today. Based on scientific evidence and philosophical arguments, many philosophers and scientists believe in the existence of a god. However, this god is not involved in our world and has not communicated with humanity through special revelation. This god is often understood as the source of the order and design of the universe.

---

[12]Thomas Paine, *The Age of Reason: Being an Investigation of True and Fabulous Theology* (New York: Liberal and Scientific Publishing House, 1877), 144.

[13]Brown, *From the Ancient World to the Age of Enlightenment*, 281.

[14]James S. Sire, *The Universe Next Door: A Basic Worldview Catalog*, 5th ed. (Downers Grove, IL: IVP Academic, 2009), 51.

[15]Wainwright, "Deism," 216.

[16]Sire, *Universe Next Door*, 59-64.

Sire argues that popular deists, in contrast to scientific and philo-sophical deists, see God as "personal and even friendly."[17] Sire points to the work of Christian Smith and Melinda Lundquist Denton, authors of *Soul Searching: The Religious and Spiritual Lives of American Teenagers*, to show the prevalence of warm deism in the United States. In their re-search they discovered that most teenagers adhered to what Smith and Denton call "Moralistic Therapeutic Deism" (MTD). They identified five main beliefs in this form of deism: (1) God created the world, orders it, and watches over humans on earth; (2) God wants people to be good, as taught in the Bible and in other religions; (3) the goal of life is to be happy and feel good about oneself; (4) God does not have to be involved in one's life except if there is a problem he can help fix; and (5) good people go to heaven when they die.[18] Sire's description of modern-day philo-sophical, scientific, or popular deists would generally include those that say they believe in a creator god, though divorced from any kind of religious tradition.

7.1.1 What is our nature? According to deism, people are rational, per-sonal, and moral creatures created by God. For warm deists, God is mildly personal, but for cold deists God is an abstract force or First Cause. Con-cerning the existence of God, Thomas Paine wrote, "The only idea man can affix to the name of God, is that of first cause, the cause of all things. And, incomprehensible and difficult as it is for man to conceive what a first cause is, he arrives at the belief of it, from the tenfold greater difficulty of disbelieving it."[19] For cold deists God is impersonal, meaning God is an "it." It does not have knowledge or awareness; it does not freely perform actions; and it does not enter into relationship with other persons. People are part of creation and therefore are bound to the mechanistic and or-derly system that God established. They have no way to transcend this mechanistic system. In addition, people do not need special revelation from God but can learn what they need to know about the universe and God solely based on human reason. According to warm deists, reason

---

[17]Ibid., 63.
[18]Christian Smith and Melinda Lundquist Denton, *Soul Searching: The Religious and Spiritual Lives of American Teenagers* (New York: Oxford University Press, 2005), 162-63.
[19]Paine, *Age of Reason*, 25.

dictates that people should worship God and live morally good lives. In moralistic therapeutic deism, God wants people to be good, feel happy, and feel good about themselves. Warm deists also tend to believe in the immortality of the soul because reason dictates that good behavior should be rewarded and bad behavior should be punished. In contrast, cold deists reject the idea of an afterlife. In summary, according to deists, humans are rational creatures created by God, personal or impersonal, and through reason alone we can determine how best to live in our world.

7.1.2 What is our world? According to deists, the world is God's orderly creation. Sire provides a helpful summary of the deist view of God and his creation. He writes that for deists the really real is "a transcendent God, as a First Cause, [who] created the universe but then left it to run on its own. God is thus not immanent, not triune, not fully personal, not sovereign over human affairs, not providential."[20] For example, Voltaire responded to the problem of evil by asserting that suffering exists not because it is deserved, nor because God allows it or is unable to stop, but because God is oblivious to it.

God created the world but then left it to run as a well-constructed self-regulating system. Voltaire once wrote in a letter, "I shall always be convinced that a watch proves a watchmaker, and that the universe proves a God."[21] For deists, the world is an orderly mechanistic system that is governed by physical laws established by God. Therefore, everything happens in the world according to these laws. Consequently, deists generally reject the miraculous and argue that miracles are against reason and rooted in superstition. Some deists reject the existence of the miraculous because they believe that miracles are contrary to God's nature, while others reject belief in miracles because they believe that there is no convincing evidence that God performs miracles.

In addition to believing that the world is an orderly system, deists also contend that the world is in its normal state. The way the world is today is the way the world has always been since creation; there has been no

---

[20]Sire, *Universe Next Door*, 51.
[21]David Beeson and Nicholas Cronk, "Voltaire: Philosopher or *Philosophe*?," in *A Cambridge Companion to Voltaire*, ed. Nicholas Cronk (New York: Cambridge University Press, 2009), 49; and Voltaire, "Letters," in *The Portable Voltaire*, ed. Ben Ray Reedman (New York: Penguin Books, 1968), 472.

fall as the Bible teaches. In other words, creation is good in its present
state. As we shall see, this belief causes problems for the deistic worldview
when attempting to deal with the problem of evil.

7.1.3 *What is our problem?* The deist worldview does not identify any
singular problem with the world. Because deism varies from deist to
deist, there is no unified answer to this question. The world is still in its
original good state. There was no fall, and nothing in creation has been
corrupted. Humans are not fallen, nor do they have a sinful nature. They
do not need forgiveness or atonement. Humans, through autonomous
reason, have the ability to live reasonable and moral lives.

Therefore, the evil in our world could be attributed to human beings
not living up to their inherent nature. Instead of using reason and following universal moral values available to all, people are choosing to do
otherwise. Warm deists, like Herbert of Cherbury, used the language of
sin and repentance, but the sin he spoke of was against general moral
values discoverable through human reason. Cold deists, who tend to be
more hostile to religion, Christianity specifically, accuse religion of being
superstitious and muddying the waters of reason. Consequently, some
cold deists might see organized religion as a problem because it keeps
people from discovering true religion based on reason. Although deism
does not identify a central problem with our world, it is reasonable to
deduce that from a deistic perspective the problems that do exist in our
world are rooted in faulty thinking. In other words, people are not using
their rational faculties as they should.

Because deism does not identify a central problem in our world, it
necessarily does not identify a solution, besides maybe living in accord
with reason. A deist's belief concerning the central problem in our world
and its solution is largely determined by whether he is a warm or cold
deist. Warm deists may contend that the solution is to follow the natural
moral law, maybe as seen in the teachings of Christ. Living a moral life
may involve repentance if one does not follow the moral dictates of
reason. In addition to this personal pursuit of virtue, some deists, like
Benjamin Franklin and Thomas Jefferson, focused on public welfare.
Living virtuously meant seeking the welfare of society through public
service. Cold deists reject the idea of an afterlife, but this does not mean

that they disregard morality. For example, Thomas Paine highly criticized organized religion and wanted people to set themselves free from it, but at the same time he devoted himself to public welfare. However, cold deists that simply affirm the existence of a First Cause would not necessarily emphasize living for the greater good as Paine did. For cold deists, there is no singular problem with the world, nor a single solution. To conclude, deists do not provide a unified vision concerning our world's problem and solution, though for many early deists the general solution to the world's problems involves living a moral life based on the virtues arrived at through human reason.

7.1.4 What is our end? A deist's perspective on humanity's end, which includes our purpose and destination, depends on whether he is a cold or warm deist. It would be safe to say that according to deists the purpose of life is to live a good moral life. Voltaire argued that the "universal religion established in all ages and throughout mankind" teaches that "there is a God, and one must be just."[22]

Cold deists reject the idea of an afterlife and therefore view death as the end of personal consciousness and existence. In contrast, warm deists believe in the afterlife and affirm that people will be rewarded or punished in the afterlife. For example, Herbert of Cherbury taught that repentance expiated sin and that moral living would be rewarded in the afterlife. Warm deists often affirm that God wants people to be happy and that this is attained through virtue, attainable through reason apart from any kind of special revelation. Similarly, those adhering to moralistic therapeutic deism believe that God wants people to be good and happy and to feel good about themselves because those who are "good" will go to heaven when they die. To conclude, cold deists believe that life ends at death, while warm deists believe that people will be rewarded or punished in the afterlife.

7.2 Deism and Life Motivation

A person's life motivation is the overarching drive that guides everyday decisions and general direction in life. Because deism does not propose a central aim in life, life motivation among deists is probably very diverse.

---

[22]Voltaire, "Philosophical Dictionary," in Reedman, *Portable Voltaire*, 196.

So on the one hand, it would be a stretch to speak of *the* life motivation in the deistic worldview. Yet on the other hand, it is still possible to identify principles that likely guide the direction of a deist's life.

A cold deist, someone who believes that God is simply an impersonal First Cause, most likely does not live his or her life with any regard for God. In this form of deism God is simply a power and not a person. Such deists might believe in the existence of a god, but for them the personal God of the Bible does not exist. The First Cause has not provided any guidance on why we exist and what we should live for. Therefore, the life motivation of cold deists may be as varied as it is for atheists. Besides assuming a desire to live a life guided by reason, deists' life motivations probably vary from person to person depending on one's life experiences.

The life motivation found among warm deists, like adherents of moralistic therapeutic deism, is probably less diverse than among cold deists. In the best-case scenario this type of deism leads to moralism, a deep desire to be good. In moralistic therapeutic deism God wants people to be good, and good people go to heaven when they die. Therefore, a warm deist may be guided by a strong desire to be a good person, probably by avoiding any major moral infraction and by being tolerant of others. When asked, "will you go to heaven when you die?," they would probably answer "yes, because I am a good person." In the worst-case scenario, this type of deism leads to a self-centered and self-absorbed life, in which one's own happiness is the guiding principle. This makes sense if (1) God created the world and watches over you, (2) the goal of life is to be happy and feel good about yourself, and (3) God does not have to be involved in your life unless there is a problem he can fix. In this paradigm, life is all about me and my happiness. God is there simply to help me be happy and feel good about myself.

REFLECTION QUESTIONS

1 Are there any similarities between deist and Christian worldviews? If so, what are they?

2 What are the most significant differences between deist and Christian worldviews?

3 What are the differences between cold and warm deists?

4 Have you come across any examples of moralistic therapeutic deism? If so, explain the context.

5 In your opinion, what is the role of deistic thought in current Western spirituality?

7.3 WORLDVIEW ANALYSIS OF DEISM

In this section the deist worldview will now be analyzed for (1) internal consistency and logical coherence, (2) external consistency and evidential correspondence, and (3) existential consistency and pragmatic satisfaction. Before highlighting some of the problems with deism, it should be noted that there are several elements of deism, especially warm deism, that align to a degree with a Christian and biblical worldview. For example, Christians can affirm warm deists' belief in a personal creator God that deserves worship and commands us to live moral lives. We can affirm the belief that humans are rational and moral creatures and that there is an afterlife. We can even agree with a cold deist that the order in creation suggests the existence of a creator.

7.3.1 Internal consistency and logical coherence. Cold deism's affirmation that the world is a closed system and warm deism's pluralistic perspective create inconsistencies in the deistic worldview. Cold deists affirm that the world is a closed system, meaning that it operates as a closed chain of cause and effect, with no intervention from the outside. The closed system is therefore determined by the natural laws that govern it, meaning that whatever is in the system is determined to behave a certain way. The problem with this perspective is that people are part of this mechanistic system as well. This calls into question the meaningfulness of the choices people make. Do we actually make real choices, or are we simply carrying out what is determined based on the laws that govern the mechanistic universe we are in? If people are simply in the mechanistic chain of cause and effect, then they are not able to change their environment as they think; they have lost the element of self-determination. The cold deist view of the world as a closed system and its affirmation of human action and responsibility appear to be

*Contemporary Cultural
Worldview Meditation*

Indie-Folk Music and Religious Pluralism

Mason Jennings, an American indie-folk singer/ songwriter, provides a vivid example of religious pluralism at the popular level with his song "I Love You and Buddha Too." Take a minute to look up this song online. Jennings begins the song by expressing his love for Jesus, Buddha, Muhammad, and other religious figures and texts. He proceeds to reject the idea that there is only one way to God and affirms that we are all part of God. Jennings implies that each religion provides a different path to the same God and that all are simply using different metaphors. Unfortunately for his position, his relatively brief song reveals some of the logical inconsistencies of religious pluralism. For example, he affirms love for Muhammad. However, true love for Muhammad, as any Muslim would agree, involves following his teachings. Since Jennings is not a Muslim, it is unlikely that he practices the Five Pillars of Islam. Muslims are unlikely to believe someone's claim to love Muhammad if that person has no desire to obey his teachings. From a Muslim perspective, Jennings's claim to love Muhammad most likely appears to be nothing more than lip service. A similar analysis could be applied to his claim that he loves Jesus and the Buddha. In addition, to support his religious perspective Jennings is forced to postulate an unknowable nonsensical deity. In the song, Jennings describes God as unnamable and unknowable and uses self-contradictory statements like "you are and you are not." Jennings's song affirms a general love for the divine in the various religions, but when one takes a minute to think through what he is saying, the logical underpinnings of his religious position are found lacking.

inconsistent. If the world is determined by natural laws, then people are not able to make real choices. Deists, like most people, live and make judgments assuming that people make real choices and are accountable for them. However, if the world is a closed system, then people are not actually making real choices. Our sense of self-determination is therefore an illusion.

Another apparent internal inconsistency in cold deism is its emphasis on living morally upright lives. Cold deists, although they reject organized religion, still affirm the importance of living up to a certain standard of morality discoverable through human reason. However, where do these moral standards come from? Are they objective moral values? Warm deists point to a good God as the source of this sense of morality. He created people with an innate sense of right or wrong or with the rational ability to distinguish right from wrong. The problem is that cold deists cannot point to a good God as the source of moral values because for them god is an impersonal First Cause. An impersonal thing does not have knowledge, does not willfully perform actions, and does not enter into relationships with other persons. Like a rock or wind or gravity, an impersonal First Cause is not a moral being but rather an amoral thing. Moral values cannot be rooted in an amoral god. Consequently, moral values are relative. They are not grounded in any source outside of humanity itself. They are socially constructed and have no basis outside of humanity. People or societies can determine for themselves what is right and wrong. Based on their understanding of god, cold deists should be moral relativists. However, this does not seem to be the case, because cold deists affirm the real difference between good and evil. Some modern cold deists might see this implication and affirm moral relativism; yet they cannot live this out consistently. Would they affirm that Hitler's murder of millions of Jews might have been morally acceptable in Nazi Germany, or would they say that what he did was objectively wrong? If one of their loved ones were raped and murdered, could they affirm that it was not objectively wrong because it might have been acceptable behavior according to the perpetrator's ethical system? Cold deists, just like everyone else, live their lives and make moral judgments as if there were objective moral values.

One weakness with warm deism is that it leads people to embrace religious pluralism, which is an internally inconsistent theological position. Religious pluralism is the belief that all religions for the most part are equally salvific. One could argue that deism does not *lead to* this belief but actually *began with* this belief, though it was not emphasized. Herbert of Cherbury's five principles of religion, also known as the five principles of deism, indirectly teach that people can access God through a variety of religions. He asserted that all religions teach morality and repentance and that those who live virtuous lives will be rewarded in the afterlife. Similarly, Voltaire postulated a "universal religion":

> All the philosophers of the world who have had a religion have said in all ages: "There is a God, and one must be just." There, then, is the universal religion established in all ages and throughout mankind. The point in which they all agree is therefore true, and the systems through which they differ are therefore false.[23]

[23]Voltaire, "Philosophical Dictionary," 196.

According to warm deists, this "true religion," which is "an expression of a universal human nature whose essence is reason," is "the same in all times and places."[24] If this "true religion" is found through human reason and is the same in all times and places, it would naturally lead to the belief that it can be found in a variety of religions. However, the pluralist position has significant weaknesses.

John Hick, a well-known and respected philosopher of religion, has one of the most developed and convincing theories of religious pluralism. For Hick, "all our concepts of God are 'images' of the infinite divine reality."[25] Thus, Christ is the Christian image of God, Yahweh is the Jewish image of God, Krishna is a Hindu image of God, and so forth. He argues that these images are finite and culturally formed conceptions of "the divine reality that exceeds all human thought."[26] Hick admits that the conflicting truth claims between religious traditions present the most difficulty for the pluralist hypothesis. In order to get around the problem of conflicting truth claims, Hick is forced to reinterpret and mythologize the central truth claims of religious traditions. For instance, Hick contends that "Jesus is the concrete image of God through whom our worship is focused, and the idea of the Incarnation is an effective mythic expression of the appropriate attitude to him."[27] In other words, the doctrine of the incarnation is simply a useful myth that helps Christians to focus on God in an appropriate manner. Ronald Nash rightly points out that Hick's reduction of religious beliefs to myth is foreign to how insiders would understand their beliefs.[28] Hick is forced to assign a completely new meaning to the doctrines of the various world religions in order to make sense of their conflicting claims. Moreover, Winfried Corduan correctly points out that to affirm that another religion's truth claims are true, as Hick does, yet at the same time affirm that the claim actually has a higher meaning behind it, does violence to or trivializes the religion.[29]

[24]Wainwright, "Deism," 216.
[25]John Hick, *God and the Universe of Faiths* (London: Collins, 1973), 178.
[26]Ibid.
[27]Ibid., 179.
[28]Ronald H. Nash, *Is Jesus the Only Savior?* (Grand Rapids: Zondervan, 1994), 65.
[29]Winfried Corduan, *A Tapestry of Faiths: The Common Threads Between Christianity & World Religions* (Downers Grove, IL: InterVarsity Press, 2002), 145.

For example, to say that the Christian belief in the incarnation of Jesus is "true" but then turn around and say that the Christian belief in the incarnation is true because it is "an effective mythic expression" of an appropriate attitude to God turns Christianity upside down. Because of his pluralist perspective, Hick must reinterpret the religious beliefs of the major world religions in such a way that they become foreign to the actual adherents of the religions.[30]

7.3.2 External consistency and evidential correspondence. Warm deists contend that the world is orderly and good because God is orderly and good. Consequently, they deny the biblical teaching of the fall. The world has always been the way it is now. The problem is that the world appears at times chaotic and the source of evil, such as natural disasters and illnesses. Diogenes Allen points out that if deists believe in God solely because of the order in the world, then any kind of disorder, like pain, suffering, and unhappiness, would reflect negatively on the wisdom and goodness of God. If there was no fall, then the brokenness in the world reflects how God created it. The warm deist position that the world is good and orderly does not seem to match our experience of the world, and it calls into question the goodness of the God they affirm.

Moreover, the belief that the world is in its normal state may imply that whatever happens in the world is good, thereby destroying ethics. If God is good and he created a good world, then whatever happens must be good. Both Allen and Sire point to the deist Alexander Pope's problematic line in his *Essay on Man*, where he writes that "whatever is, is right."[31] Pope writes:

> All nature is but art, unknown to thee;
> All chance, direction, which thou canst not see;
> All discord, harmony, not understood;
> All partial evil, universal good;
> And, spite of pride, in erring reason's spite,
> One truth is clear, Whatever is, is right.[32]

---

[30]For an extensive critique of John Hick's theory of religious pluralism, see Harold A. Netland, *Encountering Religious Pluralism: The Challenge to Christian Faith & Mission* (Downers Grove, IL: InterVarsity Press, 2001), 158-77.

[31]Diogenes Allen, *Philosophy for Understanding Theology* (Atlanta: John Knox, 1985), 169; and Sire, *Universe Next Door*, 56-57.

[32]Alexander Pope, *Essay on Man* (1733-1734), 1.288-94, www.poetryfoundation.org/poems-and

Though deists do not reject the reality of evil, their view of the world may imply this position, as evidenced by Pope's writings.

7.3.3 Existential consistency and pragmatic satisfaction. The test of existential consistency and pragmatic satisfaction has to do with the livability of a belief system and whether it is existentially satisfying. Few if any people today actually call themselves deists, yet many do fit within the deistic perspective. The fact that many could be classified as deists is actually what one would expect based on scriptural teaching. In Romans, Paul states that through creation (Rom 1:18-25) and the conscience (Rom 1:32; 2:14-16) everyone knows that God exists and that they are morally accountable to him. However, this general information is only enough to condemn us, not to save us. Similarly, the deist worldview is unsustainable in its mere affirmation of the existence of a creator and the need to live a virtuous life.

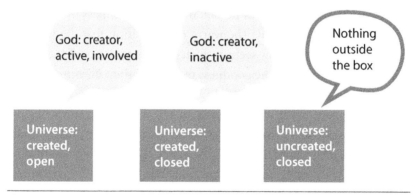

Figure 7.1. Transition from Christian theism through deism to naturalism

One of the major weaknesses of the deist worldview is that it quickly turns into naturalism. Deism began with a Christian view of God except without the Trinity, but then as it progressed away from the Christian faith God lost his omnipresence, will, and personhood, making God merely an abstract force. This god serves little to no purpose for an individual, except as an explanation for the design in the universe. When scientists proposed evolution as an explanation for the design in the universe, the god of cold deists no longer needed a reason to exist; hence naturalism. Therefore, as illustrated by figure 7.1, deism became the "isthmus between two great continents—theism and naturalism."[33]

REFLECTION QUESTIONS

1 What are the greatest strengths of deism?

2 What are some logical problems with deism?

3 What are the differences between the god of deism and the biblical God?

4 What are the social benefits for someone holding to religious pluralism?

5 Will the role of deistic thought in the Western world increase or decrease in the coming decades?

7.4 NATURALISM

In *The Oxford Companion to Philosophy*, Alan Lacey defines naturalism as "the view that everything is natural, i.e. that everything there is belongs to the world of nature, and so can be studied by the methods appropriate for studying that world, and the apparent exceptions can be explained away." In addition, he writes that in metaphysics naturalism asserts that "the world of nature should form a single sphere without incursions from outside by souls or spirits, divine or human, and without having to accommodate strange entities like non-natural values or substantive abstract universals."[34] In other words, naturalism only affirms the existence of the natural, and therefore rejects the existence of the supernatural and spiritual. Sire describes the essence of naturalism with the following words: "Prime reality is matter. Matter exists eternally and is all there is. God does not exist."[35] Alvin Plantinga provides a similar description of naturalism when he writes that it involves the view that "there is no such person as God, not anyone or anything at all like him."[36]

[33]Sire, *Universe Next Door*, 66.
[34]Alan Lacey, "Naturalism," in Honderich, *Oxford Companion to Philosophy* (1995), 604.
[35]Sire, *Universe Next Door*, 68.
[36]Alvin Plantinga, *Warranted Christian Belief* (New York: Oxford University Press, 2000), 227.

Democritus (ca. 460–370 BC), Aristotle (384–322 BC), Epicurus (341–271 BC), Lucretius (99 or 94–55 BC), Thomas Hobbes (1588–1679), and Baruch Spinoza (1632–1677) are sometimes counted as "the ancestors of naturalism," but "the major impetus to naturalism in the last two centuries" has been the explanatory power of advances in science, especially Darwin's theory of evolution.[37] Prominent adherents of naturalism include Sigmund Freud, Jean-Paul Sartre, Friedrich Nietzsche, Karl Marx, and Bertrand Russell. Some of the most prominent adherents of naturalism today include leaders of the new atheism, like Daniel Dennett, Richard Dawkins, Sam Harris, and the late Christopher Hitchens.

7.4.1 What is our nature? According to naturalism, humanity is the result of the blind and purposeless forces of evolution. Humanity is ultimately the result of matter, time, and chance. The American Humanist Association states that "humans are an integral part of nature, the result of unguided evolutionary change."[38] Bertrand Russell's "A Free Man's Worship" provides a helpful summary of a naturalist's view of humanity:

> That Man is the product of causes which had no prevision of the end they were achieving; that his origin, his growth, his hopes and fears, his loves and his beliefs, are but the outcome of accidental collocations of atoms; that no fire, no heroism, no intensity of thought or feeling, can preserve an individual life beyond the grave; that all the labours of the ages, all the devotion, all the inspiration, all the noonday brightness of human genius, are destined to extinction in the vast death of the solar system, and that the whole temple of Man's achievement must inevitably be buried beneath the debris of a universe in ruins—all these things, if not quite beyond dispute, are yet so nearly certain, that no philosophy which rejects them can hope to stand.[39]

According to Russell, humanity is "the outcome of accidental collocations of atoms." Humanity is therefore merely a further evolved form of life. Humans simply evolved from ancestral primates, Homo sapiens with bodies and brains like ours appearing at least 200,000 years ago.

---

[37]John F. Post, "Naturalism," in Audi, *Cambridge Dictionary of Philosophy*, 596.
[38]American Humanist Association, "Humanist Manifesto III," in *A World Religions Reader*, ed. Ian S. Markham and Christy Lohr, 3rd ed. (Malden, MA: Wiley-Blackwell, 2009), 292.
[39]Bertrand Russell, "A Free Man's Worship," in Markham and Lohr, *World Religions Reader*, 288.

Humanity was not created; it just happened and is "destined to extinction" just like everything else. Tom Flynn states that "no one planned the universe: it just happened. No one intended us; in Bertrand Russell's words, we humans are just 'an accident in a backwater.'"[40] Because we are part of this physical universe, we are ultimately "complex machines," our personalities arising from the interplay of chemical and physical properties. Mental phenomena, like our consciousness, are "natural biological phenomena on a par with growth, digestion, and photosynthesis."[41] Our thoughts, emotions, desires, will, and actions arise ultimately from physical properties.

7.4.2 What is our world? According to naturalism, our universe, just like humanity, is the result of matter, chance, and time. Nature, the material world, is self-existing. Our universe is probably the result of an event known as the Big Bang, when the universe began to expand from an "infinitesimally small, infinitely dense, and infinitely hot object known as a singularity," which contained "all of the energy and matter in the universe."[42] The universe is around 14 billion years old and the earth is between 4.5 and 4.6 billion years old. The universe was not planned, but just happened. Moreover, the universe is a "closed system" with certain physical laws that govern everything in it. In other words, everything that is in the natural universe is caused by what is in the natural universe; there is nothing outside the natural universe. Knowledge of the universe is best discovered through science because it is best suited for observation, experimentation, and rational analysis. However, as Russell points out, science presents a purposeless world, void of meaning.

7.4.3 What is our problem? Adherents of naturalism do not identify a problem with the world. The world is just the way it is. It is in its normal state. Therefore, naturalism does not identify a single problem that needs to be solved. Each naturalist might have his or her own opinion regarding a problem with the world, and the problem identified would most likely

---

[40]Tom Flynn, "Advocatus Diaboli," in Markham and Lohr, *World Religions Reader*, 298. This article was initially published as "Thank God I'm an Atheist," *Secular Humanist Bulletin* 11, no. 3 (1995).

[41]John Searle, "Biological Naturalism," in Honderich, *Oxford Companion to Philosophy* (1995), 93.

[42]National Academy of Sciences (U.S.) and Institute of Medicine (U.S.), *Science, Evolution, and Creationism*, 18.

be based on the norms of the individual's social context. As with most worldviews, though, naturalists often identify pain and suffering as problems in our world. For example, in "A Free Man's Worship" Russell does not identify "our problem," but he does describe the human condition in bleak terms. The present human condition is presented not as a problem to be solved but as a reality to be dealt with. He writes, "The life of Man is a long march through the night, surrounded by invisible foes, tortured by weariness and pain. . . . One by one, as they march, our comrades vanish from sight, seized by the silent orders of omnipotent Death."[43]

Other naturalists, especially secular humanists, view religion as one of the central problems in our world because, from their perspective, it produces so much pain and suffering. Secular humanism is a popular form of naturalism. Not all naturalists are secular humanists, but all secular humanists are naturalists. Secular humanism emphasizes that there is nothing higher than the human race, and therefore people should love their neighbor by seeking their good, and that all true knowledge is to be found through science. According to secular humanism, religion is "deeply destructive, violent, and intolerant."[44] Ian S. Markham and Christy Lohr describe the secular humanist perspective well when they write that "the great secular hope is that as religion fades, so peace and harmony between people will become possible." They point to John Lennon's song "Imagine" as an example of this "great secular hope," where there is nothing to live for or die for, where there is no religion, and where people live in peace.[45]

7.4.4 What is our end? Naturalism teaches that there is no ultimate meaning and purpose in life (besides what people create for themselves) and that human life ends at death. We were not created for any specific purpose, because we were not created in the first place. Rather, we came about through natural causes. Therefore, humanity and human history are not directed toward any specific end (besides eventual extinction, that is). History is simply "a linear stream of events linked by cause and effect

---

[43]Russell, "Free Man's Worship," 290.
[44]Markham and Lohr, *World Religions Reader*, 274.
[45]Ibid., 299.

but without an overarching purpose."[46] Consequently, each person has the ability to determine what to do with the time he or she has on earth. Many advocates of naturalism conclude that people should seek to enjoy life and try to make life as good as possible for themselves and others.

According to naturalism, when one's physical body perishes, the whole person—including consciousness and personal identity—is entirely dissolved. Therefore, naturalism does not concern itself with the afterlife. Rather, naturalism concerns itself with making life better in the here and now. On the one hand, the solution for human and animal suffering caused by nature (diseases and natural disasters) can be potentially solved by or at least alleviated by science. Richard Dawkins argues that science gives us the answers we need, while religion is useless and destructive. He argues that science alone, as opposed to religion, has given us information about our origin and has helped us fight diseases. He writes, "It is science, and science alone, that has given us this knowledge [about our origin] and given it, moreover, in fascinating, overwhelming, mutually confirming detail. . . . Science has eradicated smallpox, can immunize against most previously deadly viruses, and can kill most previously deadly bacteria."[47]

On the other hand, suffering caused by people can be solved or alleviated by people living ethical lives. For instance, in the "Humanist Manifesto III," the American Humanist Association describes humanism as "a progressive philosophy of life that, without supernaturalism, affirms our ability and responsibility to lead ethical lives of personal fulfillment that aspire to the greater good of humanity."[48] Moreover, it states that by treating all people "as having inherent worth and dignity" and working to benefit society, individual happiness is maximized. Thus, happiness is increased and suffering is decreased when people seek the greater good of humanity. In light of the inevitability of death, people should seek to delight in the human experience: "We aim for our fullest possible development and animate our lives with a deep sense of purpose, finding

[46]Sire, *Universe Next Door*, 80.
[47]Richard Dawkins, "Letter to *The Independent*, 20 March 1993," in Markham and Lohr, *World Religions Reader*, 276-77.
[48]American Humanist Association, "Humanist Manifesto III," 291-92.

wonder and awe in the joys and beauties of human existence, its challenges and tragedies, and even in the inevitability and finality of death."
Russell presents a similar perspective when he argues that in light of the
coming personal extinction, people should live to provide as much happiness as possible for each other:

> Be it ours to shed sunshine on their path, to lighten their sorrows by the
> balm of sympathy, to give them the pure joy of a never tiring affection, to
> strengthen failing courage, to instill faith in hours of despair. Let us not
> weigh in grudging scales their merits and demerits, but let us think only
> of their need—of the sorrows, the difficulties, perhaps the blindnesses,
> that make the misery of their lives; let us remember that they are fellow-
> sufferers in the same darkness, actors in the same tragedy with ourselves.[49]

7.5 NATURALISM AND LIFE MOTIVATION

In the naturalistic worldview there is no ultimate meaning and purpose
in our world; therefore, there is no ultimate overarching life motivation
that should guide a person's life. We are simply further evolved animals
that came about through the interplay of matter, time, and chance. God
did not place us on earth for a specific purpose; we are just here. We are
here on earth as the result of the natural process of evolution. Consequently, each adherent of naturalism is free to create his or her own
meaning and purpose in life, though bound by the belief that the supernatural and spiritual do not exist.

Secular humanism is an example of how some adherents of naturalism have sought to create meaning and purpose in their lives. Secular
humanists affirm that all people have inherent dignity and worth, and
therefore people should live ethical lives, seeking the greater good of
humanity. Consequently, secular humanists might seek to live ethically
and devote themselves to causes they feel will contribute to the happiness
of others as a way to find fulfillment in life.

Secular humanists' ethical values and beliefs concerning what is good
for humanity most likely emerge from their own life experiences and
mirror to a great extent the prevailing moral values of their society.

---

[49]Russell, "Free Man's Worship," 290.

REFLECTION QUESTIONS

1 Are there any similarities between naturalism and the Christian worldview? If so, what are they?

2 What are the most significant differences between naturalism and the Christian worldview?

3 What are the sources of morality for secular humanists?

4 What are some arguments against the societal value of religion? Are they valid arguments?

5 What would an ideal society look like from a secular humanist perspective?

7.6 WORLDVIEW ANALYSIS OF NATURALISM

As we did for deism, the naturalist worldview will also be analyzed for (1) internal consistency and logical coherence, (2) external consistency and evidential correspondence, and (3) existential consistency and pragmatic satisfaction. Though we will proceed to point out shortcomings of the naturalist worldview, there are some elements worth affirming. First, naturalism correctly affirms the reality of the natural world and the existence of objective truth, even if it is restricted to scientific knowledge. Second, naturalism correctly asserts that science has helped us understand our world and has led to numerous discoveries that have made our lives better. Finally, we would agree with secular humanists in their affirmation of human dignity and worth and in their desire to love their neighbors and live ethical lives.

7.6.1 Internal consistency and logical coherence. One major inconsistency in naturalism is its affirmation of evolution on the one hand and its optimistic view of human epistemology (our ability to know things) on the other. Alvin Plantinga convincingly argues that combining the theory of evolution with naturalism is self-defeating.[50] The naturalists' view of human origins should lead them to distrust their thinking, leading them to epistemological skepticism. Charles Darwin himself saw

---

[50]Plantinga, *Warranted Christian Belief*, 227-40.

this problem. In a letter Darwin sent to W. Graham on July 3, 1881, he writes, "The horrid doubt always arises whether the convictions of man's mind, which has developed from the mind of lower animals, are of any value or at all trustworthy. Would anyone trust the conviction of a monkey's mind, if there are any convictions in such a mind?"[51] Plantinga points out that according to naturalism human cognitive faculties were developed through random genetic mutations and natural selection. Moreover, the random mutations that led to the current human brain were selected not because they produced true beliefs but for the purpose of survival. Just because our cognitive faculties have helped our ancestors survive and reproduce says nothing about "the *truth* of our beliefs or the reliability of our cognitive faculties."[52] Naturalists have strong confidence in human reason and science, but this does not seem to fit with their understanding of our origins and the ultimate source of our cognitive faculties.

Moreover, some naturalists inconsistently affirm human dignity and worth. For example, in the "Humanist Manifesto III," the American Humanist Association promotes treating all people "as having inherent worth and dignity." However, what is the source of this inherent worth and dignity? According to naturalists, humanity is simply an accident, the result of a purposeless physical mechanism. As Russell states, we are "the outcome of accidental collocations of atoms."[53] We are simply further evolved forms of life. We are not that different from any other form of animal life. We might think ourselves more important than apes, dogs, and hamsters, but this is simply our biased opinion. We have no more value or dignity than any other animal. The value and dignity we have are self-designated; these qualities are simply something we assign ourselves. Evolution does not teach that humanity has any inherent worth or dignity. It actually teaches the opposite. Consistent naturalists will have to reject the idea that humanity has an inherent worth and dignity.

---

[51]Sire, *Universe Next Door*, 103-4. Sire references the quote in *The Autobiography of Charles Darwin and Selected Letters* (1892; repr., New York: Dover, 1958).

[52]Plantinga, *Warranted Christian Belief*, 234.

[53]Russell, "Free Man's Worship," 288.

7.6.2 External consistency and evidential correspondence. The natu-ralist worldview, though supported by the theory of evolution, is un-dercut by other scientific theories that point to the existence of God, such as the standard Big Bang model and the fine-tuning of the universe that allows life to exist. If the standard Big Bang model is true, then the uni-verse is not eternal; it began to exist at some point in the finite past. If whatever begins to exist has a cause, and if the universe began to exist as the Big Bang model suggests, then the universe must have a cause. This cause by necessity is beyond the physical universe. Theists would argue that this cause beyond the physical universe is God. Moreover, the fine-tuning of the universe that allows life to exist points to an intelligent and intentional designer. The fine-tuning of the universe usually refers to the idea that when the laws of nature are given mathematical expression, the constants and quantities are set to allow life to exist; any small deviations would make the universe life-prohibiting. Some of these fundamental constants include electromagnetic interaction, gravitation, the weak force, the strong force that binds the nuclei of atoms together, and proton-to-electron mass ratio.[54] If any of these constants were slightly different, life in the universe would be impossible. The standard Big Bang model and the fine-tuning of the universe call into question the natural-istic perspective that there is nothing beyond the physical world.

The four traditional theistic arguments for God's existence also serve as evidence that undermines the naturalistic worldview. The cosmo-logical argument for God's existence is a family of arguments that seek to show the existence of a First Cause or a Sufficient Reason for the cosmos. The teleological argument for God's existence is a family of arguments that contend that the order and structure of the cosmos point to a pow-erful and intelligent designer. Anselm of Canterbury (1033–1109) first formulated the ontological argument for God's existence. He argued that God, who is conceived of as a perfect being (something of which nothing greater can be conceived), must actually exist because he would not be a perfect being (something of which nothing greater can be conceived) if

---

[54]J. P. Moreland and William Lane Craig, *Philosophical Foundations for a Christian Worldview* (Downers Grove, IL: IVP Academic, 2003), 465, 482-90.

he exists only in our minds.[55] Finally, the moral argument for God's existence is a family of arguments that contend that the human sense of morality and the existence of objective moral values are best explained by the existence of God.[56] These classical arguments do not prove God's existence, but they show that belief in God is not irrational and at the same time call into question the ability of naturalism to account for all the evidence.

7.6.3 Existential consistency and pragmatic satisfaction. The naturalist worldview cannot be lived out consistently. If naturalism is taken to its logical conclusion, it should lead to radical epistemological skepticism and moral relativism. If our cognitive faculties are the result of the blind mechanism of evolution, why should we trust our thinking at all? Our thinking may be working for us, but this does not mean that it produces true beliefs. It may just produce beliefs that help us survive. Consequently, if naturalism is true, then we should be skeptical of our ability to know anything at all. However, naturalists do not live this way. Naturalists use human reason and the laws of logic, trusting that they help lead to true beliefs. In contrast, from the Christian perspective, we believe that God (a God of truth and order) gave us cognitive faculties that are meant to lead us to true beliefs (though we also recognize our limits because of our finitude and the fall).

In addition, if there is no God, then moral values are relative, meaning that individuals or societies simply come up with them as they see fit.[57] Moral values then have no more objective authority than personal or societal preference. According to the "Humanist Manifesto III," "ethical

---

[55]Anselm, "Anselm's Ontological Argument," in *Readings in Philosophy of Religion: Ancient to Contemporary*, ed. Linda Zagzebski and Timothy D. Miller (Malden, MA: Wiley-Blackwell, 2009), 81-82.

[56]For in-depth discussion of the classical arguments for God's existence, see Moreland and Craig, *Philosophical Foundations for a Christian Worldview*, 463-99; Michael Peterson et al., *Reason & Religious Belief: An Introduction to the Philosophy of Religion*, 5th ed. (New York: Oxford University Press, 2013), 79-107; Charles Taliaferro, *Contemporary Philosophy of Religion*, Contemporary Philosophy (Malden, MA: Blackwell, 1998), 353-93; Francis J. Beckwith, William Lane Craig, and J. P. Moreland, eds., *To Everyone an Answer: A Case for the Christian Worldview* (Downers Grove, IL: IVP Academic, 2004), 57-137.

[57]For a helpful discussions of moral relativism, see Francis J. Beckwith and Gregory Koukl, *Relativism: Feet Firmly Planted in Mid-Air* (Grand Rapids: Baker Books, 1998), 26-69; and Moreland and Craig, *Philosophical Foundations for a Christian Worldview*, 407-16.

values are derived from human need and interest as tested by experience."[58] Therefore, good and evil are subjective concepts constructed by people. Nothing is truly good or truly evil. All we can say is that some action is good or evil to an individual or in a particular society. We cannot say that an action is universally and objectively good or evil. However, naturalists do not live this way. Many naturalists, as we have seen, argue that people should live ethical lives directed toward the greater good of humanity. Even Russell recognizes the reality of good and evil: "A strange mystery it is that Nature, omnipotent but blind, in the revolutions of her secular hurryings through the abysses of space, has brought forth at last a child, subject still to her power, but gifted with sight, with knowledge of good and evil, with the capacity of judging all the worlds of his unthinking Mother."[59] But if moral values are relative, how can one distinguish ethical living from unethical living? Wouldn't moral judgments simply be one's opinion or preference, equally valid as anyone else's? Naturalists end up borrowing from a theistic worldview when they affirm the trustworthiness of our cognitive faculties and the objective reality of good and evil.

Many naturalists who have sought to live out naturalism have ended up as nihilists. As Sire argues, "nihilism is the natural child of naturalism."[60] According to Robert C. Solomon in *The Oxford Companion to Philosophy*, nihilists believe in nothing and disdain all values, in particular justification for morality. Nihilism is "the negation of everything—knowledge, ethics, beauty, reality."[61] Samuel Beckett's play *Breath* exemplifies the meaninglessness of life as felt by nihilists. Sire describes the play:

> But Beckett's nihilistic art perhaps reached its climax in *Breath*, a thirty-five-second play that has no human actors. The props consist of a pile of rubbish on the stage, lit by a light that begins to dim, brightens (but never fully) and then recedes to dimness. There are no words, only a "recorded" cry opening the play, an inhaled breath, an exhaled breath and an identical "recorded" cry closing the play. For Beckett life is such a "breath."[62]

---

[58]American Humanist Association, "Humanist Manifesto III," 292.
[59]Russell, "Free Man's Worship," 289.
[60]Sire, *Universe Next Door*, 97.
[61]Ibid., 94.
[62]Ibid., 95.

However, people cannot consistently live out nihilism; no one can live day to day with the affirmation that everything is meaningless. The inability to live out nihilism explains the development of existentialism. Existentialism's basic principle is that "existence precedes essence," which is Jean-Paul Sartre's classic formulation of existentialism. Sartre argued that because there is no God, there is no given human nature. Therefore, he argues that "people first exist, confront themselves, emerge in the world, and define themselves afterward."[63] From the existentialist perspective, human dignity is rooted in the fact that we create ourselves and that we are responsible for what we become. Both nihilism and existentialism are responses to the logical conclusion of naturalism, which Russell expresses when he states that science presents us with a purposeless world, void of meaning.

REFLECTION QUESTIONS

1 What are the strengths of naturalism?

2 What are some of the strongest arguments against naturalism?

3 Does the problem of evil support or undermine naturalism?

4 Does the theory of evolution support or undermine naturalism?

5 Will the influence of naturalism in Western society increase or decrease in the coming decades?

7.7 POSTMODERNISM

It would be helpful to begin this section on postmodernism by first looking at the trajectory from Christian theism to deism to naturalism to postmodernism in Western thought. As we have seen, deism emerged in part from a rejection of the authority of the Bible. By rejecting God's special revelation, central Christian teachings were lost, like the Trinity, the deity of Christ, the resurrection of Christ, and the gospel. This created belief in a generic, though benevolent, creator god or maybe simply an impersonal power or force. However, with new scientific discoveries and the theory of evolution, many concluded that a creator god was no longer needed in

---

[63]Samuel Enoch Stumpf and James Fieser, *Philosophy: History and Problems* (Boston: McGraw-Hill, 2003), 463.

order to explain the universe. As we have seen, denying the existence of God naturally leads to relativism and skepticism, which Russell expresses when he states that the world is purposeless, void of meaning.

Postmodernism is not technically a worldview like deism and naturalism. Nonetheless, its presence is so prevalent in North America that it cannot be ignored when discussing the topic of worldview.[64] As the term suggests, postmodernism is a reaction to modernism or, as some argue, the next stage of modernism. Modernism began in the seventeenth century with the Enlightenment and stretches to the latter half of the twentieth century. Modernism emphasizes that the "objective foundation of truth, meaning, purpose, and value is found in man, nature, and science."[65] *Postmodernism* is a broad term used in a variety of fields like architecture, literature, art, theology, and painting.

For our purposes, we will be looking at philosophical postmodernism. A universally agreed-on definition of philosophical postmodernism does not exist. Samuel Stumpf and James Fieser provide a helpful description: "Postmodernism is not a single philosophical theory; to be so would be self-defeating. Instead it is an umbrella movement that covers a variety of critiques of the modern conceptions of things."[66]

Postmodernism rejects many of the presuppositions of modernism. Although modernism rejected the premodern concept of God, it kept for the most part the premodern ideas that "the universe is real and intelligible, that language is a basically reliable tool for communicating truth and reality, and the epistemological principle that truth is found when one's ideas, beliefs, and statements correspond with reality."[67] Postmodernism rejects these ideas. Of the many characteristics of postmodernism, two of them are especially helpful for our discussion: its rejection of the correspondence theory of truth and its rejection of metanarratives.

---

[64]However, it should be noted that the topic of postmodernism is "beginning to look passé." The concept of postmodernism experienced popularity for four decades in Europe, where it began, but its popularity has waned. Although postmodernism as a concept is still alive in America, it is likely to fade away as it has in Europe. See D. A. Carson, *Becoming Conversant with the Emerging Church: Understanding a Movement and Its Implications* (Grand Rapids: Zondervan, 2005), 81-82.

[65]Kenneth Richard Samples, *A World of Difference: Putting Christian Truth-Claims to the Worldview Test* (Grand Rapids: Baker Books, 2007), 223.

[66]Stumpf and Fieser, *Philosophy*, 498.

[67]Ibid., 223.

SCENIC VIEW

*Contemporary Cultural
Worldview Meditation*

The Life of Pi—What Is Truth?

At the end of Yann Martel's best-selling novel, Pi Patel gives Japanese investigators two conflicting accounts of how he survived months in the Pacific Ocean after the catastrophic sinking of the ocean liner his family was traveling on. In the first account, Pi is accompanied by a Bengal tiger named Richard Parker and encounters magical islands and flying fish. In the second account, Pi is originally accompanied by three survivors, but the brutal ship's cook kills the other two before Pi kills the cook.

The Japanese investigators thank Pi for his cooperation, whereupon Pi asks them a series of questions.

"You can't prove which story is true and which is not. You must take my word for it."

"I guess so."

"In both stories the ship sinks, my entire family dies, and I suffer."

"Yes, that's true."

"So tell me, since it makes no factual difference to you and you can't prove the question either way, which story do you prefer? Which is the better story, the story with animals or the story without animals?"

"That's an interesting question. . . . The story with animals is the better story."

Pi Patel: "Thank you. And so it goes with God."[a]

(continued on next page)

Postmodernism rejects the correspondence theory of truth, which is "perhaps the most natural and widely held account of truth."[68] The correspondence theory of truth is that "propositions are true if and only if they correspond with the facts."[69] Postmodernism rejects the belief that there is "one objective description of reality in-dependent of us observers" and has replaced it with an antirealist position in which "all ideas are constructed and therefore his-torically, culturally, and linguisti-cally contingent."[70] This makes truth subjective.

Some postmodernists reject the idea of truth altogether, but others promote a pragmatist conception of truth. That is, truth is what works for individuals or societies. Richard Rorty (1931–2007) is a good example of this perspective. Influenced by John Dewey's (1859–1952) pragmatism, Rorty came to the conclusion that because it is impossible to be absolutely certain that a proposition corresponds to reality, it is better to think that a proposition is true if it works.

---

[68]Paul Horwich, "Truth," in Audi, *Cambridge Dictionary of Philosophy*, 930.
[69]Bede Rundle, "Correspondence Theory of Truth," in Honderich, *Oxford Companion to Philoso-phy* (1995), 166.
[70]Edward Slingerland, "Conceptual Metaphor Theory as Methodology for Comparative Religion," *Journal of the American Academy of Religion* 72 (2004): 5.

Rorty therefore holds to a form of relativism in which "objective truth" is no more than the best idea we currently have about how to explain what is going on.

In rejecting objective truth, Michel Foucault (1926-1984) argues that truth is historically conditioned and constructed by those in power. He claims that truth and knowledge cannot be separated from power. Those in power possess truth and knowledge because those in power declare what counts as truth and knowledge. Therefore, to change truth one has to change those in power because they are the ones who produce truth. In "Truth and Power," Foucault writes,

If nothing can be proven to be true, if no individual narrative or story can be established as trustworthy knowledge, then all that remains, truly, is "which story do you prefer?" So it is with God, in a postmodern worldview. Which religion is true? Well, we cannot tell for sure. All religions make truth claims and claim exclusive truths for themselves, but we have no way of discerning which truth claim is true. We are too embedded in our own cultural worldview to be able to fairly assess our own worldview or that of others. Thus, in the end, we adopt the religion that we prefer. Is it true? What is truth? No, we adopt the story that we prefer, and that's all there is to it.

Don't you want more than that? Preference doesn't make anything true. Nor does personal opinion make something worth believing. Truth matters. One of Pi's stories was true; the other was not. Don't you want to know which is which?

[a]Yann Martel, *The Life of Pi* (Boston: Houghton Mifflin, 2001), 351-52.

> The important thing here, I believe, is that truth isn't outside of power, or lacking in power. . . . Each society has its regime of truth, its "general politics" of truth: that is, the types of discourse which it accepts and makes function as true; the mechanisms and instances which enable one to distinguish true and false statements, the means by which each is sanctioned; the techniques and procedures accorded values in the acquisition of truth; the status of those who are charged with saying what counts as true. . . . "Truth" is linked in a circular relation with systems of power which produce and sustain it, and to effects of power which it induces and which extend it. A regime of truth.[71]

In addition to rejecting the correspondence theory of truth, postmodernism also rejects metanarratives and attempts to articulate whole and

---

[71]Michel Foucault, "Truth and Power," in *From Modernism to Postmodernism: An Anthology*, ed. Lawrence Cahoone, 2nd ed., Blackwell Philosophy Anthologies 2 (Malden, MA: Blackwell, 2003), 252-53.

holistic systems. In other words, postmodernism rejects worldviews, unified stories that explain reality. If the truth about reality is hidden from us, then no one can claim to have a God's-eye view. All we have are local narratives or stories that give communities structure and meaning. Each community or tribe has its own narrative, its own version of truth. Philosophical theories of the modern period, like humanism, rationalism, empiricism, and idealism, all assumed that "the world is one" and that there is a "single explanatory system that governs everything." In contrast, postmodern thinkers argue that the idea of a unified world system is a "nice fairytale." Instead of seeking a unified worldview, postmodernists call for an "infinite proliferation of images."[72] Therefore, postmodernists contend that difference is what matters; everything is unique and cannot be compared to anything else. As Wendy Doniger states, "for postmodernism, sameness is the devil, difference the angel,"[73] meaning that noting differences between religions and cultures is "good," but trying to note similarities is "evil."

Some postmodernists are suspicious of metanarratives, not simply based on epistemological reasons but also for ethical reasons. Jean-François Lyotard (1924–1998), a key figure in postmodern thought, disdained metanarratives and argued that they lead to terror. In his article "Answering the Question: What Is Postmodernism?" he writes,

> The nineteenth and twentieth centuries have given us as much terror as we can take. We have paid a high enough price for the nostalgia of the whole and the one, for the reconciliation of the concept and the sensible, for the transparent and the communicable experience. Under the general demand for slackening and for appeasement, we can hear the mutterings of the desire of a return to terror, for the realization of the fantasy to seize reality. The answer is: Let us wage war on totality.[74]

For some postmodern thinkers, all metanarratives lead to terror and are oppressive because they mask a desire to seek power. Therefore, every metanarrative is oppressive because by definition it tries to impose its

---

[72]Wendy Doniger, "Post-Modern and -Colonial -Structural Comparisons," in *A Magic Still Dwells: Comparative Religion in the Postmodern Age*, ed. Kimberley C. Patton and Benjamin C. Ray (Berkeley: University of California Press, 2000), 69.
[73]Ibid.
[74]Jean-François Lyotard, "Answering the Question: What Is Postmodernism?," in *Postmodernism: A Reader*, ed. Thomas Docherty (New York: Columbia University Press, 1993), 46.

view of reality on everyone else. Consequently, belief in a metanarrative can lead to the use of violence against those who oppose the metanarrative or are on the losing end in the metanarrative.

REFLECTION QUESTIONS

1 According to some postmodern thinkers, what is a problem with metanarratives?

2 Is postmodernism a metanarrative?

3 What is a postmodern definition of truth?

4 Identify a strength and a weakness of postmodernism's tribalism.

5 Will the influence of postmodern thought increase or decrease in the coming decades in the Western world?

7.8 WORLDVIEW ANALYSIS OF POSTMODERNISM

Even though postmodernism is not a fully developed worldview, it does make truth claims that can be analyzed for internal consistency and logical coherence, external consistency and evidential correspondence, and existential consistency and pragmatic satisfaction. Before discussing weaknesses within postmodern thought, it is important to note that there are many positive lessons we can learn from it. First, postmodernism is correct to criticize the far too optimistic view of human reason found in modernism. Human reason and science will not solve all our problems. Our potential is not limitless. The Bible affirms our cognitive limitations and the reality that the fall has affected every area of who we are, including our cognitive faculties. Consequently, we can agree with postmodernism that we have epistemological limitations.

Second, postmodernists are correct to point out that an unbiased and completely objective perspective is impossible. We are all affected by our cultural context. Complete objectivity is not attainable. We should therefore always be aware of our own biases and presuppositions. Third, postmodernism is correct to warn that power and truth are often connected. We should be aware that people (including ourselves) can manipulate truth for their own personal gain. Fourth, the postmodern

emphasis on the uniqueness of each community can help combat ethno-
centrism and promote the appreciation of cultures different from our
own.

Postmodernism has some true elements that should be heeded;
however, its weaknesses outweigh its strengths. Although postmodern
philosophers reject the criticism that their position amounts to relativism, skepticism, or nihilism, it is difficult to see how this is not the case.
Just because they might not advocate relativism, skepticism, or nihilism
does not mean that their position does not lead to them.[75]

7.8.1 Internal consistency and logical coherence. Postmodernism's
skepticism of attaining truth and its rejection of metanarratives are self-
defeating because these perspectives involve trying to deny truth, reality,
and objectivity with statements claiming truth, reality, and objectivity. In
other words, postmodern thinkers deny the ability to access truth while
at the same time claiming to be stating truth. Plantinga points out that
like many skeptical arguments, postmodernism "discredits itself if it discredits anything; it falls into the very same snare it sets for others."[76] If
truth is not objective, then the postmodern position itself is simply one
more narrative in our world. It does not present truth but rather is a nice
fairy tale that "works" for postmodern philosophers.

Inconsistency is also evident in the postmodern rejection of metanarratives. Though it is true that postmodernism is not a fully developed
cohesive worldview, it still makes claims about reality that are universal.
To deny the truthfulness of any metanarrative is itself a universal claim
that only metanarratives could make. It is ironic how postmodern philosophers reject the ability of any metanarrative to make absolute claims,
yet they are fine with making their own absolute claims.

7.8.2 External consistency and evidential correspondence. The postmodern idea that truth is merely constructed and that metanarratives
are oppressive does not fit the evidence. Postmodernism correctly points
out that our context affects our thinking. Our claims to truth are affected

---

[75]Millard J. Erickson, *Truth or Consequences: The Promise & Perils of Postmodernism* (Downers
Grove, IL: IVP Academic, 2001). See particularly pp. 185-230 for Erickson's analysis (affirmative
and critical) of postmodernism.
[76]Plantinga, *Warranted Christian Belief*, 428.

by our cultural, socioeconomic, and historical context. As Millard Erickson points out, all truth claims are affected by their context, even that of postmodern philosophers, but this says nothing regarding their truthfulness or lack thereof.[77] Simply pointing out that a belief is historically conditioned does not demonstrate its falsity. Our experience shows that some beliefs are true while others are not. For instance, Alvin Plantinga brings up the example of the statement "there was a mere illuvuuuru."[78] He argues that the statement is true or not. It does not matter what a society says about it. We do not make it true if we simply agree to it. To be sure, context does influence what we take to be true, but this does not mean that we merely construct truth. Moreover, truth claims made by postmodern philosophers are historically conditioned as well because their views did not appear in a vacuum. Does this mean that their claims are therefore not universally valid? Presumably they believe that their claims are universally true. If so, they cannot claim that truth claims are not universally true just because they are historically conditioned, since their own truth claims are historically conditioned as well.

Foucault's claim that truth is merely fabricated by those in power does not fit the evidence either. He is right in highlighting the connection between truth and power, but does this mean that any truth claim is simply an expression of power and therefore cannot be universally true? If this is the case, then is it not fair to ask if Foucault's own truth claims are tied to power? Erickson provides some thought-provoking questions.[79] Isn't Foucault simply trying to establish his own authority when he calls into question the versions of truth presented by institutional sources? Why trust Foucault's version of truth as opposed to that of institutional sources since both are attempts to exercise power? If his position is not tied to power, are there other positions also not tied to power? Just because truth claims are historically conditioned and connected to power does not mean that the claim is not universally true.

Moreover, the postmodern claim that metanarratives are necessarily oppressive does not fit the evidence. People can use metanarratives to

---

[77]Erickson, *Truth or Consequences*, 211.
[78]Plantinga, *Warranted Christian Belief*, 435.
[79]Erickson, *Truth or Consequences,* 208.

oppress others, but this is not necessarily so. For example, the Jain religion has its own metanarrative, yet it does not oppress others. Its emphasis on *ahimsa*, nonviolence, encourages Jains to avoid harming anyone, even some forms of vegetables, which Jains believe contain life. This example alone disproves that metanarratives are necessarily oppressive and violent.

Kimberley Patton correctly argues that postmodernism is in essence a reaction and not an argument.[80] She states that postmodernism appeared as a reaction to "the fascism and genocidal thinking" of the twentieth century and characterizes it as a "traumatized polemic." Postmodernists incorrectly assume that because some metanarratives lead to violence that all metanarratives will do so. In his essay "Methodology, Comparisons, and Truth," Huston Smith provides a response to Lyotard's premise that all metanarratives lead to oppressive totalism.[81] Smith points out that metanarratives do not necessarily lead to terror and violence, because respect for the rights of others can be part of the metanarrative. In other words, what matters is the moral fabric of the worldview, not the fact that the worldview presents a comprehensive metanarrative.

7.8.3 Existential consistency and pragmatic satisfaction. Postmodernism raises more questions than it answers. It rejects metanarratives and leaves people with epistemological skepticism and moral relativism. It really provides no answers for the questions of life: What is our nature? What is our world? What is our problem? What is our end? All it provides is a question mark. It does not seek truth because it believes truth is inaccessible. All we have are stories that work for different communities. Each community has its own story with its own version of truth. Any attempt to explain universal truths is disregarded as simply another narrative among many. Plantinga correctly argues that postmodernism is really an epistemology that has simply given up the search for truth:

> If we reject the very idea of truth, we needn't feel anxious about whether
> we've got it. So the thing to do is dispense with the search for truth and

---

[80]Kimberley C. Patton, "Juggling Torches: Why We Still Need Comparative Religion," in Patton and Ray, *Magic Still Dwells*, 153-71.
[81]Huston Smith, "Methodology, Comparisons, and Truth," in Patton and Ray, *Magic Still Dwells*, 172-81.

retreat into projects of some other sort: self-creation and self-redefinition as with Nietzsche and Heidegger, or Rortian irony, or perhaps playful mockery, as with Derrida. So taken, postmodernism is a kind of failure of epistemic nerve.[82]

Postmodernism also leads to moral relativism. Postmodern philosophers like Michel Foucault, Richard Rorty, and Stanley Fish argue that ethics are historically conditioned and rooted in the community; right and wrong are determined by what is considered normal or abnormal. Therefore, morality, like truth, is relative. Each community determines not only what is true but also what is right and wrong, what is good and evil. The problem is that moral relativism cannot be consistently lived out. In their book *Relativism: Feet Firmly Planted in Mid-Air*, Francis J. Beckwith and Gregory Koukl identity what they call "relativism's seven fatal flaws": (1) Relativists can't accuse others of wrongdoing. (2) Relativists can't complain about the problem of evil. (3) Relativists can't place blame or accept praise. (4) Relativists can't make charges of unfairness or injustice. (5) Relativists can't improve their morality. (6) Relativists can't hold meaningful moral discussions. (7) Relativists can't promote the obligation of tolerance.[83] Moral relativists cannot consistently do these seven things because to do them requires a belief in objective moral values that apply to all people at all times. However, relativists often do many of these things, which shows that moral relativism cannot be consistently lived out.

Finally, postmodernism can negatively affect our ability to grow in our understanding of the world by undermining various fields of academic study. For instance, in his foreword to *The Human Condition*, Peter L. Berger criticizes postmodernists, who have given up the notion of objective truth and have concluded that all that remains are personal narratives.[84] This makes religions seem "impenetrable to the outsider, sovereignly impermeable by generalizing concepts."[85] Berger is specifically

---

[82]Plantinga, *Warranted Christian Belief*, 437.
[83]Beckwith and Koukl, *Relativism*, 61-69.
[84]Peter L. Berger, foreword to *The Human Condition: A Volume in the Comparative Religious Ideas Project*, ed. Robert C. Neville (Albany: State University of New York Press, 2001), xi-xiv.
[85]Ibid., xiii.

discussing the academic study of religion, but his point applies to any field of study that involves studying the human condition. According to Berger, this postmodern epistemology encourages the insider to say that "nobody can speak for my people except me" and for the specialist to say that "nobody understands my specialty except me—and I don't have to listen to anyone outside of my specialty."[86] Berger contends that this kind of extreme relativism does not lead to tolerance but rather leads to a "peculiar fanaticism."[87] If ideas cannot be compared and evaluated, then no "science" is possible, and all people can do is "talk at and past each other—until, frustrated by the exercise, we start bashing each other's heads in."[88] To conclude, postmodernism taken to its logical conclusion not only leads to epistemological skepticism and moral relativism but can also undermine the academic study of almost any subject.[89]

REFLECTION QUESTIONS

1 If postmodernism is not a full-fledged worldview, why is it still possible to analyze it as deism and naturalism have been analyzed?

2 What are the greatest strengths of postmodern thought?

3 What are some problems with postmodern thought?

4 Can a Christian hold to elements of postmodernism? If so, what elements?

5 Does postmodern thought support or undermine religious pluralism?

---

[86]Ibid., xiv.
[87]Ibid.
[88]Ibid.
[89]For additional analysis and critique of postmodernism, see D. A. Carson, *Becoming Conversant with the Emerging Church: Understanding a Movement and Its Implications* (Grand Rapids: Zondervan, 2005), 87-156; Erickson, *Truth or Consequences*, 113-227; Douglas Groothuis, *Truth Decay: Defending Christianity Against the Challenges of Postmodernism* (Downers Grove, IL: InterVarsity Press, 2000); Moreland and Craig, *Philosophical Foundations for a Christian Worldview*, 130-53; Samples, *World of Difference*, 219-31; Sire, *Universe Next Door*, 214-43; Gene Edward Veith Jr., *Postmodern Times: A Christian Guide to Contemporary Thought and Culture* (Wheaton, IL: Crossway, 1994); and David Wells, *Above All Earthly Pow'rs: Christ in a Postmodern World* (Grand Rapids: Eerdmans, 2005), 60-90.

7.9 CONCLUSION

Deism, naturalism, and postmodernism are three significant Western philosophical alternatives to the Christian worldview. (See table 7.1 for comparisons with Christianity.) Deism retains Christianity's belief in a creator God and some of its ethical values but rejects special revelation and any uniquely Christian doctrine. Naturalism not only rejects the Bible as God's supernatural revelation as deists do but goes further and rejects belief in the existence of the supernatural altogether. Postmodernism, though not technically a worldview, makes absolute claims about truth when it rejects all metanarratives, including the Christian one. Although these three alternatives contain some elements of truth, our analysis has shown that they all contain internal, external, and existential inconsistencies that call into question the accuracy of the worldviews.

Followers of Christ need to be aware of adopting or being influenced by unbiblical beliefs found within deism, naturalism, and postmodernism. Smith and Denton's research into the religious and spiritual lives of American teenagers reveals the prevalence of moralistic therapeutic deism in American society.[90] Many Americans, including American teenagers, may speak of belief in God, but this should not be equated with being a follower of Christ with a biblically informed worldview. Contrary to what moralistic therapeutic deists believe, the goal of life is not to be happy and feel good about oneself. God does need to be involved in every area of our lives, not just when we have a problem he can fix. Also, good people do not go to heaven simply because they are good. Salvation is found only through repentance and faith in Christ. In order to protect ourselves from adopting these kinds of unbiblical religious beliefs, it is imperative that we immerse ourselves in God's Word and become active members in a local Bible-believing church.

Though naturalism may not be appealing to followers of Christ, there is still the danger of living as if God did not exist. When we constantly live with a sense of worry and fear about the future instead of trusting our sovereign heavenly Father, we are living as if God did not exist. When we disregard what God has revealed in his Word and adopt the morality of our society, we are living as if God did not exist. When we

---

[90]Smith and Denton, *Soul Searching*, 162-63.

live self-centered lives caring only about our own glory, we are living as if God did not exist. Even though we may openly deny the tenets of naturalism, we often mistakenly live as functional atheists.

Table 7.1. Comparing deism, naturalism, postmodernism, and Christianity

Worldview questions	Deism	Naturalism	Postmodernism	Christianity
What is our nature?	People are rational, personal, and moral creatures created by god (personal or impersonal).	Humanity is the result of the blind and purposeless forces of evolution.	No unified answer. People create who they are through the language they use about themselves.	Created in God's image, but now have a sinful and spiritually dead nature because of the fall.
What is our world?	The world is an orderly mechanistic system that is governed by physical laws.	The result of matter, chance, and time. Nature, the material world, is self-existing.	No unified answer. Truth about reality is hidden to us.	A creation of the triune God. It was created good but now is full of death and suffering because of the fall. However, it still declares the glory of God.
What is our problem?	No unified answer. Problems are solved through ethical living grounded in human reason.	No unified answer on this. Some may say suffering and pain. Some argue that religion is the problem. The answers are in science and in doing good to others.	No unified answer. The world is just the way it is, though the truth about reality is hidden.	Because of the fall, we live in a broken world. We have a sinful nature and are guilty before God. The solution is the gospel, the good news that God is fixing our broken world through the life, death, and resurrection of Jesus Christ. Through faith in Christ and repentance we are reconciled to God.
What is our end?	The goal is to live ethical lives. According to warm deists, heaven and hell do exist. According to cold deists, there is no afterlife.	No ultimate meaning and purpose in life beyond what we make of it. Life ends at death.	No unified answer. Metanarratives are oppressive.	Our purpose is to glorify God by enjoying him forever. Those in Christ await his return and an eternity in the new heaven and new earth. The lost await punishment in hell.

Finally, an element of postmodern thought that is probably becoming more appealing for professing Christians in North America is moral relativism. If there are no objective moral values, and morality is simply created by a community, then there is no objective right and wrong, no objective good and evil. An act or behavior may be wrong or evil for one person but not for another, and vice versa. This form of moral relativism may become more appealing for professing Christians as Western society becomes increasingly secular and accepted morality is in conflict with biblical teaching. In order to minimize tension with a secular society, some Christians may be tempted to adopt moral relativism as a feigned form of humility. Some might be tempted to say, "I know that the Bible says that a certain behavior is wrong, but who am I to judge? It may be wrong for me, but maybe not for another person. It is between that person and God." This approach may appear humble, but it undercuts the biblical teaching that God is our Creator and has revealed in his Word how humanity should live. In his mercy, our wise, perfect, and loving Creator has made it known to us what leads to our flourishing and what leads to our destruction.

MASTERING THE MATERIAL

When you finish reading this chapter, you should be able to

✔ Summarize deism using the four worldview questions.

✔ Discuss three significant weaknesses within deism.

✔ Summarize naturalism using the four worldview questions.

✔ Discuss three significant weaknesses within naturalism.

✔ Summarize the central themes of postmodern thought presented in this chapter.

✔ Discuss three significant weaknesses within postmodernism.

Glossary of Terms for Chapter Seven

deism—Affirms the existence of a creator god, but he (or it) is not involved in the world.

existentialism—The belief that existence precedes essence.

metanarrative—A complete, unique, and closed explanatory system.

naturalism—The worldview based on the belief that absolutely nothing exists except the physical realm.

nihilism—The negation of everything.

philosophical postmodernism—Rejects the presuppositions of modernism, including the beliefs that the universe is intelligible, language is a reliable tool to communicate truth and reality, and there is such a thing as objective truth.

Possible Term Paper Topics

✔ Compare and contrast the god of warm deism and the biblical God.

✔ Discuss the role that Jesus of Nazareth plays in the writings of three noted deists.

✔ Analyze the deist critique of miraculous accounts in the Bible.

✔ Select one prominent atheistic writer and analyze three of his or her arguments against the existence of God.

✔ Write a paper discussing the history of atheistic thought in North America.

✔ Read and respond to Bertrand Russell's "Why I Am Not a Christian."

✔ Write a paper discussing the most significant postmodern criticisms of modernism.

✔ Select a prominent postmodern philosopher and write a paper analyzing the major themes in his or her writings.

✔ Write a paper analyzing the possible effects of postmodern thought on biblical interpretation.

Core Bibliography for Chapter Seven

Audi, Robert, ed. *The Cambridge Dictionary of Philosophy*. 2nd ed. New York: Cambridge University Press, 1999.

Beckwith, Francis J., and Gregory Koukl. *Relativism: Feet Firmly Planted in Mid-Air*. Grand Rapids: Baker Books, 1998.

Brown, Colin. *From the Ancient World to the Age of Enlightenment*. Volume 1 of *Christianity and Western Thought: A History of Philosophers, Ideas and Movements*. Downers Grove, IL: IVP Academic, 1990.

Cahoone, Lawrence, ed. *From Modernism to Postmodernism: An Anthology*. 2nd ed. Blackwell Philosophy Anthologies 2. Malden, MA: Blackwell, 2003.

Erickson, Millard. *Truth or Consequences: The Promise & Perils of Postmodernism*. Downers Grove, IL: IVP Academic, 2001.

Inwood, M. J. "*Weltanschauung*." In *Oxford Companion to Philosophy*, edited by Ted Honderich, 909. Oxford: Oxford University Press, 1995.

Markham, Ian S., and Christy Lohr, eds. *A World Religions Reader*. 3rd ed. Malden, MA: Wiley-Blackwell, 2009.

Sire, James S. *The Universe Next Door: A Basic Worldview Catalog*. 5th ed. Downers Grove, IL: IVP Academic, 2009.

Stumpf, Samuel Enoch, and James Fieser. *Philosophy: History and Problems*. Boston: McGraw-Hill, 2003.

GLOBAL RELIGIOUS ALTERNATIVES

HINDUISM AND ISLAM

This chapter will address Hinduism and Islam, the two largest religious alternatives to Christianity. Hinduism is the third-largest world religion and will be analyzed because it serves well as a representative of Eastern religions. Other Eastern religions, such as Buddhism, Sikhism, and Jainism, all share significant features with Hinduism, especially belief in karma and reincarnation, albeit in slightly modified forms. Nonetheless, Hinduism provides an opportunity to see how different some religious worldviews can be from the Christian worldview. Islam is the second-largest world religion and, as a monotheistic religion, shares a considerable number of similarities with the Christian worldview. By studying Hinduism and Islam, we have the opportunity to analyze very different religious worldviews, each providing its own set of challenges. This chapter will ask the four worldview questions of these two major world religions: What is our nature? What is our world? What is our problem? What is our end? After describing the religious traditions by answering these four questions, we will analyze the traditions for internal consistency and logical coherence, external consistency and evidential correspondence, and existential consistency and pragmatic satisfaction.

8.1 HINDUISM

There are over one billion Hindus worldwide, making it the third-largest world religion. Around 998 million Hindus live in India, making up 79.8 percent of the nation's population.[1] The second- and third-largest Hindu

---

[1]Central Intelligence Agency, "India," The World Factbook, updated January 12, 2017, www.cia .gov/library/publications/the-world-factbook/geos/in.html.

Contemporary Cultural
Worldview Meditation

Kung Fu Panda—
Taoism in Animated Action

While Taoism is not the same as Hinduism, the worldviews bear some minor similarities and have impacted one another, particularly in China, where Hinduism-infused Buddhism has coexisted with native Taoism for nearly two thousand years.

Taoism is not a prominent worldview in Western society but has been winsomely introduced through Po, the lovable title character in the Kung Fu Panda trilogy. Some of the Taoist elements at play include:

(1) Yin-yang/balance. The ancient yin-yang symbol, black and white nearly intertwined, symbolizes the Taoist belief that seemingly contradictory forces (light/darkness, male/female, creation/destruction) are instead complementary. The yin-yang symbol recurs regularly throughout the movies and is also illustrated in the panda itself (black and white).

(2) Inner peace through meditation. Meditative Taoism was accessible only to the elites of ancient China but was the means to finding true inner peace, oneness with the flow of the universe. In *Kung Fu Panda II*, Po finally attains the inner peace that had eluded him since the

(continued on next page)

populations are found in Nepal and Bangladesh. In Nepal there are over 25 million Hindus, making up 81.3 percent of the population, while in Bangladesh there are almost 17 million Hindus, constituting only 10 percent of the population.[2] Large Hindu populations can also be found in Indonesia, Sri Lanka, and Pakistan, ranging from two to four million in each country.[3] The Hindu population in North America is growing, but as of 2011 was only around 1.5 million.[4] Although the overall Hindu population in the United States is small, Hindu beliefs and practices are far more influential than the size of the Hindu population suggests. For example, in a study done in 2009 by the Pew Forum on Religion & Public Life, among self-described Christians, 22 percent believe in reincarnation and 21 percent believe in yoga as a spiritual exercise.[5]

---

[2]Central Intelligence Agency, "Nepal," The World Factbook, updated January 12, 2017, www.cia.gov/library/publications/the-world-factbook/geos/np.html; "Bangladesh," The World Factbook, updated January 12, 2017, www.cia.gov/library/publications/the-world-factbook/geos/bg.html.

[3]Patrick Johnstone, *The Future of the Global Church: History, Trends, and Possibilities* (Colorado Springs: Biblica, 2011), 79.

[4]Hillary Rodrigues, *Introducing Hinduism* (New York: Routledge, 2006), 5; and Johnstone, *Future of the Global Church*, 79.

[5]Forum on Religion & Public Life, "Many Americans Mix Multiple Faiths," Pew Research Center, December 9, 2009, www.pewforum.org/2009/12/09/many-americans-mix-multiple-faiths.

The word *Hinduism* does not technically name one religion but is a broad term that includes the various religious beliefs and practices of India. Hinduism has no founder and no single authoritative sacred text, as are found in Christianity and Islam. When Islam entered India in the seventh century, the term *Hindu* developed as a way to distinguish Muslims from non-Muslims. Hindus view themselves as practicing the eternal dharma, which is a complete way of life, including both religious and social dimensions. The well-known scholar of Hinduism Klaus Klostermaier contends that Hindus "are arguably the most intensely religious people on earth."[6]

death of his parents, and that inner peace enables him to perform incredible physical feats.

(3) Ascension/immortality. In the original *Kung Fu Panda*, the elderly turtle Oogway is the Taoist Grand Master who chooses the very rotund and untrained Po as the leader of the new generation of Kung Fu warriors. After charging his disciple Shifu with Po's continued training, Oogway achieves Taoist immortality by becoming truly one with the universe, dissolving into a sea of peach blossoms and ascending to the heavens. To my knowledge, such a vivid representation of the quest of religious Taoism has never before been portrayed in Western popular culture.

Although diversity exists within the Hindu worldview, all Hindus share some core beliefs, including the eternality of the cosmos, reincarnation, karma, the caste system, affirmation of the Vedic scriptures, and liberation from the cycle of death and rebirth as the ultimate goal of life. Hindu teachings are rooted in the enormous collection of Hindu scriptures, including the Vedas, Upanishads, and epics like the Mahabharata and Ramayana.

Before addressing the four main worldview questions, it is important to first discuss the various Hindu philosophical schools to set a framework for our discussion. There are six traditional or orthodox schools of philosophy in Hinduism, of which only the last two survive. One of these schools is Purva Mimamsa ("earlier investigation" or "old theology"), commonly called Mimamsa.[7] Adherents of this school argue that only the four earliest Vedas are self-existent and eternal, and

[6]Klaus K. Klostermaier, *Hinduism: A Beginner's Guide* (Oxford: Oneworld, 2008), 3.
[7]For helpful discussions of Purva Mimamsa see, Klaus K. Klostermaier, *A Survey of Hinduism*, 2nd ed. (Albany: State University of New York Press, 1994), 408-11; Hillary Rodrigues, *Introducing Hinduism* (New York: Routledge, 2006), 131-32; and Klaus K. Klostermaier, *A Concise Encyclopedia of Hinduism* (Oxford: Oneworld, 1998), 118.

therefore authoritative. They do not consider any other Hindu texts to be authoritative. Consequently, this school focuses primarily on defending and justifying rituals and ceremonies that make up the samhitas, the earliest four Vedas.

The dominant Hindu philosophical school is Uttara Mimamsa ("latter investigation" or "new theology"), better known as Vedanta ("end of the Veda"). Vedanta focuses on the study of the Upanishads, Brahma Sutras, and *Bhagavad-Gita* and is concerned with speculative philosophy. There are ten principal sects of Vedanta, though the first three developed are the most significant and reveal the spectrum of belief within Vedanta thought. Only the first two sects will be addressed in this chapter, as they are the largest and most influential.

The first sect, developed in the eighth century, is Shankara's Advaita Vedanta (nonduality Vedanta), which amounts to a "radical nondualism."[8] Nondualism means that there is only one real entity in existence. Shankara, probably the most highly regarded Hindu philosopher, taught that the only entity that exists is Brahman, an impersonal ultimate reality with no attributes. Advaita Vedanta has been very influential among the intellectual elite and has become the perspective of many "modern, Western-educated, urbanized Hindus."[9] Moreover, it has become the form of Hinduism that most often appears in textbooks and other popular works on Hinduism in the West.

The second sect, developed in the eleventh to twelfth centuries, is Ramanuja's "qualified nonduality Vedanta." Ramanuja agreed with Shankara that there is only one entity that exists, but he argued that it was Saguna Brahman—that is, Brahman with attributes—which he equated with the Hindu god Vishnu. Ramanuja's qualified nonduality reflects the belief and experience of most Hindus because it has supplied the "intellectual framework" for Hindus who worship a personal god. The differences between these two major systems of Hindu philosophy significantly affect how the four worldview questions are answered.

---

[8]Rodrigues, *Introducing Hinduism*, 250. Shankara's followers see him as either an avatar (a descent) of the god Shiva or at least a person inspired by Shiva. Klostermaier, *Concise Encyclopedia of Hinduism*, 164.

[9]Lance E. Nelson, "Krishna in Advaita Vedanta: The Supreme Being in Human Form," in *Krishna: A Sourcebook*, ed. Edwin F. Bryant (New York: Oxford University Press, 2007), 309.

8.1.1 *What is our nature?* The nature of the self has been a central matter of study in all Hindu philosophical systems, leading to a variety of understandings of the self. Hindu philosophical schools reject both equating of the self with one's physical body and the Buddhist teaching of "no-self."[10]

8.1.1.1 Atman and Brahman. All Hindu schools affirm the existence of an eternal incorporeal atman. The word *atman* is translated in a variety of ways, including consciousness, soul, individual soul, human soul, eternal self, spirit, breath, self, Self, true self, innermost Self, and real self. The matter of debate is the relationship between one's atman and everything else, especially Brahman, commonly understood as Ultimate Reality. A central teaching of the Upanishads, the key texts used by the various schools of Vedanta, is that atman is Brahman. In *A Survey of Hinduism*, Klostermaier provides an account of various discussions in the Upanishads that shed light on the teaching that atman is identical to Brahman.

One Upanishad (a Hindu philosophical text) records a discussion between the great philosopher Yajñavalkya and his wife, Gargi, about Ultimate Reality. Gargi begins by asking her husband what water is woven on since the world is woven on water. He responds that water is woven on wind. She then asks what the wind is woven on. This process continues for a while until he arrives at "the world of the creator of all being" being woven on the world of Brahman. She then asks what Brahman is woven on. He responds: "Gargi. Do not question too much lest your head fall off. Verily you are asking too much about the divine being, about which we are not to question too much. Do not, Gargi, question too much."[11] In this account Brahman is presented as Ultimate Reality, "the life breath of the universe and everything in it."

In Chandogya Upanishad (another Hindu philosophical text), a father uses a fig, salt, and water to teach his son, Śvetaketu, about Brahman. The father asks his son to bring him a fig and cut it open; then asks the son what he sees. The son responds that he sees seeds. The father then tells

---

[10]Klostermaier, *Concise Encyclopedia of Hinduism*, 169. The Buddhist doctrine of "no-self" means that the "self" does not actually exist.
[11]Ibid., 205.

the son to cut open the seeds, and asks him what he sees. The son responds that he sees "nothing." The father then responds, "My dear, that subtle essence which you do not perceive, that is the source of this mighty Nyagrodha tree. That which is so tiny is the *atman* of all. This is the true, the self, that you are, Śvetaketu."[12] The father then asks his son to throw salt into a container with water, to taste it, and then to try to separate the salt from the water again. The son knows that the salt is one with the water and cannot be separated, yet he knows that the salt and water are different. The father teaches him that this is what atman is like, all-pervading and inseparable from objects but not identical with the objects. The father concludes the lesson with the well-known phrase *Tat tvam asi*, meaning "that you are." In other words, the father taught his son that the son is atman, the "invisible substance" or "subtle essence" that undergirds all things. Because of texts like these in the Upanishads, Hindus equate one's atman with Brahman (Ultimate Reality). However, the various Hindu philosophical schools interpret these texts differently.

In Shankara's Advaita Vedanta, the nondualistic perspective, all that exists is Brahman, understood as the ground of all being, Ultimate Reality. Consequently, nondualists argue that the nature of atman, the self, is "ontically identical" to Brahman. Atman is not a part of Brahman but is Brahman itself because nothing else exists. In contrast, qualified nondualists argue that atman is "in close affinity with, but ontically separate" from Brahman. Ramanuja advocated a qualified nonduality and equated Brahman with the god Vishnu. Therefore, he understood atman not as being identical to Brahman but as "modes or aspects of Brahman, wholly dependent upon the Lord."[13] Therefore, one's atman is a part of and an emanation of Vishnu.

To conclude, some Hindus understand the self as being identical to Brahman (Ultimate Reality); others understand the self to be a part of Brahman. Either way, both perspectives agree that the self is affected by karma and experiences reincarnation.

8.1.1.2 Samsara and karma. All Hindus believe that each individual goes through cycles of birth, death, and rebirth. Each person is imprisoned

---

[12]Ibid.

[13]Rodrigues, *Introducing Hinduism*, 252.

in this eternal cycle of death and rebirth, called *samsara*. This process is commonly known as reincarnation, although the technical term is *transmigration*. Samsara could be defined as the "passing through or cycling through successive lives as a consequence of moral and physical acts."[14]

Individuals accumulate karma through moral and physical acts. Karma is "non-material residue of any action performed by a person" and thereby the cause of "embodiment and samsara."[15] Almost all Hindu schools of thought have their own karma theories, yet the basic idea is that every action has a consequence that will affect this life and the next. Therefore, a person's present state of existence is explained by his or her accumulated karma. Karma has turned into the idea of a moral principle of causality: good deeds bring merit, and bad deeds bring negative consequences. Depending on one's karma, one may be born into a variety of hells, into an animal form, human form, or even a divine being.

8.1.1.3 Castes and women. Those born into human form are born into one of four castes or social classes. Within the four main castes there are hundreds of subcastes or *jatis*, meaning "birth groups."[16] The highest caste is the Brahmin priestly caste. The second caste is the Ksatriya caste, which is the warrior and politician caste. The third caste is the Vaiśya caste made up of artisans and merchants. These first three castes constitute only 15 percent of the Hindu population and are considered high-caste Hindus. They are often called the "twice-born" because of a special initiation rite performed when they enter the student stage of life in which they are "spiritually reborn." The fourth caste is the Śudra farmer caste, which makes up around 60 percent of the population.

Finally, there are Dalits ("outcastes" or "untouchables"), who belong to no caste and make up 25 percent of the population. Most Dalits have been seen as fit only for "impure and degrading work."[17] Those without a caste have been called "untouchables" (Harijans) because their touch makes others ritually impure, meaning that these others require purification

---

[14]G. R. Weldon, "Samsara," in *The Perennial Dictionary of World Religions*, ed. Keith Crim (New York: HarperCollins, 1981).

[15]Klostermaier, *Concise Encyclopedia of Hinduism*, 95.

[16]Vasudha Narayanan, "The Hindu Tradition," in *World Religions: Eastern Traditions*, ed. William G. Oxtoby, 2nd ed. (New York: Oxford University Press, 2002), 46.

[17]Klostermaier, *Concise Encyclopedia of Hinduism*, 54.

SCENIC VIEW

*Contemporary Cultural
Worldview Meditation*

Avatars and the Incarnation

At first glance, the Hindu doctrine of avatar (meaning descent) appears similar to the Christian doctrine of the incarnation, but there are significant differences. According to Hinduism, gods and goddesses appear on earth from time to time in physical form in order to combat evil and promote dharma. For example, the god Vishnu has appeared several times, including in the forms of a fish, tortoise, boar, half man–half lion, dwarf, sage, and king. His most popular forms are that of Rama and Krishna, prominent figures in the two most significant Hindu epics. These manifestations of the gods are couched in mythical terms and are only loosely tied to history.

In contrast, in the incarnation God the Son permanently took on human nature. He became and remains 100 percent God and 100 percent human. In his humanity, he became like the rest of us, except without a sinful nature. By taking on a human nature, Jesus was able to become our representative and, therefore, die as a substitute for sinful humanity. Also, the incarnation is rooted in human history rather than mythology. Jesus was born in the city of Bethlehem when Quirinius was governor of Syria (Lk 2:1-2). He grew up as any other child and eventually was crucified in Jerusalem under Pontius Pilate. Finally, the incarnation was not simply one of many attempts to temporarily defeat evil. Rather, through the incarnation, God permanently defeated Satan, sin, and death through the life, death, and resurrection of Jesus Christ.

rituals before coming in the presence of a deity again. Some Hindu texts teach extreme forms of avoidance, teaching that being touched by an untouchable's shadow or even being seen by one causes ritual impurity. Some of this understanding has changed in modern times, yet "the stigmatization of the Dalit is deeply rooted in Hindu culture."[18]

In addition to distinguishing among the different castes, traditional Hindu culture also makes a sharp distinction between the value of men and of women, leading to long-standing subordination and repression of Hindu women. Although the Vedas teach gender equality for the most part, women have not fared well in traditional Hindu society.[19] The Laws of Manu, written down between 200 BC and AD 200, is the most influential of all Hindu legal codes and contains some teachings that curtail the role of women in Hindu society. The Laws of Manu teach that women must never be independent of men. As a child, a woman is dependent on her father. As a wife she is dependent on her husband.

---

[18]Rodrigues, *Introducing Hinduism*, 66.
[19]Klostermaier, *Concise Encyclopedia of Hinduism*, 54, 114, 209.

As a widow she is dependent on her sons. A woman's only sacrament is marriage, and her salvation depends on her service to her husband. In the section on "the duties of a woman," the Laws of Manu state that "no sacrifice, no vow, no fast must be performed by women apart (from their husbands); if a wife obeys her husband, she will for that (reason alone) be exalted in heaven."[20] In addition, the Laws of Manu also teach that, though destitute of virtue, or seeking pleasure (elsewhere), or devoid of good qualities, (yet) a husband must be constantly worshipped as a god by a faithful wife."[21] Moreover, faithful wives, if childless, were expected to practice sati, which means to join their deceased husbands on their funeral pyres. If a widow did not practice sati, she could not remarry and had almost no rights. These practices have now been outlawed. Even the epics and Puranas depict women in a negative way, showing them as "vicious, sensual, fickle, untrustworthy and impure."[22] Many in traditional Hindu society considered women unfit for the study of the Vedas and believed that they should be treated as Śudras, meaning they could not eat, walk, or discuss important matters with their husbands.[23] Although there are exceptions to the rule, Hindu women for the most part are "inferior in status to men and subordinate to their power and authority."[24] Although the status and role of women in Hindu society is in transition, being born a woman is still seen as a "misfortune," and the "supreme virtue" of a woman is to give birth to sons, which confirms and improves her social status.[25]

To conclude, a Hindu's answer to the question, what is our nature?, depends on his or her philosophical perspective, caste, and gender. At the most fundamental level, they believe our nature is rooted in an ultimate reality with no attributes, or is shared with god since we are part of god.

---

[20]Ian S. Markham and Christy Lohr, eds., *A World Religions Reader*, 3rd ed. (Malden, MA: Wiley-Blackwell, 2009), 57.

[21]Ibid.

[22]Ibid.

[23]Ibid.; and C. J. Fuller, *The Camphor Flame: Popular Hinduism and Society in India*, rev. and expanded ed. (Princeton: Princeton University Press, 2004), 20.

[24]Fuller, *Camphor Flame*, 20.

[25]Sara S. Mitter, *Dharma's Daughters* (New Brunswick, NJ: Rutgers University Press, 1991) 89-90. This gender discrimination continues to this day. It has become a growing trend to use sonograms and amniocentesis to determine the sex of the unborn baby in order to abort baby girls. Narayanan, "Hindu Tradition," 109.

8.1.2 What is our world? Hinduism does not have a single authoritative story of the origin and structure of our world. Generally, Hindus believe in the existence of multiple worlds, including a variety of heavens and hells. These worlds are populated by humans, spirits, and divine, semi-divine, and demonic beings. From the Hindu perspective, the world is an eternal, alive, real, knowable, and orderly organism. It is an emanation from Brahman, whether taken to be an impersonal Ultimate Reality or a personal deity. It is governed by *rita*, which is literally "truth, divine order," meaning the cosmic law, including both the moral and the natural order in the universe. In addition, all of life is interrelated and connected. This includes the past, present, and future, as well as all life forms. With the passing of *kalpas*, or eons, the cosmos goes through cycles of creation, destruction, and re-creation. But what is the source of this orderly world?

According to Shankara, all that exists is Brahman. Technically, it is Nirguna Brahman, meaning Brahman "without attributes." He taught that the diversity we see in the world is the result of maya, which he explains is an "illusion" or "appearance." Rodrigues contends that Shankara equates maya with "ignorance."[26] In any case, maya is the source of and is identified with the "collective hallucination superimposed on the One reality."[27] Brahman uses maya to make the world appear as it does. It is the "creative power" that Brahman uses to "conjure up the world of seeming multiplicity and separate selves."[28] However, at the most fundamental level maya itself does not exist, because all that exists is Brahman. Shankara explained this through his analogy of incorrectly thinking while in the dark that a rope is a snake. The snake does not exist, but its influence is felt as long as the illusion or ignorance persists. Though he argued that the most basic attributes of Nirguna Brahman are being (*sat*), consciousness (*cit*), and bliss (*ananda*), he also contended that these "projections of qualities onto the nature of the Absolute" are also because of maya.[29] In addition to these three apparent attributes, Shankara also spoke of Saguna Brahman (Brahman with attributes) or Ishvara (the

---

[26]Rodrigues, *Introducing Hinduism*, 250.
[27]R. C. Zaehner, *Hinduism*, 2nd ed. (New York: Oxford University Press, 1966), 76.
[28]Rodrigues, *Introducing Hinduism*, 250.
[29]Ibid., 251.

Lord). Because of maya, Brahman appears conditioned and personalized and therefore seems to be a personal deity. Shankara's teaching on Saguna Brahman made it possible for Hindus to agree with his theory of nonduality yet continue to worship personal deities, though he understood these deities to be a part of maya. It should be noted though that Shankara tried to nuance his position and avoided saying that the world was a pure illusion. Rather, he taught that in regular consciousness the world is real, but at the deepest level of consciousness the world is unreal.[30]

In contrast to Shankara, Ramanuja viewed the world as an emanation of the Hindu god Vishnu. He rejected Shankara's position that all that exists is Nirguna Brahman. He argued that it is "meaningless to comprehend, relate to, or speak about a *Nirguna Brahman*."[31] He thought the idea of Ultimate Reality with no attributes was absurd. Therefore, Ramanuja taught that Ultimate Reality is Saguna Brahman (Brahman with attributes), whom he equates with Vishnu and his consort Lakshmi. From this perspective the world exists because Vishnu chose to create it. He is the material and efficient cause of everything. However, Vishnu did not create the world as something separate from himself or out of nothing. Rather, Vishnu created the world from his own body. Therefore, the world is Vishnu's body. One's atman and everything else are all "modes or aspects" of Vishnu and completely dependent on him. The world is not maya (an illusion) but rather Vishnu's body. In one sense Brahman (Vishnu) is all that exists, but in another sense Brahman is qualified by atman and matter since they are not identical to Brahman but only parts of Brahman. When discussing the production of the world, Hindus will often state that it is an expression of a deity's lila (play or sport), carrying the idea that creation does not serve a purpose for the deity. The concept of lila points to the belief that the deity has the freedom to produce and govern the world as he chooses. It does not mean, as critics often argue, that the deity does not take the world or human events seriously.

---

[30]Klostermaier, *Hinduism: Beginner's Guide*, 131. According to the Upanishads there are four stages of consciousness (from lower to higher): (1) normal waking state, (2) dreaming state, (3) dreamless state, and (4) "fourth state," which is pure awareness. Ibid., 104-6.

[31]Rodrigues, *Introducing Hinduism*, 252.

8.1.3 *What is our problem?* The ultimate problem according to the Hindu worldview is that people are trapped in samsara, the cycle of death and rebirth. Therefore, the ultimate goal in Hinduism is moksha or mukti, liberation from the cycle of death and rebirth. In their original state, however this is conceived, people were in a state of purity and bliss. Unfortunately, they somehow got themselves entangled into samsara. Various explanations have been given for this predicament, but the most common explanation is that people are trapped in samsara because of ignorance.

According to Shankara, the problem is that people are ignorant of their true nature, which is what keeps them in samsara. Instead of knowing that their atman, pure consciousness, is identical to Brahman, they incorrectly trust their senses. Therefore, people have an epistemological problem. Shankara argued that all knowledge acquired through the senses is ambiguous and cannot be held with certainty. In addition, he argued that from birth people are wired to "superimpose objective notions on the subject, and subjective notions on the object," leading to distorted knowledge.[32] This incorrect thinking is the problem.

According to Ramanuja, people are ignorant of their divine origin. They have forgotten that they are part of god, specifically Vishnu. By getting lost in "the world of sense" and living with "worldly people," the soul has forgotten where it came from.[33] It is a case of mistaken identity. Ramanuja used the parable of a young prince who gets lost in the woods and is then raised by another family. Eventually, the prince discovers his true identity and is finally reunited with his father, the king. He thought he was the son of a commoner, but he was reminded that he was actually the son of the king. Ramanuja described it as god waiting for the soul to come back and bless it with his presence, just as the father waited for his son.

Another way to ask, what is our problem?, is by asking, why do people suffer? According to Hinduism, the answer is karma. The doctrine of karma functions as a theodicy, providing an explanation for why there is evil and suffering in the world. Individuals are born as low caste rather

---

[32]Klostermaier, *Hinduism: A Beginner's Guide*, 129.
[33]Ibid., 140.

than high caste because of their bad karma. Someone is born as a woman rather than a man because of that person's bad karma. People are born with bodily defects or illnesses because of bad karma.[34] Misfortune in life is a result of accumulated bad karma. Therefore, the evil and suffering people experience is deserved. They have earned this punishment because of particular sins they have committed in previous lives.

8.1.1 What is our end? According to Hinduism, when people die, they either remain trapped in samsara because of their karma and are therefore reincarnated again or they are set free from reincarnation because they achieved moksha. In Hinduism there are three paths to achieve liberation from the cycle of death and rebirth. The first path is karma marga, the "path of works" or "path of ritual action." Initially this path involved performing sacrifices to the gods and other yearly ceremonies as described in the Vedas. Now, it involves carrying out one's caste duties in a selfless manner, with no regard to the outcome, as a sacrifice to a deity. The *Bhagavad-Gita* (one of the most, if not the most, popular Hindu texts) introduces this idea of "desireless action," by which one acts without accumulating karma. Desireless action means to perform an action for the sake of duty or fulfilling righteousness with no regard for reward or punishment. This is the highest ethical ideal in Hinduism. Arjuna, the main character in the *Gita*, though of the warrior caste, did not want to fight in the battle he was about to face because he did not want to kill his cousins on the opposing side and therefore accumulate karma. However, his charioteer Krishna, an avatar of Vishnu, told him that he had to fight because he was of the warrior caste but that if he did it with no regard for the outcome he would not accumulate karma. Krishna instructs Arjuna: "Be intent on action, not on the fruits of action; avoid attraction to the fruits and attachment to inaction! Perform actions, firm in discipline, relinquishing attachment; be impartial to failure and success—this equanimity is called discipline."[35] This path of liberation encourages Hindus to faithfully carry out their caste's ethical and ritual responsibilities, which means to live in line with dharma and the cosmic order.

[34]Ibid., 48.
[35]Barbara Stoler Miller, trans., *The Bhagavad Gita* (New York: Bantam Books, 1986), 36.

The second path is jñana marga, the "path of knowledge." This path is promoted especially by nondualists like Shankara. This path requires studying the Upanishads and gaining experiential knowledge that atman is Brahman. Achieving this state of emancipation requires "a long process of physical and spiritual discipline."[36] The goal is through meditation to travel through the four stages of consciousness: (1) normal waking state; (2) dreaming state, which is a state of higher perception because it is not tied to logic, space, and time; (3) dreamless state, where all faculties of self are unified and blissful; and (4) fourth state, which is pure awareness, freedom from all limitations, and one's true nature. Moksha is not a state attained after death but an "understanding that grants immortality" before one dies. Upon death, one is absorbed into the impersonal and attributeless Brahman.

The third and predominant way of liberation in Hinduism is bhakti marga, the "path of devotion." Bhakti marga characterizes popular Hinduism, opening the door of salvation for women and lower-caste Hindus. As would be expected, Ramanuja and others who emphasize belief in a personal deity contend that bhakti is the best way to moksha. The way of devotion is explained in various ways. For example, it may entail a general inward surrender to a deity or a more ritualistic approach involving performing prescribed rituals in front of an image of a deity. The point is that through devotion to a selected deity, one's karma is removed and one is granted liberation. Devotees trust in the grace of their selected deity to save them from samsara. The three most popular bhakti schools in Hinduism are devoted to one of three deities, Vishnu, Shiva, and the goddess. Devotees of these deities view their chosen deity as their protector and savior and view it as the supreme Being, Brahman.

Ramanuja argued that the other two paths of liberation could be helpful but that bhakti was the best path to liberation. By following Vishnu's will, a person can earn his grace and be saved, which includes going to Vishnu's heaven, becoming godlike, and enjoying his bliss in an incorruptible body, where the atman shares "profound communion with the Lord" now that it is free from illusion and karma.[37] Through devotion

---

[36]Klostermaier, *Concise Encyclopedia of Hinduism*, 108.
[37]Ibid., 149; Klostermaier, *Hinduism: A Beginner's Guide*, 141; and Rodrigues, *Introducing Hinduism*, 252.

to Vishnu and the intercession of Sri (Vishnu's female consort embodying divine grace and mercy), devotees gain the god's favor. In addition to the intercession of Sri, who functions as a divine guru, devotees must also seek the assistance of an earthly guru, who is indispensable for achieving moksha. In time, Ramanuja's school divided into two theological camps. One emphasizes the devotee's role in salvation, and the other emphasizes Vishnu's role in salvation. Vadagalai, known as the "monkey school," emphasizes the soul's "co-operation" with the Lord in the liberation. The soul must hold on to Vishnu as a baby monkey holds on to its mother. In other words, a devotee needs to perform religious activities in order to obtain grace. In contrast, Tengalai, known as the "cat school," argues that salvation is more like a kitten being picked up by the scruff of the neck and carried to safety. This school argues that trying to gain the Lord's grace by trying to do something is "audacious" because "the Lord has supreme agency and prerogative."[38]

Table 8.1. Comparing two schools of Hinduism

Worldview questions	Shankara's nonduality Vedanta	Ramanuja's qualified nonduality Vedanta
What is our nature?	Atman (self) is ontologically identical to Brahman (Ultimate Reality with no attributes).	Atman (self) is a part/mode/aspect of Brahman (personal god Vishnu).
What is our world?	World is ultimately not real, but appears real through maya (illusion). All is Brahman.	World is Vishnu's own body.
What is our problem?	Enslaved in cycle of death and rebirth through karma. Liberation through paths of work, knowledge, and devotion, though path of knowledge is more important.	Enslaved in cycle of death and rebirth through karma. Liberation through paths of work, knowledge, and devotion, though path of devotion is more important.
What is our end?	Reincarnation or moksha. Moksha leads to absorption into Brahman (Ultimate Reality with no attributes).	Reincarnation or moksha. Moksha leads to eternal bliss in Vishnu's heaven in a godlike state.

The ultimate goal of Hinduism is moksha, liberation from the cycle of death and rebirth. Hinduism teaches three ways of liberation: the way of works, the way of knowledge, and the way of devotion. This liberation is achieved during one's lifetime. Upon death, a liberated person is absorbed into an attributeless Ultimate Reality or enjoys blissful union with god in

---

[38]Rodrigues, *Introducing Hinduism*, 252-53; and Klostermaier, *Hinduism: A Short History*, 106.

*Contemporary Cultural
Worldview Meditation*

The Worldview of *Avatar*

The 2009 blockbuster *Avatar*, directed by James Cameron, has become one of the highest-grossing movies of all time (over $2 billion). It powerfully portrays a fascinating mixture of worldviews, especially the blending of scientific naturalism and pantheistic animism.

In *Avatar*, greedy capitalistic humans are determined to mine the profitable element unobtanium (thinly punned, isn't it?) from the planet Pandora. If possible, the humans would like to avoid exterminating the native Na'vi, who happen to live right on top of the mineral deposit. A wounded soldier, Jake Sully, is recruited to inhabit a Na'vi body and infiltrate the natives in order to convince them to move elsewhere on their planet.

Instead, Jake is won over by the pantheistic way of life of the Na'vi, who have intricate rituals that connect them to their planet. Their Hometree is a clear symbol of Mother Earth in modern pantheistic naturalism. As critics and fans alike note, the pantheism in Avatar is neither a byproduct nor an afterthought; rather, it is an intentional teaching point of the movie. Capitalism, rooted in Western monotheism, rapes and pillages the earth and everything valuable on it. We need, *Avatar* teaches, to abandon rampant capitalism and return to a way of natural connectedness.

Christians can "amen" the warnings against the excesses of capitalism but must resist the strong embrace of pantheistic animism. Our Hometree is not Mother Earth, to whom we are all connected; rather, our physical reality is created by the triune and transcendent God of the Bible. We can and should denounce economic and political sin, but we need not accept animism in its place.

a godlike state. Table 8.1 summarizes Shankara's nonduality Vedanta and Ramanuja's qualified nonduality Vedanta.

8.2 The Hindu Worldview and Life Motivation

The primary life motivation for a devout Hindu is achieving moksha, "the supreme and most valuable pursuit."[39] Second to moksha is gaining good karma, drawing one closer to moksha with each subsequent life. One way to gain good karma is by living in line with the eternal dharma and rita (the cosmic order). Aligning one's life with the cosmic order is largely determined by one's caste and gender.

Traditionally, the life of high-caste Hindu men was divided into four stages of life and guided by four goals or aims. The four stages of life are student, householder, forest-dweller, and renouncer. In the first stage of life the high-caste Hindu boy was expected to devote himself to studying the

---

[39]Rodrigues, *Introducing Hinduism*, 52.

Vedas under the tutelage of a guru in order to achieve one of the four aims of life—namely, dharma. Next, the boy would transition into the house-holder stage where he would get married and work, seeking the next two goals, artha and kama. Artha is "skill, attainment, power, or wealth," while kama is the experience of pleasure with "love and sexual gratification."[40]

Upon the age of retirement, some high-caste Hindu men enter the forest dwelling stage, in which they slowly cut aside the goals of artha and kama and focus on achieving moksha, the fourth and final aim of life. Traditionally, the retired man would leave his home and dwell in a hut in the forest where he could devote himself to spiritual matters, though not necessarily breaking ties with his family because his wife could go with him into the forest. On rare occasions, some men tran-sition into the renouncer stage in which they dedicate themselves more intently to achieve moksha. The renouncer stage involves renouncing one's family, friends, and possessions in order to "wander the world" in pursuit of moksha. The renouncer wears a simple robe and carries with him his staff and bowl to collect food and other offerings given to him. These four stages and aims of life provide the structure for the life of a devout high-caste Hindu. The goal in following this cosmic order is to earn good karma and hopefully achieve moksha.

Women and low-caste Hindus have their own place in the cosmic order. Traditionally, women earn good karma primarily as they carry out their role as wife and mother, especially through their devotion to their husband. A wife's devotion to her husband was historically exemplified by the act of sati, in which the wife allowed herself to be burned to death in her husband's funeral pyre. Through this act the wife avoided entry into the inauspicious state of widowhood and purified her husband of his bad karma, leading to a better rebirth for her husband. Low-caste Hindus gain good karma as they live out the duties of their caste. By suf-fering through life as an untouchable or low-caste Hindu the person pays off his or her bad karma and earns good karma, hoping to be reborn in a higher caste in future lives.

However, the path of devotion provides a shortcut to moksha, espe-cially appealing to women and low-caste Hindus. Although following

---

[40]Ibid., 91-92.

dharma and living in line with the cosmic order is still important, devotion to Vishnu, Shiva, or the goddess can take on a greater significance
because moksha can be achieved as a devotee of these deities. For Hindus
who follow the path of devotion, daily devotion and worship of their
particular deity becomes central to everyday life.

REFLECTION QUESTIONS

1 In one sentence, summarize the ultimate goal of Hinduism.

2 Are there any similarities between the Hindu and Christian worldviews? If so, what are they?

3 What are the most significant differences between the Hindu and
Christian worldviews?

4 What role does karma play in Hinduism?

5 What are the three paths to liberation in Hinduism? What do the
three paths reveal about the Hindu worldview?

8.3 WORLDVIEW ANALYSIS OF HINDUISM

Analyzing the Hindu worldview is a difficult task because it is not a
monolithic religious tradition but rather an amalgamation of various
beliefs and practices in India. Therefore, the following analysis can address only some of the more common characteristics of the Hindu
worldview that are challenged by outsiders. Special references to Shankara's nondualism and Ramanuja's qualified nondualism will be made to
guide the discussion. The Hindu worldview will be analyzed in three
areas: (1) internal consistency and logical coherence, (2) external consistency and evidential correspondence, and (3) existential consistency and
pragmatic satisfaction.

8.3.1 Internal consistency and logical coherence. It would be unfair
to test the Hindu worldview for internal consistency and logical coherence because it contains so many different conflicting schools of
thought. Therefore, instead of analyzing the Hindu worldview as a whole,
only certain elements within each of these representative schools in Hinduism will be addressed.

We will begin our analysis with Shankara's Advaita Vedanta. One apparent contradiction in this school is that Shankara affirms that all that exists is Nirguna Brahman (Ultimate Reality with no attributes) while also affirming the existence of other entities. For example, critics of Shankara point to the idea of maya as an inconsistency in the nondualist position. If maya is real, then two realities exist: Brahman and maya. If maya is unreal, then how can it be used by Brahman to create a worldwide illusion? Shankara responds by arguing that, like Brahman, maya itself is indescribable and ineffable. Critics are not convinced. Shankara is inconsistent in two ways. First, he affirms the existence of only one entity but then affirms the existence of more than one entity, Brahman and maya. Maya is real or it is not. It cannot be both. Second, he describes maya but then affirms that, just like Brahman, maya is indescribable and without attributes. Maya either has attributes or it does not. The problems with Shankara's doctrine of maya are also evident in his doctrines of Nirguna Brahman (Brahman without attributes) and Saguna Brahman (Brahman with attributes).

Shankara taught that Ultimate Reality was Brahman with no attributes; however, he was forced to postulate Brahman with attributes so that he could actually say something about Brahman. Ramanuja criticized Shankara for his concept of Nirguna Brahman, arguing that it is meaningless to try to comprehend, relate to, or even speak about an Ultimate Reality with no attributes. Because Shankara's Ultimate Reality has no attributes, we can know nothing about it, nor can we say anything meaningful about it. Problematically, Shankara had too much to say and knew far too much about an entity of which nothing could be known. This leads to the question about the relationship between Nirguna Brahman and Saguna Brahman, explained as Ishvara (lord), a personal deity. If we know nothing about Nirguna Brahman, how would we know if Ishvara has any relation to it at all? Can any statement made by a devotee about Ishvara be meaningfully applied to Brahman? Ultimately the answer is no. It seems inconsistent for Shankara to encourage people to devote themselves to the gods, because any statement about them is ultimately rooted in ignorance and says nothing about Brahman. Shankara wrote hymns of praise to Vishnu, Shiva, and the goddess, yet he still affirmed that any discussion of the gods and their attributes is rooted in maya (an illusion).

Another apparent inconsistency is Shankara's explanation about the reality of the world. He affirms that the world is real in the first three levels of knowledge: the normal waking state, dreaming state, and dreamless state. However, he also affirms that at the deepest level of knowledge there is "pure awareness" and "consciousness of consciousness" in which the world is "unreal." In this state of consciousness an enlightened person can see that the world is ultimately an illusion brought about by Brahman through maya. The question remains, is our world real or is it not? A response of "it is real in one sense but not real in another sense" does not suffice. Our world is real or it is not; it cannot be both. It is one thing to affirm that the world is different from what we perceive it to be, but it is another thing to state that the world in its entirety is not truly real.

A third apparent inconsistency in Advaita Vedanta has to do with Nirguna Brahman and the doctrine of karma. In their article "What Is Evil?" Christopher Isherwood and Swami Prabhavananda explain how good and evil relate to Brahman in Vedanta.[41] They state that Brahman is "beyond good and evil, pleasure and pain, success and disaster." Therefore, they conclude that good and evil are aspects of maya; they are ultimately unreal. This perspective should lead them to moral relativism because good and evil are ultimately not real and have no basis outside of maya. Such moral relativism leads adherents of Advaita Vedanta to a quandary. On the one hand, they have to affirm that good and evil are not ultimately real. They are part of the illusion. On the other hand, they still staunchly affirm the reality of karma, which takes good and evil very seriously. For instance, Isherwood and Prabhavananda defend the doctrine of karma and state that it is "a doctrine of absolute, automatic justice"; people get exactly what they deserve. They appear to delight in the idea of justice—that good is rewarded and evil is punished. However, their strong desire for justice does not seem

---

[41]Christopher Isherwood and Swami Prabhavananda, "What Is Evil?," in *The Inner Journey: Views from the Hindu Tradition*, ed. Margaret H. Case, Parabola Anthology (Sandpoint, ID: Morning Light, 2007), 75.

consistent with their belief that good and evil are ultimately unreal. How can one be so concerned with justice if actions are not truly either good or evil? In addition, where does karma come from if Brahman is an amoral entity? The doctrine of karma clearly has moral judgment built into it. Although karma is not technically punishment or reward, but rather the basic law of cause and effect, actions are clearly judged to be morally good or evil. Where do these moral values come from? Who or what is the judge? Who set it up that way? A response might be that karma is simply a rule of nature, similar to the laws of physics. It is simply how the world functions. However, how did this moral law found in karma proceed from an Ultimate Reality with no attributes, one that is therefore amoral?

Ramanuja avoided many of Shankara's inconsistencies by postulating Brahman as a personal god with attributes; however, this did not leave him without his own inconsistencies. The actual name of his school of thought, "qualified nondualism," appears contradictory. Nondualism means that there is only one real entity in existence. If you modify this entity and add additional distinct entities, it becomes dualistic. For example, Ramanuja affirms that all that exists is Brahman, whom he equates with the personal god Vishnu, but then at the same time he asserts the reality of atman. In one sense he affirms only the existence of Brahman because atman is a part of or a mode of Brahman. However, he also affirms that liberation is not absorption into an impersonal Brahman as Shankara taught; rather, there is fellowship between a personal Brahman and a personal atman. Brahman and atman remain two distinct entities. If Brahman and an individual's atman are not identical, then it cannot be said that all that exists is Brahman. Therefore, Ramanuja's qualified nondualism is actually a type of dualism.

8.3.2 External consistency and evidential correspondence. Testing a worldview based on external consistency and evidential correspondence is difficult because not everyone accepts the same facts. For example, Hindus assume the doctrine of karma and transmigration. They do not feel the need to provide evidence or argumentation for their position. Karma and transmigration are simply facts about the cosmos. Hindus are justified in holding their beliefs unless they are confronted with evidence or arguments that suggest otherwise. However, this principle also applies to those who do not hold to karma and transmigration. Those who do not believe in karma and transmigration are justified in not believing in these doctrines unless they are presented with evidence or arguments that show otherwise. On a side note, the same can be said about Shankara's position that all that exists is Brahman and that our world with all its dualities is ultimately unreal. This perspective contradicts our common experience. We experience our world to be real, and we see differences between entities. We would need some very strong evidence or argumentation to cause us to question the reality and dualities of the world we experience. Returning to our topic at hand, it appears that besides appealing to Hindu scriptures and personal testimony about remembering past lives, there is little to no evidence that would support belief in karma and transmigration. What agreed-on facts could Hindus and non-Hindus use to support or deny karma and transmigration? Trying to determine these facts would be very difficult.

One possible approach would be to look to science and see what it might show about the cosmos. Though scientific facts are highly debated and not agreed on by all because these facts are not free from interpretation, science might still provide data that both Hindus and non-Hindus can agree on. Science does not speak to the issue of karma and transmigration, but it might speak to the Hindu belief in the eternality of the world. Atman, karma, and transmigration are rooted in belief in the eternality of the cosmos. According to Hindu understanding, atman is eternal just like Brahman, and karma and transmigration have always been in place. If evidence can show that the cosmos is not eternal but actually had a starting point, this would undercut not only belief in the eternality of the cosmos but also the doctrines of atman, karma, and transmigration.

Space does not permit a developed discussion on the scientific evidence in support of or against the eternality of the cosmos. However, the standard Big Bang model suggests that the cosmos did have a starting point. Christian philosopher William Lane Craig uses the standard Big Bang model in his well-known Kalam cosmological argument for the existence of God.[42] The Kalam cosmological argument can be explained in the following manner: (1) Whatever begins to exist has a cause. (2) The universe began to exist. (3) Therefore, the universe has a cause. In Craig's version of the Kalam argument he uses both scientific and philosophical arguments to establish premise two, that the universe began to exist. In addition to the standard Big Bang model, Craig also points to the second law of thermodynamics, which states that "processes taking place in a closed system always tend toward a state of equilibrium."[43] From this law he argues that if the cosmos has existed eternally it would have already experienced "heat death," a state in which no change is further possible and the cosmos is therefore dead.

In addition to scientific evidence against the eternality of the cosmos, Craig also presents two philosophical arguments that support his claim that the cosmos had a beginning. He argues for "the impossibility of an actually infinite number of things" and for "the impossibility of forming an actually infinite collection of things by adding one member after another." Space does not permit an explanation of his arguments; stating his conclusion to the second argument mentioned above will suffice. He writes, "If the universe did not begin to exist a finite time ago, then the present moment would never arrive. But obviously it has arrived. Therefore, we know that the universe is finite in the past and began to exist."[44] To conclude, if scientific or philosophical arguments, like those presented by Craig, could demonstrate that the cosmos had a starting point, this would severely call into question some basic Hindu presuppositions.

8.3.3 Existential consistency and pragmatic satisfaction. The existential consistency and pragmatic satisfaction of a worldview has to do with both the livability of a belief system and whether it is existentially satisfying. Can people live out their belief system consistently? Do people find their belief system satisfying? Of the three ways to analyze a worldview, this is clearly the most subjective; nevertheless, the question of livability and existential satisfaction is critical. The inability to live out a particular

---

[42]William Lane Craig, *Reasonable Faith: Christian Truth and Apologetics*, 3rd ed. (Wheaton, IL: Crossway, 2008), 111-56.

[43]Ibid., 140-41. He discusses the standard Big Bang model and other alternative models on 125-41. He discusses the second law of thermodynamics and its implication on 140-50.

[44]Ibid., 116-24.

worldview calls into question the truth of the worldview. How does Hinduism fare in this area of analysis? On the one hand, one could argue that Hinduism passes this test because it appears that nearly one billion people find it livable and satisfying. On the other hand, many former Hindus have found the worldview unsatisfying and have left the faith.[45]

Of the two representative forms of Hinduism we have looked at, Shankara's Advaita Vedanta is the least livable. From a pragmatic perspective, Shankara recognized that to live in the world one had to accept the "reality" of the world. In this sense the world as we see it is real. However, those who have attained enlightenment are able to see that they can "no longer equate reality with the everchanging, transient world."[46] But is this position consistent? Is it not inconsistent that adherents of Advaita Vedanta believe that the world is not really real, yet they have to live as if it were? In addition, Shankara advocated the worship of the gods as a necessary step to moksha. Therefore, many adherents of Advaita Vedanta still practice bhakti, although according to their school of thought the gods and their attributes are a result of maya. Ultimately, the gods are not real, yet they worship them as if they were. They profess nonduality, yet they live the life of a dualist.

We must also examine whether the Hindu worldview is existentially satisfying. The caste system has been especially controversial. Critics often point to the harshness and inequality of the caste system, especially toward Śudras and the untouchables. The Indian government has officially abolished untouchability, but oppression persists. Many simply refer to this class as Dalit, meaning "oppressed." The Śudra and Dalit classes are socially and economically underprivileged and victims of socially pervasive discrimination. This explains, in part, why the majority of Hindu converts to Christianity and Islam come from the lower castes.

Critics also find both the status of women in Hinduism and its doctrine of karma troubling. The low status of women in traditional Hindu society, like the caste system, is controversial and unthinkable to many

---

[45]It should be noted that the same can be said about Christianity, Islam, or any other major religious tradition. Millions of people adhere to these religions, yet many adherents end up leaving their faith.

[46]Klostermaier, *Hinduism: A Beginner's Guide*, 131.

outsiders. Although there are exceptions and the status of women has improved in modern times, sexism is so ingrained in Hindu society and supported by Hindu sacred texts that it continues. In addition, some of the implications that come from the doctrine of karma are difficult to embrace. For instance, the doctrine of karma teaches that people get what they deserve: "To be born a beggar, a king, an athlete, or a helpless cripple is simply the composite consequence of the deeds of other lives. We have no one to thank but ourselves. It is no use trying to bargain with Iswara, or propitiate Him, or hold Him responsible for our troubles. It is no use inventing a Devil as an alibi for our weaknesses."[47] Therefore, those suffering deserve what they are experiencing. It is a result of their bad karma. In other words, victims of child abuse, torture, rape, and murder are not innocent but are receiving what they have earned. Karma may serve as a helpful theodicy, yet many find its implications troubling.[48]

This brief survey and analysis of the Hindu worldview clearly demonstrates the differences between the Hindu and Christian worldviews. Although Hindus and Christians share the same physical world, they appear to inhabit completely different worlds. These major worldview differences would also become evident when comparing Christianity with other religions of South Asian roots like Buddhism, Jainism, and Sikhism.

REFLECTION QUESTIONS

1 What is a good argument one could make in support of the position that it is unfair to apply an internal-consistency and logical-coherence test to the Hindu worldview?

2 What is a good argument one could make in support of the position that it is fair to apply an internal-consistency and logical-coherence test to the Hindu worldview?

---

[47]Isherwood and Prabhavanda, "What Is Evil?," 75.

[48]For additional analysis and critique of the Hindu worldview, see Timothy C. Tennent, *Christianity at the Religious Roundtable: Evangelicalism in Conversation with Hinduism, Buddhism, and Islam* (Grand Rapids: Baker Academic, 2002), 37-86; David L. Johnson, *A Reasoned Look at Asian Religions: A Critical Analysis of Eastern Thought for Better Understanding and Communication* (Minneapolis: Bethany House, 1985), 73-116; Norman L. Geisler, *Christian Apologetics* (Grand Rapids: Baker Books, 1976), 173-92; and Sire, *Universe Next Door*, 144-60.

3 What do you see as the greatest strength in the Hindu worldview?

4 What do you see as the most significant weakness in the Hindu worldview?

5 How might some Hindus respond to the logical analysis and critique of the Hindu worldview?

8.4 ISLAM

Over 1.6 billion people claim Islam as their religion, making it the second-largest world religion. The largest Muslim populations can be found in North Africa, the Middle East, Central Asia, South Asia, and Southeast Asia. Though Islam is of Arab origin, the most-populous Muslim nations are found elsewhere: Indonesia, Pakistan, India, and Bangladesh. It is estimated that there were 2.6 million Muslims in the United States in 2010, but the population is expected to grow to 6.2 million by 2030.[49] Of the 1.6 billion Muslims worldwide, around 85 percent are Sunni and 15 percent are Shiite. This chapter will focus on Sunni Islam because it is the dominant form of Islam.

Islam originated with Muhammad in the seventh century on the Arabian Peninsula, in present-day Saudi Arabia. In AD 610, at the age of forty, Muhammad reported receiving revelations from the angel Gabriel. These revelations continued for twenty-two years and were compiled into the Qur'an after his death. Muhammad rejected the polytheism of his day and called for submission to Allah, the God of Abraham. The name *Islam* comes from the Arabic word meaning "to submit." Therefore, Muslims are those who submit to Allah's will and commands as revealed in the Qur'an and through Muhammad's example. The Muslim confession of faith provides a helpful summary of the heart of Islam: "There is no god but Allah, and Muhammad is his messenger."

Sunni Muslims express their submission to Allah by practicing the Five Pillars of Islam: the confession of faith (shahada), ritual prayer (salat), religious tax (zakat), fasting during the month of Ramadan (sawm), and pilgrimage to Mecca (hajj). The Five Pillars are understood

---

[49]Forum on Religion & Public Life, "The Future Global Muslim Population," Pew Research Center, January 2011, www.pewforum.org/2011/01/27/the-future-of-the-global-muslim-population.

to be acts of worship and service. In addition to the Five Pillars, there are also five foundational beliefs in the Muslim worldview.

The first belief is that Allah is one. Committing *shirk*, associating anything with Allah, is the worst sin in Islam. The second belief is in Allah's angels. The third belief is in Allah's books—namely, the Torah, the Psalms, the Gospel, and the Qur'an. The fourth belief is in Allah's prophets and messengers. Some of the prophets mentioned in the Qur'an include Adam, Noah, Abraham, Isaac, Jacob, Joseph, Job, Moses, Aaron, David, Solomon, Elisha, Jonah, John the Baptist, and Jesus. Muhammad is the last prophet, the seal of the prophets. The fifth belief is in the final judgment. At the end of time, Allah will resurrect all people and bring them before him for judgment; he will cast some into hell, while others he will admit into paradise.

8.4.1 What is our nature? In Islam, everything originates with Allah. It is impossible to understand human nature apart from understanding Allah because he is the creator of all things. Allah is the Real, the Truth, Ultimate Reality. He is all-powerful, all-knowing, and ever-present. He is the merciful and pardoning protector. However, he is also the judge, severe in punishment. The well-known "throne verse" presents a vivid picture of Allah (Q Baqarah 2:255).[50]

> Allah! There is no god but He, the Living, the Self-subsisting, Eternal. No slumber can seize Him nor sleep. His are all things in the heavens and on earth. Who is there can intercede in His presence except as He permitteth? He knoweth what (appeareth to His creatures as) before or after or behind them. Nor shall they compass aught of His knowledge except as He willeth. His Throne doth extend over the heavens and the earth, and He feeleth no fatigue in guarding and preserving them for He is the Most High, the Supreme (in glory).

Of the various attributes mentioned in this passage, the foundational attribute is God's oneness. Surah 112 in the Qur'an is an exquisite expression of *tawhid*, the oneness of Allah, and is regarded by Muslims as

---

[50]References to the Qur'an will include *surah* (chapter) number and title along with verse. For example, Q Baqarah 2:255 indicates *surah* 2, verse 255. All qur'anic passages in English come from the Yusuf Ali translation unless otherwise noted. Abdullah Yusuf Ali, *The Meaning of the Holy Qur'an*, new ed. with rev. translation and commentary (Brentwood, MD: Amana, 1991).

"the essence of the whole Qur'an."[51] It reads, "Say: He is Allah, the One and Only; Allah, the Eternal, Absolute; He begetteth not, nor is He begotten; And there is none like unto Him."

In addition to being One, Allah is also the all-powerful creator and sustainer of the cosmos. When describing Allah, Fazlur Rahman states that he is "Creator and Sustainer of the universe and of man, and particularly the giver of guidance for man and He who judges man, individually and collectively, and metes out to him merciful justice."[52] Rahman's description highlights not only Allah's power over creation but also his relationship with humanity.

Humanity is the pinnacle of Allah's creation. Humans are different from the rest of creation in that Allah "breathed his own spirit" into them (Q Hijr 15:29; Q Sajdah 32:9; Q Sad 38:72). The Qur'an also teaches that Allah created humanity to worship and serve him: "I have only created *jinns* and men that they may serve/worship me" (Q Dhariyat 51:56).[53] Consequently, the Qur'an describes worshipers of Allah as servants or slaves of Allah.[54] Moreover, the Qur'an describes how humanity, from the very beginning, covenanted with Allah that he was their Lord and that he alone deserves worship:

> When thy Lord drew forth from the Children of Adam—from their loins—
> their descendants, and made them testify concerning themselves, (saying):
> "Am I not your Lord (who cherishes and sustains you)?"—They said: "Yea!
> We do testify!" (This), lest ye should say on the Day of Judgment: "Of this
> we were never mindful." (Q A'raf 7:172)

Moreover, Allah placed humanity as his *khalifa*, vice regent (Q Baqarah 2:30-37), and gave humanity "the Trust" (Q Ahzab 33:72-73). In simple terms, one could say that Allah has placed humanity in charge on

---

[51]Fazlur Rahman, *Major Themes of the Qur'an*, 2nd ed. (Minneapolis: Bibliotheca Islamica, 1994), 11.

[52]Ibid., 1.

[53]*Jinn* are spirit beings that Allah created out of "smokeless fire." Like people, they can embrace or reject Islam and will be brought before Allah on the day of judgment. For more information on the *jinn*, see 'Umar S. al-Ashqar, *The World of the Jinn and Devils: In the Light of the Qur'an and Sunnah*, trans. Nasiruddin Khattab, 2nd ed., Islamic Creed 3 (Riyadh: International Islamic, 2005).

[54]Ingrid Mattson, *The Story of the Qur'an: Its History and Place in Muslim Life* (Malden, MA: Blackwell, 2008), 49.

earth. Mohammad Abu-Hamdiyyah provides a helpful explanation of what it means for humanity to be Allah's *khalifa* when he states that "God put mankind in full charge on earth. This empowerment or mandate with full responsibility runs during the sojourn of man on earth."[55] S. Nomunal Haq emphasizes the moral nature of this responsibility. He argues that Allah created humanity in order to bring about, through his guidance, "a moral order *here on earth*, that is, a moral order in history."[56] Syed Abul 'Ala Maudoodi understands that people live out their role as Allah's vice regents by carrying out his will:

> Man's being the viceregent of God on this earth logically requires that the purpose of his life should be to carry out the will of God on this earth. To enforce the divine will in the portion of the world's affairs whose management has been entrusted to him by God, to create and maintain those conditions in which peace, justice, and virtue can flourish, to suppress and eradicate whatever mischief, and disorder is caused by the evil-doers among men and to foster those virtues and moral qualities which are pleasing in the sight of God and with which the Lord of the universe desires to embellish His earth and ennoble His creatures.[57]

Taking a look at Adam's sin, the first incident of humankind's disobedience, provides a helpful picture of the human condition before Allah. Allah created Adam and his wife, placed them in the garden, and commanded them not to eat from the forbidden tree (Q A'raf 7:19-26). Satan tempted them, and they ate of the tree. For their disobedience, Allah banished them from the garden and cast them down to earth. However, they quickly repented, and Allah forgave them (Q Baqarah 2:37; Q A'raf 7:23-26).

This incident of disobedience reveals some important elements of the Muslim understanding of human nature. First, Allah created Adam in a state of moral purity, which all humankind shares with him (Q Rum 30:30). In the hadiths[58] Muhammad taught that all children are born

[55]Mohammad Abu-Hamdiyyah, *The Qur'an: An Introduction* (London: Routledge, 2000), 84-85.
[56]S. Nomanul Haq, "The Human Condition in Islam," in *The Human Condition: A Volume in the Comparative Religious Ideas Project*, ed. Robert C. Neville (Albany: State University of New York Press, 2001), 162.
[57]Syed Abul 'Ala Maudoodi, *The Ethical View-Point of Islam*, 2nd ed. (Lahore: Markazi Maktaba Jamaat-e-Islami, 1953), 50.
[58]A hadith is a report about Muhammad's teachings or actions. Muslim religious scholars

muslim, meaning that they know that God exists and that they should submit to him. Therefore, Muslims generally believe that Allah created humanity with a nature that is more good than evil. Adam's disobedience resulted from Satan's temptation and Adam's own built-in human imperfections, which made it possible for him to disobey. Mustansir Mir argues that sin arises from the "willful misuses by humans of the freedom that has been accorded them."[59] Moreover, Adam and his wife's sin did not transform or corrupt human nature; rather, their sin only affected them, and Allah quickly forgave them when they repented. In opposition to the Christian doctrine of original sin, Hammudah Abdulati states that Adam and his wife's "committing a sin or making a mistake" did not "necessarily deaden the human heart, prevent spiritual reform or stop moral growth."[60] Therefore, the human condition in Islam is not about "recovery from a fall" to regain some "original glory" but is rather about "perpetually fulfilling a set of obligations, 'to enjoin good and dismiss evil,' and while fulfilling its obligations humanity reaches ever new glories."[61] To conclude, every person is born with the innate ability to obey or disobey Allah, and to repent if needed.

In light of this human condition, the Qur'an teaches that Allah gives guidance to whom he wills, guiding on the straight path those who obey him and his messengers and leading astray those who reject his guidance.[62] To those who turn to him, as the introduction to every *surah* states, Allah is "most gracious, most merciful." He is "Oft-forgiving, Most Merciful" (Q Baqarah 2:192). Allah's mercy was most clearly manifested when he sent guidance to humanity through his messengers and his books, especially Muhammad and the Qur'an. Consequently, Abdulati states that the Qur'an is "the greatest gift of God to humanity," and Gai Eaton states that Allah gave Muhammad as an act of "mercy to mankind."[63]

preserved these reports in authorized collections a couple of centuries after Muhammad's death.

[59]Mustansir Mir, "Sin," in *The Oxford Encyclopedia of the Modern Islamic World*, ed. John L. Esposito (New York: Oxford University Press, 1995), 4:73.

[60]Hammudah Abdulati, *Islam in Focus*, 3rd ed. (Indianapolis: American Trust, 1994), 31.

[61]Haq, "Human Condition in Islam," 171.

[62]Q Baqarah 2:142, 213, 272; Q An'am 6:88, 149; Q Ibrahim 14:4; Q Nahl 16:93; Q Nur 24:35; Q Qasas 28:56; Q Rum 30:29; Q Fatir 35:8.

[63]Abdulati, *Islam in Focus*, 191; and Gai Eaton, *Islam and the Destiny of Man* (Cambridge: Islamic Texts Society, 1994), 201.

8.4.2 What is our world? The world is Allah's creation and is full of
"signs" that point to his existence and goodness. Faruq Sherif argues that
Allah's "greatest and most manifest attribute" is that he is the creator and
preserver of heaven and earth.[64] Creation glorifies Allah and is a "sign"
of Allah's existence (Q Baqarah 2:164; Q Isra' 17:44). As creator and sustainer of the universe, Allah is all-powerful over its affairs. He is lord over
life and death (Q 'Imran 3:145, 156), and nothing can happen apart from
his will. In Q 'Imran 3:145 one reads, "nor can a soul die except by Allah's
leave, the term being fixed as by writing," and in Q Tawbah 9:51, "say:
Nothing will happen to us except what Allah has decreed for us: He is
our protector." Smith and Haddad state that Muslims can be assured that
"behind the flow of events, both in the natural and human orders, is a
divine plan, and that all man's life from birth to death is a microcosmic
part of that overall macrocosmic scheme."[65] The world is therefore the
field in which Allah's will is carried out.

Although the world is Allah's creation, Allah is completely separate
and different from creation. Nothing in creation is comparable to him.
The emphasis on the distinction between Allah and his creation is evident when discussing the Muslim view of Allah's attributes. Allah's attributes have been understood in various ways in the Islamic tradition.
Traditionalists, in the early history of Islam, interpreted Allah's attributes
and anthropomorphic language in the Qur'an literally. Rationalists, like
the Mu'tazilites, denied the reality of the attributes, emphasizing his distinction from creation. However, the dominant and mediating position,
that of al-Ashari, is that Allah's attributes are real and that the anthropomorphic language in the Qur'an should be accepted, yet *bila kayfa*,
"without knowing how." In other words, reason must bow to revelation.
The attributes are real, but they are not like those of creation. Allah enters
history through his revelation, but his substance or essence remains transcendent. Similarly, Allah does not reveal his person; rather, in his revelations, he provides knowledge about himself, his creation, and his will
for humanity. Allah's essence or nature is ultimately hidden from his

[64]Faruq Sherif, *A Guide to the Contents of the Qur'an* (Reading, UK: Garnet, 1995), 26.
[65]Jane I. Smith and Yvonne Yazbeck Haddad, *The Islamic Understanding of Death and Resurrection*
(Albany: State University of New York Press, 1981), 11.

*Contemporary Cultural
Worldview Meditation*

Allah as Lord and God as Father

One of the dominant images of Allah in Islam is that of lord and ruler. Muslims approach Allah primarily as his servants. Allah is the ruler and lawmaker, and Muslims are his faithful subjects. The word *Islam* means "submission," and a *Muslim* is "one who submits to Allah." Submission to Allah as lord is evident in the bodily prostration that dominates the daily ritual prayers. It is also evident in the popular Muslim name *Abdullah*, meaning "servant of Allah."

It goes without saying that the Bible also presents God as lord and ruler and believers as his servants. However, this image is balanced with the biblical teaching that believers are also adopted children of God. Therefore, God is our Father. He is not only our King and Lord but also our loving heavenly Father. Jesus called God his Father and taught his followers to approach God in the same way. God not only forgives us of our sins through Christ, but he also adopts us and makes us coheirs with Christ.

These different approaches to God highlight a key difference between Islam and Christianity. Islam emphasizes a servant's obedience to his or her lord. Christianity emphasizes a heavenly Father's loving relationship with his children.

creation. Even though Muslims accept the idea that Allah has attributes, they note that the attributes are different from attributes of his creation.

As Allah's vice regent, humankind's time on earth is a test or a trial. The Qur'an clearly states that Allah also created human beings that he might test them and determine who was the best (Q Hud 11:7-9; Q Kahf 18:7; Q Mulk 67:2; Q Insan 76:2). Fadhlalla Haeri states this idea succinctly: "Life is a trial preparing people for paradise or hell."[66] Similarly, in *The Purpose of Creation*, A. B. Philips states that "this world of life and death, wealth and poverty, sickness and health, was created to sift out the righteous souls from the evil ones. Human conduct in this world is the measure of faith."[67] Therefore, the world is the field in which humanity lives out its submission or rebellion against Allah, earning paradise or hell.

8.4.3 What is our problem? From the Muslim perspective, the main problem with the world is that the majority of people do not submit to Allah. People do not obey Allah, nor do they order society by his divine law, shari'ah, as they should. This largely explains why the world is in its current chaotic state. According to the Qur'an, the majority of people are

---

[66]Fadhlalla Haeri, *Journey of the Universe as Expounded in the Qur'an* (London: KPI, 1985), 10.
[67]A. B. Philips, *The Purpose of Creation* (Riyadh: Islamic Propagation Office in Rabwah, 2007), 47.

unbelievers. They have turned away from the signs and do not believe in Allah or worship him as they should (Q Yusuf 12:40, 103, 105-7). The Qur'an describes the majority of people as being ungrateful, in spite of all that Allah has given to them (Q Yunus 10:12, 22-23, 31, 60; Q Yusuf 12:38; Q Ibrahim 14:32-34; Q Nahl 16:51-55, 72, 83; Q Naml 27:73). The essence of unbelief is ingratitude, explaining why the word *kufr* in the Qur'an is used for both those who do not believe and those who are ungrateful. In addition, the Qur'an depicts humanity as being rebellious and as giving partners to Allah, thus committing *shirk* (Q Nisa' 4:48). Haq argues that *shirk* is "*the* cardinal sin of Islam" and that "in terms of its frequency, intensity, and rhetorical force, there exists hardly any theme in the Qur'an that matches *shirk*."[68]

The reason people do not submit to Allah and live by his commands is that they are weak, petty, and forgetful, and they succumb to Satan's temptations. The Qur'an describes humanity as weak (Q Nisa' 4:27-28). The Qur'an teaches that people are forgetful (Q Hashr 59:19), making them prone to allow the "cycles of acquisition and competition" in life to "obscure matters of ultimate concern."[69] Nevertheless, in their weakness, people are naturally capable of avoiding major sins and are able to try their best to avoid minor sins. They do not have a sinful nature, nor do they have a predisposition to rebel against Allah.

In addition to their natural weakness, people also have to contend with Satan's temptations. After Allah cast Satan away for refusing to bow down before Adam, Satan vowed to be humanity's enemy (Q A'raf 7:16-17). Although Satan cannot coerce people, he can invite and tempt them (Q A'raf 7:11-18, 27; Q Ta Ha 20:120). Satan's ultimate goal is to lead people to hell and deprive them of paradise (Q Fatir 35:6). Therefore, Allah warns humankind of Satan's temptation (Q A'raf 7:27):

> O ye Children of Adam! Let not Satan seduce you, in the same manner as He got your parents out of the Garden, stripping them of their raiment, to expose their shame: for he and his tribe watch you from a position where ye cannot see them: We made the evil ones friends (only) to those without faith.

---

[68] Haq, "Human Condition in Islam," 166.
[69] Michael Sells, *Approaching the Qur'an: The Early Revelations* (Ashland, OR: White Cloud, 1999), 40.

Believers have a variety of "weapons" in their fight against Satan's temptations: being watchful and cautious, adhering to the Qur'an and Sunnah (Muhammad's exemplary behavior), turning to Allah for his protection, keeping oneself busy with remembrance of Allah, adhering to the practices of the Muslim community, discovering "the traps and snares" of Satan, opposing Satan, repenting and seeking forgiveness from Allah, and not leaving any room for Satan to foster suspicion in people's hearts.[70]

Negative consequences await not only individuals but also entire civilizations if they reject Allah and his messengers. The Qur'an presents human history as an ongoing process of societies being created and destroyed based on Allah's unalterable moral judgment, which governs world history. In the Qur'an, Allah is quoted as saying, "Generations before you We destroyed when they did wrong: their messengers came to them with clear-signs, but they would not believe! Thus do We requite those who sin!" (Q Yunus 10:13). Before destroying a people or a civilization though, Allah first sends them a messenger to warn them, calling them back to worship Allah, and to turn away from evil (Q Yunus 10:47; Q Nahl 16:36; Q Qasas 28:59; Q Sad 38:3-4). However, every time Allah sent a messenger to a people, they rejected him (Q Mu'minun 23:44). For example, Allah destroyed pharaoh and the Egyptians for rejecting Moses (Q A'raf 7:130-32; Q Hud 11:96-99; Q Mu'minun 23:44; Q Qasas 28:40; Q Ghafir 40:26-28; Q Saffat 37). He destroyed Sodom and Gomorrah because they rejected Lot and persisted in their immorality (Q Hud 11:81-83; Q Hijr 15:61-79; Q 'Ankabut 29:28-34).

These accounts in the Qur'an serve as warnings for current and future generations. As Mahmoud Ayoub states, "History is God's court of justice and the instrument of His discipline."[71] In *Milestones*, Sayyid Qutb, one of the leading figures in the history of Muslim fundamentalism, argues that the modern world is in danger of destruction because it lacks the "vital values" needed for its progress:

> Mankind today is on the brink of a precipice, not because of the danger
> of complete annihilation which is hanging over its head—this being just
> a symptom and not the real disease—but because humanity is devoid of

---

[70]al-Ashqar, *World of the Jinn and Devils*, 165-202.
[71]Mahmoud Mustafa Ayoub, "The Problem of Suffering in Islam," *Journal of Dharma* 2 (1977): 275.

those vital values which are necessary not only for its healthy development but also for its real progress.[72]

To conclude, from the Muslim perspective what is wrong with the world is the refusal of individuals and societies to submit to Allah. Individuals are weak and forgetful; they give in to Satan's temptations. This reality leads them to be ungrateful and rebellious and to commit *shirk*, which amounts to idolatry. They end up rejecting Allah and his messenger. These same problems then extend to the societal level, and people form societies devoid of Allah's guidance. Individuals on the wrong path are heading toward hell, and societies on the wrong path are heading toward their inevitable demise.

From the Muslim perspective, the solution to what is wrong with the world is Islam, an all-encompassing way of life in submission to Allah's will. In his mercy, Allah has provided guidance by sending his messengers and his books to help remind people of their responsibilities before him. Allah's mercy toward humankind culminates with the Qur'an and Muhammad. However, the message is not new. Abul A'la Maududi argues that "the Qur'an makes it abundantly clear that Islam—the complete submission of man before God—is the one and only faith consistently revealed by God to mankind from the very beginning."[73] Similarly, Nasr contends that Muhammad came not with a new message but rather to "reaffirm the truth which always was, to re-establish the Primordial Tradition, and to expound the doctrine of Divine Unity."[74] Consequently, Islam does not provide a new solution to what is wrong with the world. Rather, it repeats what Allah's messengers and prophets have proclaimed since creation.

Allah provides guidance to individuals and to societies through Islam, especially through the Qur'an and Muhammad. Abul Hasan Ali Nadvi argues that "Islam is the most suitable religion for mankind."[75] Qutb

---

[72]Sayyid Qutb, *Milestones* (Damascus: Dar Al-Ilm, 1996), 7.

[73]Abul A'la Maududi, "What Islam Stands For," in *The Challenge of Islam*, ed. Altaf Gauhar (London: Islamic Council of Europe, 1978), 3.

[74]Seyyed Hossein Nasr, *An Introduction to Islamic Cosmological Doctrines: Conceptions of Nature and Methods Used for Its Study by the Ikhwan al-Safa, al-Biruni, and Ibn Sina*, rev. ed. (Boulder, CO: Shambhala, 1978), 5.

[75]Abul Hasan Ali Nadvi, "Islam: The Most Suitable Religion for Mankind," in Gauhar, *Challenge of Islam*, 17-30.

contends that Islam is "the only system" that has the values and way of life that can lead to the world's "healthy development" and its "real progress."[76] Suzanne Haneef states that Islam is "a complete and perfect system of life."[77] Hasan Ibn 'Abdullah al-Shaykh writes that Islam alone is capable of "saving humanity from its certain collapse."[78]

Islam provides meaning and guidance for believers. Believers know that the purpose of life is to worship and serve Allah by obeying his commands in the Qur'an and through Muhammad's example. In addition to explaining the purpose of life, Islam also provides believers with reminders of Allah, helping them to stay on the straight path. The Qur'an teaches believers to remember Allah through reciting the Qur'an and through ritual prayer: "Recite what is sent of the Book by inspiration to thee, and establish regular Prayer: for Prayer restrains from shameful and unjust deeds; and remembrance of Allah is the greatest (thing in life) without doubt. And Allah knows the (deeds) that ye do" (Q 'Ankabut 29:45). The Qur'an and Islamic rituals, especially the five daily ritual prayers, serve as reminders, helping believers to overcome their natural weakness and forgetfulness.

Moreover, the Qur'an and Muhammad's example provide moral guidance for believers. The Qur'an is a guide for humankind (Q Baqarah 2:185; Q A'raf 7:52; Q Naml 27:77), a guide that Allah gave Muhammad that he might lead humanity from "the depths of darkness into light" (Q Ibrahim 14:1). Consequently, the aim of the Qur'an is not Allah but rather humanity and its behavior. Muhammad Haykal argues that if people follow the "rules and ideals of conduct" in the Qur'an, this would enable them to attain "moral perfection."[79] In addition to the Qur'an, believers also look to Muhammad's example to see how Allah wants them to live. Muhammad is understood as the ideal man. His life exemplified complete submission and obedience to Allah. Muhammad is the "perfect model" of Islam for all generations and for all time.[80]

[76]Qutb, *Milestones*, 7-8.
[77]Suzanne Haneef, *What Everyone Should Know About Islam and Muslims*, 14th ed. (South Elgin, IL: Library of Islam, 1996), 125.
[78]Hasan Ibn 'Abdullah al-Shaykh, foreword to *The Life of Muhammad*, by Muhammad Husayn Haykal, trans. Isma'il Ragi Al-Faruqi (Indianapolis: North American Trust, 1976), x.
[79]Muhammad Haykal, "Islamic Civilization as Depicted in the Qur'an," in *Life of Muhammad*, 539.
[80]Syed Muhammad al-Naquib al-Attas, "Islam: The Concept of Religion and the Foundation of

Instead of cataloging the various morals and values found in the Qur'an, it will be enough to highlight the morals and values that two Sunni writers describe as essential to the faith. In *Islam in Focus*, Abdulati states that based on the Qur'an and the hadiths, "true believers" trust Allah with unshakable confidence, use what they have for Allah, "enjoin the right and good, and combat the wrong and evil by all lawful means at their disposal," obey Allah and Muhammad, increase in faith when the Qur'an is recited, have humility of heart when Allah's name is mentioned, show hospitality, speak the truth, and love Allah, Muhammad, and others for Allah's sake alone. In *What Everyone Should Know About Islam and Muslims*, Haneef covers an extended list of Islamic values: God-consciousness, faith, sincerity, responsibility, integrity, honesty, discipline, self-control, humility, patience, endurance, courage, thankfulness, keeping of commitments, fair dealing, dignity, honor, self-respect, purity, modesty, chastity, kindness, helpfulness, cooperation, charitableness, generosity, hospitality, consideration, good manners, brotherliness, warmth, lovingness, striving, hard work, and love of knowledge. As believers submit to Allah by obeying the Qur'an and Sunnah, believers uphold the primordial covenant and embody their roles as Allah's vice regents.

Finally, from the Muslim perspective Islam is the solution not only for individuals but also for societies. Rahman argues that there is no doubt that the "central aim" of the Qur'an is to set up a "viable social order on earth that will be just and ethically based."[81] Haneef argues that Islam has its own "social, political, legal and economic concepts and systems," and if societies implement them, they "would be as nearly ideal in moral and human terms as it is possible for a society to be."[82] These social, political, legal, and economic concepts and systems are rooted in shari'ah, God's law. Nasr provides a helpful description of shari'ah, showing its central role in Islam:

> In the Islamic perspective God has revealed the *Shari'ah* to man so that through it he can reform himself and his society. . . . The presence of

---

Ethics and Morality," in *The Challenge of Islam*, ed. Altaf Gauhar (London: Islamic Council of Europe, 1978), 66.

[81]Rahman, *Major Themes of the Qur'an*, 37.

[82]Haneef, *What Everyone Should Know About Islam and Muslims*, 111, 123.

> *Shari'ah* in the world is due to the compassion of God for his creatures so
> that he has sent an all encompassing Law for them to follow and thereby
> to gain felicity in both this world and the next. The *Shari'ah* is thus the
> ideal for human society and the individual. It provides meaning for all
> human activities and integrates human life. It is the norm for the perfect
> social and human life. . . . To live according to *Shari'ah* is to live according
> to the Divine Will, according to a norm which God has willed for man.[83]

By obeying shari'ah, humanity fulfills its charge to create a moral order
based on Allah's commands. Because only the Muslim community seeks
to obey shari'ah and thus live out Allah's purpose for humanity, it plays
a unique and crucial role in the world. In the Qur'an, Allah states, "Even
so we constituted you as a median community that you be witnesses to
humankind and that the Messenger be a witness over you" (Q Baqarah
2:143). Moreover, Allah states that the Muslim community is the "best of
peoples," for they command what is right, forbid what is wrong, and
believe in Allah (Q 'Imran 3:110).

Qutb argues that the Muslim community should therefore lead humanity:

> Islam came to create a people with a unique and distinctive character, a
> community that was to lead humanity, achieve purposes of God on earth,
> and rescue humanity from the suffering it had endured at the hands of
> misguided leaders, methodologies, and concepts.[84]

To summarize, according to the Muslim worldview, the solution to the
problems of the world is Islam. Islam provides meaning to human life,
and through the Qur'an and Islamic rituals, it provides reminders of
Allah that are needed to stay on the straight path. Moreover, shari'ah
embodies the ideal for individuals and for society. If individuals obey
shari'ah and build their societies on it, they will purify themselves and
the world. In Islam, there is no such thing as salvation; rather, there is
only success or failure in bringing about the type of world order embodied in the shari'ah.[85]

---

[83]Seyyed Hossein Nasr, *Ideals and Realities of Islam* (London: Allen & Unwin, 1985), 117-18.
[84]Sayyid Qutb, *Basic Principles of the Islamic Worldview*, trans. Rami David (North Haledon, NJ:
  Islamic Publications International, 2006), 2.
[85]Rahman, *Major Themes of the Qur'an*, 63.

8.4.4 What is our end? According to Islam, Allah created people to serve him. Therefore, humanity's purpose is to serve and worship him. The clearest way to do this is by submitting to him by obeying his commands, expressed in the Qur'an and through Muhammad's example. This time of testing on earth is leading toward a day of judgment when everyone will be held accountable for their actions, especially their response to Allah's revelation through Muhammad.

According to the Qur'an and the hadiths, people will spend eternity in either paradise or hell. In his foreword to *Paradise and Hell: In the Light of the Qur'an and Sunnah*, al-Ashqar writes, "Praise be to Allah, Who has created Paradise and Hell, and has created inhabitants for each of them, and has made Paradise the abode of His beloved and Hell the abode of His enemies."[86] The Qur'an provides a vivid contrast between paradise and hell:

> (Here is) a Parable of the Garden which the righteous are promised: in it are rivers of water incorruptible; rivers of milk of which the taste never changes; rivers of wine, a joy to those who drink; and rivers of honey pure and clear. In it there are for them all kinds of fruits; and Grace from their Lord. (Can those in such Bliss) be compared to such as shall dwell for ever in the Fire, and be given, to drink, boiling water, so that it cuts up their bowels (to pieces)? (Q Muhammad 47:15)[87]

Those who submit to Allah and obey his commands, as revealed in the Qur'an and Muhammad's example, will be rewarded with paradise. A day is coming when Allah will resurrect all people from the dead and bring them before him for judgment. Allah will judge fairly, and no one will experience injustice (Q Baqarah 2:281; Q Nisa' 4:77, 124; Q Nahl 16:111; Q Anbiya' 21:47). However, Allah's judgment is holistic in nature and not a strict quid pro quo. For example, in his mercy, Allah will multiply the weight of the good deeds of believers (Q Baqarah 2:261; Q An'am 6:160; Q Taghabun 64:17). Moreover, the hadiths record that Muhammad will

---

[86]'Umar S. al-Ashqar, *Paradise and Hell: In the Light of the Qur'an and Sunnah*, trans. Nasiruddin Khattab, 5th ed., Islamic Creed 7 (Riyadh: International Islamic, 2005), 17.

[87]The "great mass of the faithful" take the descriptions of paradise and hell "at face value." In addition, traditionally, it has been understood that there are seven levels in both paradise and hell, which amount to degrees of blessing and punishment. Jane I. Smith, "Afterlife," in Esposito, *Oxford Encyclopedia of the Modern Islamic World*, 1:42.

intercede on behalf of believers on the day of judgment (hadith nos. 3340; 3361; 4712; 4718).[88] Although the Qur'an appears to teach that there is no intercession (Q Baqarah 2:48, 254; Q An'am 6:51, 70; Q Zumar 39:23, 44), other verses state that there is no intercession without Allah's permission (Q Baqarah 2:255; Q Yunus 10:3; Q Ta Ha 20:109; Q Saba' 34:23; Q Najm 53:26), thus making intercession permissible.[89] In contrast, Allah will gather the unbelievers into hell, where they will be punished eternally in proportion to their sin.

8.5 The Islamic Worldview and Life Motivation

The heart of Islam is submission to Allah. In *What Everyone Should Know About Islam and Muslims*, Suzanne Haneef concludes by stating that her entire book can be summarized with one brief word, *submission*. She writes that the purpose of Islam is to "help the human individual, in his inward and outward aspects, his physical being as well as his mind and soul, his collective as well as his personal concerns, to live a life which is surrendered, by will and by deed, to God Most High."[90] Therefore, the life motivation for a devout Muslim is submission to Allah's commands, revealed in the Qur'an and through Muhammad's example. Allah's commands are the foundation of shari'ah law. Shari'ah not only involves religious matters but encompasses all areas of life. Muslims differ on how much they think shari'ah should be applied or modernized for today's world. Nonetheless, the desire of all devout Muslims is to align their lives to Allah's will.

One of the most significant motivating factors that compels Muslims to obey Allah's commands is a deep awareness of Allah's omniscience and the coming day of judgment. Each Muslim who develops "God-consciousness" in all things and at all times is "acutely aware that his or her every thought, word and action is known to Allah, and recorded."[91] By

---

[88] All citations of hadith in this chapter come from *Sahih al-Bukhari* unless otherwise noted. Muhammad Muhsin Khan, *The Translation of the Meanings of Sahih Al-Bukhāri*, 9 vols. (Riyadh: Darussalam, 1997).

[89] Rahman, *Major Themes of the Qur'an*, 31.

[90] Haneef, *What Everyone Should Know About Islam and Muslims*, 211.

[91] Laurence B. Brown, *Bearing True Witness (or, "Now That I've Found Islam, What Do I Do With It?")* (Riyadh: Darussalam, 2005), 73.

developing a constant awareness of Allah's omniscience and the presence of the angels that record one's actions, Muslims hope never to compromise the duties of the religion, even if they are alone. An awareness of the coming day of judgment is so significant to the everyday lives of Muslims that Abul A'la Maududi can write that belief in Allah and in Muhammad is not sufficient for "man's guidance."[92] Instead, people also need belief in the coming day of judgment in the hereafter, which functions as a powerful moral motivator and will help them conform to Allah's commands. Because "no Muslim, even the best among them, imagines that he is guaranteed paradise," a devout Muslim will try to "send on ahead for his future existence such deeds as will merit the pleasure of his Lord, so that he can look forward to it with hope for His mercy and grace."[93]

REFLECTION QUESTIONS

1 What are some similarities between the Muslim and Christian worldviews?

2 What are the most significant differences between the Muslim and Christian worldviews?

3 How does Allah compare with your understanding of God?

4 How is Muhammad's role in Islam different from Jesus' role in Christianity?

5 What is the significance of judgment day in Islam? What does it reveal about the Muslim worldview?

8.6 WORLDVIEW ANALYSIS OF ISLAM

Of all the major world religions, Islam is the most similar to Christianity. Because they are both monotheistic religions, they share common features related to their views of God, the world, and humanity. However, significant differences persist, which from a Christian perspective reveal the inadequacy of the Muslim worldview.

---

[92]Maududi, "What Islam Stands For," 13.
[93]Haneef, *What Everyone Should Know About Islam and Muslims*, 44.

8.6.1 Internal consistency and logical coherence. The most significant internal inconsistencies in the Muslim worldview have to do with the doctrine of Allah. *Tawhid*, the doctrine of the oneness of Allah, is central to Islam. Seyyed Hossein Nasr states that "Allah is first and before everything One, and it is the Oneness of God that lies at the center of both the Quranic doctrine of God and Islamic spirituality."[94] The doctrine of *tawhid* asserts not only that Allah is one but that there is no plurality in the godhead, explaining Islam's utter rejection of the Trinity. Adding partners to Allah is *shirk*, the worst sin in Islam. Because of this emphasis on radical monotheism, one early rationalist school of Islam, the Mu'tazilites, argued that the Qur'an was a creation of Allah. If not, they argued, the Qur'an would be a coeternal entity alongside Allah, which for them amounted to *shirk*. Based on this reasoning, they also argued that Allah did not have separate attributes because this would compromise the complete oneness of Allah. In contrast, the dominant Sunni position is that Allah has attributes because the Qur'an and Muhammad taught about them. Therefore, they should be accepted *bila kayf* (without knowing how). Similarly, the standard Sunni position is that the Qur'an is Allah's uncreated Word. The Qur'an, like Allah's attributes, are "not he and not other than he."[95] From the Mu'tazilite perspective, the standard Sunni position on Allah's attributes and the Qur'an is irrational and amounts to *shirk*. Sunnis affirm the oneness of Allah, with no plurality, yet at the same time they assert the eternal existence of the Qur'an and Allah's attributes, which are not identical to Allah. They appear to eschew multiplicity in the godhead, yet they allow for the eternal existence of other entities besides Allah. In response to this apparent inconsistency they simply appeal to qur'anic authority.

Another possible inconsistency in the Muslim worldview is that they affirm the goodness of Allah while also affirming the predestination of all events, with no secondary causes. Orthodox Sunni *kalam*, or theology, is most heavily influenced by Ash'arite theology, named after Abu al-Hasan al-Ash'ari (873–935). In order to explain the doctrine of

---

[94]Nasr, "God," in *Islamic Spirituality: Foundations*, ed. Seyyed Hossein Nasr, World Spirituality: An Encyclopedic History of the Religious Quest 19 (New York: Crossroad, 1987), 312.
[95]William Shepard, *Introducing Islam* (New York: Routledge, 2009), 141.

predestination found in the Qur'an and in Muhammad's teachings, al-Ash'ari developed the theory of acquisition (*kasb*) in which Allah creates the actions but people become morally responsible for those actions as they "acquire" them. Therefore, al-Ash'ari's theory of acquisition denies the existence of secondary causes. An individual's action is Allah's creation "in that it is only at the moment of action that he creates the power to act in the individual, and in that it is present to the only this act, not either this act or its opposite."[96] Every action is therefore created by Allah, either good or evil. However, this does not pose an ethical problem for this position because good and evil are determined by divine fiat. In other words, Allah simply commands what is good and evil; actions are not good or evil in themselves. Al-Ash'ari asserted that God could punish good if he so willed and send the pious to hell.[97] This in itself calls into question the goodness of Allah. How can Allah be good if he predestines and creates evil actions, with no secondary causes? The Sunni doctrine of Allah's goodness and his predestination of evil actions with no secondary causes seem to be inconsistent.

8.6.2 External consistency and evidential correspondence. Does the Muslim worldview account for the facts of our world? Compared to Eastern religions like Hinduism, Islam better accounts for the world we live in. However, some Muslim claims about the Qur'an and Muhammad do not appear to fit the evidence. According to Muslims, the Qur'an is Allah's uncreated and perfect word, true in all it affirms. Muhammad is not only Allah's last and greatest prophet but also the most perfect human being, exemplifying submission to Allah. However, these claims do not appear to fit the evidence.

First, the Qur'an's denial of Christ's crucifixion is contradicted by historical evidence (Q Nisa' 4:157-58). In determining whether particular historical claims are credible, historians look to various principles: (1) multiple, independent sources support the historical claim; (2) attestation by an enemy or unfriendly source supports the historical claim; (3) embarrassing admission supports the historical claim; (4) eyewitness testimony

---

[96]W. Montgomery Watt, *Islamic Philosophy and Theology* (Edinburgh: Edinburgh University Press, 1985), 64.

[97]Cyril Glassé, *The Concise Encyclopaedia of Islam*, rev. ed. (London: Stacey International, 2001), 62.

supports the historical claim; and (5) early testimony supports the historical claim.[98] Historical claims that satisfy more of these principles are more likely to be true than historical claims that have fewer of these principles.

The crucifixion of Christ is attested to by ancient Christian and non-Christian sources. New Testament writings that attest to the crucifixion include Paul's letters, the four Gospels, Hebrews, and 1 Peter. These reports fit four of the five historical principles. There are multiple independent reports of Christ's crucifixion. The reports are early, and some come from eyewitnesses. Finally, the report itself is an embarrassing admission that their Lord died as a criminal, experiencing such a humiliating and painful death. Early non-Christian reports of his crucifixion or execution include Josephus, Tacitus, Lucian, and Mara bar Serapion.[99] These reports fit three of the five historical principles because they are early multiple and independent reports written by "enemies," historians outside of the Christian community. Based on this historical evidence, New Testament scholars affirm the historicity of the crucifixion. John Dominic Crossan, though he rejects the reliability of the Gospels and denies the resurrection, nonetheless asserts the historicity of the crucifixion: "That he was crucified is as sure as anything historical can ever be."[100]

In contrast, the qur'anic claim that Jesus was not crucified does not fit any of the five historical principles. The claim appears more than five hundred years after the reported event. Any unbiased observer would affirm that the New Testament authors are better sources of information about Jesus' death than the Qur'an, which was written in the seventh century.[101] To deny the crucifixion, Muslims have to ignore the historical evidence. This is understandable because they believe the Qur'an is

---

[98]Gary R. Habermas and Michael R. Licona, *The Case for the Resurrection of Jesus* (Grand Rapids: Kregel, 2004), 36-40.

[99]Michael R. Licona, *The Resurrection of Jesus: A New Historiographical Approach* (Downers Grove, IL: IVP Academic, 2010), 304-5.

[100]John Dominic Crossan, *Jesus: A Revolutionary Biography* (San Francisco: HarperCollins, 1991), 145.

[101]The same argument can be applied to passages in the Qur'an that report Jesus teaching doctrines that are contrary to New Testament teaching. Common sense alone would say that the disciples are better sources of information on the teachings of Jesus than Muhammad, who lived centuries later.

Allah's perfect word. Allah's revelation trumps historical evidence. Nevertheless, the fact that central claims made by the Qur'an are not supported by historical evidence calls into question the truth of the Qur'an and the Muslim worldview.

Second, in addition to historical problems in the Qur'an, some elements of Muhammad's life call into question the Muslim claim that Muhammad was God's final and greatest prophet. Some might reject this approach as being too polemical, but it is inevitable. The truthfulness of Islam rests on the reliability of Muhammad. The content of the Qur'an rests on Muhammad as a reliable source of information about Allah.

Muhammad's prophetic call should be evaluated. According to early Muslim sources, when Muhammad first received his revelation, he thought that he was being deceived by a *jinn* (evil spirit) and feared being demon-possessed. After his initial revelation, he did not hear anything for two or three years, which led him to despair and to contemplate suicide. Also, when Muhammad received revelations, he would often be overtaken by convulsions.[102] These early Muslim accounts do raise questions about the reliability of Muhammad's prophetic call.

On one occasion Muhammad declared a revelation that he thought was from Allah but later changed it after realizing that it was from Satan. The infamous "satanic verses" come from an incident in which Muhammad got a revelation affirming the existence of three pagan deities: "Did you consider al-Hat and al-Uzza and al-Manat, the third, the other? Those are the swans exalted; Their intercession is expected; Their likes are not neglect." Soon after this revelation, Muhammad got another revelation that removed the part about interceding to the pagan gods (Q Najm 53:21-23). Muhammad explained the change by saying that the devil had initially deceived him. This account is included in al-Tabari's (AD 839–923) *History of Prophets and Kings*, which is a "definitive reference work"; however, some Muslims question the reliability of the account.[103]

---

[102]Husayn Haykal, *The Life of Muhammad*, 8th ed., trans. Isma'il Ragi Al-Faruqi (Indianapolis: North American Trust, 1976), 74-75, 79, 337; and Muhammad Ibn Ishaq, *The Life of Muhammad: A Translation of Ibn Ishaq's Sirat Rasul Allah*, ed. 'Abd al-Malik Ibn Hisham and Alfred Guillaume (Karachi, Pakistan: Oxford University Press, 2006), 106-7, 496-97.

[103]See Glassé, *Concise Encyclopaedia of Islam*, 405, 443. Also discussed in Alfred Guillaume, *New Light on the Life of Muhammad*, Journal of Semitic Studies, Monograph 1 (Manchester: Manchester University Press, 1960), 38-39.

*Contemporary Cultural
Worldview Meditation*

Jihad

The fact that self-professing Muslims have carried out terrorist attacks throughout the world in the name of Islam naturally leads to questions about Islam and violence. Is Islam a religion of violence? What about the Taliban, al-Qaeda, ISIS? Is jihad "holy war"? Some argue that these terrorist attacks are primarily the result of political problems within the Muslim world, and between the Muslim world and the West. For example, John L. Esposito and Dalia Mogahed contend that Islam is not the problem:

> But blaming Islam is a simple answer, easier and less controversial than re-examining the core political issues and grievances that resonate in much of the Muslim world: the failures of many Muslim governments and societies, some aspects of U.S. foreign policy representing intervention and dominance, Western support for authoritarian regimes, the invasion and occupation of Iraq, or support for Israel's military battles with Hamas in Gaza and Hezbollah in Lebanon.[a]

Although it is true that much of the hatred against the West is the result of perceived Western aggression against the Muslim world, it would be incorrect to hold that these terrorist groups having nothing to do with Islam. Mark Sedgwick correctly points out that "the conflict between the Muslim world and the West has so far been

(continued on next page)

Muhammad's moral character should also be evaluated. Clearly his life needs to be evaluated in context and in comparison with others in his own culture. Nonetheless, this does not mean that his actions are immune from evaluation. In particular, his view of women and his vindictiveness against his enemies deserve some attention. Before mentioning some of the negative examples of Muhammad's view of women, it is important to note that Muhammad did improve the status of women during his day. Based on the Qur'an and hadiths, shari'ah law improved the status of women as compared to the pre-Islamic period. For example, shari'ah rejects female infanticide, emphasizes the contractual nature of marriage rather than its proprietary nature, mandates that the wife rather than the father receive the dowry, and mandates that the wife retain her personal wealth and her maiden name, just to name a few improvements.[104] Nevertheless, the Qur'an allows husbands to "beat" disobedient wives (Q Nisa' 4:34),

---

[104]See Soraya Altorki, "Women and Islam," in Esposito, *Oxford Encyclopedia of the Modern Islamic World*, 323.

and Muhammad sanctioned the beating of a female servant in order to get the truth from her.[105] Also, the most authoritative collection of hadiths records Muhammad saying, "'I was shown the Hell fire and that the majority of dwellers were women who were ungrateful.' It was asked 'Do they disbelieve in Allah' (or are they ungrateful to Allah?). He replied, 'They are ungrateful to their husbands and are ungrateful for the favors and the good (charitable deeds) done to them.'"[106] In addition, although the Qur'an allows Muslim men to marry up to four wives, Muhammad claimed to have a special dispensation from Allah to marry more. According to Muslim sources, Muhammad had ten wives.[107] The youngest he married when she was six years old, though they did not consummate the marriage until she was nine years of age.[108] Muslims argue that these marriages were political in nature and that Muhammad was helping the women since the majority were

explained with little reference to religion. Religion, however, clearly matters."[b] Even Esposito and Mogahed admit that Islam is the "context" for the rise of "radicalism, extremism, and terrorism."[c]

Muhammad and those that led the Muslim community after his death spread the political domain of Islam through the sword. Sedgwick points out that "the history of early Islam (known to all Muslims) is full of stories of battles and heroic deaths. The message is not that might is right, but that right should be supported by might, and that bravery is a religious virtue."[d] In the Qur'an, jihad is not only permitted[e] but commanded,[f] and those who fight in Allah's cause are promised greater rewards in paradise.[g] Understandably, "the result is that most Muslims, whether traditional or modern, devout or not, tend to see an armed response as an appropriate response to any sort of attack."[h]

Though some Muslims understand jihad as a total endeavor or striving in the cause of Allah, armed jihad is clearly a form of jihad. The difference between Muslims that support terrorism and those that do not depends largely not on religion but on politics. For instance, for Osama Bin Laden, al-Qaeda's use of violence was justified because he believed that the West was a direct physical and moral threat to the existence of the Muslim world. He believed that because the crusaders and Jews/Zionists were using violence to destroy Islam, it was an obligation on all Muslims to respond with violence to ensure their survival. Though many may contend that Muslim terrorist organizations have hijacked Islam, it is beyond dispute that the Qur'an,

(continued on next page)

[105]Haykal, *Life of Muhammad*, 336-37; and Ibn Ishaq, *Life of Muhammad*, 496.
[106]Khan, *Translation of the Meanings of Sahih Al-Bukhāri*, hadiths 5196, 5197.
[107]Safiur-Rahman al-Mubarakpuri, *The Sealed Nectar: Biography of the Noble Prophet*, rev. ed. (Riyadh: Darussalam, 2002), 418-19.
[108]Martin Lings, *Muhammad: His Life on the Earliest Sources* (Rochester, VT: Inner Traditions International, 1983), 132-34; and al-Mubarakpuri, *Sealed Nectar*, 418.

Muhammad's example, and early Muslim history provide them with plenty of resources in their attempt to justify their actions.

[a] John L. Esposito and Dalia Mogahed, *Who Speaks for Islam? What a Billion Muslims Really Think* (New York: Gallup Press, 2007), 136-37.
[b] Mark Sedgwick, *Islam & Muslims: A Guide to a Diverse Experience in a Modern World* (Boston: Intercultural Press, 2006), 216.
[c] Esposito and Mogahed, *Who Speaks for Islam?*, 136.
[d] Sedgwick, *Islam & Muslims*, 218. For examples of jihad and martyrdom in the Qur'an and hadiths, see W. Michael Clark, "Suffering in the Sunni and Calvinist Worldviews: Demonstrating the Value of the Comparative Approach in the Study of Religion in Service of Christian Missions" (PhD diss., Southern Baptist Theological Seminary, 2010), 251-61, 298-305.
[e] "To those against whom war is made, permission is given (to fight), because they are wronged;—and verily, Allah is most powerful for their aid" (Q Hajj 22:39).
[f] "Fight in the cause of Allah those who fight you, but do not transgress limits; for Allah loveth not transgressors. And slay them wherever ye catch them, and turn them out from where they have turned you out; for tumult and oppression are worse than slaughter; but fight them not at the Sacred Mosque, unless they (first) fight you there; but if they fight you, slay them. Such is the reward of those who suppress faith. But if they cease, Allah is Oft-forgiving, Most Merciful. And fight them on until there is no more tumult or oppression, and there prevail justice and faith in Allah. But if they cease, let there be no hostility except to those who practise oppression" (Q Baqarah 2:190-93).
[g] "Not equal are those believers who sit (at home) and receive no hurt, and those who strive and fight in the cause of Allah with their goods and their persons. Allah hath granted a grade higher to those who strive and fight with their goods and persons than to those who sit (at home). Unto all (in Faith) Hath Allah promised good: But those who strive and fight Hath He distinguished above those who sit (at home) by a special reward" (Q Nisa' 4:95).
[h] Sedgwick, *Islam & Muslims*, 218.

widows, their husbands having died in battle. Although Muhammad was a man of his time and cannot be expected to have the moral ethic of today, his view and treatment of women does seem to call into question the Muslim claim that Muhammad is the ideal human being.

Muhammad also exemplified vindictiveness toward his opponents. Mehmet Aydin contends that Christians tend to object to Muhammad's use of violence because they have difficulties understanding how a prophet can also be a statesman.[109] Maybe if Christians recognized that Muhammad was also a statesman and had to use military force, they would have fewer problems with Muhammad calling for the death of his enemies. Comparing Muhammad to Moses or David shows that they were not that different. However, Christians do not view Moses, David, or anyone else in the Bible, besides Jesus, as the ideal human being. An early biography of Muhammad records that on two different occasions he ordered the assassination of people who wrote poems that

[109] Mehmet S. Aydin, "Muhammad: Prophet and Statesman," *Dialogue & Alliance* 12, no. 2 (1998): 62.

mocked him.[110] At one point, some tribesmen came to Medina, and Muhammad allowed them to drink milk and urine (as medicine) from his camels. However, the men ended up killing Muhammad's shepherd and drove away the camels. Muhammad sent men after them and ordered them "to cut their hands and feet (and it was done), and their eyes were branded with heated pieces of iron."[111] When a Jewish tribe from Medina opposed him, he killed their men and distributed their women, children, and property among the Muslims.[112] These hadiths make it clear that Muhammad often sought revenge against those who harmed him and the Muslim community.

8.6.3 Existential consistency and pragmatic satisfaction. All the basic elements of the Muslim worldview can be lived out consistently; the question is whether people find the Muslim worldview satisfying. For example, the concept of Allah's transcendence does not reveal any inconsistency or contradiction in the Muslim worldview; however, one could make an argument that Allah, as described in the Qur'an, is too transcendent to be religiously fulfilling for a believer. For instance, a majority of Muslims view Muhammad as an intercessor and also venerate saints, usually Sufi saints, believing that the saints will take their prayers to Allah. These practices could suggest that Allah is too transcendent for Muslims to relate to; therefore, Muslims resort to appealing to Muhammad and Sufi saints to have their prayers heard. One may also point to Sufism (Islamic mysticism) as further evidence that the qur'anic God is too transcendent to be religiously fulfilling for a believer.

Some scholars argue that Sufism, which emphasizes experiential knowledge and love of God, emerged to fill a spiritual void in Muslim theology and spirituality. Frederick Mathewson Denny argues that Sufism emerged as a "renewing and reforming response" to a form of Islam that had lost its "vitality and spontaneity."[113] With a similar understanding, William Chittick states that "Sufis have looked upon themselves as Muslims who *take seriously* God's call to perceive his presence

---

[110]Ibn Ishaq, *Life of Muhammad*, 136, 163, 181, 308.

[111]Khan, *Translation of the Meanings of Sahih Al-Bukhāri*, hadiths nos. 233, 1501, 3018, 4192, 4193, 4610, 5685, 5686, 5727, 6802, 6803, 6804, 6805, 6899.

[112]Ibid., hadith nos. 4028, 4121, 4122.

[113]Frederick Mathewson Denny, *An Introduction to Islam*, 2nd ed. (New York: Macmillan, 1994), 219.

in the world and in the self."[114] In other words, they stand against the
dominant form of Muslim spirituality. They emphasize "inwardness
over outwardness, contemplation over action, spiritual development
over legalism, and cultivation of the soul over social interaction."[115] They
stress God's mercy, gentleness, and beauty rather than his wrath, severity, and majesty. For example, Rabiah (713–801), an early Sufi, stressed
selfless love toward God. She wrote, "O Beloved of hearts, I have none
like unto Thee, therefore have pity this day on a sinner who comes to
Thee. O my Hope and my Rest and my Delight, the heart can love none
other but Thee."[116]

Even if the practices mentioned above are not a reaction to dissatisfaction with Allah's transcendence, the role of women in Islam and the
violence often associated with the religion are factors that have led some
Muslims to leave their faith. For instance, in their article "Conversion out
of Islam: A Study of Conversion Narratives of Former Muslims," Mohammad Hassan Khalil and Mucahit Bilici identify the two most common
explanations for why former Muslims have left Islam: (1) they disagreed
with the status of women in Islam, and (2) they came to believe that
Muslims were "cruel, oppressive, and backwards."[117] In their study they
identified a total of nine intellectual and ideological motivations for
leaving Islam: (1) status of women in Islam, (2) contradiction between
shari'ah and human rights, (3) problematic nature of the Qur'an, (4) character of Muhammad and other Muslim leaders, (5) Islam seen as illogical
and unscientific, (6) belief in the eternal damnation of good non-Muslims,
(7) the unnecessary, strict rules and expectations of Islam, (8) Islam being
not universal, but rather Arab-centric, and (9) the dubious historicity of
the Qur'an and hadiths. They also identified six social and experiential

---

[114]William C. Chittick, "Sufism," in Esposito, *Oxford Encyclopedia of the Modern Islamic World*, 4:102-3 (emphasis added).
[115]Ibid., 103.
[116]Annemarie Schimmel, *Mystical Dimensions of Islam* (Chapel Hill: University of North Carolina Press, 1975), 38-39.
[117]They gathered their data from conversion narratives found in various sources: (1) the website of Muslim-turned-Christian Nonie Darwish, (2) the works of Muslim-turned-agnostic Ibn Warraq, (3) Jeffrey Lang's *Losing My Religion: A Call for Help*, and (4) two popular websites: Answering Islam (answering-islam.org) and Apostates of Islam. Mohammad Hassan Khalil and Mucahit Bilici, "Conversion out of Islam: A Study of Conversion Narratives of Former Muslims," *Muslim World* 97 (2007): 112, 118.

motivations: (1) encounters with bad, cruel Muslims, (2) Muslims as oppressive, (3) Muslims as backward, (4) Muslim ill-treatment of women, (5) Muslim ill-treatment of non-Muslims, and (6) Muslims in a state of illusion regarding their own religion. These examples provide possible sources of dissatisfaction with the Muslim worldview, though it should be noted that many of these problems could be rooted in culture rather than in Islam itself.[118]

REFLECTION QUESTIONS

1 What do you see as the greatest strength in the Muslim worldview?

2 What do you see as the most significant weakness in the Muslim worldview?

3 How may the person of Muhammad affect a non-Muslim's view of Islam?

4 Can the Qur'an's historical accuracy or lack thereof make or break the Muslim worldview?

5 What role does radical Islam play in analyzing the Muslim worldview?

8.7 CONCLUSION

Hinduism and Islam present completely different worldviews. (See table 8.2 for a comparison of Hinduism and Islam to Christianity.) In Hinduism, people live in an eternal cosmos, which is either an illusion or an emanation from the body of god. Their true self is either identical to ultimate reality or a mode of god. They are trapped in an endless cycle of death and rebirth unless they find liberation through the paths of work, knowledge, or devotion. Upon liberation they are absorbed into

---

[118]For additional analysis and critique of the Muslim worldview, see Norman L. Geisler and Abdul Saleeb, *Answering Islam: The Crescent in Light of the Cross*, 2nd ed. (Grand Rapids: Baker Books, 2002), 135-210; Winfred Corduan, "A View from the Middle East: Islamic Theism," in Sire, *Universe Next Door*, 244-77; Tennent, *Christianity at the Religious Roundtable*, 141-94; Johnson, *Reasoned Look at Asian Religions*, 144-62; and Abdul Saleeb, "Islam," in *To Everyone an Answer: A Case for the Christian Worldview*, ed. Francis J. Beckwith, William Lane Craig, and J. P. Moreland (Downers Grove, IL: IVP Academic, 2004), 350-71.

Table 8.2. Comparing Hinduism, Islam, and Christianity

Worldview questions	Hinduism	Islam	Christianity
What is our nature?	Identical to Nirguna Brahman (Ultimate Reality with no attributes) or a mode of Saguna Brahman (personal deity with attributes).	Humanity is Allah's greatest creation, created to worship and serve him.	Created in God's image, but now have a sinful nature because of the fall.
What is our world?	An illusion brought about by Nirguna Brahman (Ultimate Reality with no attributes) since all that exists is Brahman or an emanation of the body of Saguna Brahman (personal deity with attributes).	Allah's creation filled with signs that point to his existence. Life is a test to see who will submit to Allah and who will not. Allah is all-powerful and predetermines everything in the world.	A creation of the triune God. It was created good, but now is full of death and suffering because of the fall. However, it still declares the glory of God.
What is our problem?	Trapped in samsara because of ignorance of our true nature. Three paths of liberation: works, knowledge, and devotion.	People are naturally weak and forgetful and therefore do not submit to Allah. The solution is submission to Allah as revealed in the Qur'an and Muhammad's example.	Because of the fall, we live in a broken world. We have a sinful nature and are guilty before God. The solution is the gospel, the good news that God is fixing our broken world through the life, death, and resurrection of Jesus Christ. Through faith in Christ and repentance we are reconciled to God.
What is our end?	Liberation from samsara leads to absorption into Nirguna Brahman (Ultimate Reality with no attributes) or blissful fellowship with Saguna Brahman (personal deity with attributes).	Our purpose is to serve and worship Allah by submitting to his commands as revealed in the Qur'an and Muhammad. Those who submit are rewarded with paradise on judgment day, and those who do not submit are punished in hell.	Our purpose is to glorify God by enjoying him forever. Those in Christ await his return and an eternity in the new heaven and new earth. The lost await punishment in hell.

an impersonal ultimate reality or enjoy endless bliss with a personal god. In contrast, Islam teaches that people are the pinnacle of Allah's creation, created to serve and worship Allah. They live in a real world where they are tested to see whether they will submit to Allah. However, most people have gone astray because human nature is weak and easily strays from Allah. Therefore, Allah has sent messengers to remind people of their responsibilities. Those who submit to Allah by following the teachings found in the Qur'an and exemplified by Muhammad will be rewarded with paradise on judgment day.

Even though other world religions, like Hinduism and Islam, may seem foreign and are probably unappealing to readers from a Christian background, this does not mean that Christians are immune from the influence of these worldviews. Few professing Christians would probably be tempted to convert to Hinduism. However, the belief in karma, reincarnation, and Hindu religious practices like yoga are pervasive in American culture, which could lead some Christians to unknowingly absorb elements of the Hindu worldview that are incompatible with the Christian worldview. For instance, the practice of yoga has its health benefits, but Christians should be aware that it is deeply rooted in Hinduism. In some contexts yoga is taught with all the Hindu religious trappings, but in other contexts Hindu religious elements may have been removed completely. Depending on how yoga is being taught, Christians might need to reevaluate their practice of yoga. When exposed to Eastern religious beliefs and practices, like those in Hinduism, Christians should carefully analyze whether they are compatible with what God has revealed in the Scriptures.

In contrast to Hinduism, Islam appears to be a simpler and more straightforward worldview. Allah, the creator god, created the world and has revealed his will to humanity. In response, people should submit to their creator and follow the teachings and example of Allah's final messenger and prophet—namely, Muhammad. This simple message may appeal to many because the basic premise is consistent with general revelation. In Paul's letter to the church in Rome, he writes that through general revelation everyone knows that there is a Creator God (Rom 1:19-21) and that they are morally accountable to him (Rom 1:32; 2:14-16). Islam adds to general revelation by arguing that Allah has revealed his will through the Qur'an and Muhammad. Biblically speaking, although Islam is correct in stating that everyone is morally accountable to our Creator God, Islam fails to tell the entire story.

Islam fails to proclaim a gospel of grace and rejects the person and work of Jesus Christ. Islam calls for submission and obedience to Allah as a means by which believers hope to be rewarded with paradise. In contrast, God teaches through the Scriptures that humanity has failed at submitting and obeying God (Rom 3:9-18, 23) and, therefore, stands condemned before a holy God (Rom 6:23; Eph 2:1-3). Salvation cannot be earned through our obedience (Rom 3:20; Eph 2:8-9); rather, salvation is possible only through repentance and faith in Christ's atoning work on the cross. In opposition to the gospel of grace, Islam proclaims "salvation" by works. In addition, Islam rejects the person of Christ, including his death on the cross for our sins and his resurrection. Jesus claimed to be the only way to the Father (Jn 14:6), and the apostle John makes it clear that those who do not have the Son do not have the Father (1 Jn 5:11-12). Although Muslims may claim to be submitting to the one true God, their rejection of Christ proves otherwise. To conclude, although Islam may contain many truths compatible with the Scriptures, its central message rejects the beautiful biblical truth that "it is by grace you have been saved, through faith—and this is not from yourselves, it is the gift of God—not by works, so that no one can boast" (Eph 2:8-9).

MASTERING THE MATERIAL

When you finish reading this chapter, you should be able to

✔ Summarize Hinduism using the four worldview questions.

✔ Summarize Sunni Islam using the four worldview questions.

✔ Discuss three significant weaknesses within Hinduism as presented in this chapter.

✔ Discuss three significant weaknesses within Sunni Islam as presented in this chapter.

Glossary of Terms for Chapter Eight

atman—The word *atman* is translated in a variety of ways, including consciousness, soul, individual soul, human soul, eternal self, spirit, breath, self, Self, true self, innermost Self, and real self.

eternal dharma—a complete way of life, including both religious and social dimensions.

karma—The belief that good deeds bring merit and bad deeds bring painful consequences, especially by determining what type of life form one takes on in the next life.

Laws of Manu—The most influential Hindu legal codes.

maya—This is the source of and is identified with the "collective hallucination superimposed on the One reality."

moksha—Liberation from the cycle of death and rebirth.

Nirguna Brahman—Brahman without attributes.

Purva Mimamsa—Adherents of this school argue that only the four earliest Vedas are self-existent and eternal, and therefore authoritative. They do not consider any other Hindu texts as authoritative. Consequently, this school focuses primarily on defending and justifying rituals and ceremonies that make up the samhitas, the earliest four Vedas.

Saguna Brahman—Brahman with attributes.

samsara—The eternal cycle of birth, death, and rebirth that Hindus believe everyone is imprisoned in.

shari'ah—Allah's divine law.

shirk—Refers to the sin of associating anything with Allah, the cardinal sin in Islam.

Sunnah—Muhammad's example of exemplary behavior.

tawhid—The one-ness of Allah.

Upanishads—The key philosophical texts used by the various schools of Vedanta.

Uttara Mimamsa—Better known as Vedanta ("end of the Veda"), this school focuses on the study of the Upanishads, Brahma Sutras, and the *Bhagavad Gita* and is concerned with speculative philosophy.

Possible Term Paper Topics

✔ Investigate the various theories related to the origin of the belief in karma and reincarnation within Hinduism.

✔ Investigate the importance of ritual purity within Hinduism.

✔ What are the major Hindu festivals? What is being celebrated? How do Hindus celebrate each festival?

✔ Discuss the history and religious elements of yoga.

✔ What is the role of female deities within Hinduism?

✔ What is the current role of the caste system within India?

✔ Compare and contrast how Muslims and Christians understand the person and work of Jesus of Nazareth.

✔ What are the most significant differences between Sunni and Shia Islam?

✔ Discuss the origin and role of Sufism within Islam.

✔ Investigate the Muslim views of paradise and hell.

✔ What is the role of the Arabic language within Islam?

✔ Discuss the major differences between the four major schools of shari'ah law within Sunni Islam.

Core Bibliography for Chapter Eight

Haneef, Suzanne. *What Everyone Should Know About Islam and Muslims*. 14th ed. South Elgin, IL: Library of Islam, 1996.

Haykal, Muhammad. *The Life of Muhammad*. Translated by Isma'il Ragi Al-Faruqi. Indianapolis: North American Trust, 1976.

Klostermaier, Klaus K. *A Survey of Hinduism*. 2nd ed. Albany: State University of New York Press, 1994.

Rahman, Fazlur. *Major Themes of the Qur'an*. 2nd ed. Chicago: University of Chicago Press, 2009.

Rodrigues, Hillary. *Introducing Hinduism*. New York: Routledge, 2006.

Shepard, William. *Introducing Islam*. New York: Routledge, 2009.

CONCLUSION

PURSUING (AND LIVING)

GOD'S PERSPECTIVE IN

A PLURALISTIC WORLD

Be Thou my Vision, O Lord of my heart;
Naught be all else to me, save that Thou art—
Thou my best Thought, by day or by night,
Waking or sleeping, Thy presence my light.

TRADITIONAL IRISH HYMN

Pastors arrested and convicted of sexually molesting a young parishioner. Christian accountants accused of embezzling funds from clients and firms. Christian activists charged with shooting abortion doctors or bombing abortion clinics. Young Christians engaged in rampant promiscuity and drug abuse. It seems that professing to be a follower of Jesus Christ does not always result in a life of faithful witness for Jesus Christ. Why?

Certainly the continued influence of our sinful nature is a large part of the story for Christian misconduct (see chapters four and five). Certainly we must also acknowledge that not all who profess the name of Christ do actually belong to his church universal: "Not everyone who says to me, 'Lord, Lord,' will enter the kingdom of heaven, but only the one who does the will of my Father who is in heaven" (Mt 7:21).[1] Furthermore, as noted

---

[1]Jesus goes on to warn, "Many will say to me on that day, 'Lord, Lord, did we not prophesy in your name and in your name drive out demons and perform many miracles?' Then I will tell them

in part three, Christians often embrace and live out a syncretistic worldview, combining elements of a biblical worldview with incompatible aspects of other worldviews.[2] But we are convinced there is another reason for the vast disparity between the contours of a Christian worldview (and the life motivation that emerges naturally from those contours) and the *actual lives* of Christians. Simply put, we are faced with subtle infiltrations from "worldlyviews"—perspectives or outlooks that are not full-fledged worldviews and have no articulate academic proponents, yet powerfully and persuasively prompt us to be not only *in* but also *of* the world, often without even knowing it.

Think of two commonly accepted phrases: "Cleanliness is next to Godliness." "God helps those who help themselves." Many Christians believe that these phrases are found in Scripture.[3] In actuality, the former is found in ancient Babylonian religious texts, appearing first in a Christian context in a John Wesley sermon, while the latter is an ancient Greek maxim. There is some debate, but arguably both phrases are not only abiblical (i.e., not found in the Bible) but also unbiblical (i.e., contrary to the Bible's teaching). Yet both phrases have found a home in popular Christian psychology and motivation; we are strongly influenced by these worldlyviews.

In their excellent work on such worldlyviews, Steve Wilkens and Mark Sanford argue that "the real competition for the hearts and minds of Christians and non-Christians alike does not spring from the academy . . . [but] comes from worldviews we do not see at all, even [though] they

plainly, 'I never knew you. Away from me, you evildoers!'" (Mt 7:22-23). Jesus makes it clear here and elsewhere that it is not mere *profession* of his name that brings salvation and eternal life; it is being found in him.

[2]For example, the 2009 Pew Forum survey found that 24 percent of professing Christians in America believe in reincarnation, a central belief in Hinduism and Buddhism, but an utterly unbiblical concept. See Thomas Ryan, "25 Percent of US Christians Believe in Reincarnation: What's Wrong with This Picture?," *America: The Jesuit Review*, October 21, 2015, http://america magazine.org/issue/christians-and-reincarnation.

[3]See, e.g., "What Are the Most Common Things People Think Are in the Bible That Are Not Actually in the Bible?," accessed February 20, 2017, www.gotquestions.org/not-in-the-Bible.html; and Bob Deffinbaugh, "Is Cleanliness Next to Godliness? (Act 9:32–10:23)," accessed February 20, 2017, https://bible.org/seriespage/15-cleanliness-next-godliness-acts-932-1023. Research by the Barna Group shows that a majority of Americans strongly agree with the statement "the Bible teaches that God helps those who help themselves." See George Barna and Mark Hatch, *Boiling Point: How Coming Cultural Shifts Will Change Your Life* (Ventura, CA: Regal, 2001), 90, 205.

surround us." These worldlyviews "emerge from culture . . . [and] are all around us, but are so deeply embedded in culture that we don't see them. . . . These lived worldviews are popular philosophies of life that have few intellectual proponents but vast numbers of practitioners."[4] Wilkens and Sanford identify individualism, consumerism, nationalism, moral relativism, scientific naturalism, New Age, postmodern tribalism, and salvation by therapy as the most prominent worldlyviews that "because of their stealthy nature, . . . find their way behind the church doors, mixed in with Christian ideas and sometimes identified as Christian positions."[5]

So has it always been. Thus Paul warned the church at Colossae: "See to it that no one takes you captive through hollow and deceptive philosophy, which depends on human tradition and the elemental spiritual forces of this world rather than on Christ" (Col 2:8). In chapter two, we argued that one of the benefits of worldview study is the development of a more thorough, thoughtful, and consistent Christian worldview. At the end of this work, then, it is appropriate to come full circle and examine our worldview and the way our worldview is expressed through our words, deeds, priorities, and commitments. The goal is the passionate pursuit of God's perspective in a pluralistic world—the possession of a worldview that matches up with the way God sees life, the universe, and everything. To that end, let me ask you some touchy questions regarding the potential influence of prominent worldlyviews on you.

Do you consciously or subconsciously embrace *scientism*—the belief that "human reason, especially in the form of the scientific method, can provide exhaustive knowledge of the world of nature and of mankind"?[6] What is your ultimate authority: God or science? What is the most reliable source of knowledge: God's Word or scientific consensus? If there is a real or potential conflict between what the Bible says and what a scientist says, how do you resolve that conflict?

Do you consciously or subconsciously embrace *technicism*—"an absolute faith in the inevitability of progress" and the "promise of . . .

---

[4]Steve Wilkens and Mark L. Sanford, *Hidden Worldviews: Eight Cultural Stories That Shape Our Lives* (Downers Grove, IL: IVP Academic, 2009), 12.

[5]Ibid., 13.

[6]Brian J. Walsh and J. Richard Middleton, *The Transforming Vision: Shaping a Christian World View* (Downers Grove, IL: IVP Academic, 1984), 132.

omnipotence" in solving problems?[7] Where do you look for solutions or salvation: God and his Word or technological advances? Do you believe that God can and does heal, or does healing come solely through medical treatment? When you identify problems in yourself or the world around you, where do you look for answers to the problems: God's revelation or human technical knowledge?

Do you consciously or subconsciously embrace *hedonism*—the pursuit of pleasure (physical or psychological) as the greatest good or the belief that all and only pleasure has positive importance? Do you "deserve a break today"? Where do you seek ultimate contentment or fulfillment? Is the pursuit of sexual pleasure in particular an idol in your life?

Do you consciously or subconsciously embrace *individualism*—the prioritization of self over others and over community?[8] Do you see yourself as accountable to (or in submission to) other human persons? Must you "look out for number one"? Do your family's values or preferences have any bearing on your own priorities or actions?

Do you consciously or subconsciously embrace *consumerism*, which prioritizes consumption and believes that fulfillment and satisfaction are found in the accumulation of wealth and possessions? Do you find meaning, purpose, or fulfillment via the things that you own or consume or by means of your relationship with and service to God? Are you unsatisfied with your own socioeconomic status even though you are (relatively speaking) comfortably secure financially? Do you desire to own a nicer home, a nicer vehicle, or something else that your neighbor has and you do not?

Do you consciously or subconsciously embrace *blameism*—finding others responsible for all the misfortunes, sufferings, and catastrophes in your life? If something unfortunate happens to you, where do you intuitively attribute responsibility: self, others, or God? When suffering comes into your life, do you acknowledge your own sinfulness as a potential or

---

[7]Ibid., 134-35.

[8]Individualism could also be identified as selfishness, self-orientation, or "me-ism." Individualism "is the belief that the individual is the primary reality and that our understanding of the universe and lifestyle should be centered in oneself. Individualism says that my unique interests and goals should be pursued, as much as possible, by whatever means deemed proper." Wilkens and Sanford, *Hidden Worldviews*, 27.

actual cause, either directly (bad habit of smoking => developing lung cancer) or indirectly (regular angry outbursts => estranged teenaged children)? Does your finger point more naturally inwardly or outwardly?

Do you consciously or subconsciously embrace *apatheism*—a lack of care or concern for matters regarding God or the divine?[9] How important is Bible reading to your daily or weekly routine? Do you have a desire to learn more about God and his ways? Are theological understanding and correctness important? How much do you think about the religious perspectives that your friends, neighbors, and coworkers have? How frequently do you pray for those around you? Yourself?

Do you consciously or subconsciously embrace *dogmatism*?[10] Are you convinced that all of your opinions are necessarily and obviously correct? Do you have an openness to learning from others, even those with worldviews other than your own? Are you willing to reconsider your understanding of biblical passages and teachings, or do you stubbornly cling to long-held beliefs without self-examination?

Do you consciously or subconsciously embrace *universalism*? Do you think that all people will eventually be saved, regardless of their attitude toward God the Father, Son, and Holy Spirit? Do you believe that the gate is narrow or that the road is broad when it comes to salvation and eternal life (Mt 7:13-14)?

Do you consciously or subconsciously embrace *functional atheism*? Do you embrace belief in Jesus Christ as Savior and Lord without expecting God to act in or around you? Do you believe that God has performed miracles in the past and continues to do so in the present day, or do you unwittingly assume that God leaves the world to basically run on its own? Do you consider the purposes and desires of God in all that you do before you do it, or do you act on your own wisdom and strength and hope that God will bless you?

---

[9]Apathy is a lack of care or concern, while theism regards one's attitude toward God or the divine. Apatheism then is, at its roots, "a disinclination to care all that much about one's own religion, and an even stronger disinclination to care about other people's." Jonathan Rauch, "Let It Be," *Atlantic*, May 2003, www.theatlantic.com/magazine/archive/2003/05/let-it-be/302726/.

[10]Dogmatism is "the expression of an opinion or belief as if it were fact: a positiveness in assertion of opinion especially when unwarranted or arrogant." Merriam-Webster Online, 2015.

Do you consciously or subconsciously embrace *conformism*?[11] Is your way of thinking dominated by reflection on God's character and Word? Or are you strongly influenced by societal expectations and norms? Test case: is it appropriate to expect sexual involvement on or after a first date? Do you "conform to the pattern of this world," or are you being "transformed by the renewing of your mind" (Rom 12:2)?

Plus ça change, plus c'est la même chose. (The more things change, the more they stay the same.) The particular cultural influences, or worldly-views, that affect us might be slightly different from those that plagued the first-century Roman Empire in which Paul ministered (although hedonism and blameism, at least, were well-represented in his age). But the worldview battle facing Christians today is really the same: we must identify our beliefs, loves, commitments, desires, and actions that do not fit with God's perspective and priorities and seek to eliminate them from our worldview and lifestyle. That process is not swift, nor is it one-dimensional. Clarifying our worldview and becoming more consistent is not just about thinking rightly, nor is it about merely exercising right behaviors. As James Sire reminds us, worldview is first and foremost "a commitment, a fundamental orientation of the heart."[12] The whole person is to be renewed and reoriented as we pursue God's perspective in our pluralistic world and develop a clear, consistent, critically examined Christian worldview. Our prayer is that the worldview journey we have embarked on together will aid you in that end goal.

We began (part one) with a consideration of the history and concept of worldview as "the conceptual lens through which we see, understand, and interpret the world and our place within it." We articulated four core worldview questions—What is our nature? What is our world? What is our problem? What is our end?—and evaluated the universality and diversity of worldviews. In chapter two, we looked at the fourfold impact of worldview in terms of confirmation bias, experiential accommodation, the pool of live options, and life motivation. We examined the possibility

---

[11]Conformism is here understood as the tendency "to act in accordance with prevailing standards or customs." Merriam-Webster Online, 2015.

[12]James S. Sire, *The Universe Next Door: A Basic Worldview Catalog*, 5th ed. (Downers Grove, IL: IVP Academic, 2009), 20.

of worldview adjustment and conversion before suggesting significant benefits to worldview study and responding to potential pitfalls. In chapter three, we turned our attention to worldview analysis and developed three tests for truth focused on internal, external, and existential consistency.

In part two we considered the contours of Christian worldview. First (chapter four), we viewed the narrative contours of God's story— creation, fall, redemption, and glorification. We then (chapter five) answered the four worldview questions from within a Christian worldview, focusing on God the Father, Son, and Holy Spirit as the Christian's prime reality. In chapter six we turned the critical tools of worldview analysis and truth tests on the Christian worldview, examining Christianity for internal, external, and existential consistency.

In part three we moved to a consideration of alternative worldviews, seeking to understand deism, naturalism, postmodernism, Hinduism, and Islam and subjecting them to worldview analysis.

As we study and compare significant claims of Christianity with other views, it is humbling to realize that God has both revealed and entrusted the truth of his Word to us. Our exposure to God's truth involves high stakes because responsibility always accompanies knowledge. Truth does not merely beckon each one of us to receive knowledge; it also invites us to pledge personally to live out God's truth with honesty, gratitude, humility, and commitment.

How might we meet such a pledge? Oswald Chambers, well known for his devotional book *My Utmost for His Highest*, penned these words: "The message must be part of ourselves. Our lives must be the sacrament of our message. Before God's message can liberate other souls, the liberation must be real in [us]." The apostle John said the same thing in his own words: "I have no greater joy than to hear that my children are walking in the truth" (3 Jn 4).

If you are anything like me, this journey will have brought to your attention areas of your life that do not match up with God's perspective. We are all under the conviction of the Holy Spirit. This conviction points us back, gratefully, to the basic tenets of a Christian worldview. Let us not self-righteously pat ourselves on the back, congratulating ourselves for possessing this truth. It is not ours anyway; it is God's. Instead, let us respectfully embrace a scripturally vibrant, Christ-centered, and faith-integrated worldview—one that places the work of salvation on Christ's shoulders, deposits the grace of the Father into our hearts, and liberally pours the anointing of the Spirit of God all over us.

May that be the sight of our clear, coherent, and consistent worldview!
May Christ be our vision!

SELECT BIBLIOGRAPHY

PART I—INTRODUCING WORLDVIEW

Alexander, T. Desmond. *From Eden to the New Jerusalem: An Introduction to Biblical Theology.* Grand Rapids: Kregel, 2008.

Bahnsen, Greg L. *Van Til's Apologetic: Readings and Analysis.* Phillipsburg, NJ: P&R, 1998.

Beckwith, Francis J., William Lane Craig, and J. P. Moreland, eds. *To Everyone an Answer: A Case for the Christian Worldview.* Downers Grove, IL: IVP Academic, 2004.

Blamires, Harry. *The Christian Mind: How Should a Christian Think?* Ann Arbor, MI: Servant, 1963.

Boot, Joe. *Why I Still Believe: [Hint:] It's the Only Way the World Makes Sense.* Grand Rapids: Baker Books, 2006.

Burnett, David. *Clash of Worlds.* Grand Rapids: Monarch, 2002.

Clark, Kelly James, ed. *Philosophers Who Believe: The Spiritual Journeys of 11 Leading Thinkers.* Downers Grove, IL: IVP Academic, 1993.

Colson, Charles, and Nancy Pearcey. *How Now Shall We Live?* Carol Stream, IL: Tyndale House, 2004.

Cosgrove, Mark P. *Foundations of Christian Thought: Faith, Learning, and the Christian Worldview.* Grand Rapids: Kregel, 2006.

Cowan, Steven B., and James S. Spiegel. *The Love of Wisdom: A Christian Introduction to Philosophy.* Nashville: B&H Academic, 2009.

Cupitt, Don. "The Radical Christian Worldview." *Cross Currents* 50 (2000): 56-67.

Davidson, Donald. "On the Very Idea of a Conceptual Scheme." *Proceedings and Addresses of the American Philosophical Association* 47 (1973–1974): 5-20.

Davison, Andrew, ed. *Imaginative Apologetics: Theology, Philosophy and the Catholic Tradition.* Grand Rapids: Baker Academic, 2011.

Dockery, David S. *Renewing Minds: Serving Church and Society Through Christian Higher Education.* Nashville: B&H Academic, 2008.

Downey, Deane E. D., and Stanley E. Porter, eds. *Christian Worldview and the Academic Disciplines.* Eugene, OR: Pickwick, 2009.

Ebertz, Roger P. "Beyond Worldview Analysis: Insights from Hans-Georg Gadamer on Christian Scholarship." *Christian Scholar's Review* 36, no. 1 (2006): 13-28.

Eckman, James P. *The Truth About Worldviews: A Biblical Understanding of Worldview Alternatives.* Wheaton, IL: Crossway, 2004.

Evans, A. Steven. "Matters of the Heart: Orality, Story and Cultural Transformation—The Critical Role of Storytelling in Affecting Worldview." *Missiology: An International Review* 38, no. 2 (2010): 185-99.

Geisler, Norman L., and William D. Watkins. *Worlds Apart: A Handbook on World Views.* 2nd ed. Grand Rapids: Baker Books, 1989.

Godawa, Brian. *Hollywood Worldviews: Watching Films with Wisdom and Discernment.* 2nd ed. Downers Grove, IL: InterVarsity Press, 2009.

Goheen, Michael W., and Craig G. Bartholomew. *Living at the Crossroads: An Introduction to Christian Worldview.* Grand Rapids: Baker Academic, 2008.

Groothuis, Douglas. *Christian Apologetics: A Comprehensive Case for Biblical Faith.* Downers Grove, IL: IVP Academic, 2011.

Hexham, Irving. *Understanding World Religions.* Grand Rapids: Zondervan, 2011.

Hiebert, Paul G. *Transforming Worldviews: An Anthropological Understanding of How People Change.* Grand Rapids: Baker Academic, 2008.

Hoffecker, W. Andrew, ed. *Revolutions in Worldview: Understanding the Flow of Western Thought.* Phillipsburg, NJ: P&R, 2007.

Hoffecker, W. Andrew, and Gary Scott Smith, eds. *Building a Christian World View.* Vol. 2, *The Universe, Society, and Ethics.* Phillipsburg, NJ: Presbyterian and Reformed, 1988.

Holmes, Arthur F. *Contours of a World View.* Studies in a Christian World View 1. Grand Rapids: Eerdmans, 1983.

———. *The Idea of a Christian College.* Rev. ed. Grand Rapids: Eerdmans, 1987.

Huffman, Douglas S., ed. *Christian Contours: How a Biblical Worldview Shapes the Mind and Heart.* Grand Rapids: Kregel, 2011.

Hunter, James Davison. *To Change the World: The Irony, Tragedy, and Possibility of Christianity in the Late Modern World.* Oxford: Oxford University Press, 2010.

Inwood, M. J. "*Weltanschauung.*" In *Oxford Companion to Philosophy*, edited by Ted Honderich, 909. Oxford: Oxford University Press, 1995.

Kearney, Michael. *World View.* Novato, CA: Chandler & Sharp, 1984.

———. "World View Theory and Study." *Annual Review of Anthropology* 4 (1975): 247-70.

Lewis, C. S. *Mere Christianity.* Rev. ed. New York: HarperSanFrancisco, 2001.

Licona, Michael R. *The Resurrection of Jesus: A New Historiographical Approach.* Downers Grove, IL: IVP Academic, 2010.

Marshall, Paul A., Sander Griffioen, and Richard J. Mouw, eds. *Stained Glass: Worldviews and Social Science.* Lanham, MD: University Press of America, 1989.

Meek, Esther L. "Embrace It or Replace It? The Christian and Culture." Review of *Creating a Christian Worldview: Abraham Kuyper's Lectures on Calvinism*, by Peter Heslam. *Presbyterion* 24, no. 2 (1998): 119-25.

Mendelson, E. M. "World View." In *International Encyclopedia of the Social Sciences*, edited by David L. Sills, 16:576-79. New York: Macmillan; Free Press, 1968.

Moreland, J. P. *Love Your God with All Your Mind: The Role of Reason in the Life of the Soul.* Colorado Springs, CO: NavPress, 1997.

Moreland, J. P., and William Lane Craig. *Philosophical Foundations for a Christian Worldview.* Downers Grove, IL: IVP Academic, 2003.

Nash, Ronald H. *Faith and Reason: Searching for a Rational Faith.* Grand Rapids: Zondervan, 1988.

———. *Worldviews in Conflict: Choosing Christianity in a World of Ideas.* Grand Rapids: Zondervan, 1992.

Naugle, David K. *Worldview: The History of a Concept.* Grand Rapids: Eerdmans, 2002.

Noebel, David A. *Understanding the Times: The Religious Worldviews of Our Day and the Search for Truth.* Eugene, OR: Harvest House, 1991.

Ochs, Carol. "Co-Creating My Worldview." *Cross Currents* 59 (2009): 457-66.

Olthuis, James H. "On Worldviews." *Christian Scholar's Review* 14, no. 2 (1985): 153-64.

Oswalt, John N. *The Bible Among the Myths: Unique Revelation or Just Ancient Literature?* Grand Rapids: Zondervan, 2009.

Pearcey, Nancy. *Total Truth: Liberating Christianity from Its Cultural Captivity.* Wheaton, IL: Crossway, 2004.

Prothero, Stephen. *God Is Not One: The Eight Rival Religions That Run the World—and Why Their Differences Matter.* New York: HarperOne, 2010.

Redfield, Robert. *The Primitive World and Its Transformations.* Ithaca, NY: Cornell University Press, 1953.

Ryken, Philip Graham. *What Is the Christian Worldview?* Basics of the Reformed Faith. Phillipsburg, NJ: P&R, 2006.

Samples, Kenneth Richard. *A World of Difference: Putting Christian Truth-Claims to the Worldview Test.* Grand Rapids: Baker Books, 2007.

Sire, James W. *Naming the Elephant: Worldview as a Concept.* 2nd ed. Downers Grove, IL: IVP Academic, 2015.

———. *The Universe Next Door: A Basic Worldview Catalog.* 5th ed. Downers Grove, IL: IVP Academic, 2009.

Smart, Ninian. *Worldviews: Crosscultural Explorations of Human Beliefs.* 3rd ed. Upper Saddle River, NJ: Prentice-Hall, 2000.

Smith, James K. A. *Desiring the Kingdom: Worship, Worldview, and Cultural Formation.* Cultural Liturgies 1. Grand Rapids: Baker Academic, 2009.

———. *Imagining the Kingdom: How Worship Works.* Cultural Liturgies 2. Grand Rapids: Baker Academic, 2013.

———. "Two Cheers for Worldview: A Response to Elmer John Thiessen." *Journal for Education and Christian Belief* 14, no. 1 (2010): 55-58.

Spiegel, James S. *The Making of an Atheist: How Immorality Leads to Unbelief.* Chicago: Moody, 2010.

Starr, Charlie W. "Faith Without Film Is Dull: C. S. Lewis Corrects Evangelicals on Art, Movies, and Worldview Analysis." *Christian Scholar's Review* 40 (2011): 355-74.

Taylor, Charles. *A Secular Age.* Cambridge, MA: Belknap Press, 2007.

Thiessen, Elmer John. "Educating Our Desires for God's Kingdom." Review of *Desiring the Kingdom: Worship, Worldview, and Cultural Formation,*" by James K. A. Smith. *Journal for Education and Christian Belief* 14, no. 1 (2010): 47-53.

Walsh, Brian J., and J. Richard Middleton. *The Transforming Vision: Shaping a Christian Worldview.* Downers Grove, IL: IVP Academic, 1984.

Weaver, Richard M. *Ideas Have Consequences.* Chicago: University of Chicago Press, 1948.

Wilkens, Steve, and Mark L. Sanford. *Hidden Worldviews: Eight Cultural Stories That Shape Our Lives.* Downers Grove, IL: IVP Academic, 2009.

Williams, Clifford. *Existential Reasons for God: A Defense of Desires and Emotions for Faith.* Downers Grove, IL: IVP Academic, 2011.

Wolters, Albert M. *Creation Regained: Biblical Basis for a Reformational Worldview.* Grand Rapids: Eerdmans, 2005.

Wright, N. T. *The New Testament and the People of God.* Christian Origins and the Question of God 1. Minneapolis: Fortress, 1992.

PART II—CONTOURS OF CHRISTIAN WORLDVIEW

Anselm. *Basic Writings*. Translated by S. N. Dean. La Salle, IL: Open Court, 1962.

Arndt, William F., and F. Wilbur Gingrich. *A Greek-English Lexicon of the New Testament and Other Early Christian Literature. A Translation and Adaptation of Walter Bauer's Griechisch-Deutsches Wöterbuch zu den Schriften des Neuen Testaments und der übrigen urchristlichen Literatur*. 4th rev. ed. Chicago: University of Chicago Press, 1952.

Augustine. *Concerning the City of God Against the Pagans*. Translated by Henry Bettenson. Introduction by John O'Meara. New York: Penguin, 1984.

———. *Confessions*. Translated by Henry Chadwick. Oxford World Classics. New York: Oxford University Press, 2008.

Barth, Karl, and Emil Brunner. *Natural Theology*. Translated by Peter Fraenkel. London: Geoffrey Bles, 1946.

Calvin, John. *Institutes of the Christian Religion*. Edited by John T. McNeill. Translated and indexed by Ford Lewis Battles. Library of Christian Classics 20. Philadelphia: Westminster, 1960.

Carnell, Corbin Scott. *Bright Shadow of Reality: Spiritual Longing in C. S. Lewis*. Grand Rapids: Eerdmans, 1999. Originally published in 1974.

Cowan, Steven B., ed. *Five Views on Apologetics*. Counterpoints. Grand Rapids: Zondervan, 2000.

Crouch, Andy. *Culture Making: Recovering Our Creative Calling*. Downers Grove, IL: InterVarsity Press, 2008.

Cullmann, Oscar. *Christ and Time: The Primitive Christian Conception of Time and History*. Translated by Floyd V. Filson. Rev. ed. Philadelphia: Westminster, 1964.

Demarist, Bruce A. *General Revelation: Historical Views and Contemporary Issues*. Grand Rapids: Zondervan, 1982.

Dodd, C. H. *The Parables of the Kingdom*. London: Nisbet, 1935.

Erickson, Millard J. *Christian Theology*. 3 vols. Grand Rapids: Baker Books, 1983.

Gadamer, Hans-Georg. *Truth and Method*. Translated and revised by Joel Weinsheimer and Donald G. Marshall. 2nd ed. New York: Continuum, 1993.

Galef, Julia. "Why You Think You're Right—Even if You're Wrong." TEDxPSU, February 2016. www.ted.com/talks/julia_galef_why_you_think_you_re _right_even_if_you_re_wrong.

Geisler, Norman L. *Baker Encyclopedia of Christian Apologetics*. Grand Rapids: Baker Books, 1999.

———. *Christian Apologetics*. Grand Rapids: Baker Books, 1976.

Heidegger, Martin. *Being and Time*. Translated by Joan Stambaugh. Revision and foreword by Dennis J. Schmidt. Albany: State University of New York Press, 2010.

Hodge, Charles. *Systematic Theology*. 3 vols. Reprint, Grand Rapids: Eerdmans, 1977.

Hopes, David B. *Upholding Mystery: An Anthology of Contemporary Christian Poetry*. Edited by David Impastato. New York: Oxford University Press, 1997.

Hung, Edwin. *The Nature of Science: Problems and Perspectives*. Belmont, CA: Wadsworth, 1997.

Jenson, Robert W. "How the World Lost Its Story." *First Things*, October 1993, www.firstthings.com/article/1993/10/002-how-the-world-lost-its-story.

John Paul II. *The Redeemer of Man: Redemptor Hominis*. Encyclical letter. Boston: Pauline Books & Media, 1979.

———. *The Theology of the Body: Human Love in the Divine Plan*. Boston: Pauline Books & Media, 1997.

Kaufmann, Walter, ed. and trans. *Basic Writings of Nietzsche*. Modern Library. New York: Random House, 1968.

Kuhn, Thomas S. *The Structure of Scientific Revolutions*. 2nd ed. International Encyclopedia of Unified Science 2, no. 2. Chicago: University of Chicago Press, 1970.

Kuyper, Abraham. *Principles of Sacred Theology*. Translated by J. Hendrik de Vries. Introduction by Benjamin B. Warfield. 1898. Reprint, Grand Rapids: Baker Books 1980.

Ladd, George Eldon. *A Theology of the New Testament*. Rev. ed. Grand Rapids: Eerdmans, 1993.

Leith, John, ed. *Creeds of the Churches: A Reader in Christian Doctrine from the Bible to the Present*. 3rd ed. Atlanta: John Knox, 1982.

Lewis, C. S. "Meditation in a Toolshed." In *God in the Dock: Essays on Theology and Ethics*. Edited by Walter Hooper. Grand Rapids: Eerdmans, 1970.

———. *Mere Christianity*. Rev. ed. New York: HarperSanFrancisco, 2001.

———. *The Pilgrim's Regress: An Allegorical Apology for Christianity, Reason, and Romanticism*. 1958. Reprint, Grand Rapids: Eerdmans, 1977.

———. *Surprised by Joy: The Shape of My Early Life*. New York: Harcourt Brace, 1955.

———. *The Weight of Glory and Other Addresses*. Rev. ed. Collected Letters of C. S. Lewis. New York: HarperCollins, 2001.

McDowell, Josh. *Evidence That Demands a Verdict: Historical Evidences for the Christian Faith*. Rev. ed. 2 vols. Nashville: Thomas Nelson, 1992, 1999.

McIntyre, Alasdair. *After Virtue*. 2nd ed. Notre Dame, IN: University of Notre Dame Press, 1984.

Merrell, Floyd. *A Semiotic Theory of Texts*. New York: Mouton de Gruyter, 1985.

Middleton, J. Richard. *A New Heaven and a New Earth: Reclaiming Biblical Eschatology*. Grand Rapids: Baker Academic, 2014.

Nagel, Thomas. *The View from Nowhere*. New York: Oxford University Press, 1986.

Naugle, David K. *Philosophy: A Student's Guide. Reclaiming the Christian Intellectual Tradition*. Wheaton, IL: Crossway, 2012.

———. *Reordered Love, Reordered Lives: Learning the Deep Meaning of Happiness*. Grand Rapids: Eerdmans, 2008.

———. *Worldview: The History of a Concept*. Grand Rapids: Eerdmans, 2002.

Nietzsche, Friedrich. *Beyond Good and Evil: Prelude to a Philosophy of the Future*. Translated by Helen Zimmern. 1907. Reprint, New York: Tribeca, 2010.

Opitz, Donald, and Derek Melleby. *Learning for the Love of God: A Student's Guide to Academic Faithfulness*. 2nd ed. Grand Rapids: Brazos Press, 2014.

Packer, J. I. *Knowing God*. 20th anniv. ed. Downers Grove, IL: InterVarsity Press, 1993.

Pearcey, Nancy. *Total Truth: Liberating Christianity from Its Cultural Captivity*. Wheaton IL: Crossway, 2004.

Peterson, Michael, William Hasker, Bruce Reichenbach, and David Basinger. *Reason and Religious Belief: An Introduction to the Philosophy of Religion*. 5th ed. New York: Oxford University Press, 2012.

Plantinga, Alvin. *God, Freedom, and Evil*. Grand Rapids: Eerdmans, 1977.

———. "Is Belief in God Properly Basic?" *Noûs* 15, no. 1 (1981): 41-51.

———. "Is Belief in God Rational?" In *Rationality and Religious Belief*. Edited by C. F. Delaney. Notre Dame, IN: University of Notre Dame Press, 1979.

———. *The Nature of Necessity*. Oxford: Clarendon Press, 1974.

———. "Reason and Belief in God." In *Faith and Rationality*, edited by Alvin Plantinga and Nicholas Wolterstorff, 16-93. Notre Dame, IN: University of Notre Dame Press, 1983.

———. "The Reformed Objection to Natural Theology." *Christian Scholar's Review* 11 (1982): 187-98.

Pojman, Louis P. *Philosophy of Religion: An Anthology*. Belmont, CA: Wadsworth, 1987.

Polanyi, Michael. *Personal Knowledge: Towards a Post-Critical Philosophy*. Corrected ed. Chicago: University of Chicago Press, 1962.

———. *The Tacit Dimension*. Garden City, NY: Doubleday, 1966.

Ramm, Bernard. *Varieties of Christian Apologetics: An Introduction to the Christian Philosophy of Religion.* Twin Brooks. Grand Rapids: Baker Books, 1974.

Rigney, Joe. *The Things of Earth: Treasuring God by Enjoying His Gifts.* Foreword by John Piper. Wheaton, IL: Crossway, 2015.

Schmemann, Alexander. *For the Life of the World: Sacraments and Orthodoxy.* 2nd ed. Crestwood, NY: St. Vladimir's Seminary Press, 1973.

Sire, James W. *The Universe Next Door: A Basic Worldview Catalog.* 5th ed. Downers Grove, IL: IVP Academic, 2009.

Smith, James K. A. *Desiring the Kingdom: Worship, Worldview, and Cultural Formation.* Cultural Liturgies 1-2. Grand Rapids: Baker Academic, 2009.

———. *You Are What You Love: The Spiritual Power of Habit.* Grand Rapids: Brazos Press, 2016.

Solomon, Robert C., and Kathleen M. Higgins. *The Big Questions: A Short Introduction to Philosophy.* 9th ed. Belmont, CA: Wadsworth, Cengage Learning, 2014.

Springer, William C. *This Is My Body: An Existential Analysis of the Living Body.* Lanham, MD: University Press of America, 2000.

Spykman, Gordon J. *Reformational Theology: A New Paradigm for Doing Dogmatics.* Grand Rapids: Eerdmans, 1992.

Tertullian, *On the Flesh of Christ, in Latin Christianity: Its Founder, Tertullian. Three Parts: I. Apologetic; II. Anti-Marcion; III. Ethical.* Edited by A. Cleveland Cox. Volume 3 of *Ante-Nicene Fathers,* edited by Alexander Roberts and James Donaldson. Peabody, MA: Hendrickson, 1994.

Tozer, A. W. *Knowledge of the Holy.* 1961. Reprint, New York: HarperOne, 2009.

Turner, Steve. *Popcultured: Thinking Christianly About Style, Media and Entertainment.* Downers Grove, IL: InterVarsity Press, 2013.

Wainwright, William J. *Philosophy of Religion.* Wadsworth Basic Issues in Philosophy. Belmont, CA: Wadsworth, 1988.

Walsh, Brian J., and J. Richard Middleton. *The Transforming Vision: Shaping a Christian World View.* Downers Grove, IL: IVP Academic, 1984.

Wilson, Jonathan R. *God's Good World: Reclaiming the Doctrine of Creation.* Grand Rapids: Baker Academic, 2013.

Wolters, Albert M. "Creation." *Comment Magazine* (Spring 2010). www.cardus .ca/comment/article/2022/creation/.

———. *Creation Regained: Biblical Basics for a Reformational Worldview.* Postscript coauthored by Michael W. Goheen. 2nd ed. Grand Rapids: Eerdmans, 2005.

Wolterstorff, Nicholas. "Tertullian's Enduring Question." Paper presented at Lilly Fellows Program in Humanities and the Arts Eighth Annual National Conference, University of Notre Dame, October 1998. www.lillyfellows.org /media/1406/nicholas-wolterstorff-1998.pdf.

Woznicki, Andrew N. *The Dignity of Man as a Person: Essays on the Christian Humanism of His Holiness John Paul II.* San Francisco: Society of Christ Publications, 1987.

Wright, N. T. *The Resurrection of the Son of God.* 4 vols. Christian Origins and the Question of God. Minneapolis: Fortress, 2003.

Yuasa, Yasuo. *The Body, Self-Cultivation and Ki-Energy.* Translated by Nagatomo Shigenori and Monte S. Hull. Body in Culture, History & Religion. Albany: SUNY Press, 1993.

Part III—Analyzing Worldviews

General

Allen, Diogenes. *Philosophy for Understanding Theology.* Atlanta: John Knox, 1985.

Audi, Robert, ed. *The Cambridge Dictionary of Philosophy.* 2nd ed. New York: Cambridge University Press, 1999.

Beckwith, Francis J., William Lane Craig, and J. P. Moreland, eds. *To Everyone an Answer: A Case for the Christian Worldview.* Downers Grove, IL: IVP Academic, 2004.

Berger, Peter L. Foreword to *The Human Condition: A Volume in the Comparative Religious Ideas Project,* edited by Robert C. Neville, xi-xiv. Albany: State University of New York Press, 2001.

Bowker, John, ed. *The Oxford Dictionary of World Religions.* New York: Oxford, 1997.

Corduan, Winfried. *A Tapestry of Faiths: The Common Threads Between Christianity & World Religions.* Downers Grove, IL: InterVarsity Press, 2002.

Craig, William Lane. *Reasonable Faith: Christian Truth and Apologetics.* 3rd ed. Wheaton, IL: Crossway, 2008.

Crossan, John Dominic. *Jesus: A Revolutionary Biography.* San Francisco: HarperCollins, 1991.

Forum on Religion & Public Life. *"Nones" on the Rise: One-in-Five Have No Religious Affiliation.* Pew Research Center. October 9, 2012. www.pewforum .org/uploadedFiles/Topics /Religious_Affiliation/Unaffiliated/NonesOnThe Rise-full.pdf.

Geisler, Norman L. *Christian Apologetics*. Grand Rapids: Baker Books, 1976.

Habermas, Gary R., and Michael R. Licona. *The Case for the Resurrection of Jesus*. Grand Rapids: Kregel, 2004.

Johnson, David L. *A Reasoned Look at Asian Religions: A Critical Analysis of Eastern Thought for Better Understanding and Communication*. Minneapolis: Bethany House, 1985.

Johnstone, Patrick. *The Future of the Global Church: History, Trends, and Possibilities*. Colorado Springs, CO: Biblica, 2011.

Licona, Michael R. *The Resurrection of Jesus: A New Historiographical Approach*. Downers Grove, IL: IVP Academic, 2010.

Markham, Ian S., and Christy Lohr, eds. *A World Religions Reader*. 3rd ed. Malden, MA: Wiley-Blackwell, 2009.

Moreland, J. P., and William Lane Craig. *Philosophical Foundations for a Christian Worldview*. Downers Grove, IL: IVP Academic, 2003.

Nash, Ronald H. *Is Jesus the Only Savior?* Grand Rapids: Zondervan, 1994.

———. *Worldviews in Conflict: Choosing Christianity in a World of Ideas*. Grand Rapids: Zondervan, 1992.

Peterson, Michael, William Hasker, Bruce Reichenbach, and David Basinger. *Reason & Religious Belief: An Introduction to the Philosophy of Religion*. 5th ed. New York: Oxford University Press, 2013.

Plantinga, Alvin. *Warranted Christian Belief*. New York: Oxford University Press, 2000.

Samples, Kenneth Richard. *A World of Difference: Putting Christian Truth-Claims to the Worldview Test*. Grand Rapids: Baker Books, 2007.

Sire, James S. *The Universe Next Door: A Basic Worldview Catalog*. 5th ed. Downers Grove, IL: IVP Academic, 2009.

Slingerland, Edward. "Conceptual Metaphor Theory as Methodology for Comparative Religion." *Journal of the American Academy of Religion* 72 (2004): 1-31.

Smart, Ninian. *Worldviews: Crosscultural Explorations of Human Beliefs*. New York: Scribners, 1983.

Smith, Huston. "Methodology, Comparisons, and Truth." In *A Magic Still Dwells: Comparative Religion in the Postmodern Age*, edited by Kimberley Patton and Benjamin C. Ray, 172-81. Berkeley: University of California Press, 2000.

Stumpf, Samuel Enoch, and James Fieser. *Philosophy: History and Problems*. Boston: McGraw-Hill, 2003.

Tennent, Timothy C. *Christianity at the Religious Roundtable: Evangelicalism in Conversation with Hinduism, Buddhism, and Islam.* Grand Rapids: Baker Academic, 2002.

Thiselton, Anthony C. *A Concise Encyclopedia of the Philosophy of Religion.* Grand Rapids: Baker Academic, 2002.

Deism and Naturalism

American Humanist Association. "Humanist Manifesto III." In Markham and Lohr, *World Religions Reader*, 291-92.

Brown, Colin. *From the Ancient World to the Age of Enlightenment.* Volume 1 of *Christianity and Western Thought: A History of Philosophers, Ideas and Movements.* Downers Grove, IL: IVP Academic, 1990.

Copleston, Frederick. *Modern Philosophy: From the French Enlightenment to Kant.* Volume 6 of *A History of Philosophy.* New York: Image Books, 1994.

Dawkins, Richard. "Letter to *The Independent*, 20 March 1993." In Markham and Lohr, *World Religions Reader*, 276-77.

Markham, Ian S., and Christy Lohr, eds. *A World Religions Reader.* 3rd ed. Malden MA: Wiley-Blackwell, 2009.

National Academy of Sciences (US) and Institute of Medicine (US). *Science, Evolution, and Creationism.* Washington, DC: National Academies Press, 2008.

Russell, Bertrand. "A Free Man's Worship." In Markham and Lohr, *World Religions Reader*, 288-90.

Postmodernism

Beckwith, Francis J., and Gregory Koukl. *Relativism: Feet Firmly Planted in Mid-Air.* Grand Rapids: Baker Books, 1998.

Doniger, Wendy. "Post-Modern and -Colonial -Structural Comparisons." In Patton and Ray, *A Magic Still Dwells*, 63-74.

Erickson, Millard. *Truth or Consequences: The Promise & Perils of Postmodernism.* Downers Grove, IL: IVP Academic, 2001.

Foucault, Michel. "Truth and Power." In *From Modernism to Postmodernism: An Anthology*, edited by Lawrence Cahoone, 252-53. 2nd ed. Blackwell Philosophy Anthologies 2. Malden, MA: Blackwell, 2003.

Groothius, Douglas. *Truth Decay: Defending Christianity Against the Challenges of Postmodernism.* Downers Grove, IL: InterVarsity Press, 2000.

Hick, John. *God and the Universe of Faiths.* London: Collins, 1973.

———. "Religious Pluralism." In *The Encyclopedia of Religion*, edited by Mircea Eliade. New York: Macmillan, 1987.

Lyotard, Jean-François. "Answering the Question: What Is Postmodernism?" In *Postmodernism: A Reader*, edited by Thomas Docherty, 38-46. New York: Columbia University Press, 1993.

Netland, Harold A. *Encountering Religious Pluralism: The Challenge to Christian Faith & Mission*. Downers Grove, IL: InterVarsity Press, 2001.

Patton, Kimberley C. "Juggling Torches: Why We Still Need Comparative Religion." In Patton and Ray, *A Magic Still Dwells*, 153-71.

Patton, Kimberley C., and Benjamin C. Ray, eds. *A Magic Still Dwells: Comparative Religion in the Postmodern Age*. Berkeley: University of California Press, 2000.

Hinduism

Bare, James S. "Atman." In *The Perennial Dictionary of World Religions*, edited by Keith Crim. New York: HarperCollins, 1981.

Bowker, John, ed. *The Oxford Dictionary of World Religions*. New York: Oxford, 1997.

Forum on Religion & Public Life. *Eastern, New Age Beliefs Widespread: Many Americans Mix Multiple Faiths*. Pew Research Center. December 2009. www .pewforum.org/uploadedfiles/Topics/Beliefs_and_Practices/Other_Beliefs _and_Practices/multiplefaiths.pdf.

Fuller, C. J. *The Camphor Flame: Popular Hinduism and Society in India*. Rev. and expanded ed. Princeton: Princeton University Press, 2004.

Hopkins, Thomas J. *The Hindu Religious Tradition*. The Religious Life of Man. Belmont, CA: Wadsworth, 1971.

Isherwood, Christopher, and Swami Prabhavananda. "What Is Evil?" In *The Inner Journey: Views from the Hindu Tradition*, edited by Margaret H. Case, 74-77. Parabola Anthology. Sandpoint, ID: Morning Light, 2007.

Johnson, David L. *A Reasoned Look at Asian Religions: A Critical Analysis of Eastern Thought for Better Understanding and Communication*. Minneapolis: Bethany House, 1985.

Klostermaier, Klaus K. *A Concise Encyclopedia of Hinduism*. Oxford: Oneworld, 1998.

———. *Hinduism: A Beginner's Guide*. Oxford: Oneworld, 2008.

———. *A Survey of Hinduism*. 2nd ed. Albany: State University of New York Press, 1994.

Lipner, Julius. *Hindus: Their Religious Beliefs and Practices*. New York: Routledge, 1994.

Markham, Ian S., and Christy Lohr, eds. *A World Religions Reader*. 3rd ed. Malden, MA: Wiley-Blackwell, 2009.

Mitter, Sara S. *Dharma's Daughters*. New Brunswick, NJ: Rutgers University Press, 1991.

Narayanan, Vasudha. "The Hindu Tradition." In *World Religions: Eastern Traditions*, edited by William G. Oxtoby, 12-125. 2nd ed. New York: Oxford University Press, 2002.

Nelson, Lance E. "Krishna in Advaita Vedanta: The Supreme Being in Human Form." In *Krishna: A Sourcebook*, edited by Edwin F. Bryant, 309-28. New York: Oxford University Press, 2007.

Rodrigues, Hillary. *Introducing Hinduism*. New York: Routledge, 2006.

Schuhmacher, Stephan, and Gert Woerner, eds. *The Encyclopedia of Eastern Philosophy and Religion: Buddhism, Hinduism, Taoism, and Zen*. Boston: Shambhala, 1994.

Tennent, Timothy C. *Christianity at the Religious Roundtable: Evangelicalism in Conversation with Hinduism, Buddhism, and Islam*. Grand Rapids: Baker Academic, 2002.

Weldon, G. R. "Samsara." In *The Perennial Dictionary of World Religions*, edited by Keith Crim. New York: HarperCollins, 1981.

Zaehner, R. C. *Hinduism*. 2nd ed. New York: Oxford University Press, 1966.

Islam

Abdulati, Hammudah. *Islam in Focus*. 3rd ed. Indianapolis: American Trust, 1994.

Abrahamov, Binyamin. *Islamic Theology: Traditionalism and Rationalism*. Edinburgh: Edinburgh University Press, 1998.

Abu-Hamdiyyah, Mohammad. *The Qur'an: An Introduction*. London: Routledge, 2000.

Ali, Abdullah Yusuf. *The Meaning of the Holy Qur'an*. New edition with revised translation and commentary. Brentwood, MD: Amana, 1991.

Altorki, Soraya. "Women and Islam." In Esposito, *Oxford Encyclopedia of the Modern Islamic World*.

Ashqar, 'Umar S. al-. *Divine Will and Predestination: In the Light of the Qur'an and Sunnah*. Translated by Nasiruddin Khattab. 3rd ed. Islamic Creed 8. Riyadh: International Islamic, 2005.

———. *The Messengers and the Messages: In the Light of the Qur'an and Sunnah*. Translated by Nasiruddin Khattab. 3rd ed. Islamic Creed 4. Riyadh: International Islamic, 2005.

———. *Paradise and Hell: In the Light of the Qur'an and Sunnah*. Translated by Nasiruddin Khattab. 5th ed. Islamic Creed 7. Riyadh: International Islamic, 2005.

———. *The World of the Jinn & Devils: In the Light of the Qur'an and Sunnah.* Translated by Nasiruddin Khattab. 2nd ed. Islamic Creed 3. Riyadh: International Islamic, 2005.

———. *The World of the Noble Angels: In the Light of the Qur'an and Sunnah.* Translated by Nasiruddin Khattab. 2nd ed. Islamic Creed 2. Riyadh: International Islamic, 2005.

Attas, Syed Muhammad Naquib al-. "Islam: The Concept of Religion and the Foundation of Ethics and Morality." In Gauhar, *Challenge of Islam*, 32-67.

Aydin, Mehmet S. "Muhammad: Prophet and Statesman." *Dialogue & Alliance* 12, no. 2 (1998): 58-68.

Ayoub, Mahmoud Mustafa. "The Problem of Suffering in Islam." *Journal of Dharma* 2 (1977): 267-94.

Badawi, Jamal. "The Earth and Humanity: A Muslim View." In Hick and Meltzer, *Three Faiths—One God*, 87-98.

———. "Islam: A Brief Look." In Hick and Meltzer, *Three Faiths—One God*, 187-95.

Bakker, Dirk. *Man in the Qur'an.* Amsterdam: Drukkerij Holland, 1965.

Bowker, John, ed. *The Oxford Dictionary of World Religions.* New York: Oxford, 1997.

Brown, Daniel. *A New Introduction to Islam.* Malden, MA: Blackwell, 2004.

Brown, Laurence B. *Bearing True Witness (or, "Now That I've Found Islam, What Do I Do With It?").* Riyadh: Darussalam, 2005.

Chittick, William C. "Sufism." In Esposito, *Oxford Encyclopedia of the Modern Islamic World*.

Corduan, Winfried. "A View from the Middle East: Islamic Theism." In *Universe Next Door*, edited by James Sire, 244-77. 5th ed. Downers Grove, IL: IVP Academic, 2009.

Cornell, Vincent J. "Fruit of the Tree of Knowledge: The Relationship Between Faith and Practice in Islam." In Esposito, *Oxford History of Islam*, 63-105.

Denny, Frederick Mathewson. *An Introduction to Islam.* 2nd ed. New York: Macmillan, 1994.

Eaton, Gai. *Islam and the Destiny of Man.* Cambridge: Islamic Texts Society, 1994.

Edalatnejad, Saeid. "The Islamic Point of View on the Problem of Evil." In *Probing the Depths of Evil and Good: Multireligious Views and Case Studies*, edited by Jerald Gort, Henry Jansen, and H. M. Vroom, 305-18. Currents of Encounter 33. Amsterdam: Rodopi, 2007.

Esposito, John, ed. *The Oxford Encyclopedia of the Modern Islamic World.* 4 vols. New York: Oxford University Press, 1995.

———, ed. *The Oxford History of Islam*. Oxford: Oxford University Press, 1999.

Fakhry, Majid. *Ethical Theories in Islam*. Islamic Philosophy, Theology, and Science 8. Leiden: Brill, 1991.

———. "Philosophy and Theology: From the Eighth Century C.E. to the Present." In Esposito, *Oxford History of Islam*, 269-303.

Forum on Religion & Public Life. *The Future Global Muslim Population: Projections for 2010–2030*. Pew Research Center. January 2011. www.pewforum.org /uploadedFiles/Topics/Religious_Affiliation/Muslim/FutureGlobalMuslim Population-WebPDF-Feb10.pdf.

Gauhar, Altaf, ed. *The Challenge of Islam*. London: Islamic Council of Europe, 1978.

Geisler, Norman L., and Abdul Saleeb. *Answering Islam: The Crescent in Light of the Cross*. 2nd ed. Grand Rapids: Baker Books, 2002.

Glassé, Cyril. *The New Encyclopaedia of Islam*. Rev. ed. London: Stacey International, 2001.

Haeri, Fadhlalla. *Journey of the Universe as Expounded in the Qur'an*. London: KPI, 1985.

Hafeez, Abdul. "Allah's Omnipotence and Freedom of Will for Man." *Hamdard Islamicus* 25 (2002): 31-40.

Haneef, Suzanne. *What Everyone Should Know About Islam and Muslims*. 14th ed. South Elgin, IL: Library of Islam, 1996.

Haq, S. Nomanul. "The Human Condition in Islam." In *The Human Condition: A Volume in the Comparative Religious Ideas Project*, edited by Robert C. Neville, 157-74. Albany: State University of New York Press, 2001.

———. "The Taxonomy of Truth in the Islamic Religious Doctrine and Tradition." In *Religious Truth: A Volume in the Comparative Religious Ideas Project*, edited by Robert Cummings Neville, 127-44. Albany: State University of New York Press, 2001.

———. "Ultimate Reality: Islam." In *Ultimate Realities: A Volume in the Comparative Religious Ideas Project*, edited by Robert C. Neville, 75-94. Albany: State University of New York Press, 2001.

Haykal, Muhammad. "Islamic Civilization as Depicted in the Qur'an." In *The Life of Muhammad*, 517-55. Indianapolis: North American Trust, 1976.

———. *The Life of Muhammad*. Translated by Isma'il Ragi Al-Faruqi. Indianapolis: North American Trust, 1976.

Hick, John, and Edmund S. Meltzer, eds. *Three Faiths—One God: A Jewish, Christian, Muslim Encounter*. Albany: State University of New York Press, 1989.

Hodgson, Marshall. "A Comparison of Islam and Christianity as Frameworks for Religious Life." *Diogenes* 32 (1960): 49-74.

Ibn Ishaq, Muhammad. *The Life of Muhammad: A Translation of Ibn Ishaq's Sirat Rasul Allah.* Edited by 'Abd al-Malik Ibn Hisham and Alfred Guillaume. Karachi, Pakistan: Oxford University Press, 2006.

Jomier, Jacques. *The Great Themes of the Qur'an.* Translated by Zoe Hersov. London: SCM Press, 1997.

Khalil, Mohammad Hassan, and Mucahit Bilici. "Conversion out of Islam: A Study of Conversion Narratives of Former Muslims." *Muslim World* 97 (2007): 111-24.

Khan, Muhammad Muhsin. *The Translation of the Meanings of Sahih Al-Bukhāri.* 9 vols. Riyadh: Darussalam, 1997.

Lings, Martin. *Muhammad: His Life on the Earliest Sources.* Rochester, VT: Inner Traditions International, 1983.

Mattson, Ingrid. *The Story of the Qur'an: Its History and Place in Muslim Life.* Malden, MA: Blackwell, 2008.

Maudoodi, Syed Abul 'Ala. *The Ethical View-Point of Islam.* 2nd ed. Lahore: Markazi Maktaba Jamaat-e-Islami, 1953.

Maududi, Abul A'la. "What Islam Stands For." In Gauhar, *Challenge of Islam,* 2-14.

McAuliffe, Jane Dammen, and Daniel A. Madigan. "Themes and Topics." In *The Cambridge Companion to the Qur'an,* edited by Jane Dammen McAuliffe, 79-95. Cambridge Companions to Religion. Cambridge: Cambridge University Press, 2007.

Mir, Mustansir. "Sin." In Esposito, *Oxford Encyclopedia of the Modern Islamic World.*

Mubarakpuri, Safiur-Rahman al-. *The Sealed Nectar: Biography of the Noble Prophet.* Rev. ed. Riyadh: Darussalam, 2002.

Nadwi, Abul Hasan Ali. "Islam: The Most Suitable Religion for Mankind." In Gauhar, *Challenge of Islam,* 16-30.

Nasr, Seyyed Hossein. "God." In *Islamic Spirituality: Foundations,* edited by Seyyed Hossein Nasr, 311-23. World Spirituality: An Encyclopedic History of the Religious Quest 19. New York: Crossroad, 1987.

———. *Ideals and Realities of Islam.* London: Allen & Unwin, 1985.

———. *An Introduction to Islamic Cosmological Doctrines: Conceptions of Nature and Methods Used for Its Study by the Ikhwan al-Safa, al-Biruni, and Ibn Sina.* Rev. ed. Boulder, CO: Shambhala, 1978.

Philips, A. B. *The Purpose of Creation.* Riyadh: Islamic Propagation Office in Rabwah, 2007.

Qutb, Sayyid. *Basic Principles of the Islamic Worldview.* Translated by Rami David. North Haledon, NJ: Islamic Publications International, 2006.

———. *Milestones.* Damascus: Dar Al-Ilm, 1996.

———. *Social Justice in Islam.* Translated by John B. Hardie. Rev. ed. Oneonta, NY: Islamic Publications International, 2000.

Rahman, Fazlur. *Major Themes of the Qur'an.* 2nd ed. Chicago: University of Chicago Press, 2009.

Rauf, Feisal Abdul. *Islam: A Search for Meaning.* Costa Mesa, CA: Mazda, 1995.

Rippin, Andrew. *Muslims: Their Religious Beliefs and Practices.* Volume 1 of *The Formative Period.* London: Routledge, 1990.

Schimmel, Annemarie. *Islam: An Introduction.* Albany: State University of New York Press, 1992.

———. *Mystical Dimensions of Islam.* Chapel Hill: University of North Carolina Press, 1975.

Sells, Michael. *Approaching the Qur'an: The Early Revelations.* Ashland, OR: White Cloud, 1999.

Shaykh, Hasan Ibn 'Abdullah al-. Foreword to *The Life of Muhammad*, by Muhammad Husayn Haykal, trans. Isma'il Ragi Al-Faruqi. Indianapolis: North American Trust, 1976.

Shepard, William. *Introducing Islam.* New York: Routledge, 2009.

Sherif, Faruq. *A Guide to the Contents of the Qur'an.* Reading, UK: Garnet, 1995.

Siddiqi, Muzammil H. "God: A Muslim View." In Hick and Meltzer, *Three Faiths—One God*, 63-76.

Smith, Jane I. "Afterlife." In Esposito, *Oxford Encyclopedia of the Modern Islamic World.*

Smith, Jane I., and Yvonne Yazbeck Haddad. *The Islamic Understanding of Death and Resurrection.* Albany: State University of New York Press, 1981.

Tabari, Abu Ja'far Muhammad B. Jarir al-. *The Commentary on the Qur'an.* Edited by W. F. Madelung and A. Jones. Translated by John Cooper. Vol. 1. Oxford: Oxford University Press, 1987.

Tennent, Timothy C. *Christianity at the Religious Roundtable: Evangelicalism in Conversation with Hinduism, Buddhism, and Islam.* Grand Rapids: Baker Academic, 2002.

Watt, W. Montgomery, trans. *Islamic Creeds: A Selection.* Islamic Surveys. Edinburgh: Edinburgh University Press, 1994.

———. *Islamic Philosophy and Theology.* Edinburgh: Edinburgh University Press, 1985.

AUTHOR INDEX

SUBJECT INDEX

SCRIPTURE INDEX